译者前言

本书一如前三个选译本，是从约翰逊编辑的1955年集注版《艾米莉·狄金森诗歌全集》中按顺序选取第901～1200首诗，译为中文，仍取英汉对照体例。约翰逊编的1955年集注版与其编的1960年阅读版在文本上有些许不同，包括字词、标点等。字词、标点方面的差异已在附录的对照表中列出，读者可自行查阅。本书对一些难读、难懂之处提供了题解或注释，比之前三本选译本提供的量要多一些，但远未涵盖全部。

本书收录的300首诗大致有以下三个特点：一是在形式表现上，除少数例外，罕见明显的语法跳跃和断裂而导致难读难懂的情况，形式连接大多较为明显，换言之，形式特异性数量及其变动幅度均较小，这或许体现了作者诗艺形式上的圆熟；诗歌形式特征关联其承载的情感内容特点。二是在情感表达上，该300首诗表达的情感状态相对稳定，甚少极悲极喜、情绪大起大落的情况；同时由于形式的原因，其情感表达也较为连贯。三是在情感特征上，由连接的形式所表达的连贯的情感，更多地体现了深沉、克制、浓缩的特点，也表明了作者思想情感在此一阶段的成熟及其深度；有些诗非因形式特异，而因情感克制或浓缩，又或因其思想的深度而可能令人感到难懂，甚至晦涩。总之，本书中的诗歌形式连接，表达连贯，情感和思想内容有相当的深度和厚度，其深沉、克制有时令人动容，其浓缩、隐匿有时令人费解，但无论如何，这厚重的300首相比之前三本选译本中的诗歌，整体而言更适宜阅读。

本书译文之不足在所难免，请读者诸君不吝批评指正。由于艾米莉·狄金森的诗歌一般都没有标题，本书目录中取每首诗第一行作为标题，书中诗歌的序号均按约翰逊版中的序号排列。题解或注释中所引《圣经》原文均来自King James版。提及艾米莉·狄金森书信全集中的某一封信时，以"L"开头，后接信的序号。以上提到的约翰逊两个诗歌全集本以及狄金森书信全集是指：

Dickinson, Emily. *The Poems of Emily Dickinson: Including Variant Readings Critically Compared with All Known Manuscripts*. Ed. Thomas H. Johnson. 3 vols. Cambridge, MA: Belknap Press of Harvard University Press, 1955.

Dickinson, Emily. *The Letters of Emily Dickinson*. Eds. Thomas Herbert Johnson, Theodora Van Wagenen Ward. 3 vols. Cambridge, MA: Belknap Press of Harvard University Press, 1958.

Dickinson, Emily. *The Complete Poems of Emily Dickinson*. Ed. Thomas H. Johnson. Boston: Little, Brown and Company, 1960.

译者
2024 年 8 月

本书获中央高校基本科研业务费专项资金资助（项目编号：CBZZ202303）

The Poems of Emily Dickinson
艾米莉·狄金森诗选 ①
901~1200首

[美]艾米莉·狄金森 著　周建新 译

·广州·

图书在版编目（CIP）数据

艾米莉·狄金森诗选. 1, 901～1200首: 英汉对照/(美)艾米莉·狄金森（Emily Dickinson）著; 周建新译. —广州: 华南理工大学出版社, 2024.12

ISBN 978-7-5623-7443-5

Ⅰ.①艾…　Ⅱ.①艾…②周…　Ⅲ.①诗集-美国-近代-英、汉　Ⅳ.①I712.24

中国国家版本馆 CIP 数据核字（2023）第 209441 号

艾米莉·狄金森诗选. 1（901～1200首）

(美) 艾米莉·狄金森（Emily Dickinson）著　周建新　译

出 版 人：房俊东
出版发行：华南理工大学出版社
　　　　　(广州五山华南理工大学17号楼，邮编510640)
　　　　　http://hg.cb.scut.edu.cn　　E-mail: scutc13@scut.edu.cn
　　　　　营销部电话：020-87113487　87111048（传真）
策划编辑：吴翠微
责任编辑：陈　蓉
责任校对：梁樱雯
印 刷 者：广州小明数码印刷有限公司
开　　本：787mm×1092mm　1/20　印张：12.7　字数：276千
版　　次：2024年12月第1版　印次：2024年12月第1次印刷
定　　价：168.00元（全三册）

版权所有　盗版必究　印装差错　负责调换

目 录

901	Sweet, to have had them lost	1
	真好，失去了他们	1
902	The first Day that I was a Life	1
	我生命的第一天	2
903	I hide myself within my flower,	3
	我躲藏在我的花里，	3
904	Had I not This, or This, I said,	3
	我说，如果没有这个，或这个，	4
905	Between My Country—and the Others—	5
	在我的国度——和其他疆域之间——	5
906	The Admirations—and Contempts—of time—	5
	时间的——轻蔑——与仰慕——	6
907	Till Death—is narrow Loving—	6
	直到死——是那窄窄的爱——	7
908	'Tis Sunrise—Little Maid—Hast Thou	7
	已是日出——小姑娘——你在白昼	8
909	I make His Crescent fill or lack—	8
	我能让他的新月盈或缺——	9
910	Experience is the Angled Road	9
	经验是一条曲折的路	10
911	Too little way the House must lie	10
	那房子肯定离得很近	10
912	Peace is a fiction of our Faith—	11
	宁静是我们信仰的虚构——	11
913	And this of all my Hopes	11
	在我所有的希冀里这个	12
914	I cannot be ashamed	12
	我不会感到羞愧	12
915	Faith—is the Pierless Bridge	13

	信念——是没有桥墩的桥	13
916	His Feet are shod with Gauze—	14
	他脚着薄纱鞋——	14
917	Love—is anterior to Life—	15
	爱——先于生命——	15
918	Only a Shrine, but Mine—	15
	只有一个神龛，但它属于我——	15
919	If I can stop one Heart from breaking	16
	如果我能使一颗心免于破碎	16
920	We can but follow to the Sun—	16
	我们只能追随太阳——	17
921	If it had no pencil	17
	如果它没有铅笔	17
922	Those who have been in the Grave the longest—	18
	那些已长久待在坟墓	18
923	How the Waters closed above Him	18
	水面怎样在他头顶合拢	19
924	Love—is that later Thing than Death—	19
	爱——是死之后的事——	20
925	Struck, was I, not yet by Lightning—	20
	我，被击倒，非因闪电——	21
926	Patience—has a quiet Outer—	22
	忍耐——有平静的外表——	22
927	Absent Place—an April Day—	23
	未知的地方——四月的一天——	23
928	The Heart has narrow Banks	23
	心有窄窄的堤	24
929	How far is it to Heaven?	24
	去天堂有多远？	25
930	There is a June when Corn is cut	25
	玉米收割时正是六月	26
931	Noon—is the Hinge of Day—	27
	正午——是一日的枢纽——	27
932	My best Acquaintances are those	27

	我最熟识的那些	28
933	Two Travellers perishing in Snow	28
	两位旅者在雪地死去	29
934	That is solemn we have ended	29
	我们的结束是一件庄严的事	30
935	Death leaves Us homesick, who behind,	30
	死亡让我们思乡，作为身后人，	30
936	This Dust, and it's Feature—	31
	这一粒尘，及其形骸——	31
937	I felt a Cleaving in my Mind—	32
	我感觉我思想有一道裂痕——	32
938	Fairer through Fading—as the Day	32
	慢慢消逝更显美丽——当那白日	33
939	What I see not, I better see—	33
	我看不见的，看得更清晰——	34
940	On that dear Frame the Years had worn	34
	看那可爱的框架被岁月侵蚀	35
941	The Lady feeds Her little Bird	35
	那女士喂她的小鸟	35
942	Snow beneath whose chilly softness	36
	冰雪下寒冷的温柔乡里	36
943	A Coffin—is a small Domain,	36
	棺材——是一块小小领地，	37
944	I learned—at least—what Home could be—	38
	我了解了——至少——什么是家——	39
945	This is a Blossom of the Brain—	40
	这是大脑长出的一枝花——	41
946	It is an honorable Thought	41
	这是一个荣耀的想法	42
947	Of Tolling Bell I ask the cause?	42
	我问丧钟为何敲响？	42
948	'Twas Crisis—All the length had passed—	43
	这是一次危机——终于全部结束——	43
949	Under the Light, yet under,	44

	在光的下面，再下面，	45
950	The Sunset stopped on Cottages	45
	落日停于木屋旁	46
951	As Frost is best conceived	46
	正如寒霜最能被估计	47
952	A Man may make a Remark—	47
	一个人可以发言——	48
953	A Door just opened on a street—	48
	一扇当街的门刚开启——	48
954	The Chemical conviction	49
	化学的断言	49
955	The Hollows round His eager Eyes	49
	他渴望的双眼四周深陷	50
956	What shall I do when the Summer troubles—	50
	当夏日陷入苦恼——	51
957	As One does Sickness over	51
	像一个人大病初愈	52
958	We met as Sparks—Diverging Flints	52
	我们相遇似火花——燧石光激射	52
959	A loss of something ever felt I—	53
	我感到某些事物的失去——	53
960	As plan for Noon and plan for Night	54
	正如正午和夜晚的计划不一	54
961	Wert Thou but ill—that I might show thee	55
	假如你生病——我就能展示给你	56
962	Midsummer, was it, when They died—	56
	正是在，仲夏，他们死去——	57
963	A nearness to Tremendousness—	57
	接近宏大之极——	57
964	"Unto Me?" I do not know you—	58
	"来接我？"我可不认识你——	58
965	Denial—is the only fact	59
	遗弃，是被遗弃者	59
966	All forgot for recollecting	60

	忘记一切只因记起	60
967	Pain—expands the Time—	61
	痛苦——拉长了时间——	61
968	Fitter to see Him, I may be	61
	我更适宜见他了，或许	63
969	He who in Himself believes—	64
	相信自己的人——	64
970	Color—Caste—Denomination—	64
	颜色——地位——和名称——	65
971	Robbed by Death—but that was easy—	66
	被死神夺去——但那倒容易——	66
972	Unfulfilled to Observation—	67
	仔细观察尚未完全——	67
973	'Twas awkward, but it fitted me—	68
	它有点笨拙，但适合我——	68
974	The Soul's distinct connection	69
	灵魂与永生	69
975	The Mountain sat upon the Plain	69
	山峦端坐在平原	70
976	Death is a Dialogue between	70
	死亡是一场对话	70
977	Besides this May	71
	除了这个五月	71
978	It bloomed and dropt, a Single Noon—	71
	它绽放继而坠落，在一个正午——	72
979	This Merit hath the worst—	73
	这功绩糟到极点——	73
980	Purple—is fashionable twice—	74
	紫色——是双倍的时尚——	74
981	As Sleigh Bells seem in summer	74
	正如雪橇铃声仿佛响在夏天	74
982	No Other can reduce	75
	没有别的可以贬低	75
983	Ideals are the Fairly Oil	75

	理想相当于润滑油	76
984	'Tis Anguish grander than Delight	76
	这巨痛比欢乐宏大	76
985	The Missing All—prevented Me	76
	错过一切，阻止了我	77
986	A narrow Fellow in the Grass	77
	一个细长的家伙	78
987	The Leaves like Women interchange	79
	树叶像女人在交流	79
988	The Definition of Beauty is	79
	美的定义就是	80
989	Gratitude—is not the mention	80
	感激——并非提及	80
990	Not all die early, dying young—	81
	并非所有早亡，都是夭折——	81
991	She sped as Petals of a Rose	81
	她奔忙像玫瑰的花瓣	82
992	The Dust behind I strove to join	82
	后面的尘土我努力将它	82
993	We miss Her, not because We see—	82
	我们思念她，非因我们看见——	83
994	Partake as doth the Bee,	83
	像蜜蜂一样品尝，	83
995	This was in the White of the Year—	83
	此时是一年中白色时节——	84
996	We'll pass without the parting	84
	我们会不辞而别	85
997	Crumbling is not an instant's Act	85
	崩溃非一瞬之功	85
998	Best Things dwell out of Sight	86
	最美好的事物不在眼见的现场	86
999	Superfluous were the Sun	87
	太阳显得多余	87
1000	The Fingers of the Light	88

	光的手指 ……………………………………	88
1001	The Stimulus, beyond the Grave …………	89
	与他谋面，在坟墓以远 …………………	89
1002	Aurora is the effort ………………………	89
	极光 …………………………………………	90
1003	Dying at my music! ………………………	90
	在我的音乐里死去！ ………………………	90
1004	There is no Silence in the Earth—so silent …	90
	大地上不存在寂静——如此寂静 ………	90
1005	Bind me—I still can sing— ………………	91
	捆住我——我仍能歌吟—— ……………	91
1006	The first We knew of Him was Death— ……	91
	我们知道他的第一件事是死 ……………	91
1007	Falsehood of Thee could I suppose ………	91
	你的虚假我若能猜到 ……………………	92
1008	How still the Bells in Steeples stand ……	92
	多安静那些钟在尖塔上屹立 ……………	92
1009	I was a Phebe—nothing more— …………	92
	我是一只霸鹟——不多—— ……………	93
1010	Up Life's Hill with my little Bundle ……	93
	我带着小小行囊爬上生活的高山 ………	93
1011	She rose as high as His Occasion …………	94
	她升到与他的情形齐高 …………………	94
1012	Which is best? Heaven— …………………	94
	哪一个最好？天堂—— …………………	94
1013	Too scanty 'twas to die for you, …………	95
	为你去死太没价值， ……………………	95
1014	Did We abolish Frost ………………………	95
	纵然我们把寒霜消除 ……………………	96
1015	Were it but Me that gained the Height— …	96
	假如唯有我升到那高度—— ……………	96
1016	The Hills in Purple syllables ……………	96
	群山用紫色的声音 ………………………	96
1017	To die—without the Dying ………………	96

	死去——却未消逝	97
1018	Who saw no Sunrise cannot say	97
	看不见日出的人不能说	97
1019	My Season's furthest Flower—	98
	我的季节中最后的花儿——	98
1020	Trudging to Eden, looking backward,	98
	跋涉去伊甸园，回头望，	98
1021	Far from Love the Heavenly Father	99
	全无爱怜的天父	99
1022	I knew that I had gained	99
	我知我已得到	100
1023	It rises—passes—on our South	100
	它升起——经过——我们南方	100
1024	So large my Will	100
	我的愿望如此大	101
1025	The Products of my Farm are these	102
	我农庄的产品都在这里	102
1026	The Dying need but little, Dear,	102
	垂死的人所需甚少，亲爱的，	102
1027	My Heart upon a little Plate	103
	我的心在一个小盘上	103
1028	'Twas my one Glory—	103
	这是我的一份荣誉——	103
1029	Nor Mountain hinder Me	104
	没有山可阻止我	104
1030	That Such have died enable Us	104
	那些死去的使我们	104
1031	Fate slew Him, but He did not drop—	104
	命运杀了他，但他并未仆倒——	105
1032	Who is the East?	105
	谁是东方？	105
1033	Said Death to Passion	106
	死神对激情说	106
1034	His Bill an Augur is	106

	他的喙像螺丝钻	107
1035	Bee! I'm expecting you!	107
	蜜蜂！我期盼着你！	107
1036	Satisfaction—is the Agent	108
	满足——会导致	108
1037	Here, where the Daisies fit my Head	109
	这里，雏菊适合戴我头上	109
1038	Her little Parasol to lift	110
	她将小阳伞举起	110
1039	I heard, as if I had no Ear	110
	我听见，仿佛我没耳朵	111
1040	Not so the infinite Relations—Below	112
	并非万物无限关联——在下界	112
1041	Somewhat, to hope for,	112
	不管怎么说，有所期待，	112
1042	Spring comes on the World—	113
	春天来到世界——	113
1043	Lest this be Heaven indeed	113
	为防这个真是天堂	113
1044	A Sickness of this World it most occasions	113
	一种对当世的厌烦往往被触发	114
1045	Nature rarer uses Yellow	114
	大自然更少用黄色	114
1046	I've dropped my Brain—My Soul is numb—	115
	我已垂下头颅——灵魂麻木——	116
1047	The Opening and the Close	116
	存在的开启	117
1048	Reportless Subjects, to the Quick	117
	难于描述的主题，向急智者	118
1049	Pain has but one Acquaintance	118
	痛苦只有一位相识	118
1050	As willing lid o'er weary eye	118
	正如甘愿的眼睑将疲惫的眼遮住	119
1051	I cannot meet the Spring unmoved—	119

	我无法邂逅春天而无动于衷——	119
1052	I never saw a Moor—	120
	我从未见过荒野——	120
1053	It was a quiet way—	120
	就这么轻轻地——	121
1054	Not to discover weakness is	122
	不去发掘软弱	122
1055	The Soul should always stand ajar	122
	灵魂应保持半敞开	123
1056	There is a Zone whose even Years	123
	有这么一个地带那里长年	123
1057	I had a daily Bliss	124
	我有一份日常的快乐	124
1058	Bloom—is Result—to meet a Flower	124
	遇见一朵花——总看到——花娇艳丽	125
1059	Sang from the Heart, Sire,	125
	从心中唱出，先生，	126
1060	Air has no Residence, no Neighbor,	127
	空气没有住处，没有邻居，	127
1061	Three Weeks passed since I had seen Her—	127
	与她晤面后才过三周——	128
1062	He scanned it—staggered—	128
	他审视它——摇晃着	129
1063	Ashes denote that Fire was—	129
	灰烬表明曾经有火——	129
1064	To help our Bleaker Parts	130
	救助自身更羸弱的部分	130
1065	Let down the Bars, Oh Death—	130
	放下栅栏，啊死神——	130
1066	Fame's Boys and Girls, who never die	131
	声名的少男少女，永不死去	131
1067	Except the smaller size	131
	除了那较小的	131
1068	Further in Summer than the Birds	132

	比鸟儿还要深入夏天 …………………………………	132
1069	Paradise is of the option. …………………………	133
	极乐园是一个选项。…………………………………	133
1070	To undertake is to achieve ………………………	133
	答应就是做到 ………………………………………	134
1071	Perception of an object costs ……………………	134
	对一个物体的感知须支出 …………………………	135
1072	Title divine—is mine! ……………………………	135
	神圣的头衔——我今得添!……………………	135
1073	Experiment to me …………………………………	136
	对我的考验 …………………………………………	136
1074	Count not that far that can be had, ……………	137
	别以为真如此遥远,…………………………………	137
1075	The Sky is low—the Clouds are mean. ………	137
	天空低垂——云层暗淡。…………………………	137
1076	Just Once! Oh least Request! ……………………	138
	就一次!啊最低的要求!……………………………	138
1077	These are the Signs to Nature's Inns— ………	138
	这些是指向大自然酒馆的标记—— ……………	139
1078	The Bustle in a House ……………………………	139
	屋里的喧闹 …………………………………………	140
1079	The Sun went down—no Man looked on— …	140
	太阳下山——没人在看—— ……………………	140
1080	When they come back—if Blossoms do— ……	141
	当它们归来——假如群芳真归来—— …………	141
1081	Superiority to Fate ………………………………	142
	想超越命运 …………………………………………	142
1082	Revolution is the Pod ……………………………	143
	革命是那豆荚 ………………………………………	143
1083	We learn it in Retreating ………………………	143
	退却时我们知悉 ……………………………………	144
1084	At Half past Three, a single Bird ………………	144
	三点半,一只鸟儿 …………………………………	145
1085	If Nature smiles—the Mother must ……………	145

	如果自然露出笑容——那是母亲	145
1086	What Twigs We held by—	146
	我们被怎样的细枝托住——	146
1087	We miss a Kinsman more	147
	我们对亲人愈加思念	147
1088	Ended, ere it begun—	147
	还没开始,就已结束——	148
1089	Myself can read the Telegrams	148
	我能读懂那些电报	148
1090	I am afraid to own a Body—	149
	我害怕拥有肉身——	149
1091	The Well upon the Brook	149
	水井依赖小溪	150
1092	It was not Saint—it was too large—	150
	它不是圣徒——它太大——	150
1093	Because 'twas Riches I could own,	150
	因为那是我能拥有的财富,	150
1094	Themself are all I have—	151
	他们是我全部所有——	151
1095	To Whom the Mornings stand for Nights,	151
	对于清晨代表夜晚的人来说,	151
1096	These Strangers, in a foreign World,	151
	这些陌生人,在异域,	152
1097	Dew—is the Freshet in the Grass—	152
	晨露——是草中的流溪——	152
1098	Of the Heart that goes in, and closes the Door	153
	对于那颗心一进去,就把门关	153
1099	My Cocoon tightens—Colors teaze—	153
	我的茧收紧——色若丝缕——	154
1100	The last Night that She lived	154
	她活着的最后一夜	155
1101	Between the form of Life and Life	157
	生命的形式和生命	157
1102	His Bill is clasped—his Eye forsook—	157

	他的钩嘴合拢——他的目光散逸——	158
1103	The spry Arms of the Wind	158
	在风轻捷的臂间	158
1104	The Crickets sang	159
	蟋蟀歌唱	159
1105	Like Men and Women Shadows walk	160
	仿佛男男女女的影子	160
1106	We do not know the time we lose—	160
	我们失去的光阴我们不知——	161
1107	The Bird did prance—the Bee did play—	161
	鸟儿雀跃——蜂儿嬉戏——	162
1108	A Diamond on the Hand	162
	钻石戴在手上	162
1109	I fit for them—	163
	我适宜他们——	163
1110	None who saw it ever told it	163
	见过它的人从未提起	164
1111	Some Wretched creature, savior take	164
	某个不幸的生灵,被救世主带走	164
1112	That this should feel the need of Death	164
	这一位会感到死亡的必要	165
1113	There is strength in proving that it can be bourne	166
	有一种力量证明它能承重	166
1114	The largest Fire ever known	166
	世上最大的火灾	167
1115	The murmuring of Bees, has ceased	167
	蜜蜂的嗡嗡,已经止息	167
1116	There is another Loneliness	168
	有另一种孤独	168
1117	A Mine there is no Man would own	169
	有一座矿藏没人能拥有	169
1118	Exhiliration is the Breeze	169
	欢欣是一阵轻风飞扬	170
1119	Paradise is that old mansion	170

	天堂是那所老宅	170
1120	This slow Day moved along—	171
	这缓慢的一天向前行进——	171
1121	Time does go on—	171
	时光确实在前进——	171
1122	'Tis my first night beneath the Sun	172
	这是我在太阳下的第一夜	172
1123	A great Hope fell	172
	一个巨大的希望坠落	173
1124	Had we known the Ton she bore	174
	假如我们知道她背负的吨量	174
1125	Oh Sumptuous moment	174
	啊奢侈的时刻	175
1126	Shall I take thee, the Poet said	175
	诗人说,我是否该选你	176
1127	Soft as the massacre of Suns	176
	像对阳光的杀戮那般柔软	176
1128	These are the Nights that Beetles love—	176
	这是甲虫喜爱的夜晚——	177
1129	Tell all the Truth but tell it slant—	177
	说出所有的真理但曲折地说出——	178
1130	That odd old man is dead a year—	178
	那古怪的老人已死了一年——	179
1131	The Merchant of the Picturesque	179
	贩卖奇思的商人	179
1132	The smouldering embers blush—	180
	闷燃的余烬露出羞红——	180
1133	The Snow that never drifts—	180
	那从不堆砌的雪——	181
1134	The Wind took up the Northern Things	182
	风卷起北边各种物件	182
1135	Too cold is this	183
	这太冷冰	183
1136	The Frost of Death was on the Pane—	184

	死亡的寒霜附在窗玻璃上——	184
1137	The duties of the Wind are few,	185
	风的职责很少,	186
1138	A Spider sewed at Night	187
	一只蜘蛛在夜里织网	187
1139	Her sovereign People	187
	对自己高贵的子民	188
1140	The Day grew small, surrounded tight	188
	白昼逐渐萎缩,陷于牢牢围住	188
1141	The Face we choose to miss—	188
	我们喜欢思念的那张脸——	189
1142	The Props assist the House	189
	支架给房子支撑	189
1143	The Work of Her that went,	190
	她已完结的工作,	190
1144	Ourselves we do inter with sweet derision.	190
	我们确实用甜蜜的嘲弄埋葬自己。	190
1145	In thy long Paradise of Light	190
	身处你漫长的光明乐园	191
1146	When Etna basks and purrs	191
	当埃特纳火山晒着太阳发出呼噜	191
1147	After a hundred years	191
	百年以后	192
1148	After the Sun comes out	192
	太阳一露出光芒	193
1149	I noticed People disappeared	193
	我注意到有人消失	193
1150	How many schemes may die	194
	有多少计划会消失	194
1151	Soul, take thy risk.	195
	灵魂,尽管冒险一试	195
1152	Tell as a Marksman—were forgotten	195
	退尔作为神射手——早已被遗忘	196
1153	Through what transports of Patience	197

	通过在忍耐里沉迷 ……………………………………	198
1154	A full fed Rose on meals of Tint …………………………	198
	一朵饱满的玫瑰秀色可餐 …………………………………	198
1155	Distance—is not the Realm of Fox ……………………	198
	距离——并非狐狸的领地 …………………………………	199
1156	Lest any doubt that we are glad that they were born Today ……	199
	毫无疑问我们高兴她们出生在今日 ………………………	199
1157	Some Days retired from the rest ………………………	199
	一些日子从其他日子中退隐 ……………………………	199
1158	Best Witchcraft is Geometry ……………………………	200
	最好的魔法就是几何学 …………………………………	200
1159	Great Streets of silence led away ……………………	200
	寂静的大街延伸出去 ……………………………………	200
1160	He is alive, this morning— ……………………………	201
	他活着——今晨—— ………………………………………	201
1161	Trust adjust her "Peradventure"— ……………………	201
	信任调整了她的"或许"—— ……………………………	201
1162	The Life we have is very great. ………………………	202
	我们现有的生活非常美好。………………………………	202
1163	God made no act without a cause, ……………………	202
	上帝不会无故行动,………………………………………	203
1164	Were it to be the last …………………………………	203
	假如那是最后一次 …………………………………………	203
1165	Contained in this short Life …………………………	203
	这短暂的生命所含 ………………………………………	204
1166	Of Paul and Silas it is said …………………………	204
	据说保罗和西拉 …………………………………………	204
1167	Alone and in a Circumstance …………………………	205
	独处一隅 …………………………………………………	206
1168	As old as Woe— …………………………………………	207
	像悲伤一样古老—— ……………………………………	207
1169	Lest they should come—is all my fear ………………	208
	唯恐他们会来——就是我全部的恐惧 …………………	208
1170	Nature affects to be sedate …………………………	208

	大自然假装镇定	208
1171	On the World you colored	209
	在你彩绘的世界	209
1172	The Clouds their Backs together laid	210
	乌云拥挤背对背	210
1173	The Lightning is a yellow Fork	210
	闪电是一把黄色的叉子	210
1174	There's the Battle of Burgoyne—	211
	伯戈因的战斗——	211
1175	We like a Hairbreadth 'scape	212
	我们喜欢九死一生的逃亡	212
1176	We never know how high we are	212
	我们从不知我们多高	212
1177	A prompt—executive Bird is the Jay—	213
	一只敏捷——实干的鸟叫松鸦——	213
1178	My God—He sees thee—	214
	我的上帝——他看见你——	214
1179	Of so divine a Loss	214
	对如此神圣的损失	214
1180	"Remember me" implored the Thief!	215
	"请记着我"小偷恳求！	215
1181	When I hoped I feared—	216
	当我怀着希望我就恐惧——	216
1182	Remembrance has a Rear and Front—	216
	回忆有前有后——	217
1183	Step lightly on this narrow spot—	217
	轻轻踏足这方寸之地——	217
1184	The Days that we can spare	218
	我们忙里偷闲的日子	218
1185	A little Dog that wags his tail	218
	一只小狗摇着尾巴	219
1186	Too few the mornings be,	220
	清晨寥寥，	220
1187	Oh Shadow on the Grass,	220

	啊草地上的阴影，	221
1188	'Twas fighting for his Life he was—	221
	这是关乎他生存的战斗——	221
1189	The Voice that stands for Floods to me	222
	那在我听来如洪水的声音	222
1190	The Sun and Fog contested	222
	太阳和雾霭竞赛	223
1191	The pungent atom in the Air	223
	空气中刺鼻的微粒	223
1192	An honest Tear	224
	一滴真诚的泪	224
1193	All men for Honor hardest work	224
	人人都尽力争取荣誉	224
1194	Somehow myself survived the Night	225
	我好歹熬过了黑夜	225
1195	What we see we know somewhat	225
	我们眼见的多少有所了解	226
1196	To make Routine a Stimulus	226
	就让常规成为一种刺激	226
1197	I should not dare to be so sad	227
	我不该再次胆敢如此悲伤	227
1198	A soft Sea washed around the House	227
	一片温柔的海在房屋四周荡漾	228
1199	Are Friends Delight or Pain?	228
	朋友是欢乐还是痛苦？	228
1200	Because my Brook is fluent	229
	因为我的小溪顺畅流淌	229

附录 1955年集注版与1960年阅读版词汇和标点差异一览表 …… 230

901

Sweet, to have had them lost
For news that they be saved—
The nearer they departed Us
The nearer they, restored,

Shall stand to Our Right Hand—
Most precious are the Dead—
Next precious
Those that rose to go—
Then thought of Us, and stayed.

901①

真好,失去了他们
因听说他们会得救——
他们越早离开我们
就越早,返回,

站在我们右手边——
最重要的是死者——
其次
是那些起身欲走——
而后想起我们,又留下的。

902

The first Day that I was a Life
I recollect it—How still—
That last Day that I was a Life
I recollect it—as well—

---

① 题解:死去原属不幸,但若得救上天堂,则也是好事,越早上天堂和上帝(Our Right Hand)在一起越好,此时死去相当于返回来处。因此,最重要的是死者,因其得救会上天堂,其次是因不舍而留下陪我们的人。

'Twas stiller—though the first
Was still—
'Twas empty—but the first
Was full—

This—was my finallest Occasion—
But then
My tenderer Experiment
Toward Men—

"Which choose I"?
That—I cannot say—
"Which choose They"?
Question Memory!

902①
我生命的第一天
我能记起——多么静谧——
我生命的最后一天
我——也能记起——

它更静谧——虽然那第一天
也寂静——
它也虚空——但那第一天
却丰盈——

这——是我最后的机会——
但也是
我更温柔的尝试
对人类——

---

① 题解:"我"来到世上成为一个生命的第一天,静谧又丰盈;"我"作为一个生命存在的最后一天,更静谧但虚空。"我"无法确定自己更喜欢哪一个,那就去问问人类(人们)。这是"我"最后的机会,也是一个柔情的试验,测试一下他们选哪个,他们一定会搜索记忆才能回答。

"我该选哪个"?
那,我难以说清——
"他们会选哪个"?
去向记忆打听!

903

I hide myself within my flower,
That fading from your Vase,
You, unsuspecting, feel for me—
Almost a loneliness.

903①

我躲藏在我的花里,
它正自你的花瓶消弥,
你,毫无察觉,会为我感到——
隐约的孤寂。

904

Had I not This, or This, I said,
Appealing to Myself,
In moment of prosperity—
Inadequate—were Life—

"Thou hast not Me, nor Me"—it said,
In Moment of Reverse—
"And yet Thou art industrious—
No need—hadst Thou—of us"?

My need—was all I had—I said—
The need did not reduce—

---

① 题解:这是狄金森给朋友寄送一束花时随附的一首诗。花瓶里的花凋枯了,"你"自然会为此感到一丝孤寂,但"你"绝未想到,"你"同时也是为"我"感到孤寂,因为"我"就躲藏在花里。

Because the food—exterminate—
The hunger—does not cease—

But diligence—is sharper—
Proportioned to the Chance—
To feed upon the Retrograde—
Enfeebles—the Advance—

904①
我说，如果没有这个，或这个，
激励我，
在成功的时刻——
生命——将不完整——

"你不拥有我，我也没拥有你"——它说，
在逆境时——
"但你仍勤奋不已——
难道你——不需要——我们"？

对你的需要——是我全部渴求——我说——
它不会减少——
因为食物——消失——
饥饿——并不会停止——

但勤奋——更急需——
并视情况增递——
滋养退缩——
会削弱——前进的动力——

---

① 题解：在成功或顺境之时，若无"它"（"这个"）吸引着"我"、激励着"我"，"我"的生命将不完满；但在逆境时，即使没有"它"，"我"也会勤奋努力，难道"我"其实是不需要"它"的吗？非也，"我"全部身心都需要"它"，但即使"我"没有激励"我"的外部精神食粮（"它"），"我"内心中对目标的饥渴也不会消失，因此，更需要（sharper）的是按实际际遇的需要发奋努力。若任由退缩之念滋生，就会削弱奋进的意志。

905

Between My Country—and the Others—
There is a Sea—
But Flowers—negotiate between us—
As Ministry.

905

在我的国度——和其他疆域之间——
隔着一片海洋——
但众多花朵——在我们间穿梭——
像事务部一样繁忙。

906

The Admirations—and Contempts—of time—
Show justest—through an Open Tomb—
The Dying—as it were a Hight①
Reorganizes Estimate
And what We saw not
We distinguish clear—
And mostly—see not
What We saw before—

'Tis Compound Vision—
Light—enabling Light—
The Finite—furnished
With the Infinite—
Convex—and Concave Witness—
Back—toward Time—
And forward—
Toward the God of Him—

---

① "Hight"在1960年阅读版中为"Height"。

906①

时间的——轻蔑——与仰慕——
最显公正——通过敞开的坟墓——
将逝者——曾经的权贵
重新预估
过往看不见的
如今辨得清楚——
过往曾见的
现在却看不见——几乎

这是繁复的景象——
光——使光发亮——
有限——被蒙上
无限——
凸——与凹碰面——
后退——退向时间——
前进——
前往上帝那边——

907

Till Death—is narrow Loving—
The scantest Heart extant
Will hold you till your privilege
Of Finiteness—be spent—

But He whose loss procures you
Such Destitution that
Your Life too abject for itself
Thenceforward imitate—

---

① 题解：临进坟墓的垂死者处在两个世界的连接处，那里景象繁复，有现世和来世的光交接，有有限和无限的混杂，有凹和凸的接触。退，是有生老病死的时间之域；进，是上帝的永恒之境。临进坟墓的垂死者重新估计，那曾亲历的现世，将无缘再看到，而那不曾见过的来世，将清晰展现。

Until—Resemblance perfect—
Yourself, for His pursuit
Delight of Nature—abdicate—
Exhibit Love—somewhat—

907①
直到死——是那窄窄的爱——
最些微的关心
将支撑你直至你有限的
生的特权——耗尽——

但他的逝去使你
如此贫乏以至于
你的人生凄惨之极
从此就效拟——

直至——完全相似——
你自己，为追寻他
把天生的欢愉——放弃——
展现了爱——有点——

908
'Tis Sunrise—Little Maid—Hast Thou
No Station in the Day?
'Twas not thy wont, to hinder so—
Retrieve thine industry—

'Tis Noon—My little Maid—
Alas—and art thou sleeping yet?

---

① 题解：只需些微的关心，就可以让对方感受到温暖，直至他过完一生。但对方的逝去会使你的人生仿佛一无所有，凄凉不已，困苦至极，于是你无限怀念，只想效仿对方，追寻对方而去。最后，抛弃了人生的欢愉，终于和对方一样死去了。这时的死，多少显示了爱，所以才有诗开头的一句——爱是窄窄的，因为只专注于一个人。

The Lily—waiting to be Wed—
The Bee—Hast thou forgot?

My little Maid—'Tis Night—Alas
That Night should be to thee
Instead of Morning—Had'st thou broached
Thy little Plan to Die—
Dissuade thee, if I c'd not, Sweet,
I might have aided—thee—

908

已是日出——小姑娘——你在白昼
就没有工作?
这可不像你的习惯,这样停顿——
请重拾你的忙活——

已是正午——我的小姑娘——
啊——你还在沉睡吗?
百合花——等着出嫁——
还有蜜蜂——你忘记它了吗?

我的小姑娘——已是夜晚——啊
夜晚对于你
绝不像清晨——你是否已开始
盘算着死去——
亲爱的,我要劝阻你,即使不成,
我也已——帮过你——

909

I make His Crescent fill or lack—
His Nature is at Full
Or Quarter—as I signify—
His Tides—do I control—

He holds superior in the Sky
Or gropes, at my Command
Behind inferior Clouds—or round
A Mist's slow Colonnade—

But since We hold a Mutual Disc—
And front a Mutual Day—
Which is the Despot, neither knows—
Nor Whose—the Tyranny—

909
我能让他的新月盈或缺——
他的天性是满
或亏——听从我指示——
他的潮汐——也由我控制——

他高挂天空
或听我号令,探步
在暗云后面——或绕过
薄雾缓慢的一列廊柱——

但由于我们彼此掌控一个圆盘——
面对彼此的日子——
不知,哪一位是暴君——
也不知谁施行——专制——

910
Experience is the Angled Road
Preferred against the Mind
By—Paradox—the Mind itself—
Presuming it to lead

Quite Opposite—How Complicate
The Discipline of Man—

Compelling Him to Choose Himself
His Preappointed Pain—

910①
经验是一条曲折的路
非头脑所好
矛盾的——是——头脑——
愿受它引导

相当对立——多么奇丽
人类的制度——
竟是强迫自己
选择预定的痛苦——

911
Too little way the House must lie
From every Human Heart
That holds in undisputed Lease
A white inhabitant—

Too narrow is the Right between—
Too imminent the chance—
Each Consciousness must emigrate
And lose it's neighbor once—

911②
那房子肯定离得很近

---

① 题解：头脑中的思想（mind），是观念性和直线性的，经验则是实践性的和曲折的；人的所思所想往往是自由适意的，而来自现实的经验则常令人苦痛和委屈，因为理想与现实毕竟有差距。不过人好奇怪，竟然愿意受他不喜欢的经验的引导，强迫自己去领受那仿佛命中注定的（preappointed）的苦痛。

② 题解：坟墓如房子一般，距离每个人很近，且据无法提出异议的租约，那里可住下一位白色的宾客。人与坟墓间的权利基本对等，即人总要归于坟墓，而坟墓总会容纳死去的人类，这种情况随时可能出现，毕竟人生短暂，时时都可能有人死去。每个活着的（有意识的）人都必然会搬入坟墓中，也必有一次机会失去其近邻。

就在每一颗人心之侧
根据无异议的租约
可容留一位白色房客——

两者的权利差异甚小——
机遇随时迫近——
每个有意识的必须搬迁
也必有一次失去近邻——

912

Peace is a fiction of our Faith—
The Bells a Winter Night
Bearing the Neighbor out of Sound
That never did alight.

912①

宁静是我们信仰的虚构——
钟声在一个冬夜
将邻居送出声音之外
但从未降落安歇。

913

And this of all my Hopes
This, is the silent end
Bountiful colored, my Morning rose
Early and sere, it's end

Never Bud from a Stem
Stepped with so gay a Foot
Never a Worm so confident
Bored at so brave a Root

---

① 题解:安宁,只是我们信念的虚构。比如在一个冬夜,我们为一位死去的邻居鸣钟,想象着钟声会将死者携至钟声之上的天堂安顿下来。灵魂获得安宁,但事实上死者从未获得降落安歇。

913

在我所有的希冀里这个
这个，是无言的结局
曾经色彩夺目，我清晨的蔷薇
如今早早枯萎，死去

从未有哪朵茎上的花蕾
曾如此欢欣迈步
从未有哪只蠕虫如此自信
钻洞在如此坚毅的根部

914

I cannot be ashamed
Because I cannot see
The love you offer—
Magnitude
Reverses Modesty

And I cannot be proud
Because a Hight① so high
Involves Alpine
Requirements
And Services of Snow.

914②

我不会感到羞愧
因我看不见
你给予的爱——

---

① "Hight"在1960年的阅读版中为"Height"。
② 题解："你"不在我眼前，"我"看不见"你"给予的爱，但"我"不会感到羞愧，因为"你"对"我"的爱的巨大，已扭转了"我"原来的谦逊心态；但"我"也不会感到自豪或骄傲，因为"你"的爱已达到如此之高度，"我"要达到同样的高度，简直就如攀登阿尔卑斯山以及应付山上的白雪一样不易，设备需要达到很高的要求才可以成功。

它的巨大
扭转了谦逊之态

我也不会自豪
因如此的高度
已和阿尔卑斯山
的要求
以及白雪的事务相关。

915

Faith—is the Pierless Bridge
Supporting what We see
Unto the Scene that We do not—
Too slender for the eye

It bears the Soul as bold
As it were rocked in Steel
With Arms of Steel at either side—
It joins—behind the Vail①

To what, could We presume
The Bridge would cease to be
To Our far, vascillating② Feet
A first Necessity.

915

信念——是没有桥墩的桥
支撑我们所见
进入看不见的境地——
它对眼睛而言过于纤细

---

① "Vail"在1960年阅读版中为"Veil"。
② "vascillating"在1960年阅读版中为"vacillating"。

它英勇地承载灵魂
如同它在钢铁间摇曳
两边伸出无数钢臂——
它就在轻纱后面——连接

连接什么，我们若能猜到，
那桥就不再是
对我们远行、踌躇的脚
首要的必需。

916

His Feet are shod with Gauze—
His Helmet, is of Gold,
His Breast, a Single Onyx
With Chrysophras①, inlaid.

His Labor is a Chant—
His Idleness—a Tune—
Oh, for a Bee's experience
Of Clovers, and of Noon!

916

他脚着薄纱鞋——
头戴，纯金盔，
前胸，似玛瑙
绿玉，镶在内。

他的劳作是一首歌——
他的闲暇——一支曲调——
啊，一只蜜蜂流连
在苜蓿花丛，在午间！

---

① "Chrysophras" 在 1960 年阅读版中为 "Chrysophrase"。

917

Love—is anterior to Life—
Posterior—to Death—
Initial of Creation, and
The Exponent of Earth—

917

爱——先于生命——
后于——死亡——
是创造的源泉，和
世界的执掌——

918

Only a Shrine, but Mine—
I made the Taper shine—
Madonna dim, to whom all Feet may come,
Regard a Nun—

Thou knowest every Woe—
Needless to tell thee—so—
But can'st thou do
The Grace next to it—heal?
That looks a harder skill to us—
Still—just as easy, if it be thy Will
To thee—Grant me—
Thou knowest, though, so Why tell thee?

918

只有一个神龛，但它属于我——
是我把长烛挑得光彩灼灼——
让圣像暗淡，四面八方的步履，
都走来敬奉这位修女——

你了解人间所有悲伤——

所以——无须再告诉你——
但你难道不能
就当施恩——把它们治愈?
这对我们要难得多——
但对你——却容易,只要你愿意
请允许我——求你治愈——
你本就,知道,为何还要我告诉你?

919

If I can stop one Heart from breaking
I shall not live in vain
If I can ease one Life the Aching
Or cool one Pain

Or help one fainting Robin
Unto his Nest again
I shall not live in Vain.

919

如果我能使一颗心免于破碎
我此生就不会虚度
如果我能给一个疼痛的生命以抚慰
或舒缓其痛楚

或帮助一只昏厥的知更鸟
回到它的巢屋
我此生就不会虚度。

920

We can but follow to the Sun—
As oft as He go down
He leave Ourselves a Sphere behind—
'Tis mostly—following—

We go no further with the Dust
Than to the Earthen Door—
And then the Panels are reversed—
And we behold—no more

920

我们只能追随太阳——
像日落一样平常
他遗给我们一个地球——
让我们——紧随其后——

我们和尘土
只能走到大地的门边——
然后门板翻转——
我们就什么都——不再看见

921

If it had no pencil
Would it try mine—
Worn—now—and dull—sweet,
Writing much to thee.
If it had no word,
Would it make the Daisy,
Most as big as I was,
When it plucked me?

921[①]

如果它没有铅笔

---

① 题解：狄金森于1863年在一张纸条上写下此诗，把它与一截铅笔一起送到附近她哥哥奥斯汀家中的访客鲍尔斯（Samuel Bowles, 1826—1878）手里。鲍尔斯是传说中的狄金森的恋人之一。诗歌表明狄金森想从鲍尔斯那里获得只言片语的回复。诗中的"it"，一个可指狄金森本人，一个可指鲍尔斯。诗中暗示，狄金森的一截铅笔又旧又钝，是因为已用它写了很多字给鲍尔斯，如果鲍尔斯无笔，可用狄金森的笔来写，如果鲍尔斯没有话要说给狄金森，也可以画一朵雏菊，大小如鲍尔斯当年摘取"我"（狄金森）时一样。Judith Farr 把诗中的"plucked"理解为"taken"，认为具有性意味。

它会不会换我的来试——
如今——既旧——又钝——亲爱的,
曾写了许多给你,
如果它无词落笔,
它会不会画一朵雏菊,
大小几乎如我,
当它把我摘取?

922

Those who have been in the Grave the longest—
Those who begin Today—
Equally perish from our Practise—
Death is the other way—

Foot of the Bold did least attempt it—
It—is the White Exploit—
Once to achieve, annuls the power
Once to communicate—

922

那些已长久待在坟墓——
那些今日才刚起步——
都同样在我们的劳碌中消逝——
死亡正是那另一条路——

勇敢者的脚也不敢尝试——
这——是白色的功绩——
一旦获取,就丧失
曾用以交流的力气——

923

How the Waters closed above Him
We shall never know—
How He stretched His Anguish to us

That—is covered too—

Spreads the Pond Her Base of Lilies
Bold above the Boy
Whose unclaimed Hat and Jacket
Sum the History—

923
水面怎样在他头顶合拢
我们无从得知——
他怎样向我们伸出他的痛苦
那——也已被掩盖——

池塘铺展它满池的百合花
在那个男孩头上恣意摇曳
他无人认领的帽子和上衣
说明了发生的一切——

924
Love—is that later Thing than Death—
More previous—than Life—
Confirms it at it's entrance—And
Usurps it—of itself—

Tastes Death—the first—to hand the sting
The Second—to it's friend—
Disarms the little interval—
Deposits Him with God—

Then hovers—an inferior Guard—
Lest this Beloved Charge
Need—once in an Eternity—
A smaller than the Large—

924①

爱——是死之后的事——
远在——生之前——
在入口处确认——然后
就推翻——这个概念——

品尝死——是第一步——传递痛
是第二步——给它的朋友——
消除那小间隙——
将他和上帝放在一起——

随后一位谦逊的警卫——盘桓不去——
以防这位亲爱的事主
一进入永生——就要求——
入微门不入大户——

925

Struck, was I, not yet by Lightning—
Lightning—lets away
Power to perceive His Process
With Vitality.

Maimed—was I—yet not by Venture—
Stone of stolid Boy—
Nor a Sportsman's Peradventure—
Who mine Enemy?

Robbed—was I—intact to Bandit—
All my Mansion torn—

---

① 题解：爱是生之前和死之后的事情。生之前确认确实有爱的存在，随后就再无此概念，可见人生即是苦。死后，朋友才感受到痛，才显示有爱，同时死者也才能越过人境和天境之间的间隙，和上帝同处，并被一位普通警卫（天使）看护，以防这位死去的事主，一进入永生之境，就仍如以往一般企盼尘世间微门小户人家的爱，而非天庭大户（上帝）之爱。

Sun—withdrawn to Recognition—
Furthest shining—done—

Yet was not the foe—of any—
Not the smallest Bird
In the nearest Orchard dwelling
Be of Me—afraid.

Most—I love the Cause that slew Me.
Often as I die
It's beloved Recognition
Holds a Sun on Me—

Best—at Setting—as is Nature's—
Neither witnessed Rise
Till the infinite Aurora
In the other's eyes.

925

我,被击倒,非因闪电——
闪电——释放能量
全程可见
活力激荡。

我——被残害——非因意外——
自冷漠男孩的石头——
也非猎户失手——
谁与我为仇?

我——被劫掠——与盗匪无关——
我的屋宅夷为平地——
太阳——退往天宇——
渺远的光明——消弭——

但并非仇敌——所致——
也非那微小鸟只
在附近果园里
对我——猜忌。

深深地——我爱杀我之因。
时常当我死去
它亲爱的天宇
托着太阳照我躯——

最美——是落日——一如自然的景致——
再看不见升起
直至无垠的曙光
映在他人眼里。

926

Patience—has a quiet Outer—
Patience—Look within—
Is an Insect's futile forces
Infinites—between—

'Scaping one—against the other
Fruitlesser to fling—
Patience—is the Smile's exertion
Through the quivering—

926①

忍耐——有平静的外表——
忍耐——看里面——
是一只昆虫的无力
在无限——之间——

---

① 题解：忍耐，表面平静，内里无力；表面微笑，内里战栗。忍耐，只能继续忍耐，无处可逃，两头都是无限，无法抵达彼岸。

奔逃行为——是向另一个
更徒劳地冲去——
忍耐——是微笑的体现
通过颤栗——

927

Absent Place—an April Day—
Daffodils a-blow
Homesick curiosity
To the Souls that snow—

Drift may block within it
Deeper than without—
Daffodil delight but
Him it duplicate—

927①

未知的地方——四月的一天——
黄水仙
把思乡的执念
吹进覆雪的灵魂间——

飘雪会积于其中
更深厚若非——
黄水仙的欢愉但
对他却是双倍——

928

The Heart has narrow Banks
It measures like the Sea

---

① 题解：在心内心外都积雪的冬天，四月某个地方的黄水仙自然激起人思乡的欲念，让人感到温暖欢乐，从而内心积雪变薄。但对人而言，欢乐是双倍的，不仅内心，身外的冬天也似没那么寒冷，令人欢欣。

In mighty—unremitting Bass
And Blue Monotony

Till Hurricane bisect
And as itself discerns
Its insufficient Area
The Heart convulsive learns

That Calm is but a Wall
Of unattempted Gauze
An instant's Push demolishes
A Questioning—dissolves.

928
心有窄窄的堤
它宽广似大海
不间断的呢喃——低沉而有力
蔚蓝的色彩从不更改

直至飓风劈它成两半
而它也自知
自己地盘有限
这才惊恐地认识

宁静不过是一面墙
一面静止的薄纱
瞬间一推就可摧垮
一个疑问——就能溶化。

929
How far is it to Heaven?
As far as Death this way—
Of River or of Ridge beyond
Was no discovery.

How far is it to Hell?
As far as Death this way—
How far left hand the Sepulchre
Defies Topography.

929①

去天堂有多远?
像死亡之路那么远——
前方有河流或山峦
无法预先发现。

去地狱有多远?
像死亡之路那么远——
左手边的坟墓有多远
难以描绘所见。

930

There is a June when Corn is cut
And Roses in the Seed—
A Summer briefer than the first
But tenderer indeed

As should a Face supposed the Grave's
Emerge a single Noon
In the Vermilion that it wore
Affect us, and return—

---

① 题解：站在上帝右手边，表示将获奖赏留在天堂得永生，在左手边，表示将被惩罚下地狱受永劫。《圣经·新约·马太福音》第 25 章第 32～46 节有描述："And before him shall be gathered all nations: and he shall separate them one from another, as a shepherd divideth his sheep from the goats: And he shall set the sheep on his right hand, but the goats on the left. Then shall the King say unto them on his right hand, Come, ye blessed of my Father, inherit the kingdom prepared for you from the foundation of the world…Then shall he say also unto them on the left hand, Depart from me, ye cursed, into everlasting fire, prepared for the devil and his angels… And these shall go away into everlasting punishment: but the righteous into life eternal."（Matthew 25：32 - 46）。

Two Seasons, it is said, exist—
The Summer of the Just,
And this of Ours, diversified
With Prospect, and with Frost—

May not our Second with it's First
So infinite compare
That We but recollect the one
The① other to prefer?

930②
玉米收割时正是六月
自种子中成长——
这夏季比上一个短暂
但更温凉

仿佛一张来自坟墓的脸
在一个正午出现
红颜尽显
惊扰我们,随即凯旋——

据说,有,两个季节——
有正义的夏季,
而我们这一季,多变

---

① "The"在1960年阅读版中为"Tho"。

② 题解:6月的夏季(也许是Indian Summer)随种子一起生长,至6月成熟。它不如另一个夏季漫长,但却更温凉。它短暂得如坟墓中的人在正午归家省亲,虽有栩栩生气,但只叨扰我们一阵就返回坟墓了。一个是上天正义的夏季,一个是人间多变的夏季,既给人温暖希冀,也带来霜露寒意。第二个夏季是属于人间的短暂的夏季,无法与天上漫长的那第一个夏季相比,我们只能一面怀想和渴望天上的那第一个,一面心里却更喜欢人间的那第二个。本诗写于1864年,狄金森1864年4—11月在波士顿治疗眼疾,住在剑桥,她在6月写给嫂子苏珊(Susan Huntington Gilbert,即Sue)的一封信里有此表述:"I knew it was 'November', but then there is a June when Corn is cut, whose option is within."(L292)。

既有希冀,也有霜期——

我们的第二季难比
如此漫长的第一季
就只能想念一个
却偏爱另一个?

931

Noon—is the Hinge of Day—
Evening—the Tissue Door—
Morning—the East compelling the sill
Till all the World is ajar—

931

正午——是一日的枢纽——
夜晚——是薄纱门——
清晨——东方推挤门槛
直至全世界半开——

932

My best Acquaintances are those
With Whom I spoke no Word—
The Stars that stated come to Town
Esteemed Me never rude
Although to their Celestial Call
I failed to make reply—
My constant—reverential Face
Sufficient Courtesy.

932①

我最熟识的那些
我从未与之言语——
称到镇里来的群星
从不觉得我无礼
虽然对它们来自天上的呼唤
我并未给予回应——
我脸上一贯——景仰的表情
已显示了十足的恭敬。

933

Two Travellers perishing in Snow
The Forests as they froze
Together heard them strengthening
Each other with the words

That Heaven if Heaven—must contain
What Either left behind
And then the cheer too solemn grew
For language, and the wind

Long steps across the features took
That Love had touched the Morn
With reverential Hyacinth—
The taleless Days went on

Till Mystery impatient drew
And those They left behind
Led absent, were procured of Heaven
As Those first furnished, said—

---

① 题解:"我"与天上的群星很熟悉,也一直对它们很恭敬,所以群星不会认为"我"无礼。第三行原文"The Stars that stated come to Town"中的"come to Town"可以理解为星星发出的邀请,如此,"town"应该是指天堂。诗歌体现了说话人和群星的关系,以及其对上天的态度。

933①

两位旅者在雪地死去
树林都听说
他们冻僵前用言语
鼓励对方振作

说如果有天堂——天堂会收留
各自所抛下的
随后欢欣变得肃穆
不再言语,而风啊

大步跨过两具尸体
他们的爱打动了那个早上
以虔诚的紫蓝——
无聊的日子一如既往

直至神秘变得不安
而他们抛下的那些
走失,被救上天堂
一如先到者,所言——

934

That is solemn we have ended
Be it but a Play
Or a Glee among the Garret
Or a Holiday

Or a leaving Home, or later,
Parting with a World

---

① 题解:两位旅者虽被雪冻死,但他们笃信天堂,相信他们死后所抛下的亲友们也会如他们一样能上天堂。他们被冻成紫色,他们对天堂的爱感动了清晨,但风吹过无动于衷,日子流逝得无声无息,他们死去的消息无人传递,日久成谜。直至他们的亲友们也如他们一样在某天消失了,得救上了天堂,才与先到的他们相聚。一切诚如他们所言。

We have understood for better
Still to be explained.

934①
我们的结束是一件庄严的事
不论它只是一场戏
或阁楼上一支欢曲
或一个假期

或一次离家而去，或随后，
作别我们已知的世界
对它的更深认识
需待进一步解释。

935
Death leaves Us homesick, who behind,
Except that it is gone
Are ignorant of it's Concern
As if it were not born.

Through all their former Places, we
Like Individuals go
Who something lost, the seeking for
Is all that's left them, now—

935②
死亡让我们思乡，作为身后人，
除了它消失不见

---

① 题解：任何结束都是一件庄严的事情，包括最后我们结束自己的生命，与我们已了解的这个世界作别。但若想了解这个世界更多，我们还需获得更多的解释。

② 题解：亲人们的死亡令我们思念，但除了他们（死亡）已经消失不见之外，我们对他们（死亡）一无所知，仿佛没发生过一样。满怀思念的我们只能重访他们生前的足迹，在其中一个个找寻谁遗落下了什么。而这种找寻，就是死者遗留给身后人的全部工作。

我们不知其中意味
仿佛从未出现

他们从前所有居所，我们
像个人一样走进
为谁遗落了什么，而找寻
这就是他们身后的全部，如今——

936

This Dust, and it's Feature—
Accredited—Today—
Will in a second Future—
Cease to identify—

This Mind, and it's measure—
A too minute Area
For it's enlarged inspection's
Comparison—appear—

This World, and it's species
A too concluded show
For it's absorbed Attention's
Remotest scrutiny—

936

这一粒尘，及其形骸——
今天——可辨认——
在下个未来——
无法鉴定身份——

这一思想，及其宽度——
只占很小面积
对它更广的查看
对比——显示——

这个世界,及其万物
只是几近尾声的表演
若对它全神贯注
最渺远的审验——

937

I felt a Cleaving in my Mind—
As if my Brain had split—
I tried to match it—Seam by Seam—
But could not make it fit.

The thought behind, I strove to join
Unto the thought before—
But Sequence ravelled out of Sound
Like Balls—upon a Floor.

937

我感觉我思想有一道裂痕——
仿佛我的大脑已裂开——
我极力缝合———针接一针——
但无法恢复如原来。

后面的思绪,我努力将它
接上前面的思绪——
但顺序难以梳理
像一个个线团——散落在地。①

938

Fairer through Fading—as the Day
Into the Darkness dips away—
Half Her Complexion of the Sun—

---

① 本节与第992首基本相同。

Hindering—Haunting—Perishing—

Rallies Her Glow, like a dying Friend—
Teasing with glittering Amend—
Only to aggravate the Dark
Through an expiring—perfect—look—

938①
慢慢消逝更显美丽——当那白日
在黑暗里渐渐消弭——
她的太阳的半张脸——
阻挡——盘桓——将要离去——

像一位垂死的朋友,重振她的光芒——
戏显她飘忽的残辉——
却只让黑暗更加浓重
因她临终——完满的——面容——

939
What I see not, I better see—
Through Faith—my Hazel Eye
Has periods of shutting—
But, No lid has Memory—

For frequent, all my sense obscured
I equally behold
As someone held a light unto
The Features so beloved—

---

① 题解:事物一点点地消逝,更加显得美丽迷人,就像白日渐渐沉入黑暗一样。在日将落时分,半个太阳似乎不愿落下(Hindering),随后有些盘桓犹疑(Haunting),最后终将离去(Perishing)。这就像人临死前回光返照,重焕光辉(Rallies Her Glow),似如戏弄(Teasing),以其闪闪烁烁、强弱不定的生命之光(glittering Amend)。但最终气数已绝(expiring),生命完满(perfect),面容定格,黑暗凝固,更显浓重。

And I arise—and in my Dream—
Do Thee distinguished Grace—
Till jealous Daylight interrupt—
And mar thy perfectness—

939

我看不见的，看得更清晰——
借助信念——我淡褐色的眼
有时关闭——
但，眼睑没有记忆——

时常，我所有的感觉模糊
我依然能看见
仿佛某人掌一盏灯
照亮如此尤物——

我飘然起身——在我的梦里——
赋予你卓绝的光辉——
直至嫉妒的日光插足——
损害了你的完美——

940

On that dear Frame the Years had worn
Yet precious as the House
In which We first experienced Light
The Witnessing, to Us—

Precious! It was conceiveless fair
As Hands the Grave had grimed
Should softly place within our own
Denying that they died.

940①
看那可爱的框架被岁月侵蚀
却珍贵如那房子
在里面我们首次体验了光明
这一次目睹,对我们——

太宝贵!真是难以想象的神奇
仿佛有沾着坟墓尘埃的许多手
轻轻放入我们手心里
说他们欲去还留。

941

The Lady feeds Her little Bird
At rarer intervals—
The little Bird would not dissent
But meekly recognize

The Gulf between the Hand and Her
And crumbless and afar
And fainting, on Her yellow Knee
Fall softly, and adore—

941②
那女士喂她的小鸟
次数越来越少——
小鸟没有异议
只怯怯地意识到

---

① 题解:看着被岁月消磨了生命而最终死去的人的躯体(frame),仍然觉得如此可爱,那种感觉真的太神奇了,仿佛死去的人会活过来,会拉着我们的手说他们没有死,而眼前的死者也同样会活过来。由此可见生者对于死者有多么不舍。对诗中"frame"和"house"的不同理解会带来不同的解读。

② 题解:一只小鸟渴望得到女士的喂食和关心,但两者距离遥远,见面次数越来越少,也没有了面包粒,饥饿的小鸟头晕脚软,但依然对女士没有异议,依然对对方膜拜不已。

手和它之间的距离
以及既遥远也无面包粒
它感到晕眩，黄色的膝
软软地跪下，膜拜不已——

942

Snow beneath whose chilly softness
Some that never lay
Make their first Repose this Winter
I admonish Thee

Blanket Wealthier① the Neighbor
We so new bestow
Than thine acclimated Creature
Wilt Thou, Austere Snow?

942

冰雪下寒冷的温柔乡里
有些从未躺过的
今冬第一次安息
我提醒你

我们新送那邻居的毛毯
要厚重一些
比起你那已适应环境的生灵
你会么，严苛的②雪？

943

A Coffin—is a small Domain,
Yet able to contain

---

① wealthier 意为 "more heavily, with a deeper cover"。
② 严苛的：原文 austere 意为 "严厉，简朴"，也有表达严寒之意，尤其考虑到狄金森为此词提供了异文（variant） "Russian"，或许是想用 "Russian" 表达遥远而寒冷之意。

A Citizen of Paradise
In it's diminished Plane.

A Grave—is a restricted Breadth—
Yet ampler than the Sun—
And all the Seas He populates
And Lands He looks upon

To Him who on it's small Repose
Bestows a single Friend—
Circumference without Relief—
Or Estimate—or End—

943①

棺材——是一块小小领地,
却可安置
一位天堂的公民
在它狭窄的面积里。

坟墓——是一片有限的疆土——
却比太阳宽广——
包涵他养育的全部海洋
和他巡顾的陆地四方

在他小憩时
一位孤身友伴给予他——
一个宇宙无法轻视——
无可估计——无边无涯——

---

① 题解:一位死后将上天堂的公民被一位单身朋友放入棺材,葬在坟墓里,仿佛是在他小憩时将他送到了一个浩瀚的宇宙或世界里。"circumference"一词在狄金森诗里有多种含义,主要指无边无涯、混沌无际的无限状态或包涵、包容一切的全包全含的境界。

944

I learned—at least—what Home could be—
How ignorant I had been
Of pretty ways of Covenant—
How awkward at the Hymn

Round our new Fireside—but for this—
This pattern—of the Way—
Whose Memory drowns me, like the Dip
Of a Celestial Sea—

What Mornings in our Garden—guessed—
What Bees—for us—to hum—
With only Birds to interrupt
The Ripple of our Theme—

And Task for Both—
When Play be done—
Your Problem—of the Brain—
And mine—some foolisher effect—
A Ruffle—or a Tune—

The Afternoons—Together spent—
And Twilight—in the Lanes—
Some ministry to poorer lives—
Seen poorest—thro' our gains—

And then Return—and Night—and Home—

And then away to You to pass—
A new—diviner—care—
Till Sunrise take us back to Scene—
Transmuted—Vivider—

This seems a Home—
And Home is not—
But what that Place could be—
Afflicts me—as a Setting Sun—
Where Dawn—knows how to be—

944①

我了解了——至少——什么是家——
我曾多么无知
对圣约的细节——
也朦胧不解赞美诗

围在我们新炉火旁——但就这样——
这样的——形式——
想起就令我窒息,像沉入
天空的海洋——

我们花园里是怎样的早晨——猜猜——
什么蜜蜂——为我们——嗡唱——
只有鸟儿来打断
我们思绪的飘扬——

还有两人的任务——
当嬉戏结束——
你的——要费脑力——
我的——傻傻地沉迷于
一阵忙乱——或一支乐曲——

---

① 题解:两人曾经在一起,让"我"体验到了家的生活,不再像从前那样不了解在教堂中颂唱赞美诗和山盟海誓的神圣意味,仅仅是一起围坐炉火旁的情景,想起来都幸福得令人窒息。那时的生活是蜂吟鸟唱,快乐嬉戏。工作既有分工,也一起帮助他人。到夜晚则共度良宵,直至第二天清晨日出才醒来。生活是如此美好,一切都变了样,更加精彩。仿佛已经真的有家了,但事实并非如此。这令"我"感到困扰:事情为何会变成那样?正如夕阳,其中如何孕育着明日的黎明,一个真切的黎明,而非虚幻如"我"曾经的家。

下午——我们共度——
薄暮——笼罩小巷——
给贫寒的生命些许帮助——
对比我们所获——它们最显凄凉——

然后返回——夜里——到家——

然后去和你经历——
一个新的——更神圣的——呵护——
直到日出把我们带回原地——
已变了样——精彩胜过当初——

这看似一个家——
事实却非如此——
但那是什么地——
颇费我思量———如夕阳——
那里黎明知道——怎样成为自己——

945

This is a Blossom of the Brain—
A small—italic Seed
Lodged by Design or Happening
The Spirit fructified—

Shy as the Wind of his Chambers
Swift as a Freshet's Tongue
So of the Flower of the Soul
It's process is unknown.

When it is found, a few rejoice
The Wise convey it Home
Carefully cherishing the spot
If other Flower become.

When it is lost, that Day shall be
The Funeral of God,
Upon his Breast, a closing Soul
The Flower of our Lord.

945

这是大脑长出的一枝花——
一颗小小的——斜斜的种子
因天意或巧合埋下
精神结出了果实——

如他室内的风那么羞怯
像洪流的话语那么迅捷
就是这枝灵魂的花朵
它生长的过程无人了解。

当它被发现,给人些许欢愉
智者将它带回家
爱护它小心翼翼
看会否长出更多花。

当它遗失,那天就是
上帝的葬礼,
在他胸前①,一个闭合的灵魂
那是上主之花。

946

It is an honorable Thought
And make One lift One's Hat
As One met sudden Gentlefolk
Upon a daily Street

---

① 据说在死者胸前放一枝花是维多利亚时期葬礼的一个传统。

That We've immortal Place
Though Pyramids decay
And Kingdoms, like the Orchard
Flit Russetly away

946
这是一个荣耀的想法
令人举帽
就像突然遇见乡绅
在寻常街道

想到我们有永生之地
纵然金字塔变成废墟
王国，像果园
带着赤褐色逝去

947
Of Tolling Bell I ask the cause?
"A Soul has gone to Heaven"
I'm answered in a lonesome tone—
Is Heaven then a Prison?

That Bells should ring till all should know
A Soul had gone to Heaven
Would seem to me the more the way
A Good News should be given.

947
我问丧钟为何敲响？
"有一个灵魂已到天堂去"
回答的调子有些凄凉——
难道天堂是一座监狱？

那钟会一直敲到众所周知

有一个灵魂已到天堂去
我听来更像是
告诉大家一个好消息。

948

'Twas Crisis—All the length had passed—
That dull—benumbing time
There is in Fever or Event—
And now the Chance had come—

The instant holding in it's claw
The privilege to live
Or warrant to report the Soul
The other side the Grave.

The Muscles grappled as with leads
That would not let the Will—
The Spirit shook the Adamant—
But could not make it feel.

The Second poised—debated—shot—
Another had begun—
And simultaneously, a Soul
Escaped the House unseen—

948①

这是一次危机——终于全部结束——

---

① 题解：生命奄奄一息的危机时刻，生死只在一念之间（the instant，瞬间），生，则活下来；死，则到坟墓的另一极（天堂）报到。它虽是难捱和无言，但并不平静，而是狂热和多变故。在那一瞬间里，肌肉挣扎着，避免不能动弹；躯体（adamant，坚石）失去感觉，不论心灵如何想要晃醒它。那一秒（the second）那一瞬现在又开始了，（危机）机会又在眼前。那一秒摆好姿势，在争议中射出死亡之箭，另一次危机开始，此时，一个灵魂逃离（肉体的）房子，没人看见，或许是到天堂去报到了，或许是逃脱了被击中的命运。最后一行中的 unseen 可修饰 house，也可修饰 soul。

那段难捱——无言的时间
狂热而多变故——
而今机会来到眼前——

瞬间把生的特权
紧拽在它爪里
或保证汇报灵魂
给坟墓的另一极。

肌肉似与铅扭斗
不愿放走意志——
心灵摇晃着坚石——
但无法让它觉知。

那一秒——以有争议的姿势——射击——
另一次已开始——
与此同时,一个灵魂
逃离房子消失——

949

Under the Light, yet under,
Under the Grass and the Dirt,
Under the Beetle's Cellar
Under the Clover's Root,

Further than Arm could stretch
Were it Giant long,
Further than Sunshine could
Were the Day Year long,

Over the Light, yet over,
Over the Arc of the Bird—
Over the Comet's chimney—
Over the Cubit's Head,

Further than Guess can gallop
Further than Riddle ride—
Oh for a Disc to the Distance
Between Ourselves and the Dead!

949①

在光的下面,再下面,
在草和尘的下面,
在甲虫的地窖下面
在红花草的根下面,

比手臂探出的还要深
假如有巨人的手那么长,
比阳光照射的还要深
假如日子像流年那么长,

在光的上面,再上面,
在鸟的弧顶上面——
在彗星的烟囱上面——
在腕尺②的头顶上面,

比猜测飞奔的还要高远
比谜语骑行的还要高远——
啊多想只有一个圆盘的距离
在死者和我们之间!

950

The Sunset stopped on Cottages

---

① 题解:死者既在阳光下面,在地下的坟墓里,可以说是很深很深,因为死者再不可能回来了;死者也在阳光之上,在天堂里,可以说是很高很远,比月亮还要高远。要是我们和死者离得近,那该多好呀。

② 腕尺(cubit):《圣经·新约·马太福音》第 6 章第 27 节有表述:"Which of you by taking thought can add one cubit unto his stature?"(Matthew 6:27)第 240 首诗中也有"cubit"一词。

Where Sunset hence must be
For treason not of His, but Life's,
Gone Westerly, Today—

The Sunset stopped on Cottages
Where Morning just begun—
What difference, after all, Thou mak'st
Thou supercilious Sun?

950①

落日停于木屋旁
那里便是落日时段
非因它的背叛，而是生命的变迁
奔向西边，今天——

落日停于木屋旁
那里却刚开启了早上——
你到底，制造了，什么变化
你这傲慢的太阳？

951

As Frost is best conceived
By force of it's Result—
Affliction is inferred
By subsequent effect—

If when the sun reveal,
The Garden keep the Gash—
If as the Days resume
The wilted countenance

---

① 题解：同一个落日，停于这些木屋前，是夕阳时段；停于那些木屋前，却是清晨时分。因此，造成这种差异的不是落日，而是生命（生活）的变迁。

Cannot correct the crease
Or counteract the stain—
Presumption is Vitality
Was somewhere put in twain.

951
正如寒霜最能被估计
借助它后果的威力——
烦忧也可被推算
依据其后的效力——

假如当太阳显露，
花园仍遗创痛——
假如当白昼重续
那萎靡的面容

皱纹仍未修复
或斑渍无法消除——
推测意味着活力
曾被一分为二在某处。

952
A Man may make a Remark—
In itself—a quiet thing
That may furnish the Fuse unto a Spark
In dormant nature—lain—

Let us deport—with skill—
Let us discourse—with care—
Powder exists in Charcoal—
Before it exists in Fire.

952①

一个人可以发言——
这本是———一件平静的事
那也会点燃导火线
原本处于——休眠态势——

让我们发话——巧用技艺——
让我们交谈——小心应变——
火药本在木炭里——
它在火中出现之前。

953

A Door just opened on a street—
I—lost—was passing by—
An instant's Width of Warmth disclosed—
And Wealth—and Company.

The Door as instant shut—And I—
I—lost—was passing by—
Lost doubly—but by contrast—most—
Informing—misery—

953

一扇当街的门刚开启——
我——内心失落——正巧过路——
顿时一片温馨显示——
还有财富——和陪护。

那门又瞬间关闭——而我——
我——内心失落——正巧过路——
更倍感失落——但前后对比——最——
喻示——凄楚——

---

① 第1261首诗中也提到了语言的力量:"A Word dropped careless on a Page/May stimulate an eye."

954

The Chemical conviction
That Nought be lost
Enable in Disaster
My fractured Trust—

The Faces of the Atoms
If I shall see
How more the Finished Creatures
Departed me!

954①

化学的断言
说物质不灭
使我陷入灾难
我的信念本不坚决——

假如那些原子的脸
我能看清晰
更多已结束的生灵
将离我而去!

955

The Hollows round His eager Eyes
Were Pages where to read
Pathetic Histories—although
Himself had not complained.
Biography to All who passed
Of Unobtrusive Pain

---

① 题解：人死肉体即灭，本来"我"是这么认为的，虽然不是很坚定，但如今科学却断言物质不灭，这就使"我"陷入灾难中。想象一下：假如人肉体已灭，但其物质分子还在，且"我"还能一一看见无数原子的脸，那样的情形，相当于看见更多已结束的生命在离"我"而去！那是多么令人痛苦的事情，犹如灾难！

Except for the italic Face
Endured, unhelped—unknown.

955

他渴望的双眼四周深陷
如纸页展示出
他悲惨的过去——虽然
他从未有怨诉。
对所有经过身边的人
不啻是默默痛苦的记录
除了那沧桑的脸
隐忍,无助——没人关注。

956

What shall I do when the Summer troubles—
What, when the Rose is ripe—
What when the Eggs fly off in Music
From the Maple Keep?

What shall I do when the Skies a'chirrup
Drop a Tune on me—
When the Bee hangs all Noon in the Buttercup
What will become of me?

Oh, when the Squirrel fills His Pockets
And the Berries stare
How can I bear their jocund Faces
Thou from Here, so far?

'Twouldn't afflict a Robin—
All His Goods have Wings—
I—do not fly, so wherefore
My Perennial Things?

956

当夏日陷入苦恼——
玫瑰红遍——
无数的蛋在音乐中飞远
脱离枫叶的怀抱,我该怎么办?

当喃喃的天空滴下一曲清音
我该怎么办——
当蜜蜂整个正午在金凤花上盘桓
我会变成什么样?

啊,当松鼠填满他的口袋
浆果圆瞪着眼
我如何忍见他们快乐的脸
你离这里,这么遥远?

知更鸟不会苦恼——
他的货物都有翅膀——
而我——不会飞,该去往何处
我经年轮回的事物?

957

As One does Sickness over
In convalescent Mind,
His scrutiny of Chances
By blessed Health obscured—

As One rewalks a Precipice
And whittles at the Twig
That held Him from Perdition
Sown sidewise in the Crag

A Custom of the Soul
Far after suffering

Identity to question
For evidence't has been—

957
像一个人大病初愈
精神正在复原，
他对各种可能性的体察
因身体健康而模糊——

像一个人重走绝壁
削那根细杖
曾使他免于坠亡
撒落于崖石旁

这是灵魂的惯例
在痛苦过后很久
怀疑自己的身份
要找回曾经的证据——

958
We met as Sparks—Diverging Flints
Sent various—scattered ways—
We parted as the Central Flint
Were cloven with an Adze—
Subsisting on the Light We bore
Before We felt the Dark—
We knew by change between itself
And that etherial Spark. ①

958
我们相遇似火花——燧石光激射

---

① "We knew by change between itself/And that etherial Spark." 在1960年的阅读版中为 "A Flint unto this Day—perhaps—/But for that single Spark."。

朝不同方向——播光散彩——
我们分离似那中央燧石
被一把扁斧劈开——
靠自带的光存活
在感受到黑暗之前——
我们偶然相识
在它与那幻妙的火花之间①。

959

A loss of something ever felt I—
The first that I could recollect
Bereft I was—of what I knew not
Too young that any should suspect

A Mourner walked among the children
I notwithstanding went about
As one bemoaning a Dominion
Itself the only Prince cast out—

Elder, Today, a session wiser
And fainter, too, as Wiseness is—
I find myself still softly searching
For my Delinquent Palaces—

And a Suspicion, like a Finger
Touches my Forehead now and then
That I am looking oppositely
For the site of the Kingdom of Heaven—

959

我感到某些事物的失去——
自从懂得回忆

---

① "我们偶然相识/在它与那幻妙的火花之间"在1960年的阅读版中对应译文为"一颗燧石带给这一天——也许——/仅是那一刻火花的闪现"。

失去了什么——我并不知道
当时太年轻从未注意

一个哀悼者行走在孩童间
我依然游弋
像一个人在悲叹一个王国
它自身是唯一遭放逐的王子——

如今,比以前年长,一个更睿智的时期
也更淡定,一如智慧,使然——
我发现自己仍在暗暗找寻
我远逸的宫殿——

一个疑虑,像一根手指
不时轻触我额前
当我正朝相反方向
寻找天国的地点——

960

As plan for Noon and plan for Night
So differ Life and Death
In positive Prospective—
The Foot upon the Earth

At Distance, and Achievement, strains,
The Foot upon the Grave
Makes effort at conclusion
Assisted faint of Love.

960①

正如正午和夜晚的计划不一

---

① 题解:立足于生,想要让人生有成绩,而非虚度,就会费心费力去生活;立足于死,认为人生终究归结于坟墓,就会想如何在死时更得安宁,着重把努力放在死时,且祈愿得到爱些微的帮助。

生与死也各异
从积极的角度看问题——
立足于大地

远处看,获得成绩,费心费力,
立足于坟墓
在结束时才努力
有爱些微的帮助。

961

Wert Thou but ill—that I might show thee
How long a Day I could endure
Though thine attention stop not on me
Nor the least signal, Me assure—

Wert Thou but Stranger in ungracious country—
And Mine—the Door
Thou paused at, for a passing bounty—
No More—

Accused—wert Thou—and Myself—Tribunal—
Convicted—Sentenced—Ermine—not to Me
Half the Condition, thy Reverse—to follow—
Just to partake—the infamy—

The Tenant of the Narrow Cottage, wert Thou—
Permit to be
The Housewife in thy low attendance
Contenteth Me—

No Service hast Thou, I would not achieve it—
To die—or live—
The first—Sweet, proved I, ere I saw thee—
For Life—be Love—

961①

假如你生病——我就能展示给你
我一天能忍耐多长
虽然你对我已不在意
没一丝痕迹,慰我衷肠——

假如你是路人在村野他乡——
我——是那门口
你经停,讨过路的打赏——
别无他求——

假如你——被控告——而我——是法庭——
穿白鼬皮袍的法官——不是对我——定罪——判刑
只要有一半的条件,就给你——平反——
就为分担——那恶名——

假如你是,狭窄小屋的租户——
如若可以
做侍奉你的卑微主妇
也令我满意——

没有你的协助,我不可能完成——
死——还是生——
第一个——亲爱的,请向我确认,在我见你之前
因为生命——就是爱情——

962

Midsummer, was it, when They died—
A full, and perfect time—
The Summer closed upon itself
In Consummated Bloom—

---

① 题解:因为爱"你",所以愿意为"你"做一切,若没有"你",这一切都不可能发生,"我"活着的一生是爱"你"的一生,即使去死,也是因为"你",只要"你"愿意。

The Corn, her furthest kernel filled
Before the coming Flail—
When These—leaned unto Perfectness—
Through Haze of Burial—

962
正是在,仲夏,他们死去——
一个丰盈,完美的时间——
夏季结束它自己
在圆满谢世的花里面——

谷物,充胀她最后的颗粒
在打谷枷到来之前——
此时所有这一切——都接近完美——
透过葬礼的薄烟——

963
A nearness to Tremendousness—
An Agony procures—
Affliction ranges Boundlessness—
Vicinity to Laws

Contentment's quiet Suburb—
Affliction cannot stay
In Acres—It's Location
Is Illocality—

963
接近宏大之极——
由痛苦引起——
烦恼无边无际——
几近规律

幸福宁静的周际——
烦恼无法落户

庭除——它的栖息地
是无处——

964

"Unto Me?" I do not know you—
Where may be your House?

"I am Jesus—Late of Judea—
Now—of Paradise" —

Wagons—have you—to convey me?
This is far from Thence—

"Arms of Mine—sufficient Phaeton—
Trust Omnipotence" —

I am spotted— "I am Pardon" —
I am small— "The Least
Is esteemed in Heaven the Chiefest[①]—
Occupy my House" —

964

"来接我?"我可不认识你——
你的房子在哪里?

"我是耶稣——从前在朱迪亚[②]——

---

① 参见《圣经·新约·马太福音》第 18 章第 4 节: "Whosoever therefore shall humble himself as this little child, the same is greatest in the kingdom of heaven." (Matthew 18: 4)。

② 朱迪亚 (Judea): 原文 "Judea" 也作 "Judaea" (犹太), 位于古巴勒斯坦的南部地区, 是犹太人故土, 包括今巴勒斯坦的南部地区和约旦的西南部地区, 是耶稣生活、传教、受难、复活之地 (参见《圣经·新约·路加福音》第 1~24 章记载)。《圣经·新约·马太福音》第 2 章第 1 节记载耶稣出生地: "Now when Jesus was born in Bethlehem of Judaea in the days of Herod the king, behold, there came wise men from the east to Jerusalem." (Matthew 2: 1)。朱迪亚是古代罗马统治的一个行省, 本丢·彼拉多 (Pontius Pilate) 曾任该地总督, 《圣经·新约·路加福音》第 3 章第 1 节描述: "Now in the fifteenth year of the reign of Tiberius Caesar, Pontius Pilate being governor of Judaea." (Luke 3: 1)。彼时, 彼拉多下令把耶稣钉死在十字架上。

现在——住天国"——

你可带有——车驾——来接我?
这儿离你那里很远——

"挽我的手臂——相当于车马——
请相信神的话"——

我已被玷污——"我是宽恕"——
我很微小——"在天堂
最微小的最重要——
请来我的房居住"——

965

Denial—is the only fact
Perceived by the Denied—
Whose Will—a numb significance—
The Day the Heaven died—

And all the Earth strove common round—
Without Delight, or Beam—
What Comfort was it Wisdom—was—
The spoiler of Our Home?

965

遗弃,是被遗弃者
唯一认识的事实——
其愿望——毫无意义——
在天堂消失的那一日——

地球如常运转——
没有光明,或欢乐——
有何慰藉说智慧——是——
我们家园的破坏者?

966

All forgot for recollecting
Just a paltry One—
All forsook, for just a Stranger's
New Accompanying—

Grace of Wealth, and Grace of Station
Less accounted than
An unknown Esteem possessing—
Estimate—Who can—

Home effaced—Her faces dwindled—
Nature—altered small—
Sun—if shone—or Storm—if shattered—
Overlooked I all—

Dropped—my fate—a timid Pebble—
In thy bolder Sea—
Prove—me—Sweet—if I regret it—
Prove Myself—of Thee—

966

忘记一切只因记起
微不足道的一位——
抛弃一切，只因一个陌生人
新的相陪——

财富的荣耀，地位的荣耀
也比不了
一种未知的尊重显得重要——
估计——谁能做到——

家园被抹去——她面容日渐萎缩——
自然——很小的改变——

阳光——是否普照——或暴雨——是否破坏——
我都视而不见——

把我的命运———块胆怯的卵石——投入——
你勇敢的海里——
请向我——证实——亲爱的——我是否该后悔——
请证实我——对你的意义——

967

Pain—expands the Time—
Ages coil within
The minute Circumference
Of a single Brain—

Pain contracts—the Time—
Occupied with Shot
Gamuts of Eternities
Are as they were not—

967

痛苦——拉长了时间——
岁月盘绕在里面
在一个大脑
小小的空间——

痛苦——缩短了时间——
永恒的全境
被枪击占据
仿佛未曾被占领——

968

Fitter to see Him, I may be
For the long Hindrance—Grace—to Me—
With Summers, and with Winters, grow,

Some passing Year—A trait bestow

To make Me fairest of the Earth—
The Waiting—then—will seem so worth
I shall impute with half a pain
The blame that I was chosen—then—

Time to anticipate His Gaze—
It's first—Delight—and then—Surprise—
The turning o'er and o'er my face
For Evidence it be the Grace—

He left behind One Day—So less
He seek Conviction, That—be This—

I only must not grow so new
That He'll mistake—and ask for me
Of me—when first unto the Door
I go—to Elsewhere go no more—

I only must not change so fair
He'll sigh— "The Other—She—is Where?"
The Love, tho', will array me right
I shall be perfect—in His sight—

If He perceive the other Truth—
Upon an Excellenter Youth—

How sweet I shall not lack in Vain—
But gain—thro' loss—Through Grief—obtain—
The Beauty that reward Him best—
The Beauty of Demand—at Rest—

968
我更适宜见他了,或许
经过长久阻隔——我的——魅力——
与夏季,和冬季,同长,
逝去的年岁——给我特别的模样

要能使我变成世上最美丽——
那么——等待——就有所值
我该有些心痛
那时——竟然怪罪我被选中——

是时候憧憬他注视我的神采——
首先——愉快——接着——意外——
对我的脸反复审视
以确证是那种魅力——

他曾在某天遗弃——如此稀少的光辉
如今他要确认,那位——就是这位——

我一定不能长得太新奇
以免他认不出——还向我问起
我自己——当首次走到那门口
我再不会——往别处走——

我一定不能变得太美丽
他会叹气说——"那另一位——她——在哪里?"
爱,确实,会令我举止得体
我会完美——在他眼里——

假如他从一个更绚烂的青春——
看到另一个真——

多幸福我的退隐就并非徒劳——
而是通过失去——收获——通过悲伤——得到——

他最赏心悦目的美丽——
他需要的美丽——在平静里——

969

He who in Himself believes—
Fraud cannot presume—
Faith is Constancy's Result—
And assumes—from Home—

Cannot perish, though it fail
Every second time—
But defaced Vicariously—
For Some Other Shame—

969

相信自己的人——
欺骗不敢近前——
信仰是坚持的结果——
来自——家传——

它不会丧失,虽然会受挫
一次接一次——
但会黯然失色——
因其他一些丑事——

970

Color—Caste—Denomination—
These—are Time's Affair—
Death's diviner Classifying
Does not know they are—

As in sleep—All Hue forgotten—
Tenets—put behind—
Death's large—Democratic fingers

Rub away the Brand—

If Circassian—He is careless—
If He put away
Chrysalis of Blonde—or Umber—
Equal Butterfly—

They emerge from His Obscuring—
What Death—knows so well—
Our minuter intuitions—
Deem unplausible①

970②
颜色——地位——和名称——
这些——是时间的事务——
死神更神圣的分类里
不知他们为何物——

就如在睡眠里——所有色彩都已忘记——
所有的信条——也置之不理——
死神巨大——可亲的手指
擦掉了所有标记——

是否切尔克斯人③——他并不在乎——
他带走
浅黄——或棕红的蛹——
都同样是蝴蝶——

---

① "Deem unplausible"在1960年阅读版中为"Deem unplausible—"。
② 题注：人生前，有各种标记，比如肤色、地位、名分等，但人死后，没有差异。死亡如同睡眠，死神擦掉了人生前的所有标记，他并不在乎带走什么人，就像不在乎带走的是浅黄或棕红的蛹，反正如同蝴蝶，死神对人的区分是懵懂的，也不在乎，因为死后都一样，没有分别。因此说，凡是死神大智若愚，清楚明白的事情，人类的直觉再细腻敏锐，也难以理解。
③ 切尔克斯人是高加索人的一支。

他们在他的懵懂中显现——
凡死神——所知详尽——
我们的直觉再敏锐——
也觉难以置信

971

Robbed by Death—but that was easy—
To the failing Eye
I could hold the latest Glowing—
Robbed by Liberty

For Her Jugular Defences—
This, too, I endured—
Hint of Glory—it afforded—
For the Brave Beloved—

Fraud of Distance—Fraud of Danger,
Fraud of Death—to bear—
It is Bounty—to Suspense's
Vague Calamity—

Staking our entire Possession
On a Hair's result—
Then—Seesawing—coolly—on it
Trying if it split—

971

被死神夺去——但那倒容易——
对那垂闭的眼
我还可擎起最后一缕光——
被自由夺去

为她做生死博弈——
这一点,我,也能忍耐——

应享——一丝荣耀——
我那勇敢的所爱——

距离的假象——危险的假象,
死亡的假象——要一一忍受——
真够慷慨——对于悬而未决
模棱两可的灾难——

把我们全部所有
赌在一根发丝的结果上——
然后——在其上——冷冷地——拉锯——
试试会否绷断——

972

Unfulfilled to Observation—
Incomplete—to Eye—
But to Faith—a Revolution
In Locality—

Unto Us—the Suns extinguish—
To our Opposite—
New Horizons—they embellish—
Fronting Us—with Night.

972

仔细观察尚未完全——
也不完整——对于眼——
但对于信仰——却是一场革命
在具体地点——

对于我们——太阳已熄灭——
在对面的世界——
新的地平线升起——熠熠美丽——
我们面对——黑夜。

973

'Twas awkward, but it fitted me—
An Ancient fashioned Heart—
It's only lore—it's Steadfastness—
In Change—unerudite—

It only moved as do the Suns—
For merit of Return—
Or Birds—confirmed perpetual
By Alternating Zone—

I only have it not Tonight
In it's established place—
For technicality of Death—
Omitted in the Lease—

973①

它有点笨拙，但适合我——
一颗古老作派的心——
它唯一的学识——它的坚定执着——
在变动方面——不属博学多知——

它就像太阳运行——
总会复返——
或像鸟——肯定永远
将地域轮换——

只是今夜我找不到它
在它的常居地——
因为死神耍了个诡计——
没将它写在租约里——

---

① 题解："我"的心忠贞专一，像太阳周而复始地运行，像鸟儿年年迁徙，永不改变，只是今夜"我"心不复从前，因为在死神的租约里，今夜"我"未被给予它（心）。今夜"我"心不再，因为死神，带走了"我"的所爱。

974

The Soul's distinct connection
With immortality
Is best disclosed by Danger
Or quick Calamity—

As Lightning on a Landscape
Exhibits Sheets of Place—
Not yet suspected—but for Flash—
And Click—and Suddenness.

974

灵魂与永生
明显的关联
在危险或突然的灾难面前
最能体现——

正如陆上的闪电
展示了一片地段——
未曾料见——但只是一闪——
一刹——猛然间。

975

The Mountain sat upon the Plain
In his tremendous Chair—
His observation omnifold,
His inquest, everywhere—

The Seasons played around his knees
Like Children round a sire—
Grandfather of the Days is He
Of Dawn, the Ancestor—

975

山峦端坐在平原
在他巨大的椅子上——
他视野辽阔,
探视,四方——

四季嬉戏在他膝旁
像孩子们围绕在父亲身边——
他是白昼的祖父
黎明的,祖先——

976

Death is a Dialogue between
The Spirit and the Dust.
"Dissolve" says Death—The Spirit "Sir
I have another Trust ["]—

Death doubts it—Argues from the Ground—
The Spirit turns away
Just laying off for evidence
An Overcoat of Clay.

976①

死亡是一场对话
在灵魂和尘土间。
"消散吧"死神说——灵魂答"先生
我有另一个寓居点"——

死神不信——从地里发出质疑——
那灵魂则转身离去
只脱下一件凡人的外衣
作为证据。

---

① 题解:人死后,躯体(凡人的外衣)入土,灵魂升天(到另一个寓居点)。

977

Besides this May
We know
There is Another—
How fair
Our Speculations of the Foreigner!

Some know Him whom We knew—
Sweet Wonder—
A Nature be
Where Saints, and our plain going Neighbor
Keep May!

977①

除了这个五月
我们知道
还有另一个——
多美好
我们对这外邦人的猜测!

有人知道他而我们早已认识——
多奇妙——
有这样一个自然
那里圣人们,和我们朴实的邻居一道
欢度五月!

978

It bloomed and dropt, a Single Noon—
The Flower—distinct and Red—

---

① 题解:天堂的五月对于尘世的五月而言,像一个外邦人,想想还有另一个五月在另一个世界,多美好!想想在那另一个自然里,圣人们和我们去世的邻居一起欢度五月,多奇妙!

I, passing, thought another Noon
Another in it's stead

Will equal glow, and thought no More
But came another Day
To find the Species disappeared—
The Same Locality—

The Sun in place—no other fraud
On Nature's perfect Sum—
Had I but lingered Yesterday—
Was my retrieveless blame—

Much Flowers of this and further Zones
Have perished in my Hands
For seeking it's Resemblance—
But unapproached it stands—

The single Flower of the Earth
That I, in passing by
Unconscious was—Great Nature's Face
Passed infinite by Me—

978①

它绽放继而坠落,在一个正午——
这株花——绛红而突出——
我,经过,心想另一个正午
会有另一株

---

① 本诗中所提及的花,研究者们有不同解读,Judith Farr 认为是萱草:"Yet there was indeed one flower grown by the Dickinsons that blooms for only one day and then drops from the stem, often in noontide heat: the daylily or Hemerocallis."(见 Farr, Judith. *The Gardens of Emily Dickinson*. Cambridge, Massachusetts: Harvard University Press, 2004: 135.)

也同样绽红,由此再无他念
但第二天来看
发现那物种已不见——
在同一地点——

太阳还在原位——并无其他欺骗
对大自然完美的计算——
要是我前一天曾流连——
这是无法挽回的遗憾——

此处和别处的许多花
曾消亡在我手里
想找出它的同类——
但始终难以企及——

大地上的一株花
我,曾经过旁边
浑然不觉——是大自然的脸
从我身旁走向无限——

979

This Merit hath the worst—
It cannot be again—
When Fate hath taunted last
And thrown Her furthest Stone—

The Maimed may pause, and breathe,
And glance securely round—
The Deer attracts no further
Than it resists—the Hound—

979

这功绩糟到极点——
不再是功绩——

当命运发出最后的嘲笑
掷出她最远的石子——

重伤者就可停步,喘气,
放心环顾四周——
鹿的魅力远不及
它抵抗——猎狗——

980

Purple—is fashionable twice—
This season of the year,
And when a soul perceives itself
To be an Emperor.

980

紫色——是双倍的时尚——
在一年中的这一季,
当一颗灵魂发觉自己
是个皇帝。

981

As Sleigh Bells seem in summer
Or Bees, at Christmas show—
So fairy—so fictitious
The individuals do
Repealed from observation—
A Party that we knew—
More distant in an instant
Than Dawn in Timbuctoo.

981

正如雪橇铃声仿佛响在夏天
或蜜蜂,在圣诞节出现——
如此神奇——如此虚幻

以至于人们
不再察看——
我们熟知的一个热闹场面——
刹那间显得更远
比起廷巴克图①的黎明。

982

No Other can reduce

Our mortal Consequence

Like the remembering it be nought

A Period from hence

But Contemplation for

Contemporaneous Nought

Our Single Competition

Jehovah's Estimate.

982②

没有别的可以贬低

我们凡世的结局

能像忆起它只是虚无

当一段时期过去

但关于沉思

当世的虚无

我们唯一的竞争

是耶和华的评估。

983

Ideals are the Fairly Oil

With which we help the Wheel

---

① 廷巴克图：原文为"Timbuctoo"，现为"Timbuktu"，西非撒哈拉沙漠南边的历史名城，19世纪时只有三位白人到过那里。在本诗中喻指遥远之地。
② 题解：对人生的结局或意义，在过后去回忆，发现一切都是虚无，这是最能贬低人生的。但对于人生当世是否是虚无的，有另一位评估者，那就是上帝。

But when the Vital Axle turns
The Eye rejects the Oil.

983

理想相当于润滑油
我们用以把车轮润滑
一旦生命的轮轴转动
眼睛就看不上它。

984

'Tis Anguish grander than Delight
'Tis Resurrection Pain—
The meeting Bands of smitten Face
We questioned to, again.

'Tis Transport wild as thrills the Graves
When Cerements let go
And Creatures clad in Miracle
Go up by Two and Two.

984

这巨痛比欢乐宏大
这是复活的痛苦——
遇见如此多愁苦的脸
我们再次，心生疑雾。

这狂野的激情如坟墓的颤栗
当解去裹尸衣
这些创造物身着奇迹
一对接一对上去。

985

The Missing All—prevented Me
From missing minor Things.

If nothing larger than a World's
Departure from a Hinge—
Or Sun's extinction, be observed—
'Twas not so large that I
Could lift my Forehead from my work
For Curiosity.

985
错过一切,阻止了我
错过次要的东西。
如果没什么事大于世界
从铰链脱离——
或能看到,太阳熄灭——
那就不够重大足以
让我从工作中抬头
就为好奇。

986
A narrow Fellow in the Grass
Occasionally rides—
You may have met Him—did you not
His notice sudden is—

The Grass divides as with a Comb—
A spotted shaft is seen—
And then it closes at your feet
And opens further on—

He likes a Boggy Acre
A Floor too cool for Corn—
Yet when a Boy, and Barefoot—
I more than once at Noon
Have passed, I thought, a Whip lash
Unbraiding in the Sun

When stooping to secure it
It wrinkled, and was gone—

Several of Nature's People
I know, and they know me—
I feel for them a transport
Of cordiality—

But never met this Fellow
Attended, or alone
Without a tighter breathing
And Zero at the Bone—

986
一个细长的家伙
有时在草丛中穿行——
你或许见过——不是么
看见他会猛然一惊——

草向两边岔开像被梳子梳理——
一支带斑点的箭露了出来——
随后草丛在你脚下合拢
又在前方分开——

他喜欢沼泽地
那里太阴凉不适宜种谷物——
但孩提时,赤着脚——
我不止一次在正午
经过,我以为,是一根鞭
伸展在阳光下面
刚要弯腰去捡
它一扭身,倏忽不见——

有几位大自然的子民

我认识，他们对我也熟悉——
我对他们怀着
由衷的欢喜——

但每次遇见这个家伙
不论有人陪伴，还是单独
都会呼吸紧促
骨头冷到零度——

987
The Leaves like Women interchange
Exclusive Confidence—
Somewhat of nods and somewhat
Portentous inference.

The Parties in both cases
Enjoining secrecy—
Inviolable compact
To notoriety.

987
树叶像女人在交流
推心置腹的私语——
时而点头时而
煞有介事地推理。

不论哪种情形
都告诫对方保密——
不可违反的约定
已声名狼藉。

988
The Definition of Beauty is

That Definition is none—①
Of Heaven, easing Analysis,
Since Heaven and He are one.

988
美的定义就是
没有定义——
至于天堂，无须分析，
既然天堂和他是一体。

989
Gratitude—is not the mention
Of a Tenderness,
But it's still appreciation
Out of Plumb of Speech.

When the Sea return no Answer
By the Line and Lead
Proves it there's no Sea, or rather
A remoter Bed?

989
感激——并非提及
一种温情，
而是静静的谢意
来自语言铅锤的测定。

如果大海无回应
借助连线和测锤
可证明根本没海，又或者
海床更深邃？

---

① 第797首诗中有类似的表述："The Definition of Melody—is—/That Definition is none—"。

990

Not all die early, dying young—
Maturity of Fate
Is consummated equally
In Ages, or a Night—

A Hoary Boy, I've known to drop
Whole statured—by the side
Of Junior of Fourscore—'twas Act
Not Period—that died.

990

并非所有早亡,都是夭折——
命运成熟的实现
完全可以
或历经岁月,或一夜间——

一位白发少年,我知道
全身仆倒——邻近于
一位耄耋稚儿——这是行为
而非一生——死去。

991

She sped as Petals of a Rose
Offended by the Wind—
A frail Aristocrat of Time
Indemnity to find—
Leaving on nature—a Default
As Cricket or as Bee—
But Andes in the Bosoms where
She had begun to lie—

991①

她奔忙像玫瑰的花瓣

被风冒犯——

一位时间的脆弱贵族

想找到补偿——

在大自然留下——一份拖欠

像蟋蟀或像蜜蜂——

但就在安第斯山中间

她已开始安躺其中——

992

The Dust behind I strove to join

Unto the Disk before—

But Sequence ravelled out of Sound

Like Balls upon a Floor—

992②

后面的尘土我努力将它

接上前面的圆盘——

但顺序难以梳理

像一个个线团散落地板——

993

We miss Her, not because We see—

The Absence of an Eye—

Except it's Mind accompany

Abridge Society

---

① 题解:一位时间的脆弱贵族,早早夭折,像玫瑰的花瓣被风吹落,忙着奔向永生找补偿,在自然里留下一份拖欠或一个空缺,一如蟋蟀或蜜蜂死去。但无论如何,她已开始被埋在安第斯山中间。本诗写于1865年11月,作者将它送给嫂子苏珊。苏珊的姐姐玛莎(Martha Isabella Gilbert Smith, 1828—1895) 2岁的女儿也叫苏珊,于1865年11月3日去世。

② 本诗与第937首第二节基本相同。

As slightly as the Routes of Stars—
Ourselves—asleep below—
We know that their superior Eyes
Include Us—as they go—

993

我们思念她,非因我们看见——
缺席了一只眼——
除非她思绪的萦绕
限制社交

轻微似群星的路线——
我们——在下面入眠——
知道他们高高在上的眼
在他们走时——定将我们包含——

994

Partake as doth the Bee,
Abstemiously.
The Rose is an Estate—
In Sicily.

994①

像蜜蜂一样品尝,
浅尝辄止。
玫瑰是一座庄园——
在西西里。

995

This was in the White of the Year—

---

① 艾米莉·狄金森的艾默斯特学院(Amherst College)校友,她的表弟佩雷兹·狄金森·考恩(Perez Dickinson Cowan, 1843—1923)在1864年4月26日的日记中记载,他收到艾米莉·狄金森送的一束花,随附一张字条,字条上就是这首诗。

That—was in the Green—
Drifts were as difficult then to think
As Daisies now to be seen—

Looking back is best that is left
Or if it be—before—
Retrospection is Prospect's half,
Sometimes, almost more.

995

此时是一年中白色时节——
彼时——是绿色期间——
彼时难得想到积雪
正如此时雏菊难得一见——

之后能做的最好就是回望
或者假如是——之前——
回顾就相当于展望的一半,
有时, 几乎更多一点。

996

We'll pass without the parting
So to spare
Certificate of Absence—
Deeming where

I left Her I could find Her
If I tried—
This way, I keep from missing
Those that died.

996①
我们会不辞而别
也就不必
缺席证明——
想着在哪里

我离开她我还能找到她
如果我努力不懈——
这样,我就无须老是想念
死去的那些。

997

Crumbling is not an instant's Act
A fundamental pause
Dilapidation's processes
Are organized Decays.

'Tis first a Cobweb on the Soul
A Cuticle of Dust
A Borer in the Axis
An Elemental Rust—

Ruin is formal—Devil's work
Consecutive and slow—
Fail in an instant, no man did
Slipping—is Crash's law.

997
崩溃非一瞬之功

---

① 艾米莉·狄金森诗信的早期编辑托德夫人(Mabel Loomis Todd, 1856—1932)为本诗做了说明:"On the occasion of Mrs Maria Avery Howard's departure from Amherst after a visit, Emily's good-by was embodied in the following lines, accompanied by an oleander blossom tied with black ribbon." (见 Todd, Mabel Loomis, ed. *Letters of Emily Dickinson*, vol. 1. Boston: Roberts Brothers, 1894: 154). 艾米莉·狄金森在本诗中表明不会与霍华德夫人(Mrs Maria Avery Howard, 1833—1893)当面道别,这样就不必确证她已离去,可随时想象着想见她就能见。

一个根本的停歇
破败的过程
是有组织的瓦解。

先是灵魂结了蛛网
蒙一层尘垢
轴心有只蛀虫
生薄薄的锈——

毁坏是有条不紊的——恶行
缓慢而连续——
瞬间消灭,没人做到
悄悄进行——则是碎裂的规律。

998

Best Things dwell out of Sight
The Pearl—the Just—Our Thought.

Most shun the Public Air
Legitimate, and Rare—

The Capsule of the Wind
The Capsule of the Mind

Exhibit here, as doth a Burr—
Germ's Germ be where?

998

最美好的事物不在眼见的现场
珍珠——正义——和我们的思想。

大多避开公众的注意
合理,也稀奇——

那风的荚膜
那心思的蒴果

在此展现,像一个牛蒡——
它胚芽的胚芽在何方?

999

Superfluous were the Sun
When Excellence be dead
He were superfluous every Day
For every Day be said

That syllable whose Faith
Just saves it from Despair
And whose "I'll meet You" hesitates
If Love inquire "Where"?

Upon His dateless Fame
Our Periods may lie
As Stars that drop anonymous
From an abundant sky.

999①

太阳显得多余
当精彩已死去
他每天都显得多余
因为每天都被提及

---

① 题解:太阳如果失去其精彩(光亮),就显得多余。爱也一样,如果失去了爱的真正内涵,只靠单纯的信仰才能令人不对它绝望的话,爱就只有形式,没有内容,只会承诺说"我会去见你",但当对方询问具体在哪里见面时,又犹豫不决了。我们均把有限的一生用于信仰爱,因为它永久以来的声名,但我们终将失败,不会找寻到爱,终会像无名的群星从广袤的天空坠落。

那个字是谁因信仰
才避免它令人绝望
又是谁说"我会去见你"又犹豫
一碰上爱询问"在哪里"?

仰赖他永久的声名
我们将毕生安放其中
像无名的群星坠落
从广袤的天空。

1000
The Fingers of the Light
Tapped soft upon the Town
With "I am great and cannot wait
So therefore let me in."

"You're soon," the Town replied,
"My Faces are asleep—
But swear, and I will let you by,
You will not wake them up."

The easy Guest complied
But once within the Town
The transport of His Countenance
Awakened Maid and Man

The Neighbor in the Pool
Upon His Hip elate
Made loud obeisance and the Gnat
Held up His Cup for Light.

1000
光的手指
轻拍小镇

表示"我很庞大且我等不及
所以请让我进。"

"你来早了,"小镇回答,
"我的脸都在安眠——
但请保证,我让你经过,
你不会唤醒他们。"

和气的客人应许
但一入城里
他面容上的狂喜
惊醒了男男女女

水池里的邻居
兴奋得一屁股坐起
大声表示敬意
而蚊蚋为光把杯高举。

1001

The Stimulus, beyond the Grave
His Countenance to see
Supports me like imperial Drams
Afforded Day by Day.

1001

与他谋面,在坟墓以远
那种激励
支撑着我像宫廷酒
天天供给。

1002

Aurora is the effort
Of the Celestial Face
Unconsciousness of Perfectness
To simulate, to Us.

1002

极光
是天空的努力
没意识到是把完美
给我们，模拟。

1003

Dying at my music!
Bubble! Bubble!
Hold me till the Octave's run!
Quick! Burst the Windows!
Ritardando!
Phials left, and the Sun!

1003

在我的音乐里死去!
沸腾! 沸腾!
扶住我直至八度音奏响!
快! 推开窗!
渐缓之曲!
那些小瓶走了，还有太阳!

1004

There is no Silence in the Earth—so silent
As that endured
Which uttered, would discourage Nature
And haunt the World.

1004

大地上不存在寂静——如此寂静
只因隐忍
一旦爆发，会让自然灰心
令世界不宁。

1005

Bind me—I still can sing—
Banish—my mandolin
Strikes true within—

Slay—and my Soul shall rise
Chanting to Paradise—
Still thine.

1005

捆住我——我仍能歌吟——
放逐我——我的曼陀林
弹奏内心真情——

杀死我——我的灵魂会向上
歌唱到天堂——
依然为你而唱。

1006

The first We knew of Him was Death—
The second—was—Renown—
Except the first had justified
The second had not been.

1006

我们知道他的第一件事是死
第二件——是——声名——
除第一件已证实
第二件尚未确定。

1007

Falsehood of Thee could I suppose

'Twould undermine the Sill
To which my Faith pinned Block by Block
Her Cedar Citadel.

1007
你的虚假我若能猜到
根基会被动摇
在那上面我的信仰把一块块钉牢
建造她的雪松城堡。

1008
How still the Bells in Steeples stand
Till swollen with the Sky
They leap upon their silver Feet
In frantic Melody!

1008
多安静那些钟在尖塔上屹立
直至没入天际
他们银足跃起
在狂野的旋律里!

1009
I was a Phebe①—nothing more—
A Phebe—nothing less—
The little note that others dropt
I fitted into place—

I dwelt too low that any seek—
Too shy, that any blame—
A Phebe makes a little print

---

① Phebe：在1960年阅读版中为Phoebe。其中文名称为霸鹟，为产于北美东部的一种小鸟，其名源于对其叫声的模拟。

Upon the Floors of Fame—

1009

我是一只霸鹟——不多——
一只霸鹟——也不少——
其他鸟发出的轻啼
我一一放好——

我住得太低没人会找——
太羞怯，没人责难——
一只霸鹟留一个小印记
在声名的地板——

1010

Up Life's Hill with my little Bundle
If I prove it steep—
If a Discouragement withhold me—
If my newest step

Older feel than the Hope that prompted—
Spotless be from blame
Heart that proposed as Heart that accepted
Homelessness, for Home—

1010

我带着小小行囊爬上生活的高山
如果我觉得道路险阻——
如果我泄气沮丧——
如果我刚迈出的脚步

感觉比激励我的希望还苍老——
那无可责难
一颗主张不回家的心和一颗接受不回家的心
没什么两样，对家而言——

1011

She rose as high as His Occasion
Then sought the Dust—
And lower lay in low Westminster
For Her brief Crest—

1011①

她升到与他的情形齐高
然后把尘土寻找——
并在低矮的威斯敏斯特躺得更低
为她短暂的巅峰期——

1012

Which is best? Heaven—
Or only Heaven to come
With that old Codicil of Doubt?
I cannot help esteem

The "Bird within the Hand"
Superior to the one
The "Bush" may yield me
Or may not
Too late to choose again.

1012

哪一个最好？天堂——
或是那带着怀疑的古遗嘱附件
即将要来的天堂？
我无法不下论断

"已在手里的鸟"

---

① 题解：她终于能与他齐高，随即归于尘土，而这竟是她短暂的高光时刻。

好过"林子"
可能给我的那只
又或许不会给予
再选已经太迟。

1013

Too scanty 'twas to die for you,
The merest Greek could that.
The living, Sweet, is costlier—
I offer even that—

The Dying, is a trifle, past,
But living, this include
The dying multifold—without
The Respite to be dead.

1013

为你去死太没价值，
只有最无头脑的希腊人才干。
活着，亲爱的，更难坚持——
即便那样我也愿——

死，是小事，终会过去，
但活着，它包括
各种死亡——却无
死的解脱。

1014

Did We abolish Frost
The Summer would not cease—
If Seasons perish or prevail
Is optional with Us—

1014

纵然我们把寒霜消除
夏天也不会结束——
即便季节的消逝或欣荣
任由我们做主——

1015

Were it but Me that gained the Height—
Were it but They, that failed!
How many things the Dying play
Might they but live, they would!

1015

假如唯有我升到那高度——
假如唯有他们,功亏一篑!
垂死的人玩弄多少事物
假如他们还活着,一定会!

1016

The Hills in Purple syllables
The Day's Adventures tell
To little Groups of Continents
Just going Home from School.

1016

群山用紫色的声音
诉说白昼的历险
给一小群大陆
正离校往家赶。

1017

To die—without the Dying
And live—without the Life
This is the hardest Miracle
Propounded to Belief.

1017①

死去——却未消逝
活着——却无生气
这是最艰难的奇迹
向信仰呈递。

1018

Who saw no Sunrise cannot say
The Countenance 'twould be.
Who guess at seeing, guess at loss
Of the Ability.

The Emigrant of Light, it is
Afflicted for the Day.
The Blindness that beheld and blest—
And could not find it's Eye.

1018②

看不见日出的人不能说
那个形象就是。
靠猜看见的人,是猜
那种能力的丧失。

这光的移民,它是困扰
对白昼而言。
那看见并祝福的失明——
找不到自己的眼。

---

① 题解:爱已离去,所以,活着如行尸走肉。像死人,却未离世;像活人,却了无生气。这是一个奇迹,艰难的奇迹,只因信仰爱,才会发生这奇迹。

② 题解:看不见日出的人就不能说那个形象是日出;靠猜测看见,那正表明自己看见它的能力已经丧失。日出(光的移民)对白昼来讲是个困扰,因为在白昼肉眼难以看见太阳,能看见它的是失明(blindness),而失明看不见自己的眼。原文"the Day"也可指"那一天",在那一天,失明者看到了日出,并祝福日出。

1019

My Season's furthest Flower—
I tenderer commend
Because I found Her Kinsmanless,
A Grace without a Friend.

1019

我的季节中最后的花儿——
我温情的推荐
因我发现她没有亲戚,
是一个无朋友的恩典。

1020

Trudging to Eden, looking backward,
I met Somebody's little Boy
Asked him his name—He lisped me "Trotwood"—
Lady, did He belong to thee?

Would it comfort—to know I met him—
And that He did'nt look afraid?
I could'nt weep—for so many smiling
New Acquaintance—this Baby made—

1020

跋涉去伊甸园,回头望,
我遇见谁家的小男孩
问他姓名——他含糊说"特洛特伍德"① ——
女士,他是你的吗?

---

① 特洛特伍德(Trotwood):应是指英国小说家狄更斯(Charles Dickens, 1812—1870)的小说《大卫·科波菲尔》(*David Copperfield*)中的小主人公大卫。在第14章(Chapter 14 My aunt makes up her mind about me)中,大卫跑到贝西姑妈(Miss Betsy Trotwood)家,贝西姑妈给他起名"Trotwood Copperfield"。《大卫·科波菲尔》是艾米莉·狄金森最喜爱的书之一。

是否令人欣慰——知道我与他碰面——
而且他看来也不胆怯?
我不能哭——为这么多笑颜
这新相识——这小孩给的这些——

1021

Far from Love the Heavenly Father
Leads the Chosen Child,
Oftener through Realm of Briar
Than the Meadow mild.

Oftener by the Claw of Dragon
Than the Hand of Friend
Guides the Little One predestined
To the Native Land.

1021

全无爱怜的天父
领那得救的孩子,
往往穿过荆棘的疆土
而非柔美的草地。

往往用虬龙似的爪
而非朋友般的手
引那命定的小娃
朝故土走。

1022

I knew that I had gained
And yet I knew not how
By Diminution it was not
But Discipline unto

A Rigor unrelieved
Except by the Content
Another bear it's Duplicate
In other Continent.

1022
我知我已得到
但不知如何实现
非借助逐渐减少
而通过自律谨严

一种严酷从未缓解
只是内涵有所不一
有人有它的翻版
就在其他陆地。

1023
It rises—passes—on our South
Inscribes a simple Noon—
Cajoles a Moment with the Spires
And infinite is gone—

1023
它升起——经过——我们南方
题献一个简单的正午——
跟塔尖唠叨片刻
然后踪迹全无——

1024
So large my Will
The little that I may
Embarrasses
Like gentle infamy—

Affront to Him
For whom the Whole were small
Affront to me
Who know His Meed of all.

Earth at the best
Is but a scanty Toy—
Bought, carried Home
To Immortality.

It looks so small
We chiefly wonder then
At our Conceit
In purchasing.

1024
我的愿望如此大
我还几乎无所成
令人尴尬
像轻微的恶行——

冒犯了他
全部对于他显得微小
冒犯了我
我知道他对全部的酬劳。

地球至多是个
寒碜的玩具——
买下，带回家
抵达永生之域。

它看起来如此小
我们主要惊愕于
我们的自负
在购买时。

1025

The Products of my Farm are these
Sufficient for my Own
And here and there a Benefit
Unto a Neighbor's Bin.

With Us, 'tis Harvest all the Year
For when the Frosts begin
We just reverse the Zodiac
And fetch the Acres in.

1025

我农庄的产品都在这里
对我已可自足自给
处处都有收益
进入邻居的箱子。

对于我们,全年都是收获季
每当霜降开启
我们就翻转黄道带
纳入这些田地。

1026

The Dying need but little, Dear,
A Glass of Water's all,
A Flower's unobtrusive Face
To punctuate the Wall,

A Fan, perhaps, a Friend's Regret
And Certainty that one
No color in the Rainbow
Perceive, when you are gone.

1026

垂死的人所需甚少,亲爱的,

一杯水而已，
一朵花朦胧的脸
把墙壁标记，

一把扇，或许，一位友人的悔意
而且肯定有一位察知
彩虹无一丝
彩色，当你离世。

1027

My Heart upon a little Plate
Her Palate to delight
A Berry or a Bun, would be,
Might it an Apricot!

1027①

我的心在一个小盘上
让她的腭欢喜
一枚浆果或一个圆面包，就可以，
但愿是一颗杏子！

1028

'Twas my one Glory—
Let it be
Remembered
I was owned of Thee—

1028②

这是我的一份荣誉——
请让此
得以永记
我属于你——

---

① 本诗显然是写来随水果送人的。
② 本诗可能是一首写花的诗，随花送人。

1029

Nor Mountain hinder Me
Nor Sea—
Who's Baltic—
Who's Cordillera?

1029①

没有山可阻止我
也没有海能这样做——
波罗的海算什么——
科迪勒拉山算什么?

1030

That Such have died enable Us
The tranquiller to die—
That Such have lived,
Certificate for Immortality.

1030

那些死去的使我们
死得更平静——
那些已然活着的,
获得了永生证。

1031

Fate slew Him, but He did not drop—
She felled—He did not fall—
Impaled Him on Her fiercest stakes—
He neutralized them all—

---

① 本诗可能是一首写来随花送人的诗。

She stung Him—sapped His firm Advance—
But when Her Worst was done
And He—unmoved regarded Her—
Acknowledged Him a Man.

1031
命运杀了他，但他并未仆倒——
她砍——他也不倒地——
钉他上最恐怖的火刑柱——
他令它们全失去效力——

她刺他——削弱他勇往直前的意志——
但当她最坏的手段都用完
他仍——无动于衷看着她——
她承认他是个好汉。

1032
Who is the East?
The Yellow Man
Who may be Purple if He can
That carries in the Sun.

Who is the West?
The Purple Man
Who may be Yellow if He can
That lets Him out again.

1032
谁是东方？
那黄人
会变紫如果他能
带太阳归隐。

谁是西方？

那紫人
会变黄假如他能
让他再次现身。

1033

Said Death to Passion
"Give of thine an Acre unto me."
Said Passion, through contracting Breaths
"A Thousand Times Thee Nay."

Bore Death from Passion
All His East
He—sovereign as the Sun
Resituated in the West
And the Debate was done.

1033

死神对激情说
"把你的地分一块给我。"
激情,气息越来越弱
"我对你说一千个不。"

死神从激情那里
携走他所有的东方
他自己——像太阳般威仪
重新端坐在西方
争论就此停息。

1034

His Bill an Augur① is
His Head, a Cap and Frill

---

① "Augur" 在 1960 年阅读版中为 "Auger"。

He laboreth at every Tree
A Worm, His utmost Goal.

1034①
他的喙像螺丝钻
他的头,像褶边帽
他在每棵树上忙碌
虫子,是他的终极目标。

1035

Bee! I'm expecting you!
Was saying Yesterday
To Somebody you know
That you were due—

The Frogs got Home last Week—
Are settled, and at work—
Birds, mostly back—
The Clover warm and thick—

You'll get my Letter by
The seventeenth; Reply
Or better, be with me—
Yours, Fly.

1035
蜜蜂!我期盼着你!
昨天还通知
你认识的某人
说你会如期而至——

---

① 本诗曾被1896年版狄金森诗集的编辑赋予诗题"The Woodpecker"(啄木鸟)。

青蛙上周已到家——
已安顿，开始忙活计——
鸟儿，大多已返回——
红花草热烈而茂密——

你会收到我的信
在十七日；请给个回音
或最好，和我在一起——
你的，苍蝇。

1036
Satisfaction—is the Agent
Of Satiety—
Want—a quiet Comissary①
For Infinity.

To possess, is past the instant
We achieve the Joy—
Immortality contented
Were Anomaly.

1036
满足——会导致
腻烦——
匮乏——是无声的表示
无限。

拥有，转瞬成过去
一旦我们获得欢愉——
得享永生
只是特例。

---

① "Comissary" 在1960年阅读版中为 "Commissary"。

1037

Here, where the Daisies fit my Head
'Tis easiest to lie
And every Grass that plays outside
Is sorry, some, for me.

Where I am not afraid to go
I may confide my Flower—
Who was not Enemy of Me
Will gentle be, to Her.

Nor separate, Herself and Me
By Distances become—
A single Bloom we constitute
Departed, or at Home—

1037

这里，雏菊适合戴我头上
这里躺下最舒坦
外面戏耍的每株草
都为我感到，有些，遗憾。

我并不怕来这里①
我会嘱咐我的花——
她并非我仇敌
我会温柔，对她。

我和她，不会分离
纵使相距天涯——
我们同是一枝花
不论分开，或在家——

---

① 这句也可直译为"在我不惧去之地"。约翰逊版和富兰克林版对此诗有不同处理方式，译者翻译时把"Where"等同于第一节中的"Here"，希望使诗意更连贯紧凑，中心更突出。

1038

Her little Parasol to lift
And once to let it down
Her whole Responsibility—
To imitate be Mine.

A Summer further I must wear,
Content if Nature's Drawer
Present me from sepulchral Crease
As blemishless, as Her.

1038[①]

她将小阳伞举起
有时又放低
她全部的职责——
我意欲模拟。

我定要将夏季消磨得更远,
假如大自然的抽屉
自坟墓的皱痕里将我展现
如她一般无瑕,我将深感满意。

1039

I heard, as if I had no Ear
Until a Vital Word
Came all the way from Life to me
And then I knew I heard.

I saw, as if my Eye were on
Another, till a Thing
And now I know 'twas Light, because

---

① 本诗随一朵牵牛花 (morning glory) 赠人。

It fitted them, came in.

I dwelt, as if Myself, were out,
My Body but within
Until a Might detected me
And set my kernel in.

And Spirit turned unto the Dust
"Old Friend, thou knowest me,"
And Time went out to tell the News
And met Eternity

1039
我听见,仿佛我没耳朵
直到一个充满生机的字眼
径直从生命来到我这里
我才知我已听见。

我看见,仿佛我眼盯着别处
直到进来,一样东西
我现在知道那是光,因为
它,对它们适宜。

我安居,仿佛我自己在外,
我身体却在内住
直到一股力量找到我
把我的内核搬入。

灵魂转向尘土
"老伙计,你我可不陌生,"
时间出去传播消息
并会见永恒

1040

Not so the infinite Relations—Below
Division is Adhesion's forfeit—On High
Affliction but a Speculation—And Woe
A Fallacy, a Figment, We knew—

1040①

并非万物无限关联——在下界
隔离恰是联结所弃——在上界
苦恼仅是推测——而悲伤
是谬论，是虚构，我们知道这些——

1041

Somewhat, to hope for,
Be it ne'er so far
Is Capital against Despair—

Somewhat, to suffer,
Be it ne'er so keen—
If terminable, may be borne.

1041

不管怎么说，有所期待，
只要不太遥远
是对抗绝望的资产——

不管怎么说，受苦，
只要不太痛楚——
若有结束之时，也能承受住。

---

① 本诗阅读顺序应该是：并非万物无限关联。在下界，隔离恰是联结所弃；在上界，苦恼仅是推测，而悲伤是谬论，是虚构。我们知道这些。

1042

Spring comes on the World—
I sight the Aprils—
Hueless to me until thou come
As, till the Bee
Blossoms stand negative,
Touched to Conditions
By a Hum.

1042

春天来到世界——
我看见四月——
色彩全无直至你到来
就像，花朵无精打采
直至蜜蜂，
触而发动
用一阵嗡嗡。

1043

Lest this be Heaven indeed
An Obstacle is given
That always gauges a Degree
Between Ourself and Heaven.

1043

为防这个真是天堂
一个屏障被推出
以便在我们和天堂之间
总能测定一个刻度。

1044

A Sickness of this World it most occasions
When Best Men die.
A Wishfulness their far Condition
To occupy.

A Chief indifference, as Foreign
A World must be
Themselves forsake—contented,
For Deity

1044①
一种对当世的厌烦往往被触发
当那些人杰死去。
一种渴望想对他们遥远的情形
占据。

一种明显的冷漠,仿佛完全陌生
这一世界肯定
为他们所弃——安心满意,
为了神性

1045
Nature rarer uses Yellow
Than another Hue.
Saves she all of that for Sunsets
Prodigal of Blue

Spending Scarlet, like a Woman
Yellow she affords
Only scantly and selectly
Like a Lover's Words.

1045
大自然更少用黄色
比起用其他色彩。

---

① 题解:人杰死去可上天堂,往往引发世人对当前世界的厌烦,心里渴望能和人杰一样占据在遥远的世界。对当世的态度就主要是冷漠,似乎完全陌生,觉得这个世界就是人杰抛弃的世界,还颇感满意,为得那居于天堂的神性。

她储存它就专为日落
蓝色的慷慨

红色的挥霍,像一位妇人
她供给黄色时
总是精简而谨慎
像一位恋人的用词。

1046
I've dropped my Brain—My Soul is numb—
The Veins that used to run
Stop palsied—'tis Paralysis
Done perfecter on stone

Vitality is Carved and cool.
My nerve in Marble lies—
A Breathing Woman
Yesterday—Endowed with Paradise.

Not dumb—I had a sort that moved—
A Sense that smote and stirred—
Instincts for Dance—a caper part—
An Aptitude for Bird—

Who wrought Carrara in me
And chiselled all my tune
Were it a Witchcraft—were it Death—
I've still a chance to strain

To Being, somewhere—Motion—Breath—
Though Centuries beyond,
And every limit a Decade—
I'll shiver, satisfied.

1046

我已垂下头颅——灵魂麻木——
曾经奔流的血脉
止于麻痹——这叫瘫痪
石头上完成更精彩。

活力被切割而变得冰凉。
我的神经在大理石里躺——
一位气息盈盈的妇人
昨日——得上天堂。

并非喑哑——我也还在动——
一种感觉在翻搅和冲击——
一种本能想舞蹈——一种雀跃的本领——
一种鸟的能力——

谁在我身上锻造卡拉拉①大理石
凿出我所有的乐曲
假如这是巫术——假如这是死——
我尚有机会争取

活着,在某处——移动——呼吸——
纵有几世纪的距离,
且每十年为一限——
我也会在颤栗中,感到满意。

1047

The Opening and the Close
Of Being, are alike

---

① 卡拉拉(Carrara):意大利中部地名,以出产白色和蓝灰色大理石闻名。艾米莉·狄金森在 1862 年 5 月下旬写给路易丝·诺克罗斯(Louise Norcross)和弗朗西斯·诺克罗斯(Frances Norcross)两位表妹的一封信里提到过这个词:"Do they dwell in Carrara? Did they find the garden in the gown?"(L264)。

Or differ, if they do,
As Bloom upon a Stalk.

That from an equal Seed
Unto an equal Bud
Go parallel, perfected
In that they have decayed.

1047①
存在的开启
和关闭,相似
或相异,假如真如此,
犹如花朵在枝。

从一粒同样的种子
长成一苞同样的蓓蕾
一路相伴,直至圆满
最后他们都已枯萎。

1048
Reportless Subjects, to the Quick
Continual addressed—
But foreign as the Dialect
Of Danes, unto the rest.

Reportless Measures, to the Ear
Susceptive—stimulus—
But like an Oriental Tale
To others, fabulous—

---

① 题解:存在(生命)的开始和结束都是相似的,或者也有不同。如果相似,那就跟枝干上的花朵类似,同是从一粒种子长出,历经相似的萌芽期、成熟期,最后全都枯萎腐败。如果有不同,那就是人在死后也许仍有来生。

1048

难于描述的主题,向急智者
诉说不停——
却像丹麦人的方言
那般陌生,对其他人。

难于描述的节律,对于耳朵
是强烈的——刺激——
却像一个东方故事
对于别人,那般神奇——

1049

Pain has but one Acquaintance
And that is Death—
Each one unto the other
Society enough.

Pain is the Junior Party
By just a Second's right—
Death tenderly assists Him
And then absconds from Sight.

1049

痛苦只有一位相识
那就是死亡——
各自对于对方
都是满意的依傍。

痛苦是较小的一方
只有次一等的权利——
死亡就温柔地扶助他
然后一同逃匿。

1050

As willing lid o'er weary eye

The Evening on the Day leans
Till of all our nature's House
Remains but Balcony

1050

正如甘愿的眼睑将疲惫的眼遮住
傍晚倚在白昼身上
直至我们自然的整座大屋
仅有阳台露出

1051

I cannot meet the Spring unmoved—
I feel the old desire—
A Hurry with a lingering, mixed,
A Warrant to be fair—

A Competition in my sense
With something hid in Her—
And as she vanishes, Remorse
I saw no more of Her.

1051①

我无法邂逅春天而无动于衷——
我感受到那古老的冲动——
一种急促加流连,混杂在一起,
一种确保公平的保证——

我感受到一种竞争
与她内心某种东西——
而当她消失,真懊悔呀
我再无法与她相遇。

---

① 题解:我邂逅春天,感受到她那古老的冲动,既要匆匆离去,也愿欲去还留,二者均有,以保持平衡公正。我感受到内心与春天存在某种竞争,或许是抗拒,或许是妒忌,但是呀,当春天离去,我懊悔不已,再无法与她相遇。

1052

I never saw a Moor—
I never saw the Sea—
Yet know I how the Heather looks
And what a Billow be.

I never spoke with God
Nor visited in Heaven—
Yet certain am I of the spot
As if the Checks were given—

1052

我从未见过荒野——
我从未见过大海——
但我知道石南的模样
和波涛的风采。

我从未与上帝交谈
也未到访过天堂——
但我确信有那个地方
仿佛已有车票①在手上——

1053

It was a quiet way—
He asked if I was his—
I made no answer of the Tongue
But answer of the Eyes—
And then He bore me on
Before this mortal noise
With swiftness, as of Chariots
And distance, as of Wheels.

---

① 车票（checks）：火车票（railway tickets）的通俗称谓。

This World did drop away
As Acres from the feet
Of one that leaneth from Balloon
Upon an Ether street.
The Gulf behind was not,
The Continents were new—
Eternity it was before
Eternity was due.
No Seasons were to us—
It was not Night nor Morn—
But Sunrise stopped upon the place
And fastened it in Dawn.

1053

就这么轻轻地——
他问我是否属于他——
我的舌头没有回话
但眼睛已作答——
随后他携我前行
面对凡世的嘈杂
迅捷,如乘车马
遥远,如藉车轮。
这个世界确实在远逝
仿佛土地远离双脚
它们的主人在气球上
倾身向苍天的街道。
背后没有海湾,
大陆焕然一新——
永恒就在前面
永恒即将来到。
我们没有四季——
没有暗夜与清早——
只有朝阳停在那个地方
把自己栓紧在拂晓。

1054

Not to discover weakness is
The Artifice of strength—
Impregnability inheres
As much through Consciousness

Of faith of others in itself
As Pyramidal Nerve
Behind the most unconscious clock
What skilful Pointers move—

1054

不去发掘软弱
正是力量的诡计——
固有的牢不可破
源于意识到

别人对它的信念
正如金字塔似的机件
密集在毫不知情的钟后面
那些指针转动多灵便——

1055

The Soul should always stand ajar
That if the Heaven inquire
He will not be obliged to wait
Or shy of troubling Her

Depart, before the Host have slid
The Bolt unto the Door—
To search for the accomplished Guest,
Her Visitor, no more—

1055

灵魂应保持半敞开
以便天堂有事要找
他不必被迫等待
或羞于打扰

就离开,在主人
插上门闩——
不再找寻贵宾,
她的访客,之前——

1056

There is a Zone whose even Years
No Solstice interrupt—
Whose Sun constructs perpetual Noon
Whose perfect Seasons wait—

Whose Summer set in Summer, till
The Centuries of June
And Centuries of August cease
And Consciousness—is Noon.

1056

有这么一个地带那里长年
没有夏至或冬至出入——
那里太阳营造永恒的正午
那里完美的四季常驻——

那里夏季紧接夏季,直至
几个世纪的六月
以及几个世纪的八月停止
而意识——是正午时节。

1057

I had a daily Bliss
I half indifferent viewed
Till sudden I perceived it stir—
It grew as I pursued

Till when around a Height
It wasted from my sight
Increased beyond my utmost scope
I learned to estimate.

1057

我有一份日常的快乐
我几乎一直对它漠视
直至突然发现它躁动——
它成长在我追求时

直至到某个高度
它逐渐淡出我视域
增大到超出
我能估量的最远距离。

1058

Bloom—is Result—to meet a Flower
And casually glance
Would scarcely cause one to suspect
The minor Circumstance

Assisting in the Bright Affair
So intricately done
Then offered as a Butterfly
To the Meridian—

To pack the Bud—oppose the Worm—

Obtain its right of Dew—
Adjust the Heat—elude the Wind—
Escape the prowling Bee

Great Nature not to disappoint
Awaiting Her that Day—
To be a Flower, is profound
Responsibility—

1058
遇见一朵花——总看到——花娇艳丽
不经意的一瞥
几乎不会令人注意
周边不起眼的一切

在帮助灿烂的事业
如此细微呵护
然后像一只蝴蝶
献给辉煌的正午——

将蓓蕾包住——以防虫蛀——
让它有权沐浴甘露——
调节温度——避开狂风——
躲闪逡巡的蜜蜂

不辜负大自然
在那天等候她——
作为一朵花，肩负重大
责任——

1059
Sang from the Heart, Sire,
Dipped my Beak in it,
If the Tune drip too much

Have a tint too Red

Pardon the Cochineal—
Suffer the Vermillion①—
Death is the Wealth
Of the Poorest Bird.

Bear with the Ballad—
Awkward—faltering—
Death twists the strings—
'Twas'nt my blame—

Pause in your Liturgies—
Wait your Chorals—
While I repeat your
Hallowed name—

1059

从心中唱出，先生，
把我的喙浸入其中，
如果曲子滴水太多
颜色太红

请原谅那胭脂红——
染上太多红朱——
对那只最清贫的鸟
死是一笔财富。

携着那歌谣——
笨拙——又孱弱——
是死神扭曲了琴弦——

---

① "Vermillion" 在1960年阅读版中为"Vermilion"。

那不是我的错——

暂止于你的礼拜仪式——
等你的唱诗班响起——
当我不断重复你
神圣的名字——

1060

Air has no Residence, no Neighbor,
No Ear, no Door,
No Apprehension of Another
Oh, Happy Air!

Ethereal Guest at e'en an Outcast's Pillow—
Essential Host, in Life's faint, wailing Inn,
Later than Light thy Consciousness accost me
Till it depart, persuading Mine—

1060

空气没有住处,没有邻居,
没有耳朵,没有门户,
没有对别人的恐惧
呵,快乐的空气!

空灵的客人甚至枕着被弃者的枕头——
必需的主人,在生命衰弱、哀嚎的旅馆,
你的意识在光之后来与我搭讪
直至它离开,劝服我也同往——

1061

Three Weeks passed since I had seen Her—
Some Disease had vext
'Twas with Text and Village Singing
I beheld Her next

And a Company—our pleasure
To discourse alone—
Gracious now to me as any—
Gracious unto none—

Borne without dissent of Either
To the Parish night—
Of the Separated Parties
Which be out of sight?

1061

与她晤面后才过三周——
某种疾病已发难
透过文告和村庄的吟唱
我与她再次相见

还有众人——我们曾愉快
促膝交谈——
如今我感觉亲切无比——
但无人有同感——

双方均无异议
忍受着这教区的夜晚——
在散去的人群里
谁已消逝不见?

1062

He scanned it—staggered—
Dropped the Loop
To Past or Period—
Caught helpless at a sense as if
His Mind were going blind—

Groped up, to see if God was there—

Groped backward at Himself
Caressed a Trigger absently
And wandered out of Life.

1062

他审视它——摇晃着——
松开环扣
扫过或停住——
感到无助仿佛
他的大脑正变得盲目——

向上摸索，看上帝是否在那里——
摸索他身后一带
茫然按动扳机
便游离生命之外。

1063

Ashes denote that Fire was—
Revere the Grayest Pile
For the Departed Creature's sake
That hovered there awhile—

Fire exists the first in light
And then consolidates
Only the Chemist can disclose
Into what Carbonates.

1063

灰烬表明曾经有火——
请敬畏那最灰色的一堆
为那离去的生灵
他曾在那里低徊——

火起初存在于光里

随后合为一体
唯有化学家能揭示
是什么碳酸盐物质。

1064

To help our Bleaker Parts
Salubrious Hours are given
Which if they do not fir for Earth
Drill silently for Heaven—

1064

救助自身更羸弱的部分
我们有怡人的时光
如若它们不宜活在尘世
悄然磨砺它们去往天堂——

1065

Let down the Bars, Oh Death—
The tired Flocks come in
Whose bleating ceases to repeat
Whose wandering is done—

Thine is the stillest night
Thine the securest Fold
Too near Thou art for seeking Thee
Too tender, to be told.

1065

放下栅栏,啊死神——
让疲惫的羊群进入
它们的悲鸣已不再
它们的流浪已结束——

你就是最安宁的夜

你就是最安全的羊圈
你离得太近无须找寻
你太温柔,不劳多言。

1066

Fame's Boys and Girls, who never die
And are too seldom born—

1066

声名的少男少女,永不死去
也极少有新的诞生——

1067

Except the smaller size
No lives are round—
These—hurry to a sphere
And show and end—
The larger—slower grow
And later hang—
The Summers of Hesperides
Are long.

1067①

除了那较小的
没有生命是圆形的——
这些——迅速长成球体
展现并结束生命——
那较大的——成长缓慢
随后悬荡——

---

① 本诗是艾米莉·狄金森1866年3月17日写给文学导师希金森(Thomas Wentworth Higginson)的一封信(L316)的结尾;作者也把本诗赠给了嫂子苏珊,据说可能是作为送给嫂子的苹果礼物的附诗。

金苹果园①的夏季
漫长。

1068

Further in Summer than the Birds
Pathetic from the Grass
A minor Nation celebrates
It's unobtrusive Mass.

No Ordinance be seen
So gradual the Grace
A pensive Custom it becomes
Enlarging Loneliness.

Antiquest felt at Noon
When August burning low
Arise this spectral Canticle
Repose to typify

Remit as yet no Grace
No Furrow on the Glow
Yet a Druidic Difference
Enhances Nature now

1068

比鸟儿还要深入夏天
来自青草的悲怜
一个微小的国度在举行
它不引人注目的弥撒宴。

---

① 金苹果园：原文 Hesperides 指古希腊神话中看守金苹果园的赫斯珀洛斯（Hesperus）神的女儿们。有神话说是姐妹 3 人，也有说是 4 人，还有说是 7 人，其中 4 人名为 Aegle、Arethusa、Erythia 和 Hesperethusa。本词也可喻指金苹果园或金苹果园所在的西方世界中的一个海岛。

没有仪式可见
那种庄严渐渐
形成一种忧郁的气氛
使孤独更为明显。

在正午感觉最为古老
当八月低低地燃烧
怪异的幽歌升起
暂停以彰显灵妙

没有减损一点庄严
火光中没有一丝愁郁
但却给此刻的大自然
增添了别样的神秘

1069

Paradise is of the option.
Whosoever will
Own① in Eden notwithstanding
Adam and Repeal.

1069②

极乐园是一个选项。
无论谁住
在伊甸园尽管
有亚当和废除。

1070

To undertake is to achieve

---

① Own in：本诗草稿中原是"Dwell in"。
② 本诗是艾米莉·狄金森1866年6月9日写给文学导师希金森的一封信（L319）的结尾，信中本诗之前有这一句："To escape enchantment, one must always flee."本诗大意或许是：不论是谁，住在伊甸园总是人类一个选项，尽管曾经发生了亚当在其中犯事以及伊甸园已被废除这样的事情。

Be Undertaking blent
With fortitude of obstacle
And toward encouragement

That fine Suspicion, Natures must
Permitted to revere
Departed Standards and the few
Criterion Sources here

1070①
答应就是做到
假如答应结合与
阻力的坚毅
以及鼓励

那精细的怀疑,大自然一定
允许敬慕
偏离的标准和少数
此处的准则基础

1071
Perception of an object costs
Precise the Object's loss—
Perception in itself a Gain
Replying to it's Price—
The Object Absolute—is nought—
Perception sets it fair
And then upbraids a Perfectness
That situates so far—

---

① 题解:能答应去做已经相当于成功做到了,假如答应已经意味着承担了艰巨的阻力和各种受到鼓励的、精细入微的、难以言表的怀疑。上天一定会允许有人去崇敬那些偏离传统的标准,以及订立属于自己的少数的准则。本诗似可理解为诗人对自己选择的非传统的人生发展道路和诗歌创作道路的辩护。按她的逻辑,不论她最终能否成功,她能这么选择,本身就已意味着一种成就。

1071

对一个物体的感知须支出
物体本身的遗失——
感知本身是一种收获
对应于它的付出——
纯粹的物体——不存在——
感知令它美丽
随后责备那种完美
竟至如此渺远境地——

1072①

Title divine—is mine!
The Wife—without the Sign!
Acute Degree—conferred on me—
Empress of Calvary!
Royal—all but the Crown!
Betrothed—without the swoon
God sends us Women—
When you—hold—Garnet to Garnet—
Gold—to Gold—
Born—Bridalled—Shrouded—
In a Day—
"My Husband"—women say—
Stroking the Melody—
Is this—the way?

1072

神圣的头衔——我今得添!
成为妻子——无须牌匾!

---

① 本诗当作一封信寄给朋友鲍尔斯,诗后附言:"Here's—what I had to 'tell you'—You will tell no other? Honor—is it's own pawn—"(L250)。随后她也把本诗赠给了嫂子苏珊,但第七行变成了"God gives us Women—",在第 11 行"In a Day—"后增加了一行"Tri Victory—"。

非一般的地位——向我颁授——
髑髅地①的皇后!
高贵——只差王冠!
订了婚——但无迷恋
上帝给我们送来了女人——
当你——拥有——宝石对宝石——
黄金——对黄金——
出生——成为新娘——罩着尸衣——
就在一天——
"我的夫君"——女人们说话——
边奏着乐曲——
是——这样吗?

1073

Experiment to me
Is every one I meet
If it contain a Kernel?
The Figure of a Nut

Presents upon a Tree
Equally plausibly,
But Meat within, is requisite
To Squirrels, and to Me

1073

对我的考验
就是我遇见的每一位
是否都有内核?
一枚坚果的形象

---

① 髑髅地 (Calvary):即耶稣受难地,指耶稣被钉上十字架的地方,位于耶路撒冷以西的一座山上。参见《圣经·新约·路加福音》第23章第33节记载:"And when they were come to the place, which is called Calvary, there they crucified him, and the malefactors, one on the right hand, and the other on the left."(Luke 23:33)

呈现于树上
貌似同样不错,
但内有果肉,是必需
对于松鼠,和我

1074

Count not that far that can be had,
Though sunset lie between—
Nor that adjacent, that beside,
Is further than the sun.

1074①

别以为真如此遥远,
纵有落日横在中间——
也别以为毗邻,是近旁,
它远过太阳。

1075

The Sky is low—the Clouds are mean.
A Travelling Flake of Snow
Across a Barn or through a Rut
Debates if it will go—

A Narrow Wind complains all Day
How some one treated him
Nature, like Us is sometimes caught
Without her Diadem.

1075

天空低垂——云层黯淡。
一片雪花漂游

---

① 这是作者1866年5月上旬写给朋友霍兰夫人(Mrs. J. G. Holland,即Elizabeth Luna Chapin Holland)的一封信中的附诗。

越过谷仓或掠过路沟
犹豫是去还是留——

一缕轻风整天抱怨
别人待它如何轻浅
大自然,像我们有时被人看见
不戴冠冕。

1076

Just Once! Oh least Request!
Could Adamant refuse
So small a Grace
So scanty put,
Such agonizing terms?
Would not a God of Flint
Be conscious of a sigh
As down His Heaven dropt remote
"Just Once" Sweet Deity?

1076

就一次! 啊最低的要求!
难道顽石会拒绝
如此微小的恩典
如此寒碜地提起,
那样令人悲痛的字眼?
难道铁石心肠的上帝
留意到一声叹息
不会自遥远的天堂掷下一句
"就一次"亲爱的上帝?

1077

These are the Signs to Nature's Inns—
Her invitation broad

To Whosoever famishing
To taste her mystic Bread—

These are the rites of Nature's House—
The Hospitality
That opens with an equal width
To Beggar and to Bee

For Sureties of her staunch Estate
Her undecaying Cheer
The Purple in the East is set
And in the North, the Star—

1077
这些是指向大自然酒馆的标记——
她广为相邀
但凡饥饿的人
去品尝她神秘的面包——

这些是大自然屋宅举行的典礼——
殷勤款待
用同等的胸怀恭迎
蜜蜂和乞丐

为使大家找到她坚固的大宅
她永不消退的欢欣
东方的紫色落下
北方,升起了星星——

1078
The Bustle in a House
The Morning after Death
Is solemnest of industries
Enacted upon Earth—

The Sweeping up the Heart
And putting Love away
We shall not want to use again
Until Eternity.

1078
屋里的喧闹
在人死后的清早
是世间上演的
最庄严的操劳——

把心扫起
将爱收捡
我们不再用它
直至永远。

1079
The Sun went down—no Man looked on—
The Earth and I, alone,
Were present at the Majesty—
He triumphed, and went on—

The Sun went up—no Man looked on—
The Earth and I and One
A nameless Bird—a Stranger
Were Witness for the Crown—

1079
太阳下山——没人在看——
只有，我和大地，
出席那种庄严——
他得胜，继续进击——

太阳升起——没人注意——

我和大地还有一位
是只无名鸟儿———一位陌生客
共同见证王冠的光辉——

1080

When they come back—if Blossoms do—
I always feel a doubt
If Blossoms can be born again
When once the Art is out—

When they begin, if Robins may,
I always had a fear
I did not tell, it was their last Experiment
Last Year,

When it is May, if May return,
Had nobody a pang
Lest in a Face so beautiful
He might not look again?

If I am there—One does not know
What Party—One may be
Tomorrow, but if I am there
I take back all I say—

1080

当它们归来——假如群芳真归来——
我总感一丝怀疑
群芳能否再开
当那艺术已绽放一次——

当它们开始,假如知更鸟愿意,
我总有一丝恐惧
我并未透露,那是它们最后的尝试

去年此时,

正当五月,假如五月回返,
是否已无人悲痛
以防他不再顾盼
如此美丽的面容?

假如我在那里——没人知道
自己属于——哪一方
明天,但假如我真在那里
我收回我所讲——

1081

Superiority to Fate
Is difficult to gain
'Tis not conferred of Any
But possible to earn

A pittance at a time
Until to Her surprise
The Soul with strict economy
Subsist till Paradise.

1081

想超越命运
很难破阻力
世无凭白授予
但有可能争取

一次获得一点
直至令她吃惊
灵魂竟靠严苛的节俭
存活到了天庭。

1082

Revolution is the Pod
Systems rattle from
When the Winds of Will are stirred
Excellent is Bloom

But except it's Russet Base
Every Summer be
The Entomber of itself,
So of Liberty—

Left inactive on the Stalk
All it's Purple fled
Revolution shakes it for
Test if it be dead.

1082

革命是那豆荚
从中嘎嘎产生体系
当意志的风被搅动
美丽的是花期

但除了它红褐色的基地
每个夏季都是
自己的埋葬者,
自由也如此——

留在枝上无精打采
它所有紫色都已逃逸
革命摇晃它以检查
它是否已死。

1083

We learn it in Retreating

How vast an one
Was recently among us—
A Perished Sun

Endear in the departure
How doubly more
Than all the Golden presence
It was—before—

1083
退却时我们知悉
有一位多么宽广
最近和我们在一起——
一个逝去的太阳

别离时更感
加倍地爱恋
胜过它金色的显现
曾经——从前——

1084
At Half past Three, a single Bird
Unto a silent Sky
Propounded but a single term
Of cautious melody.

At Half past Four, Experiment
Had subjugated test
And lo, Her silver Principle
Supplanted all the rest.

At Half past Seven, Element
Nor Implement, be seen—
And Place was where the Presence was
Circumference between.

1084①

三点半，一只鸟儿
向宁静的天宇
提议仅唱一段
小心翼翼的旋律。

四点半，试验
压过了测试
看，它银色的原则
接替了其余。

七点半，既无元素
也无工具，可见——
地点是那曾经的显现之所
在寰宇之间。

1085

If Nature smiles—the Mother must
I'm sure, at many a whim
Of Her eccentric Family—
Is She so much to blame?

1085

如果自然露出笑容——那是母亲
我肯定，笑对诸多突发的奇念
来自她古怪的家庭——
她需为此承受批判吗？

---

① 题解：三点半，鸟儿开始小心翼翼地试唱；四点半，测试（尝试）结束，进入真正的试验（歌唱），因此银色的原则（嘹亮的歌声）四处传遍；七点半，元素（歌声）和工具（鸟儿）均已不见，在曾经的场所，在宇宙之间。

1086

What Twigs We held by—
Oh the View
When Life's swift River striven through
We pause before a further plunge
To take Momentum—
As the Fringe

Upon a former Garment shows
The Garment cast,
Our Props disclose
So scant, so eminently small
Of Might to help, so pitiful
To sink, if We had labored, fond
The diligence were not more blind

How scant, by everlasting Light
The Discs that satisfied Our Sight—
How dimmer than a Saturn's Bar
The Things esteemed, for Things that are!

1086

我们被怎样的细枝托住——
啊那画面
当生活的急流激荡
又一次跌入前我们停步
以积蓄力量——
正如流苏

在旧衣上可映衬出
衣服的模样,
我们的支撑物也揭露
多微小,多明显不足
我们可借助的力量,多凄楚

这样沉入,如果我们曾劳作,并乐享
那样的勤奋并非更盲目

借助永恒的光,毫不显眼
那使我们悦目的圆盘——
比土星的栅栏还暗淡
那曾经景仰的万物,比起万物在眼前!

1087

We miss a Kinsman more
When warranted to see
Than when withheld of Oceans
From possibility

A Furlong than a League
Inflicts a pricklier pain,
Till We, who smiled at Pyrenees—
Of Parishes, complain.

1087

我们对亲人愈加思念
当相见得以确定
甚于当大海阻止
这种可能性

是一弗隆①而非一里格②
令痛苦更艰险,
等到我们,曾笑对比利牛斯山——
把教区,抱怨。

1088

Ended, ere it begun—

---

① 弗隆(furlong):长度单位,相当于220码、201米或⅛英里。
② 里格(league):长度单位,约为3英里或4.8千米。

The Title was scarcely told
When the Preface perished from Consciousness
The Story, unrevealed—

Had it been mine, to print!
Had it been yours, to read!
That it was not Our privilege
The interdict of God—

1088

还没开始，就已结束——
题目还几乎未提及
当序言从意识里消失
故事，尚未揭示——

假如它是我的，拿去刊印！
假如它是你的，拿来阅览！
可这不是我们的特权
据上帝的禁令所言——

1089

Myself can read the Telegrams
A Letter chief to me
The Stock's advance and Retrograde
And what the Markets say

The Weather—how the Rains
In Counties have begun.
'Tis News as null as nothing,
But sweeter so—than none.

1089

我能读懂那些电报
对我主要是一封信在讲

股市的升与降
还有市场的情况

还有天气——雨如何开始
在各县显露。
这些消息毫无价值,
但聊胜于——无。

1090
I am afraid to own a Body—
I am afraid to own a Soul—
Profound—precarious Property—
Possession, not optional—

Double Estate—entailed at pleasure
Upon an unsuspecting Heir—
Duke in a moment of Deathlessness
And God, for a Frontier.

1090
我害怕拥有肉身——
我害怕拥有灵魂——
深——不可测的财产——
拥有,没有选择——

双重财产——随性地遗给
一位毫无戒心的继承人——
一位公爵在不死的时刻
和一位边疆的,神。

1091
The Well upon the Brook
Were foolish to depend—
Let Brooks—renew of Brooks—
But Wells—of failless Ground!

1091

水井依赖小溪
真愚蠢之极——
让小溪——延续自其他小溪——
而水井——自不竭的大地!

1092

It was not Saint—it was too large—
Nor Snow—it was too small—
It only held itself aloof
Like something spiritual—

1092

它不是圣徒——它太大——
也不是白雪——它太小——
它只是置身事外
像有灵之物那一套——

1093

Because 'twas Riches I could own,
Myself had earned it—Me,
I knew the Dollars by their names—
It feels like Poverty

An Earldom out of sight to hold,
An Income in the Air,
Possession—has a sweeter chink
Unto a Miser's Ear—

1093

因为那是我能拥有的财富,
我已挣到它——我自己,

我知道它们名叫美元——
感觉像是贫瘠

拥有一个看不见的伯爵爵位,
一份收入悬于半空,
财产——有一种更迷人的叮当声
在守财奴耳中——

1094

Themself are all I have—
Myself a freckled—be—
I thought you'd choose a Velvet Cheek
Or one of Ivory—
Would you—instead of Me?

1094①

他们是我全部所有——
我自己——长满斑点——
我想你会选一张丝绒
或乳白的脸——
你会否——对我视而不见?

1095

To Whom the Mornings stand for Nights,
What must the Midnights—be!

1095

对于清晨代表夜晚的人来说,
午夜又代表——什么!

1096

These Strangers, in a foreign World,

---

① 本诗是作为礼物送人的鲜花的附诗。诗中说话人问对方会不会只选花而不选自己。

Protection asked of me—
Befriend them, lest Yourself in Heaven
Be found a Refugee—

1096①

这些陌生人,在异域,
请求我保护——
做他们朋友,以免你在天堂
也无依无助——

1097

Dew—is the Freshet in the Grass—
'Tis many a tiny Mill
Turns unperceived beneath our feet
And Artisan lies still—

We spy the Forests and the Hills
The Tents to Nature's Show
Mistake the Outside for the in
And mention what we saw.

Could Commentators on the Sign
Of Nature's Caravan
Obtain "Admission" as a Child
Some Wednesday Afternoon.

1097
晨露——是草中的流溪——

---

① 参见《圣经·新约·马太福音》第 25 章第 41～43 节记载,若未迎陌生人进屋进行救助,在审判日会受到惩罚:"Then shall he say also unto them on the left hand, Depart from me, ye cursed, into everlasting fire, prepared for the devil and his angels: For I was an hungred, and ye gave me no meat: I was thirsty, and ye gave me no drink: I was a stranger, and ye took me not in: naked, and ye clothed me not: sick, and in prison, and ye visited me not."(Matthew 25: 41 - 43)

是许多小磨坊
难以觉察地涌现在我们脚底
而工匠还在静静躺——

我们窥察森林和山岗
还有为大自然表演准备的营帐
错把帐外当帐里
还提及我们所见的景象。

大自然商旅旗号的评说员
可否获得"许可"进入
当作一个孩童
在某个周三下午。

1098

Of the Heart that goes in, and closes the Door
Shall the Playfellow Heart complain
Though the Ring is unwhole, and the Company broke
Can never be fitted again?

1098

对于那颗心一进去,就把门关
它的玩伴是否该抱怨
尽管圈子已不完整,队伍已离散
难道再不可能破镜重圆?

1099

My Cocoon tightens—Colors teaze①—
I'm feeling for the Air—
A dim capacity for Wings
Demeans the Dress I wear—

---

① "teaze"在1960年的阅读版中为"tease"。

A power of Butterfly must be—
The Aptitude to fly
Meadows of Majesty concedes
And easy Sweeps of Sky—

So I must baffle at the Hint
And cipher at the Sign
And make much blunder, if at last
I take the clue divine—

1099
我的茧收紧——色若丝缕——
我在摸索感受空气——
翅翼的些许能力
都会贬低我穿的外衣——

蝴蝶的能力之一——
一定指飞翔的潜力
辽阔的牧场向后退去
掠过长空轻而易举——

所以我得苦思这个暗示
解读这个征兆
相信会犯许多错误，如果最终
我把神圣的线索找到——

1100
The last Night that She lived
It was a Common Night
Except the Dying—this to Us
Made Nature different

We noticed smallest things—
Things overlooked before
By this great light upon our Minds
Italicized—as 'twere.

As We went out and in
Between Her final Room
And Rooms where Those to be alive
Tomorrow were, a Blame

That Others could exist
While She must finish quite
A Jealousy for Her arose
So nearly infinite—

We waited while She passed—
It was a narrow time—
Too jostled were Our Souls to speak
At length the notice came.

She mentioned, and forgot—
Then lightly as a Reed
Bent to the Water, struggled scarce—
Consented, and was dead—

And We—We placed the Hair—
And drew the Head erect—
And then an awful leisure was
Belief to regulate—

1100[①]
她活着的最后一夜

---

① 本诗描绘的是狄金森家邻居希尔斯夫妇（Mr. and Mrs. Leonard Mariner Hills）的小女儿劳拉（Laura Hills, 1838—1866）之死。劳拉 1866 年 5 月 1 日（约翰逊误认为是 5 月 3 日）在爱默斯特（Amherst）其父母家中去世，希尔斯夫妇的家紧挨艾米莉·狄金森家房子的东面。劳拉 1860 年与密歇根州的迪基（Franklin Wakeman Dickey, 1839—1917）结婚。劳拉去世后，迪基两次再婚，先在 1869 年和萨丽娜（Salina Caroline Gillett, 1850—1873）结婚，后又在 1874 年和玛丽（Mary Alice Perry, 1844—1932）再婚。迪基于 1917 年在密歇根州巴特克里克市（Battle Creek）去世。

是个平常夜
除了临死者——我们感觉
令大自然有别

我们注意到最细微的事物——
以往我们竟视而不见
借助这强光照着我们头脑
它好似——更凸显。

当我们进出
她弥留的房间
和那些活人的房间
简直是罪孽，活到明天

因为他人还能存活
而她必须了结
因她而起的妒意
几乎不会绝灭——

我们等着她过世——
这是难捱的时间——
我们灵魂动荡无法言辞
那迹象终于出现。

她提及，又忘记——
然后轻似一根芦苇
弯身喝水，微微挣扎——
表示赞许，然后死去——

我们——我们梳好她的头发——
把头颅摆正——
然后一种可怕的空闲
成了需调整的信念——

1101

Between the form of Life and Life
The difference is as big
As Liquor at the Lip between
And Liquor in the Jug
The latter—excellent to keep—
But for ecstatic need
The corkless is superior—
I know for I have tried

1101

生命的形式和生命
大不相同
有如酒在唇上
和酒在罐中
后者———一直保存固然很好——
但若为狂喜的需要
开盖的酒更妙——
我试过所以我知道

1102

His Bill is clasped—his Eye forsook—
His Feathers wilted low—
The Claws that clung, like lifeless Gloves
Indifferent hanging now—
The Joy that in his happy Throat
Was waiting to be poured
Gored through and through with Death, to be
Assassin of a Bird
Resembles to my outraged mind
The firing in Heaven,
On Angels—squandering for you
Their Miracles of Tune—

1102①

他的钩嘴合拢——他的目光散逸——
还有他低垂的羽毛——
那紧抓的双爪,像了无生气的手套
如今无精打采的悬吊——
他兴奋的喉咙中的欢欣
还等着一吐为快
被刺伤,刺伤而亡
就这样杀死了一只鸟
如同我愤怒的思想
在天堂开枪,
射向天使们——而他们正向你挥洒
他们歌声的美妙——

1103

The spry Arms of the Wind
If I could crawl between
I have an errand imminent
To an adjoining Zone—

I should not care to stop
My Process is not long
The Wind could wait without the Gate
Or stroll the Town among.

To ascertain the House
And is the soul at Home
And hold the Wick of mine to it
To light, and then return—

1103

在风轻捷的臂间

---

① 题解:刺死一只鸟,如同枪杀天上的天使,鸟和天使同样都为我们奉献美妙的歌声。

我可否爬行
我有一件紧急差事
需要去附近的地点——

我不乐意停下
我的手续不长
风可在大门外等
或在城内闲逛。

只需找到那所房子
而灵魂也在屋内
把我的灯芯递给它
点燃,然后返回——

1104

The Crickets sang
And set the Sun
And Workmen finished one by one
Their Seam the Day upon.

The low Grass loaded with the Dew
The Twilight stood, as Strangers do
With Hat in Hand, polite and new
To stay as if, or go.

A Vastness, as a Neighbor, came,
A Wisdom, without Face, or Name,
A Peace, as Hemispheres at Home
And so the Night became.

1104

蟋蟀歌唱
太阳西落
工人们一个个结束

他们白日的劳作。

浅草含着露珠
薄暮站立,像个陌生人
手里拿着帽子,彬彬有礼又有些拘束
仿佛欲留,还去。

一种浩瀚,像一位邻人,走来,
一种智慧,看不到脸,不知姓名,
一种宁静,像家园的氛围
夜晚就这样降临。

1105

Like Men and Women Shadows walk
Upon the Hills Today—
With here and there a mighty Bow
Or trailing Courtesy
To Neighbors doubtless of their own
Not quickened to perceive
Minuter landscape as Ourselves
And Boroughs where we live—

1105

仿佛男男女女的影子
今天在山上行走——
到处是殷勤的鞠躬
或不绝如缕的问候
向他们自己的邻居
却未能快速辨认
我们这样更微小的风景
和我们居住的城镇——

1106

We do not know the time we lose—

The awful moment is
And takes it's fundamental place
Among the certainties—

A firm appearance still inflates
The card—the chance—the friend—
The spectre of solidities
Whose substances are sand—

1106

我们失去的光阴我们不知——
是可怕的瞬息
它在已确知的万物里
找到了最终的位置——

清晰的表象依然充斥
纸牌——意外——友朋——
那物化的幽灵
由沙子组成——

1107

The Bird did prance—the Bee did play—
The Sun ran miles away
So blind with joy he could not choose
Between his Holiday

The morn was up—the meadows out
The Fences all but ran,
Republic of Delight, I thought
Where each is Citizen—

From Heavy laden Lands to thee
Were seas to cross to come
A Caspian were crowded—
Too near thou art for Fame—

1107

鸟儿雀跃——蜂儿嬉戏——
太阳跑开好几英里
无比的欢愉使他莫辩东西
一味沉浸于他的假期

清晨已升起——草地已展开
篱笆只知跑不停,
这是欢乐的共和国,我猜
那里万物都是它的公民——

从沉甸甸的大地抵达你
若需过海穿洋
整个里海都显拥挤——
而你太近难把名扬——

1108

A Diamond on the Hand
To Custom Common grown
Subsides from it's significance
The Gem were best unknown—
Within a Seller's Shrine
How many sight and sigh
And cannot, but are mad for fear
That any other buy.

1108

钻石戴在手上
习惯后就觉平常
但意义也会降低
宝石最好不张扬——
放在卖家橱窗里

引来诸多目光和叹息
却无能为力,只十分恐惧
别人把它买去。

1109①

I fit for them—
I seek the Dark
Till I am thorough fit.
The labor is a sober one
With the austerer sweet—an—this—
With this sufficient sweet
That abstinence of mine produce
A purer food for them, if I succeed,
If not I had
The transport of the Aim—

1109

我适宜他们——
我找寻黑暗
直至我完全适宜。
这努力是一件严肃的事
会带来更艰苦的甜蜜——这——甜蜜——
因了这充足的甜蜜
我的斋戒会给他们产出
更纯洁的食物,如果我成功,
如果未成功我也有
对目标的神迷——

1110

None who saw it ever told it

---

① 题注:约翰逊指出第1行(I fit for them—)其实是第3行(Till I am thorough fit)的草稿版,而第5行(With the austerer sweet—an—this—)是第6行(With this sufficient sweet)的草稿版,诗人意将第6行替代第5行,因此,在约翰逊1960年出版的阅读版全集中,第5行被删除了。此外,约翰逊认为第5行中的"an—this—"是诗人拟以替换行中的"the"。

'Tis as hid as Death
Had for that specific treasure
A departing breath—
Surfaces may be invested
Did the Diamond grow
General as the Dandelion
Would you serve it so?

1110

见过它的人从未提起
它的隐藏就像死亡
对那特别的宝藏
只有一口临别的气息那样——
表面可以有所蕴含
假如钻石处处存在
像蒲公英一样平常
你是否还对它同样对待?

1111

Some Wretched creature, savior take
Who would exult to die
And leave for thy sweet mercy's sake
Another Hour to me

1111

某个不幸的生灵,被救世主带走
他们乐意赴死
主慈心宽厚
多给了我一个小时

1112

That this should feel the need of Death
The same as those that lived
Is such a stroke

    Hight—Feat—pass—
of Irony
As never was ~~beheld~~—achieved—
~~As makes one hide it's head—~~
    hang

Not satisfied to ape the Great in his simplicity
The small must die, the same as he—as well as He—
   do
~~What a Pomposity—~~
  ~~an absurdity—~~
   Perversity—
~~Oh the pomposity~~
Oh the Audacity—

1112①
这一位会感到死亡的必要
那些活着的也同感
这真是一个打击
   高捧——伟绩——经过——
属于讽刺
从未见过——实现——
就像让一个人把头藏起——
    挂起

不满足于模仿伟人行为的简单
微小的必定死去，像他一样——他也未能免——

---

 ① 本诗是一份草稿，显示了诗人修改的痕迹和思路。大意：这一位（伟人）觉得死是必要的，其他（微小的）人竟然也有同样的看法，这真是一个讽刺，一个以前从未取得和实现过的伟绩。这些微小的人并不满足于模仿伟人的行为，他们还想像他（伟人）一样死去，真是太大胆了。1960年阅读版把"as well as He—"之前的"the same as he—"删除了。

肯定
多么傲慢——
　荒诞——
　错乱——
啊这么傲慢——
啊这么大胆——

1113

There is strength in proving that it can be bourne①
Although it tear—
What are the sinews of such cordage for
Except to bear
The ship might be of satin had it not to fight—
To walk on seas requires cedar Feet

1113

有一种力量证明它能承重
虽然它也会拉伤——
那种绳索的筋肉起何作用
除了承受力量
航船可用缎布来造若非用于战斗——
在海面行走需雪松般的脚

1114

The largest Fire ever known
Occurs each Afternoon—
Discovered is without surprise
Proceeds without concern—
Consumes and no report to men
An Occidental Town,
Rebuilt another morning
To be burned down again

---

① "bourne"在1960年的阅读版中为"borne"。

1114

世上最大的火灾
每个下午都发生——
发现后无人惊奇
燃烧过程无人理睬——
烧成灰烬也没人报道
一座西方小镇,
在次日早晨重建
只为再度被毁

1115

The murmuring of Bees, has ceased
But murmuring of some
Posterior, prophetic,
Has simultaneous come.
The lower metres of the Year
When Nature's laugh is done
The Revelations of the Book
Whose Genesis was June.
Appropriate Creatures to her change
The Typic Mother sends
As Accent fades to interval
With separating Friends
Till what we speculate, has been
And thoughts we will not show
More intimate with us become
Than Persons, that we know.

1115①

蜜蜂的嗡嗡,已经止息

---

① 题解:季节变换之际,蜜蜂嗡鸣之后便是其他昆虫(比如蟋蟀)的呢喃,就在六月,既是新生(创世纪)也是重生(启示录)时节。当离去的昆虫(朋友)鸣声时断时续,即将消失,大自然母亲自会送来适宜新季节的生灵,此时,我们所猜测的季节变换,已然成真,我们此前不愿显露的内心的这些想法,此时更显亲切,胜过认识的外部的人。

但随即
某种预言似的,呢喃,
立时响起。
那是年光低低的乐音
当大自然的欢笑已止歇
那是圣经的启示录
它的创世纪就在六月。
原生的母亲为她的变化
送来了适宜的生灵
当临别的朋友
话语时续时停
直至我们猜测的,已成真
而我们不愿显露的思路
变得更亲切
胜过我们认识的,那些人物。

1116

There is another Loneliness
That many die without—
Not want of friend occasions it
Or circumstances of Lot

But nature, sometimes, sometimes thought
And whoso it befall
Is richer than could be revealed
By mortal numeral—

1116

有另一种孤独
许多人至死未曾尝试——
非由缺少朋友引起
也非命运的境遇所致

而是天性,有时,有时是所思

不论它落到谁头上
谁的富有都无法揭示
用人间的数字——

1117

A Mine there is no Man would own
But must it be conferred,
Demeaning by exclusive wealth
A Universe beside—

Potosi never to be spent
But hoarded in the mind
What Misers wring their hands tonight
For Indies in the Ground!

1117

有一座矿藏没人能拥有
但可以被转授,
其巨量财富足以贬低
旁边的宇宙——

波托西①永不会耗尽
而是存于心中的巨宝
有多少财迷今夜扼腕
为地下的印度群岛!

1118

Exhiliration② is the Breeze
That lifts us from the Ground
And leaves us in another place
Whose statement is not found—

---

① 波托西(Potosi):玻利维亚一城市,以产银矿闻名。该地在第119首诗和书信(L205)中也提到过。
② "Exhiliration"在1960年阅读版中为"Exhilaration"。

Returns us not, but after time
We soberly descend
A little newer for the term
Upon Enchanted Ground—

1118

欢欣是一阵轻风飞扬
使我们离地飘起
把我们带到另一地方
那里的情况无法获悉——

一去不返,但随即
我们徐徐降低
其间一切都有些新奇
落到一个销魂地——

1119

Paradise is that old mansion
Many owned before—
Occupied by each an instant
Then reversed the Door—
Bliss is frugal of her Leases
Adam taught her Thrift
Bankrupt once through his excesses—

1119

天堂是那所老宅
曾有许多主人——
各自都住过一阵
然后就反转房门——
欢愉对她的租约严管
是亚当教会她节俭
他因为放纵曾经破产——

1120

This slow Day moved along—
I heard it's axles go
As if they could not hoist themselves
They hated motion so—

I told my soul to come—
It was no use to wait—
We went and played and came again
And it was out of sight

1120

这缓慢的一天向前行进——
我听到它的轴运转沉重
仿佛它们自己提不起劲
它们如此讨厌移动——

我告诉我的灵魂过来——
不必再做无用的等待——
我们出去嬉戏再回来
而它已在视线之外

1121

Time does go on—
I tell it gay to those who suffer now—
They shall survive—
There is a sun—
They don't believe it now—

1121

时光确实在前进——
我欣然给正受难的人讲——

他们会活下来——
总会有阳光——
他们现在就是不信——

1122

'Tis my first night beneath the Sun
If I should spend it here—
Above him is too low a height
For his Barometer
Who Airs of expectation breathes
And takes the Wind at prime—
But Distance his Delights confides
To those who visit him

1122①

这是我在太阳下的第一夜
假如我要在这里度过——
他之上的高度太低
对他的气压计来说
它呼出期盼的气息
并将劲风迎接——
但距离把他的欢愉倾诉
给他那些来访者

1123②

A great Hope fell
You heard no noise
The Ruin was within

---

① 题解：我首次在太阳下幻想着与他过夜，我是他的气压计（晴雨表），每天计量他的情况，但他对我的期待却并不高。尽管我每天呼出期盼他来的气息，并准备迎接他带来的劲风，但我俩之间的距离，却成为他欢愉的条件，他每天就在接待各种来访者中乐此不疲，并未把我记念在心里。

② 富兰克林版全集把本诗前两节（第 1～9 行）视为一首诗，后两节（第 10～17 行）视为另外一首诗。

Oh cunning wreck that told no tale
And let no Witness in

The mind was built for mighty Freight
For dread occasion planned
How often foundering at Sea
Ostensibly, on Land

A not admitting of the wound
Until it grew so wide
That all my Life had entered it
And there were troughs beside

A closing of the simple lid
That opened to the sun
Until the tender Carpenter
Perpetual nail it down—

1123

一个巨大的希望坠落
你听不到一点声响
这种崩溃发生在内部
啊这诡秘的事故啥也不讲
也不让任何证人进入

头脑为巨大货物而建
为可怕事件而设计
海上的沉没多么频繁
表面上，像在陆地

受伤总不愿承认
直至伤口变得够宽

令我的一生都陷入
还有沟渠在旁边

那简单的盖子合闭
它曾向太阳开放
直至那温情的木匠
将它永远钉上——

1124

Had we known the Ton she bore
We had helped the terror
But she straighter walked for Freight
So be hers the error—

1124

假如我们知道她背负的吨量
我们就帮助了恐怖
但她更径直地走向货物
那就是她的错误——

1125

Oh Sumptuous moment
Slower go
That I may gloat on thee—
'Twill never be the same to starve
Now I abundance see—

Which was to famish, then or now—
The difference of Day
Ask him unto the Gallows led—
With morning in the sky

1125①
啊奢侈的时刻
请慢些走
好让我自得地看看你——
再也不会那样挨饿
我如今看到丰裕无比——

哪一回挨饿,那时还是现在——
问他日子有何不同
他被领向绞刑台——
当晨曦初现天空

1126
Shall I take thee, the Poet said
To the propounded word?
Be stationed with the Candidates
Till I have finer tried—

The Poet searched Philology
And when about to ring
For the suspended Candidate
There came unsummoned in—

That portion of the Vision
The Word applied to fill
Not unto nomination
The Cherubim reveal—

---

① 题解:或许"我"曾经挨饿,但现在"我"看到的是丰裕富足,再也不会挨饿了,因此"我"可以面对奢侈时刻,洋洋自得。"我"是哪一回挨过饿,是那时还是现在?问这个问题,犹如问清晨被领向绞刑台的囚犯,那天的日子有何异样。本诗写于 1868 年,诗歌具有一种欢庆的情绪。据约翰逊提示,1868 年底有消息称艾米莉·狄金森心仪的牧师沃兹华斯 (Charles Wadsworth) 即将从旧金山返回费城。

1126

诗人说，我是否该选你
当拟用的那个字？
请与其他候选静待
直至我尝试更好的词——

诗人去查找文献
正当他要摇铃
叫那被搁置的候选
就有一位擅自闯进——

视野中的那部分
就这个字适宜填补
二级天使对于提名
不会透露——

1127

Soft as the massacre of Suns
By Evening's Sabres slain

1127①

像对阳光的杀戮那般柔软
被黄昏的大刀挥砍

1128

These are the Nights that Beetles love—
From Eminence remote
Drives ponderous perpendicular
His figure intimate
The terror of the Children
The merriment of men

---

① 题解：或指黄昏对落日宁静余晖的屠杀。

Depositing his Thunder
He hoists abroad again—
A Bomb upon the Ceiling
Is an improving thing—
It keeps the nerves in progress①
Conjecture flourishing—
Too dear the Summer evening
Without discreet alarm—
Supplied by Entomology
With it's remaining charm

1128
这是甲虫喜爱的夜晚——
从渺远的高地里
轰隆隆垂直驶来
他小巧的身影
孩子们感到恐惧
大人们觉得有趣
搁下他的雷霆
他再次舒展羽翼——
做一颗炸弹在空中②嗡鸣
也是一件有意思的事情——
它能持续引起注意
感觉一切欣欣向荣——
夏夜真令人动容
没有小心翼翼的惊惧——
各种各样的昆虫
展现它们最后的魅力

1129
Tell all the Truth but tell it slant—

---

① "It keeps the nerves in progress" 在 1960 年阅读版中为 "It keeps the nerves progressive"。
② 空中（Ceiling）：喻指 "sky" 和 "heaven"。

Success in Circuit lies
Too bright for our infirm Delight
The Truth's superb surprise
As Lightning to the Children eased
With explanation kind
The Truth must dazzle gradually
Or every man be blind—

1129
说出所有的真理但曲折地说出——
成功在于迂回战术
对于我们脆弱的欢愉
真理奇异的光彩过于炫目
正如闪电时孩子们的压力
要好言讲解才得以舒缓
真理绚丽的光辉须一点点释放
否则每个人都会瞎眼——

1130
That odd old man is dead a year—
We miss his stated Hat.
'Twas such an evening bright and stiff
His faded lamp went out.

Who miss his antiquated Wick—
Are any hoar for him?
Waits any indurated mate
His wrinkled coming Home?

Oh Life, begun in fluent Blood
And consummated dull!
Achievement contemplating thee—
Feels transitive and cool.

1130

那古怪的老人已死了一年——
我们想念他气派的帽子。
在这样明亮肃静的夜晚
他微弱的灯盏终于飘逝。

有谁想念他老朽的灯芯——
有无为他生灰白的头发？
有没有身躯僵硬的老伴
等满脸皱纹的他回家？

啊生命，在汩汩的血中诞生
在平凡无聊中结束！
想起你一生的成就——
顿感人生凄凉与飘忽。

1131

The Merchant of the Picturesque
A Counter has and sales
But is within or negative
Precisely as the calls—
To Children he is small in price
And large in courtesy—
It suits him better than a check
Their artless currency—
Of Counterfeits he is so shy
Do one advance so near
As to behold his ample flight—

1131

贩卖奇思的商人
有一个柜台在卖它
但买得起或买不起
全凭人喊价——

对于孩子们他价格不高
而礼节上却不低——
最好别给他支票
而给实实在在的货币——
对于仿冒他总尽力避开
若真有人凑向前去
就会看到他满脸逃避的神采——

1132①

The smouldering embers blush—
Oh Cheek within the Coal
Hast thou survived so many nights?
The smouldering embers smile—
Soft stirs the news of Light
The stolid Rafters glow
One requisite has Fire that lasts
Prometheus never knew—

1132

闷燃的余烬露出羞红——
啊炭火中的面颊
你就这样历经了无数暗夜重重?
闷燃的余烬笑啦——
是光的消息轻轻地激励
迟钝的椽子容光奕奕
让火持续的一个前提
是普罗米修斯决不能知悉——

1133

The Snow that never drifts—

---

① 题注:在1960年阅读版中,第二行的"nights"应为"years";第六行"Rafters"应为"seconds";而第二行"Cheek"应为"Hearts",是印刷错误,按艾米莉·狄金森原稿,实际应是"Heart"。

The transient, frag[r]ant snow
That comes a single time a Year
Is softly driving now—

So thorough in the Tree
At night beneath the star
That it was February's Foot
Experience would swear—

Like Winter as a Face
We stern and former knew
Repaired of all but Loneliness
By Nature's Alibi—

Were every storm so spice
The Value could not be—
We buy with contrast—Pang is good
As near as memory—

1133
那从不堆砌的雪——
那匆匆、芬芳的雪
每年仅有一次
正悄悄驶至——

痛快淋漓洒向树木
星空下的暗夜无边
那定是二月的脚步
经验如此断言——

犹如冬天就似一张脸
我们早知其严酷
能平复一切除却孤独
凭大自然作的不在此处的供述——

假如每场暴风雪都那么有趣
也就没什么意义——
有对比我们才欢喜——剧痛是好事
容易让人回忆——

1134

The Wind took up the Northern Things
And piled them in the south—
Then gave the East unto the West
And opening his mouth

The four Divisions of the Earth
Did make as to devour
While everything to corners slunk
Behind the awful power—

The Wind—unto his Chambers went
And nature ventured out—
Her subjects scattered into place
Her systems ranged about

Again the smoke from Dwellings rose
The Day abroad was heard—
How intimate, a Tempest past
The Transport of the Bird—

1134

风卷起北边各种物件
在南边堆成堆——
又把东边移到西边
还张开他的嘴

对地球八方四面
仿佛真要吞噬

万物向各处逃窜
躲避那可怕的暴力——

风——进入了他的房间
大自然就冒险露面——
将她的臣民散置于各点
把她的秩序整理一遍

炊烟再次从屋舍升起
已然听到外面白昼的声息——
多么甜蜜,暴风雨已过去
鸟儿心旷神怡——

1135

Too cold is this
To warm with Sun—
Too stiff to bended be,
To joint this Agate were a work—
Outstaring Masonry—

How went the Agile Kernel out
Contusion of the Husk
Nor Rip, nor wrinkle indicate
But just an Asterisk.

1135

这太冷冰
无法用阳光温暖——
也难以弯曲因太僵硬,
拼接这颗玛瑙的工作——
足以令石匠举棋不定——

到底那灵活的内核如何出去
瘀伤在外壳

既无裂口,也无皱折痕迹
只有星号一个。

1136

The Frost of Death was on the Pane—
"Secure your Flower" said he.
Like Sailors fighting with a Leak
We fought Mortality.

Our passive Flower we held to Sea—
To Mountain—To the Sun—
Yet even on his Scarlet shelf
To crawl the Frost begun—

We pried him back
Ourselves we wedged
Himself and her between,
Yet easy as the narrow Snake
He forked his way along

Till all her helpless beauty bent
And then our wrath begun—
We hunted him to his Ravine
We chased him to his Den—

We hated Death and hated Life
And nowhere was to go—
Than Sea and continent there is
A larger—it is Woe

1136

死亡的寒霜附在窗玻璃上——
"护好你的花"他讲。
像船员为堵船漏奔忙

我们与无常拼抢。

我们把无精打采的花带给大海——
带给高山——带给太阳——
但就在他鲜红架子上
已开始爬上了寒霜——

我们把他撬回来
把我们自己堵在
他和她之间
但像一只灵活的小蛇
他岔开方向继续向前

等到她无助的美全都垂枯
我们就无比愤怒——
我们搜寻到他的深谷
我们追踪到他的住处——

我们怨恨死也怨恨生
我们已无处可往——
除了大海和陆地
更宽广的——是悲伤

1137

The duties of the Wind are few,
To cast the ships, at Sea,
Establish March, the Floods escort,
And usher Liberty.

The pleasures of the Wind are broad,
To dwell Extent among,
Remain, or wander,
Speculate, or Forests entertain.

The kinsmen of the Wind are Peaks
Azof ①—the Equinox,
Also with Bird and Asteroid
A bowing intercourse.

The limitations of the Wind
Do he exist, or die,
Too wise he seems for Wakelessness,
However, know not I.

1137
风的职责很少，
在海上，推船行走，
确立三月，护送洪水，
以及迎接自由。

风的快乐很广，
寓居天地间，
逗留，或漫游，
沉思，或给森林消遣。

风的亲戚有山峰
亚速海——昼夜平分点②，
还与鸟儿和小行星
摇头晃脑地交谈。

风的局限
不论他存，或逝，
都似乎太聪明而难得酣睡，
不过，我不得而知。

---

① Azof：即 Azov，指亚速海。
② 昼夜平分点（equinox）：指春分或秋分，当天昼和夜的长短相同。

1138

A Spider sewed at Night
Without a Light
Upon an Arc of White.

If Ruff it was of Dame
Or Shroud of Gnome
Himself himself inform.

Of Immortality
His Strategy
Was Physiognomy.

1138

一只蜘蛛在夜里织网
没有一丝亮光
在一个白色圆弧上。

轮状皱领是给女士
或是地精的尸衣
他自己给自己喻示。

对永生的前途
他的策略之路
是依靠相面术。

1139

Her sovreign① People
Nature knows as well
And is as fond of signifying
As if fallible—

---

① "sovreign" 在 1960 年阅读版中为 "sovereign"。

1139①

对自己高贵的子民
大自然甚是熟悉
而且同样喜欢喻示
仿佛常有闪失——

1140

The Day grew small, surrounded tight
By early, stooping Night—
The Afternoon in Evening deep
It's Yellow shortness dropt—
The Winds went out their martial ways
The Leaves obtained excuse—
November hung his Granite Hat
Upon a nail of Plush—

1140

白昼逐渐萎缩,陷于牢牢围住
被早到的,佝偻的夜幕——
午后短暂的黄艳
坠入向晚的深渊——
风退出战斗之路
叶子获得了宽恕——
十一月挂它花岗岩的帽
在一颗长毛绒的钉上——

1141

The Face we choose to miss—
Be it but for a Day
As absent as a Hundred Years,
When it has rode away.

---

① 这是艾米莉·狄金森送给嫂子苏珊的一首书信诗（L336），可能还随附有一枝花。诗前的抬头是："Rare to the Rare—"。

1141①

我们喜欢思念的那张脸——
哪怕只离开了一天
仿佛已过了一百年,
自它驶离的那一瞬间。

1142

The Props assist the House
Until the House is built
And then the Props withdraw
And adequate, erect,
The House support itself
And cease to recollect
The Augur② and the Carpenter—
Just such a retrospect
Hath the perfected Life—
A past of Plank and Nail
And slowness—then the Scaffolds drop
Affirming it a Soul.

1142

支架给房子支撑
直至房子建成
随后支架被撤去
房屋已足以,自立,
可以撑起自己
不再想起
螺旋钻和木匠——
正是这样的回想
才有生活的圆满——
那曾经的板条和铁钉

---

① 这是艾米莉·狄金森送给嫂子苏珊的诗。
② "Augur" 在1960年阅读版中为 "Auger"(螺旋钻)。

以及缓慢——接着脚手架倒塌
证实它也有魂灵。

1143

The Work of Her that went,
The Toil of Fellows done—
In Ovens green our Mother bakes,
By Fires of the Sun.

1143

她已完结的工作,
男人们已结束的活——
都在绿色烤炉里由我们的母亲烘烤,
用太阳的火。

1144

Ourselves we do inter with sweet derision.
The channel of the dust who once achieves
Invalidates the balm of that religion
That doubts as fervently as it believes.

1144①

我们确实用甜蜜的嘲弄埋葬自己。
那条人们曾到过的黄尘路
让宗教的慰藉毫无用处
它既满腹狐疑又执迷不悟。

1145

In thy long Paradise of Light

---

① 本诗是艾米莉·狄金森 1877 年写给朋友鲍尔斯的一封信的结尾,诗之前的信是这样:"You have the most triumphant Face out of Paradise—probably because you are there constantly, instead of ultimately—"(L489)。艾米莉·狄金森诗歌全集编者约翰逊和富兰克林均推测其中的"triumphant face"是指鲍尔斯的照片,因为他之前寄过照片给艾米莉·狄金森,故艾米莉·狄金森在此信中予以回应,表示他的照片改变了她对来生的看法。

No moment will there be
When I shall long for Earthly Play
And mortal Company—

1145

身处你漫长的光明乐园
我就不再有片刻的闲隙
可以怀想凡间的嬉戏
和尘世的伴侣——

1146

When Etna basks and purrs
Naples is more afraid
Than when she show her Garnet Tooth—
Security is loud—

1146①

当埃特纳火山晒着太阳发出呼噜
更令那不勒斯恐慌
比起她把石榴石的牙展露——
安全警报震天响——

1147

After a hundred years
Nobody knows the Place
Agony that enacted there
Motionless as Peace

Weeds triumphant ranged
Strangers strolled and spelled
At the lone Orthography

---

① 题解：火山喷火冒烟，随时有爆发的风险，比起真正爆发时喷出石榴石般深红色的岩熔，然后安全警报大作所引起的恐慌更甚。

Of the Elder Dead

Winds of Summer Fields
Recollect the way—
Instinct picking up the Key
Dropped by memory—

1147
百年以后
无人知道那片地
那里曾经的苦痛
已静寂平息

曾经荒草深深
有闲逛的陌客辨读
死去的先人
名字中的孤独

夏季田野上的风
还将那条路记起——
本能拾起了回忆
丢掉的钥匙——

1148
After the Sun comes out
How it alters the World—
Waggons like messengers hurry about
Yesterday is old—

All men meet as if
Each foreclosed a news—
Fresh as a Cargo from Batize
Nature's qualities—

1148

太阳一露出光芒
就改变了世界的面貌——
马车像信使一样匆忙
昨天已经古老——

大家相互碰面
仿佛各藏一条消息——
像鲜货来自巴蒂斯①
有着大自然的质地——

1149

I noticed People disappeared
When but a little child—
Supposed they visited remote
Or settled Regions wild—
Now know I—
　　　　or I know now
　　　　They both visited
And settled Regions wild
But vaster——that
　　vaster
　　did because they died
A Fact withheld the little child—
　a

1149②

我注意到有人消失
那时还只是个孩子——

---

① 巴蒂斯（Batize）：原文"Batize"在富兰克林版全集中改作"Balize"，均是指中美洲国家伯利兹（Belize），该国1862年成为英国的直辖殖民地，定名为英属洪都拉斯，1964年实行自治，1973年更名为伯利兹，1981年独立。该国以出口红木等自然资源闻名。
② 这是一首未完成的诗的手稿，显示了诗人的修改痕迹。

以为他们去拜访远方
或安顿在荒野之地——
我现在才知——
　　　　或我知道现在
　　　　他们既去拜访
也安顿在荒野之地
但更宽广——缘于
　　更宽广
　　如此是因为他们已死
这事实瞒过了那个孩子——
一个

1150

How many schemes may die
In one short Afternoon
Entirely unknown
To those they most concern—
The man that was not lost
Because by accident
He varied by a Ribbon's width
From his accustomed route—
The Love that would not try
Because beside the Door
It must be competitions①
Some unsuspecting Horse was tied
Surveying his Despair

1150

有多少计划会消失
在一个短暂的下午

---

① 在富兰克林版全集中，本行被删除。富兰克林和约翰逊两位全集编者均发现本诗是远未完成的草稿。约翰逊虽然保留了本行，但也认为就诗歌上下文来看，本行没有意义（"meaningless"）。

完全不被那些
最相关的人所知——
有人没有消失不见
是因为碰巧
他相差一条飘带这么远
离他平时走的道——
有爱不去尝试
是因为在那门边
肯定有争抢
一匹毫无戒心的马被拴着
正审视他的绝望

1151

Soul, take thy risk.
With Death to be
Were better than be not
With thee

1151

灵魂，尽管冒险一试
即便与死神相依
也胜过不能在一起
与你

1152

Tell as a Marksman—were forgotten
Tell—this Day endures
Ruddy as that coeval Apple
The Tradition bears—

Fresh as Mankind that humble story
Though a statelier Tale
Grown in the Repetition hoary
Scarcely would prevail—

Tell had a son—The ones that knew it
Need not linger here—
Those who did not to Human Nature
Will subscribe a Tear—

Tell would not bare his Head
In Presence
Of the Ducal Hat—
Threatened for that with Death—by Gessler—
Tyranny bethought

Make of his only Boy a Target
That surpasses Death—
Stolid to Love's supreme entreaty
Not forsook of Faith—

Mercy of the Almighty begging—
Tell his Arrow sent—
God it is said replies in Person
When the cry is meant—

1152
退尔①作为神射手——早已被遗忘
退尔——今天依然持续
红火似当时那个苹果
传统就是它的载体——

---

① 退尔（Tell）：威廉·退尔（William Tell），瑞士 14 世纪传奇故事中反抗奥地利统治、争取瑞士独立斗争中的英雄。相传在 1307 年，瑞士阿尔特多夫镇（Altdorf）的奥地利执行官盖斯勒（Albrecht Gessler 或 Hermann Gessler）在镇市集广场上竖立一杆，杆上挂着他自己的一顶帽子，要求所有居民经过时须脱帽向杆上的帽子鞠躬行礼。神弓手退尔不从，被盖斯勒下令逮捕，并被迫作出选择：要么被处死，要么以箭射落置于其儿子头顶的苹果，若成功，则可被赦免。后退尔成功射中其儿子头顶的苹果，盖斯勒赦免退尔死罪，将他押上船送到别处地牢中度过余生。后退尔逃脱返回，以箭射死盖斯勒。现今阿尔特多夫当地建有退尔父子的铜像以表纪念。

鲜活如人类那卑微的传说
虽能变成更堂皇的故事
经过多年的老生常谈
但不可能人人尽知——

退尔有一个儿子——知道的人
不必在此徘徊——
不知道的人出于人类的天性
会献出一滴泪水——

退尔不会光着头
出现
面对公爵的帽——
因此受到死亡威胁——被盖斯勒——
暴君想到

把他唯一的儿子当活靶
那就不仅仅是死亡——
要对爱崇高的恳求无动于衷
还不能丧失信仰——

仁慈的主也百般恳请——
退尔还是射出了箭
上帝据说会亲自回应
如果是真心的呼唤

1153

Through what transports of Patience
I reached the stolid Bliss
To breathe my Blank without thee
Attest me this and this—
By that bleak exultation
I won as near as this
Thy privilege of dying
Abbreviate me this

1153

通过在忍耐里沉迷
我获得了麻木的欢愉
能呼吸我的虚空而无须你
印证了我现在这个样子——
凭那凄凉的狂喜
我才基本赢得这个样子
是你死去的权利
使我褪变成这个样子

1154

A full fed Rose on meals of Tint
A Dinner for a Bee
In process of the Noon became—
Each bright Mortality
The Forfeit is of Creature fair
Itself, adored before
Submitting for our unknown sake
To be esteemed no more

1154

一朵饱满的玫瑰秀色可餐
足够一只蜜蜂饱享
在临近正午时分——
每一次绚烂的死亡
消逝的都是美丽的生灵
它,曾广受爱戴
由于我们未知的原因
如今风光不再

1155

Distance—is not the Realm of Fox
Nor by Relay of Bird
Abated—Distance is
Until thyself, Beloved.

1155①
距离——并非狐狸的领地
也不因鸟儿的接力
缩短——距离是
亲爱的，等到你为止。

1156
Lest any doubt that we are glad that they were born Today
Whose having lived is held by us in noble Holiday
Without the date, like Consciousness or Immortality—

1156②
毫无疑问我们高兴她们出生在今日
她们的人生由我们谨记在高贵的节日
没有具体日期，像永生或意识——

1157
Some Days retired from the rest
In soft distinction lie
The Day that a Companion came
Or was obliged to die

1157
一些日子从其他日子中退隐
那一天有些许别致
一位同伴来到
或者说不得不死

---

① 题解：本诗可能是艾米莉·狄金森送给住在附近的嫂子苏珊的一首诗，在狄金森去世前多年，两人甚少来往。因此诗中所指距离并非狐狸或鸟儿国度中的空间距离，而是两人心中的情感疏离，直至对方出现，距离才可能消失。

② 这是艾米莉·狄金森 1870 年 12 月 19 日写给嫂子苏珊祝福她 40 岁生日的书信诗 (L356)，还附送了鲜花。苏珊 50 岁生日时，艾米莉·狄金森也写了一首赠诗给苏珊（约翰逊版第 1488 首诗；L679）。苏珊生于 1830 年 12 月 19 日，艾米莉·狄金森生于 1830 年 12 月 10 日，仅相差 9 天。这或许是诗中出现"她们""我们"之称的原因。

1158

Best Witchcraft is Geometry
To the magician's mind—
His ordinary acts are feats
To thinking of mankind.

1158

最好的魔法就是几何学
对于魔术师的头脑——
他平常的表演都是壮举
对于人类的思考

1159

Great Streets of silence led away
To Neighborhoods of Pause—
Here was no Notice—no Dissent
No Universe—no laws—

By Clocks, 'twas Morning, and for Night
The Bells at Distance called—
But Epoch had no basis here
For Period exhaled.

1159

寂静的大街延伸出去
至邻近歇脚的社区——
这里没有通告——没有异议
没有宇宙——没有法律——

看时钟，正是早上，到了晚上
远处的钟会呼唤——
但时代在这里没有基地
容纳呼出的那段时间。

1160

He is alive, this morning—
He is alive—and awake—
Birds are resuming for Him—
Blossoms—dress for His Sake.
Bees—to their Loaves of Honey
Add an Amber Crumb
Him—to regale—Me—Only—
Motion, and am dumb.

1160①

他活着——今晨——
他活着——并醒来——
百鸟为他重新歌唱——
百花——为他盛装抹彩。
群蜂——在它们蜜块上
添一粒琥珀黄
对他——极力取悦——而我——仅仅——
点头示意，一句话不讲。

1161

Trust adjust her "Peradventure" —
Phantoms entered "and not you."

1161②

信任调整了她的"或许"——
进来的是幻影"而不是你"。

---

① 这是艾米莉·狄金森约在 1870 年 6 月写给朋友鲍尔斯的诗，写在一张字条上（L341），但最终没有送出去。当时鲍尔斯偕夫人到狄金森家拜访并留宿一夜。

② 这是艾米莉·狄金森 1870 年 9 月 26 日写给文学导师希金森的一封信（L352）中的两行诗，诗之前写道："I remember your coming as serious sweetness placed now with the Unreal—"。希金森在当年 8 月首次到艾米莉·狄金森家拜访。这两行诗表明作者不相信希金森"或许"还会再来，所来者一定是幻影，"而不是你"。

1162

The Life we have is very great.
The Life that we shall see
Surpasses it, we know, because
It is Infinity.
But when all Space has been beheld
And all Dominion shown
The smallest Human Heart's extent
Reduces it to none.

1162①

我们现有的生活非常美好。
我们的未来生活能预见
会胜过现在,我们知道,因为
它是无限。
但当所有空间都已看见
全部的疆土都已显露
人类心灵最小的天地
会将它缩小为无。

1163

God made no act without a cause,
Nor heart without an aim,
Our inference is premature,
Our premises to blame.

---

① 本诗是艾米莉·狄金森1870年10月初写给霍兰夫人的一封信(L354)的结尾。霍兰夫人1870年5月才与丈夫霍兰先生(Josiah Gilbert Holland, 1819—1881)到欧洲游历了5个月返回。艾米莉·狄金森不喜出门,她在信里表明了她目前生活的美好,表达了对出门旅行的看法:"We are by September and yet my flowers are bold as June. Amherst has gone to Eden. …To shut our eyes is Travel. /The Seasons understand this. /How lonesome to be an Article! I mean—to have no soul." 本诗后半部分表明,出门旅行把所有空间所有异国疆土都看遍后,最终这些外在的内容还是相当于无。人终究是活在自我心灵的感受里。

1163①

上帝不会无故行动，
心也一样如果缺乏目标，
我们的推论为时尚早，
我们的假设没有必要。

1164

Were it to be the last
How infinite would be
What we did not suspect was marked—
Our final interview.

1164②

假如那是最后一次
将是多么无限
那我们没想到的事——
竟成最后的会面。

1165

Contained in this short Life
Are magical extents
The soul returning soft at night
To steal securer thence
As Children strictest kept
Turn soonest to the sea
Whose nameless Fathoms slink away
Beside infinity

---

① 本诗是艾米莉·狄金森 1870 年 12 月写给弗朗西斯·诺克罗斯和路易丝·诺克罗斯两位表妹的一封信（L357）的结尾。

② 本诗是艾米莉·狄金森 1870 年 2 月写给凯蒂姑姑（"Aunt Katie"，即 Mrs Joseph A. Sweetser）的一封慰问信（L338）的一部分。凯蒂，即凯瑟琳（Catherine Dickinson, 1814—1895）是艾米莉·狄金森父亲爱德华（Edward Dickinson, 1803—1874）的妹妹，她的大儿子亨利（Henry Edwards Sweetser, 1837—1870）于 1870 年 2 月 17 日在纽约市去世，年仅 33 岁。

1165①

这短暂的生命所含
是奇妙的宽广
灵魂在夜里悄悄潜返
从那里窃取更安全保障
恰如越被严管的孩子
越快转向海边
那莫名的深邃悄悄隐退
在无限的边缘

1166

Of Paul and Silas it is said
They were in Prison laid
But when they went to take them out
They were not there instead.

Security the same insures
To our assaulted Minds—
The staple must be optional
That an Immortal binds.

1166②
据说保罗和西拉

---

① 题解：在宽广的空间里，灵魂更觉自由和安全，正如孩子被看管得越严，越受束缚，就越想到海边求得心灵解放，看无边宽广和深邃的大海，悄悄退隐，在夜幕或在退潮时，在无限的时空里。诗中"strictest…soonest"同"the stricter…the sooner"结构。

② 《圣经·新约·使徒行传》第5章第17～23节描述使徒被天使从牢中救出："And laid their hands on the apostles, and put them in the common prison. But the angel of the Lord by night opened the prison doors, …when the officers came, and found them not in the prison…"（Acts 5: 17-23）第16章第23～40节描述保罗和西拉被关进监狱后向上帝祈祷，于是牢门打开，手上的锁链松脱，但保罗和西拉并未逃走，最后是长官派卫兵把两人领出了牢房："…they cast them into prison, …And at midnight Paul and Silas prayed, and sang praises unto God…And suddenly there was a great earthquake, so that the foundations of the prison were shaken: and immediately all the doors were opened, and every one's bands were loosed…. But Paul said…let them come themselves and fetch us out…And they came and besought them, and brought them out, and desired them to depart out of the city. And they went out of the prison…and departed."（Acts 16: 23-40）艾米莉·狄金森应该是把这两个圣经故事混淆了。

被关进了监狱
但当他们去救时
却发现不在那里。

我们受攻击的心灵
有同样安全的保障——
枷锁一定是随意
由一位天神套上。

1167

Alone and in a Circumstance
Reluctant to be told
A spider on my reticence
Assiduously crawled

And so much more at Home than I
Immediately grew
I felt myself a visitor
And hurriedly withdrew

Revisiting my late abode
With articles of claim
I found it quietly assumed
As a Gymnasium
Where Tax asleep and Title off
The inmates of the Air
Perpetual presumption took
As each were special Heir—
If any strike me on the street
I can return the Blow—
If any take my property
According to the Law
The Statute is my Learned friend
But what redress can be

For an offense nor here nor there
So not in Equity—
That Larceny of time and mind
The marrow of the Day
By spider, or forbid it Lord
That I should specify.

1167①

独处一隅
不愿被提及
一只蜘蛛在我的无言里
勤勉爬行不息

很快就变得
比我更自在
我反觉自己像一位访客
就匆忙退出来

重回我的故居
带着申领条款
我发现它颇像
一个体育馆
那里捐税休眠,产权离场
空气的住户们
一如既往地臆想
以为个个是特别继承人——
如果有人在大街上打我

---

① 题解:本诗写于半张信纸上,约写于1870年6月。纸的正面中央贴有一张没用过的1869年发行的3美分面值邮票,邮票下面一侧贴有从1870年5月号的《哈泼斯》杂志(Harper's Magazine)上撕下的两张小字条,一张上面写着"George Sand",指法国小说家乔治·桑(1804—1876),另一张上面写"Mauprat",指乔治·桑于1837年出版的有关爱与教育的小说《莫普拉》。本诗是在邮票和纸条贴在这半张纸上以后才开始写的。诗全集编者约翰逊据此猜测,本诗或是意指艾米莉·狄金森被乔治·桑的这本小说吸引,从而该书无形中窃取了狄金森的"时间和心灵"("time and mind")。

我还可以回击——
如果有人夺走我财产
根据的是法律
那法令是我博学的朋友
但有什么可以反击
如果侵犯了无痕迹
所以很不公平——
那蜘蛛窃取时间和心灵
那岁月的精华
或者主啊,请阻止我
别让我一一指明。

1168

As old as Woe—
How old is that?
Some eighteen thousand years—
As old as Bliss
How old is that
They are of equal years

Together chiefest they are found
But seldom side by side
From neither of them tho' he try
Can Human nature hide

1168

像悲伤一样古老——
有多古老?
大约一万八千年——
像欢乐一样古老
有多古老?
同样这么久远

他们基本同时被发现

但很少互相靠近
他努力却没看见
哪一个隐藏得了人性

1169

Lest they should come—is all my fear
When sweet incarcerated here

1169①

唯恐他们会来——就是我全部的恐惧
当被美美地囚在此地

1170

Nature affects to be sedate
Upon occasion, grand
But let our observation shut
Her practices extend

To Necromancy and the Trades
Remote to understand
Behold our spacious Citizen
Unto a Juggler turned—

1170

大自然假装镇定
在壮丽的，时辰
但就让我们的观察关闭
让她的活动延伸

至魔幻和忙碌之境
远至难以理解

---

① 题解：当诗人把自己关在自己屋子里写诗时，很害怕被他人打扰。

看我们这位庞大的公民
变成了杂耍者——

1171

On the World you colored
Morning painted rose—
Idle his Vermillion①
Aimlessly crept the Glows
Over Realms of Orchards
I the Day before
Conquered with the Robin—
Misery, how fair
Till your wrinkled Finger
Shored the sun away
Midnight's awful Pattern
In the Goods of Day—

1171

在你彩绘的世界
浓妆的清晨升起——
他的朱红慵懒
那辉光漫无目的
爬行在果园上面
我在一日之前
和知更鸟一起——
镇服了苦难,多美满
直至你起皱的手指
推开太阳的巡护
午夜可怕的样品
混入白昼的货物——

---

① "Vermillion" 在 1960 年阅读版中为 "Vermilion"。

1172

The Clouds their Backs together laid
The North begun to push
The Forests galloped till they fell
The Lightning played like mice

The Thunder crumbled like a stuff
How good to be in Tombs
Where Nature's Temper cannot reach
Nor missile ever comes

1172

乌云拥挤背对背
北边开始起冲突
森林飞跑直至跌倒
闪电迅如老鼠

雷霆炸响像物体崩溃
躲在坟墓里多好
不受大自然情绪的影响
飞弹也不来袭扰

1173

The Lightning is a yellow Fork
From Tables in the sky
By inadvertent fingers dropt
The awful Cutlery

Of mansions never quite disclosed
And never quite concealed
The Apparatus of the Dark
To ignorance revealed.

1173

闪电是一把黄色的叉子

从天空的餐桌那里
被粗心的手指碰落
这可怕的餐具

大宅从未清晰揭示
也未完全隐匿
这黑暗的器械
显露给了无知。

1174

There's the Battle of Burgoyne—
Over, every Day,
By the Time that Man and Beast
Put their work away
"Sunset" sounds majestic—
But that solemn War
Could you comprehend it
You would chastened stare—

1174

伯戈因①的战斗——
进行着,每天,
等到人和兽
把各自工作搁置一边
"日落"听来甚是宏伟——
但那场庄严的战争
假如你能领会
一定心怀愧疚双眼圆瞪——

---

① 伯戈因(Burgoyne):即约翰·伯戈因(John Burgoyne,1722—1792),英国将军,他在美国独立战争期间率军占领了泰孔德罗加要塞(Fort Ticonderoga,1777年7月6日),但在萨拉托加战役(Saratoga Campaign)中被北美军队包围,被迫于1777年10月17日率军投降。回到英国后,他从事戏剧创作,《女继承人》(*The Heiress*,1786)是他最受欢迎的剧本。

1175

We like a Hairbreadth 'scape
It tingles in the Mind
Far after Act or Accident
Like paragraphs of Wind

If we had ventured less
The Breeze were not so fine
That reaches to our utmost Hair
It's Tentacles divine.

1175

我们喜欢九死一生的逃亡
它仍令心灵激动
在行动或事故过去很久后
像一股一股清风

假如我们少一点历险
那微风不会如此美妙
能抵达我们最远的发尖
用它神圣的触角。

1176

We never know how high we are
Till we are asked to rise
And then if we are true to plan
Our statures touch the skies—

The Heroism we recite
Would be a normal thing
Did not ourselves the Cubits warp
For fear to be a King—

1176

我们从不知我们多高

直到被要求站起
假如我们严格按照计划
我们的身躯会高与天齐——

我们唱诵的英雄主义
也不过稀松平常
要不是我们弯曲了丝毫
生怕成为国王——

1177

A prompt—executive Bird is the Jay—
Bold as a Bailiff's Hymn—
Brittle and Brief in quality—
Warrant in every line—

Sitting a Bough like a Brigadier
Confident and straight—
Much is the mien of him in March
As a Magistrate—

1177①

一只敏捷——实干的鸟叫松鸦——
像执行官的诵唱一样嘹亮——
清脆又简短——
每一句都够分量——

端坐枝头像一位准将
自信而笔挺——
他在三月的风采
真像一位治安警——

---

① 关于松鸦的叫声，艾米莉·狄金森在书信里有提到："The Wind blows gay today and the Jays bark like Blue Terriers."（L315）她在书信中共提到松鸦 7 次（其余见第 184、360、401、665、882、976 封信），在诗中提到 6 次（见第 386、797、1381、1561、1635、1690 首诗）。

1178

My God—He sees thee—
Shine thy best—
Fling up thy Balls of Gold
Till every Cubit play with thee
And every Crescent hold—
Elate the Acre at his feet—
Upon his Atom swim—
Oh Sun—but just a Second's right
In thy long Race with him!

1178

我的上帝——他看见你——
光彩熠熠——
抛起你金球无数
直至每一腕尺都与你嬉戏
每一弯新月都接住——
他脚下的土地无比欢喜——
在他的微粒上游泳——
啊太阳——就只有获第二名的权利
在你和他的长途赛跑中!

1179

Of so divine a Loss
We enter but the Gain,
Indemnity for Loneliness
That such a Bliss has been.

1179[①]

对如此神圣的损失

---

① 这是艾米莉·狄金森 1871 年 9 月写给嫂子苏珊的一封信(L364)里的一首诗,信的开头写道:"To miss you, Sue, is power. The stimulus of Loss makes most Possession mean." 苏珊在当年 9 月到纽约州的吉尼瓦(Geneva, New York)看望自己的姐姐玛莎(Martha Isabella Gilbert Smith)。信中表达了写信人内心的寂寞和对苏珊的思念之情。本诗表达说话者对待得与失时,只对收获进行记账,损失的则不记入。收获就是和苏珊在一起时的幸福,是对寂寞的补偿。

我们只将收获记入,
这是对寂寞的补偿
那曾经如此的幸福。

1180
"Remember me" implored the Thief!
Oh Hospitality!
My Guest "Today in Paradise"
I give thee guaranty.

That Courtesy will fair remain
When the Delight is Dust
With which we cite this mightiest case
Of compensated Trust.

Of all we are allowed to hope
But Affidavit stands
That this was due where most we fear
Be unexpected Friends.

1180①
"请记着我"小偷恳求!
啊殷勤热忱!
我的客人"今天在天堂"
我向你保证。

---

① 题解:《圣经·新约·路加福音》第23章42~43节记载被钉在十字架上的耶稣临死前与旁边同样被钉在十字架上的一个犯人的对话:"And he said unto Jesus, Lord, remember me when thou comest into thy kingdom. And Jesus said unto him, Verily I say unto thee, Today shalt thou be with me in paradise."(Luke 23: 42-43)本诗说话人赞赏耶稣这种殷勤好客的慷慨,赞赏其不计小偷的罪行,保证客人(小偷)可以上天堂,这算是补偿给小偷的信任,虽其本应因罪不该得到信任,不应得以上天堂;说话人相信耶稣的慷慨会一直持续,有罪的世人归于尘土之后都会得耶稣赦免和信任,升入天堂,小偷的例子就是最有力的例子;在世人各种憧憬或期待里,至少有耶稣的誓言不会变,即死后上天堂一定会实现,虽然担心在天堂里遇见的大多是意想不到的朋友。本诗第1节与第1305首诗第1节语境相似。

那慷慨定然惠传
当欢乐褪成尘
我们就引此为最有力个案
关于补偿的信任。

我们可憧憬的一切
至少誓言依旧
即这会来临虽然我们担心那里
大多是意想不到的朋友。

1181

When I hoped I feared—
Since I hoped I dared
Everywhere alone
As a Church remain—
Spectre cannot harm—
Serpent cannot charm—
He deposes Doom
Who hath suffered him—

1181①

当我怀着希望我就恐惧——
从我怀着希望我就敢于——
独自闯荡
像一座教堂屹立不败——
鬼怪无法加害——
毒蛇无法使坏——
他将厄运罢黜
它曾使他受苦——

1182

Remembrance has a Rear and Front—

---

① 本诗及第1182、1183和1184首诗同是1871年11月艾米莉·狄金森写给文学导师希金森的一封信（L368）中随附的4首诗。

'Tis something like a House—
It has a Garret also
For Refuse and the Mouse.

Besides the deepest Cellar
That ever Mason laid—
Look to it by it's Fathoms
Ourselves be not pursued—

1182
回忆有前有后——
有点像一栋房屋——
还带一个阁楼
容留杂物和老鼠。

还有那最深的地窖
由石匠竭力造出——
当心它的深度
我们可别被追逐——

1183
Step lightly on this narrow spot—
The broadest Land that grows
Is not so ample as the Breast
These Emerald Seams enclose.

Step lofty, for this name be told
As far as Cannon dwell
Or Flag subsist or Fame export
Her deathless Syllable.

1183①
轻轻踏足这方寸之地——

---

① 题解：本诗像是描述墓园中一座在战斗中牺牲的战士之墓。

再广大的疆土
也不如这小丘辽阔
由翠绿的缝线围出。

昂首阔步,因这名字被传扬
远如大炮落地
或旗帜飘起或声名溢出
她不朽的絮语。

1184

The Days that we can spare
Are those a Function die
Or Friend or Nature—stranded then
In our Economy

Our Estimates a Scheme—
Our Ultimates a Sham—
We let go all of Time without
Arithmetic of him—

1184

我们忙里偷闲的日子
唯在某项功能丧失
或是朋友或大自然——困顿之时
因我们如此吝惜

我们的憧憬仅是一个计划——
我们的目标无异于一个骗局——
我们放逐全部光阴
从未——算计——

1185

A little Dog that wags his tail
And knows no other joy

Of such a little Dog am I
Reminded by a Boy

Who gambols all the living Day
Without an earthly cause
Because he is a little Boy
I honestly suppose—

The Cat that in the Corner dwells
Her martial Day forgot
The Mouse but a Tradition now
Of her desireless Lot

Another class remind me
Who neither please nor play
But not to make a "bit of noise"
Beseech each little Boy—

1185①
一只小狗摇着尾巴
不知有其他欢愉
这样一只小狗
我因一个男孩而想起

他整日里蹦蹦跳跳
没有具体的原因
就因他是一个小男孩
我真心这么认定——

---

① 本诗约写于 1871 年 12 月，诗中提到的小男孩是艾米莉·狄金森的侄子奈德（Edward [Ned] Dickinson, 1861—1898），当时他 10 岁，是艾米莉·狄金森哥哥奥斯汀和嫂子苏珊的长子，深受艾米莉·狄金森喜爱。诗中提到的"另一类"可能指艾米莉·狄金森的母亲诺克罗斯（Emily Norcross Dickinson, 1804—1882）（参见艾米莉·狄金森在 1866 年 8 月奈德 5 岁时写给嫂子苏珊的信［L320］）。

猫蜷居在角落
已忘却她威风的日子
老鼠如今只是一个传说
在她无欲求的生活里

有另一类使我想起
既不讨喜也不嬉戏
但却恳请每一个小男孩
别发出"一点声息"——

1186

Too few the mornings be,
Too scant the nights.
No lodging can be had
For the delights
That come to earth to stay,
But no apartment find
And ride away.

1186①

清晨寥寥,
夜晚又那么稀少。
让欢乐
无处落脚
它来到地球定居,
但找不到一套公寓
只好驶离。

1187

Oh Shadow on the Grass,
Art thou a Step or not?

---

① 本诗是艾米莉·狄金森 1871 年 7 月写给表妹路易丝·诺克罗斯的一封信(L362)的一部分,在信中本诗是以书信散文体的形式出现的。

Go make thee fair my Candidate
My nominated Heart—
Oh Shadow on the Grass
While I delay to guess
Some other thou wilt consecrate—
Oh Unelected Face—

1187
啊草地上的阴影，
你是否是一个脚印？
去好好做我的候选人吧
我那被提名的心——
啊草地上的阴影
趁我耽搁了猜想
你就会捧其他为神圣——
啊未被选中的脸庞——

1188
'Twas fighting for his Life he was—
That sort accomplish well—
The Ordnance of Vitality
Is frugal of it's Ball.

It aims once—kills once—conquers once—
There is no second War
In that Campaign inscrutable
Of the Interior.

1188①
这是关乎他生存的战斗——
他骁勇善战——

---

① 题解：一个人在内心与死亡交锋，并饶有成果。生命之死，只需一颗子弹，瞄准一次，屠杀一次，很节省子弹。

生命力的军械署
一向节省炮弹。

瞄准一次——屠杀一次——征服一次——
就不再有第二次战争
在那不可思议的
内部战役中。

1189

The Voice that stands for Floods to me
Is sterile borne to some—
The Face that makes the Morning mean
Glows impotent on them—

What difference in Substance lies
That what is Sum to me
By other Financiers be deemed
Exclusive Poverty!

1189

那在我听来如洪水的声音
对于某些人无关痛痒——
那赋予清晨意义的脸庞
其光辉对他们毫无影响——

到底有何本质上的差异
那对我是总数的东西
竟被其他金融客视为
一贫如洗!

1190

The Sun and Fog contested
The Government of Day—
The Sun took down his Yellow Whip
And drove the Fog away—

1190

太阳和雾霭竞赛
看谁可以独占白昼——
太阳摘下他的黄鞭
把雾霭赶走——

1191

The pungent atom in the Air
Admits of no debate—
All that is named of Summer Days
Relinquished our Estate—

For what Department of Delight
As positive are we
As Limit of Dominion
Or Dams—of Ecstasy—

1191①

空气中刺鼻的微粒
不容任何争议——
凡背负夏日之名的
都撤离了我们的领地——

对哪个欢乐的部门
我们有如此确定它
疆地之极限
或狂喜——之堤坝——

---

① 题解：一年有春、夏、秋、冬四个部门，我们对哪个部门统治的疆地面积及其堤坝围起的狂喜范围都不如对夏季的那般确定，那就是，夏季已经放弃其领地，离开我们的地盘，空气中弥漫的刺鼻微粒已经不容置辩地表明夏季已离去，秋天已莅临。

1192

An honest Tear
Is durabler than Bronze—
This Cenotaph
May each that dies—

Reared by itself—
No Deputy suffice—
Gratitude bears
When Obelisk decays

1192

一滴真诚的泪
比青铜更经久——
这座纪念碑
愿每位逝者都享有——

它兀自挺拔——
无可替代——
感激依旧流传
纵使方碑已腐坏

1193

All men for Honor hardest work
But are not known to earn—
Paid after they have ceased to work
In Infamy or Urn—

1193

人人都尽力争取荣誉
但并不知能否获得——
直至停止努力后才得回报
以骂名或骨灰盒——

1194

Somehow myself survived the Night
And entered with the Day—
That it be saved the Saved suffice
Without the Formula.

Henceforth I take my living place
As one commuted led—
A Candidate for Morning Chance
But dated with the Dead.

1194①

我好歹熬过了黑夜
与白昼一同来到——
对于获救者而言得救已足够
无须遵循俗套。

因此我将生身之所
看作转换的站点——
一个候选人等待清晨的机会
只不过是与死神约见。

1195

What we see we know somewhat
Be it but a little—
What we don't surmise we do
Though it shows so fickle

I shall vote for Lands with Locks
Granted I can pick 'em—

---

① 题解："我"熬过了一夜，成功熬到了第二天，虽然不知道是如何活过来的，但接着还有挑战，因此，"我"觉得目前的生身之所，不过是转换的站点，"我"在那里作为一个候选人，还要继续等，看能否有熬到第二天清晨的机会，看是否会遇见死神。

Transport's doubtful Dividend
Patented by Adam.

1195①
我们眼见的多少有所了解
即使只是一点点——
我们眼不见的我们就猜测
不论它如何幻变

我该选择众锁横陈的大地
愿我能将它们拾起——
狂喜可疑的股息
是亚当的专利。

1196
To make Routine a Stimulus
Remember it can cease—
Capacity to Terminate
Is a Specific Grace—
Of Retrospect the Arrow
That power to repair
Departed with the Torment
Become, alas, more fair—

1196②
就让常规成为一种刺激
并记住它终会停止——
那结束的能力

---

① 题解：如果我要猜测我看不见的，我该选取那片到处上锁的土地（伊甸园），但愿我能将它们拾起打开，这样就可以尝到吃禁果的狂喜，不过能否分到这狂喜的股息，是令人怀疑的，因为这是亚当的专利。

② 题解：让日复一日的常规日子成为一种刺激，促使生活每一天成为乏味的惯例，不过它终会停止，虽然终结它的能力来自上天。追忆之箭具有修复的能力，只要它带着修复日子的苦恼而去，啊，过往的日子经过追忆之箭的修复，一定变得更美丽。

是一种特别的恩赐——
追忆之箭
有修复的能力
携着那折磨离去
变得,啊,更美丽——

1197

I should not dare to be so sad
So many Years again—
A Load is first impossible
When we have put it down—

The Superhuman then withdraws
And we who never saw
The Giant at the other side
Begin to perish now.

1197

我不该再次胆敢如此悲伤
在这么多年后——
负担起初不可能有
当我们已将它放手——

超人于是撤退
而从未谋面
那位彼岸巨人的我们
如今也开始崩陷。

1198

A soft Sea washed around the House
A Sea of Summer Air
And rose and fell the magic Planks
That sailed without a care—
For Captain was the Butterfly

For Helmsman was the Bee
And an entire universe
For the delighted crew.

1198①
一片温柔的海在房屋四周荡漾
一片夏季空气的海洋
那些魔幻的舟楫起落
无忧无虑起航——
蝴蝶是船长
蜜蜂是舵手
而整个宇宙
是快乐的船员帮手。

1199
Are Friends Delight or Pain?
Could Bounty but remain
Riches were good—

But if they only stay
Ampler to fly away
Riches are sad.

1199
朋友是欢乐还是痛苦？
假如恩惠常驻
这财富就可取——

但假如他们仅是暂留
等更丰足后就飞走
这财富就可弃。

---

① 本诗原稿写在1871年马萨诸塞州农业学院（Massachusetts Agricultural College）毕业典礼日程表的纸张背面，本诗或许就是描绘毕业典礼那种盛大、欢乐的场面的。

1200

Because my Brook is fluent
I know 'tis dry—
Because my Brook is silent
It is the Sea—

And startled at it's rising
I try to flee
To where the Strong assure me
Is "no more Sea" —

1200①

因为我的小溪顺畅流淌
我知道这很平凡——
因为我的小溪不声不响
这是大海的浩瀚——

惊恐于溪水上涨
我设法逃到某个地方
那里强者向我保证
"不再有海洋"——

---

① 题解：当"我"写诗时文思顺畅，"我"知道写出的诗句会是很一般、很平凡的；当"我"写诗时凝神静气，"我"就知道自己进入了浩瀚的文思之海；当"我"写诗时文思泉涌，灵感如潮，"我"感到惊恐，想逃离这样的场景，去到无"海"之地。

附录　1955年集注版与1960年阅读版词汇和标点差异一览表

序号	1955年集注版	1960年阅读版	诗序号
1	are	and	901
2	Hight	Height	906、914
3	c'd	could	908
4	it's	its	911、913、924、925、930、935、936、943、945、948、951、963、973、978、989、993、1018、1022、1068、1071、1082、1106、1108、1120、1128、1140、1175、1182、1188、1200
5	Vail	Veil	915
6	vascillating	vacillating	915
7	Chrysophras	Chrysophrase	916
8	no more	no more.	920
9	Once to achieve, annuls the power	Once to achieve annuls the power	922
10	The	Tho	930
11	We knew by change between itself/And that etherial Spark.	A Flint unto this Day—perhaps—/But for that single Spark.	958
12	Deem unplausible	Deem unplausible—	970
13	Trust["]	Trust"	976
14	did'nt	didn't	1020
15	could'nt	couldn't	1020
16	Augur	Auger	1034、1142
17	Comissary	Commissary	1036
18	to Her.	to Her	1037
19	my kernel in.	my kernel in	1039

续表

序号	1955 年集注版	1960 年阅读版	诗序号
20	For Deity	For Deity.	1044
21	'Twas'nt	'Twasn't	1059
22	Vermillion	Vermilion	1059、1171
23		Tri Victory—	1072（第 11 行"In a Day—"后加本行）
24	to Me	to Me.	1073
25	teaze	tease	1099
26	With the austerer sweet—an—this—		1109（第 5 行在 1960 版中无）
27	bourne	borne	1113
28	down again	down again.	1114
29	June.	June	1115
30	Exhiliration	Exhilaration	1118
31	out of sight	out of sight—	1120
32	who visit him	who visit him—	1122
33	in the sky	in the sky—	1125
34	It keeps the nerves in progress	It keeps the nerves progressive	1128
35	remaining charm	remaining charm—	1128
36	Cheek	Hearts	1132
37	nights	years	1132
38	Rafters	seconds	1132
39	frag[r]ant	fragrant	1133
40	it is Woe	it is Woe—	1136
41	sovreign	sovereign	1139
42	me this	me this—	1153
43	no more	no more—	1154
44	there instead.	there instead	1166

本书获中央高校基本科研业务费专项资金资助（项目编号：CBZZ202303）

The Poems of Emily Dickinson

艾米莉·狄金森诗选 ②
1201~1500首

[美]艾米莉·狄金森 著　周建新 译

华南理工大学出版社
SOUTH CHINA UNIVERSITY OF TECHNOLOGY PRESS

·广州·

图书在版编目（CIP）数据

艾米莉·狄金森诗选.2，1201～1500首：英汉对照/（美）艾米莉·狄金森（Emily Dickinson）著；周建新译. —广州：华南理工大学出版社，2024.12

ISBN 978-7-5623-7443-5

Ⅰ.①艾… Ⅱ.①艾… ②周… Ⅲ.①诗集-美国-近代-英、汉 Ⅳ.①I712.24

中国国家版本馆 CIP 数据核字（2023）第 209440 号

艾米莉·狄金森诗选.2（1201～1500首）
（美）艾米莉·狄金森（Emily Dickinson）著　周建新　译

出 版 人：房俊东
出版发行：华南理工大学出版社
　　　　　（广州五山华南理工大学17号楼，邮编510640）
　　　　　http://hg.cb.scut.edu.cn　　E-mail: scutc13@scut.edu.cn
　　　　　营销部电话：020-87113487　87111048（传真）
策划编辑：吴翠微
责任编辑：陈　蓉
责任校对：梁樱雯
印　刷　者：广州小明数码印刷有限公司
开　　本：787mm×1092mm　1/20　印张：12.7　字数：276千
版　　次：2024年12月第1版　印次：2024年12月第1次印刷
定　　价：168.00元（全三册）

版权所有　盗版必究　　印装差错　负责调换

译者前言

本书一如前四个选译本,是从约翰逊编辑的 1955 年集注版《艾米莉·狄金森诗歌全集》中按顺序选取第 1201～1500 首诗,译为中文,仍取英汉对照体例。约翰逊编的 1955 年集注版与其编的 1960 年阅读版在文本上有些许不同,包括字词、标点等。字词、标点方面的差异已在附录的对照表中列出,读者可自行查阅。本书对一些难读、难懂之处提供了题解或注释,比之前四本选译本提供的量要多一些,但远未涵盖全部。

本书收录的 300 首诗有以下三个特点:一是开始具有鲜明的理性玄思特征。相比第 901～1200 首体现的深沉、克制、浓缩的情感,本书体现艾米莉·狄金森是一个将感性的情感内化为理性思考和探索的人,似乎人世间的悲欢离合罕能令她如从前一样或啼笑或落泪,或狂喜或极悲。她冷静地观察、探究其内里的法则和因果,并平静地说出,少有第 901～1200 首中体现的那种克制和深沉,更多的是淡定超然的玄想玄思,仿佛一个阅遍人间苦乐,已处变不惊,且淡然旁观的思考者。感性的淡退,理性的增涨,或是人生的必然,译者见此,未知该悲该喜。本集诗歌的玄思特征,使书中更多的诗歌显得晦涩难懂,作者在诗中的所思所想、所探所指,时常是模糊或不确定的,需要读者对照原文,反复揣摩。诗歌的晦涩,不源于诗歌形式,而在其内容。二是本集诗歌在形式上并无多少特异之处,除偶有句子前后或上下行的倒装。可见大约自前一选译本至本书,除了短横杠符号之外,艾米莉·狄金森诗歌形式的特异性已不再是其诗歌突出特征。三是与前一本相似,本书中的诗其情感特点也总体平稳,无明显上下起伏。本书中的诗歌最晚的写作年代是 1880 年,此时诗人已 50 岁,至知天命之年。可见人生至此的艾米莉·狄金森已是思多见广之人,思想和情感成熟稳定,并逐渐走向通达。

艾米莉·狄金森初期诗歌的格律和行句表述具有模仿传统的特点,其风格和内容让人眼熟,情感热情奔放,充满好奇与天真,正是初写诗者所常有。中期的诗歌更多愁善感，情感波动甚大。现实或憧憬中的爱情使她悲喜交加，对宗教、自然、死亡、永生等的思考亦深深触动其内心，思想和情感的冲动、呐喊、质疑、彷徨使此时期的诗歌较有力量和动感，诗歌形式特异性也明显，此时期的诗歌最具鲜明特色。到后期的诗歌，大约从第901首（写于1864年）或第1000首诗（写于1865年）起，艾米莉·狄金森的思想、感情、诗艺逐渐走向成熟稳定，诗歌形式特异性减少，思想渐具深度，情感走向深沉。到了本书，则稍微向前了一步，更多的是作者对世界冷静超然的玄思，预显其晚期超脱的征兆。

本书译文之不足在所难免，请读者诸君不吝批评指正。由于艾米莉·狄金森的诗歌一般都没有标题，本书目录中取每首诗第一行作为标题，书中诗歌的序号均按约翰逊版中的序号排列。题解或注释中所引《圣经》原文均来自King James版。提及艾米莉·狄金森书信全集中的某一封信时，以"L"开头，后接信的序号。以上提到的约翰逊两个诗歌全集本以及狄金森书信全集是指：

Dickinson, Emily. *The Poems of Emily Dickinson: Including Variant Readings Critically Compared with All Known Manuscripts*. Ed. Thomas H. Johnson. 3 vols. Cambridge, MA: Belknap Press of Harvard University Press, 1955.

Dickinson, Emily. *The Letters of Emily Dickinson*. Eds. Thomas Herbert Johnson, Theodora Van Wagenen Ward. 3 vols. Cambridge, MA: Belknap Press of Harvard University Press, 1958.

Dickinson, Emily. *The Complete Poems of Emily Dickinson*. Ed. Thomas H. Johnson. Boston: Little, Brown and Company, 1960.

译者
2024年9月

目 录

1201	So I pull my Stockings off	1
	我因此脱去长袜	1
1202	The Frost was never seen—	2
	寒霜从不让人看到——	2
1203	The Past is such a curious Creature	3
	过去是个如此奇特的生灵	4
1204	Whatever it is—she has tried it—	4
	不管怎样——她已尝试——	4
1205	Immortal is an ample word	5
	永生只是一个堂皇的字眼	5
1206	The Show is not the Show	6
	演出就不是演出	6
1207	He preached upon "Breadth" till it argued him narrow—	7
	他鼓吹"大度"直至它反驳他为狭隘——	7
1208	Our own possessions—though our own—	7
	我们的财物——虽已属于我们——	8
1209	To disappear enhances—	8
	消失平添魅力——	9
1210	The Sea said "Come" to the Brook—	9
	大海对小溪说"来吧"——	10
1211	A Sparrow took a Slice of Twig	10
	一只麻雀衔起一截细枝	10
1212	A word is dead	11
	一个字会死亡	11
1213	We like March.	11
	我们喜爱三月。	12
1214	We introduce ourselves	13
	我们介绍自己	14
1215	I bet with every Wind that blew	14

	我与吹过的每一阵风都打赌 ……………………………	14
1216	A Deed knocks first at Thought ………………………	14
	一个行动先敲击想法 ……………………………………	14
1217	Fortitude incarnate ………………………………………	15
	坚毅的体现 ………………………………………………	15
1218	Let my first Knowing be of thee ………………………	16
	愿我最先感知的是你 ……………………………………	16
1219	Now I knew I lost her— …………………………………	16
	如今我知道失去了她—— ………………………………	17
1220	Of Nature I shall have enough …………………………	17
	我对大自然的拥有已足够 ………………………………	18
1221	Some we see no more, Tenements of Wonder ………	18
	有些人我们不会再见，那些奇妙的房屋 ………………	18
1222	The Riddle we can guess …………………………………	19
	我们能猜出的谜 …………………………………………	19
1223	Who goes to dine must take his Feast …………………	19
	去赴宴的人要么欢享美餐 ………………………………	19
1224	Like Trains of Cars on Tracks of Plush ………………	20
	像长毛绒轨道上的一列列车厢 …………………………	20
1225	It's Hour with itself ……………………………………	20
	它自在自省的时间 ………………………………………	21
1226	The Popular Heart is a Cannon first— ………………	21
	大众倾心的首先是一门大炮—— ………………………	21
1227	My Triumph lasted till the Drums ……………………	22
	我获胜的感觉持续 ………………………………………	22
1228	So much of Heaven has gone from Earth ……………	23
	如此多的天堂已离开人间 ………………………………	23
1229	Because He loves Her …………………………………	24
	因为他爱她 ………………………………………………	24
1230	It came at last but prompter Death ……………………	25
	它终于来临但更迅捷的死神 ……………………………	25
1231	Somewhere upon the general Earth ……………………	26
	在大地上的某处 …………………………………………	26
1232	The Clover's simple Fame ………………………………	27

	红花草简朴的名声	27
1233	Had I not seen the Sun	27
	假如我没见到太阳	27
1234	If my Bark sink	27
	如果我的小船沉没	28
1235	Like Rain it sounded till it curved	28
	它听起来像雨直到它拐弯	28
1236	Like Time's insidious wrinkle	29
	像时光隐隐的痕印	29
1237	My Heart ran so to thee	30
	我的心急奔向你	30
1238	Power is a familiar growth—	31
	权力是一种常见的生长物——	31
1239	Risk is the Hair that holds the Tun	32
	冒险是那头发悬着大桶	32
1240	The Beggar at the Door for Fame	32
	在门口讨要声名的乞丐	33
1241	The Lilac is an ancient shrub	33
	紫丁香是一种古老的灌木	33
1242	To flee from memory	34
	逃离记忆	34
1243	Safe Despair it is that raves—	35
	喊叫的绝望往往安然无恙——	35
1244	The Butterfly's Assumption Gown	35
	蝴蝶那假想的长袍	36
1245	The Suburbs of a Secret	36
	一个秘密的郊区	36
1246	The Butterfly in honored Dust	36
	蝴蝶在荣耀的尘里	36
1247	To pile like Thunder to it's close	37
	似天雷般高高堆积	37
1248	The incidents of love	37
	爱的琐事	37
1249	The Stars are old, that stood for me—	38

	群星已衰老，那代表我自己——	38
1250	White as an Indian Pipe	38
	白如一株水晶兰	38
1251	Silence is all we dread.	39
	寂静是我们所惧。	39
1252	Like Brooms of Steel	39
	像无数钢制的扫帚	39
1253	Had this one Day not been.	40
	假如没有这一天。	40
1254	Elijah's Wagon knew no thill	40
	以利亚的马车没有车把	41
1255	Longing is like the Seed	41
	渴望就像种子	42
1256	Not any higher stands the Grave	42
	坟墓并没有更高	42
1257	Dominion lasts until obtained—	42
	控制会持续直至完全得到——	43
1258	Who were "the Father and the Son"	43
	谁是"圣父与圣子"	44
1259	A Wind that rose	45
	一阵风刮起	46
1260	Because that you are going	46
	因为你将要离去	48
1261	A Word dropped careless on a Page	49
	一个字无意中掉落纸页	50
1262	I cannot see my soul but know 'tis there	50
	我看不见我的灵魂但知道它就在那里	50
1263	There is no Frigate like a Book	51
	没有一艘快艇比得上一本书	51
1264	This is the place they hoped before,	52
	此地是他们从前的期待，	52
1265	The most triumphant Bird I ever knew or met	52
	我认识或见过的最得意的鸟	53
1266	When Memory is full	53

	当记忆满涨 ···	53
1267	I saw that the Flake was on it ······················	53
	我看见雪片覆在上面 ··································	54
1268	Confirming All who analyze ·························	54
	所有在民意市集 ·······································	54
1269	I worked for chaff and earning Wheat ··············	55
	我找寻麦麸却得到麦粒 ·······························	55
1270	Is Heaven a Physician? ······························	55
	天堂是个医生么? ·····································	56
1271	September's Baccalaureate ···························	56
	九月的告别演讲 ·······································	56
1272	So proud she was to die ·····························	56
	她如此骄傲地赴死 ····································	57
1273	That sacred Closet when you sweep— ···············	57
	当你打扫那个神圣的密室—— ·······················	58
1274	The Bone that has no Marrow, ······················	58
	没有骨髓的骨头, ·····································	58
1275	The Spider as an Artist ······························	59
	蜘蛛作为艺术家 ·······································	60
1276	'Twas later when the summer went ··················	60
	夏日的离去 ··	60
1277	While we were fearing it, it came— ················	61
	我们害怕它,它就出现—— ·························	61
1278	The Mountains stood in Haze— ·····················	62
	山峦在暮霭中屹立—— ·······························	62
1279	The Way to know the Bobolink ······················	62
	了解食米鸟的方式 ····································	63
1280	The harm of Years is on him— ······················	64
	岁月对他的伤害—— ·································	65
1281	A stagnant pleasure like a Pool ······················	65
	迟钝的欢愉像个水池 ·································	65
1282	Art thou the thing I wanted? ························	66
	你是我曾需要的东西? ·······························	66
1283	Could Hope inspect her Basis ·······················	67

	假如希望能检视她的基础 ·················	68
1284	Had we our senses ·················	68
	假如我们有理智 ·················	68
1285	I know Suspense—it steps so terse ·················	68
	我知道悬念——它举步若轻 ·················	69
1286	I thought that nature was enough ·················	69
	我以为大自然已足够 ·················	70
1287	In this short Life ·················	70
	这个短暂的生命 ·················	70
1288	Lain in Nature—so suffice us ·················	71
	对我们已足够——安置于大自然 ·················	71
1289	Left in immortal Youth ·················	71
	遗留在不朽的青春里 ·················	72
1290	The most pathetic thing I do ·················	72
	我做的最令人伤感的事 ·················	72
1291	Until the Desert knows ·················	73
	直至沙漠得知 ·················	73
1292	Yesterday is History, ·················	74
	昨日已成历史, ·················	74
1293	The things we thought that we should do ·················	74
	我们认为该去做的事情 ·················	75
1294	Of Life to own— ·················	75
	把生命拥有—— ·················	76
1295	Two Lengths has every Day— ·················	76
	每一天都有两个长度—— ·················	76
1296	Death's Waylaying not the sharpest ·················	77
	死亡的拦截对时间的窃取 ·················	77
1297	Go slow, my soul, to feed thyself ·················	78
	慢些走,我的灵魂,去获取滋养 ·················	78
1298	The Mushroom is the Elf of Plants— ·················	78
	蘑菇是植物的精灵—— ·················	79
1299	Delight's Despair at setting ·················	80
	欢乐消退时的绝望 ·················	80
1300	From his slim Palace in the Dust ·················	81

	自他尘土中的狭长宫殿 ………………………………… 81
1301	I cannot want it more— ………………………………… 81
	我无法想要更多—— …………………………………… 82
1302	I think that the Root of the Wind is Water— ……… 82
	我认为风植根于水—— ………………………………… 82
1303	Not One by Heaven defrauded stay— ………………… 82
	并非受天堂蒙骗的就会留下—— ……………………… 83
1304	Not with a Club, the Heart is broken ………………… 83
	心碎,不是因为棍棒 …………………………………… 83
1305	Recollect the Face of me ……………………………… 84
	请想起我的脸庞 ………………………………………… 85
1306	Surprise is like a thrilling—pungent— ……………… 85
	惊奇像一阵战栗——那么刺激—— …………………… 85
1307	That short—potential stir ……………………………… 85
	那短暂——潜在的轰动 ………………………………… 86
1308	The Day she goes ……………………………………… 86
	她离开的日子 …………………………………………… 86
1309	The Infinite a sudden Guest …………………………… 87
	无限是一位不速之客 …………………………………… 87
1310	The Notice that is called the Spring ………………… 87
	那被称为春天的通告 …………………………………… 87
1311	This dirty—little—Heart ……………………………… 88
	这颗肮脏——小小的——心 …………………………… 88
1312	To break so vast a Heart ……………………………… 88
	让如此巨大的一颗心破碎 ……………………………… 89
1313	Warm in her Hand these accents lie ………………… 89
	这些话语暖暖地躺在她手里 …………………………… 89
1314	When a Lover is a Beggar …………………………… 89
	当恋人是个乞丐 ………………………………………… 90
1315	Which is the best—the Moon or the Crescent? …… 90
	哪个最好——满月还是弦月? ………………………… 90
1316	Winter is good—his Hoar Delights …………………… 91
	冬天挺好——他灰白的欢愉 …………………………… 91
1317	Abraham to kill him …………………………………… 91

	亚伯拉罕要杀他	92
1318	Frigid and sweet Her parting Face—	93
	寒冷又甜蜜是她离别的脸——	93
1319	How News must feel when travelling	93
	如果消息有心	94
1320	Dear March—Come in—	94
	亲爱的三月——请进——	95
1321	Elizabeth told Essex	96
	伊丽莎白告诉埃塞克斯	96
1322	Floss won't save you from an Abyss	97
	丝线不会救你出深渊	97
1323	I never hear that one is dead	97
	我从未听说一个人死了	98
1324	I send you a decrepit flower	99
	我寄你一枝枯萎的花	99
1325	Knock with tremor—	99
	战战兢兢地敲门——	100
1326	Our little secrets slink away—	100
	我们的小秘密已逃潜——	100
1327	The Symptom of the Gale—	101
	大风的征兆——	101
1328	The vastest earthly Day	102
	尘世最宏大的一天	102
1329	Whether they have forgotten	102
	不论他们已忘记	103
1330	Without a smile—Without a Throe	103
	没有欢笑——没有苦痛	103
1331	Wonder—is not precisely Knowing	103
	疑惑——既非全部了解	104
1332	Pink—small—and punctual—	104
	粉红——小巧——准时——	105
1333	A little Madness in the Spring	105
	春天里的一点疯狂	105
1334	How soft this Prison is	106

	这座牢狱多安宁	106
1335	Let me not mar that perfect Dream	106
	我还是别玷污那完美的梦	107
1336	Nature assigns the Sun—	107
	大自然指派太阳——	107
1337	Upon a Lilac Sea	108
	在一片紫丁香的海域	108
1338	What tenements of clover	108
	哪些红花草的公寓	109
1339	A Bee his burnished Carriage	109
	一只蜜蜂乘它锃亮的车驾	110
1340	A Rat surrendered here	110
	一只耗子在此屈服于	111
1341	Unto the Whole—how add?	111
	往全部里——怎能再加？	111
1342	"Was not" was all the Statement.	112
	"不在世"就是全部所记。	112
1343	A single Clover Plank	112
	是一根红花草的茎条	113
1344	Not any more to be lacked—	114
	不再为人所需——	114
1345	An antiquated Grace	115
	一种古雅的恩典	115
1346	As Summer into Autumn slips	116
	正如夏天溜进了秋天	116
1347	Escape is such a thankful Word	117
	逃跑是个令人感激的词	117
1348	Lift it—with the Feathers	118
	提起它——与羽毛一起	118
1349	I'd rather recollect a setting	118
	我宁愿回忆夕阳场景	118
1350	Luck is not chance—	119
	幸运并非偶然——	119
1351	You cannot take itself	119

	从任何人的心灵	120
1352	To his simplicity	120
	对于他单纯的想法	120
1353	The last of Summer is Delight—	120
	夏季最后的日子属于欢乐——	121
1354	The Heart is the Capital of the Mind—	121
	头脑自成一国——	122
1355	The Mind lives on the Heart	122
	头脑依靠心而活	122
1356	The Rat is the concisest Tenant.	123
	耗子是最简便的租户。	123
1357	"Faithful to the end" Amended	123
	"忠心至终" 修改	124
1358	The Treason of an accent	125
	对口音的背离	126
1359	The long sigh of the Frog	126
	青蛙长长地叹息	126
1360	I sued the News—yet feared—the News	127
	我既渴求那消息——又害怕——那消息	127
1361	The Flake the Wind exasperate	127
	风惹怒的雪花	128
1362	Of their peculiar light	128
	对于他们独特的光	128
1363	Summer laid her simple Hat	128
	夏日将她朴素的帽子	129
1364	How know it from a Summer's Day?	129
	从一个夏日如何得知？	129
1365	Take all away—	130
	一切已拿去——	130
1366	Brother of Ingots—Ah Peru—	130
	金锭的兄弟——啊，秘鲁——	130
1367	"Tomorrow"—whose location	131
	"明天"——它的所在	131
1368	Love's stricken "why"	131

	爱重伤后的一声"为何" …………………………	132
1369	Trusty as the stars ………………………………	132
	像群星一样可信 …………………………………	132
1370	Gathered into the Earth, ……………………	133
	聚集到地里去, …………………………………	133
1371	How fits his Umber Coat ……………………	133
	他赭色的外套有多合身 …………………………	133
1372	The Sun is one—and on the Tare …………	134
	太阳就一个——而对莠草 ………………………	134
1373	The worthlessness of Earthly things ………	134
	世间一切毫无价值 ………………………………	134
1374	A Saucer holds a Cup ………………………	135
	在污秽的人类生活里 ……………………………	135
1375	Death warrants are supposed to be ………	136
	死刑令被看作是 …………………………………	136
1376	Dreams are the subtle Dower ………………	136
	梦是上天的赠予 …………………………………	137
1377	Forbidden Fruit a flavor has ………………	137
	禁果有一种滋味 …………………………………	137
1378	His Heart was darker than the starless night …	137
	他的心比无星光的夜晚还暗 ……………………	137
1379	His Mansion in the Pool ……………………	138
	青蛙遗弃 …………………………………………	138
1380	How much the present moment means ……	139
	此刻还有多大意义 ………………………………	139
1381	I suppose the time will come ………………	139
	我猜那个时候会来到 ……………………………	140
1382	In many and reportless places ……………	140
	在许多难以言明之地 ……………………………	141
1383	Long Years apart—can make no …………	141
	常年的分离——不会造成 ………………………	142
1384	Praise it—'tis dead— ………………………	142
	赞美它吧——它已死亡—— ……………………	142
1385	"Secrets" is a daily word ……………………	143

	"秘密"是一个日常词语	143
1386	Summer—we all have seen—	143
	夏天——我们都曾见过——	145
1387	The Butterfly's Numidian Gown	146
	在蝴蝶努米底亚式的长衣上面	146
1388	Those cattle smaller than a Bee	146
	那些牛比蜜蜂还小	147
1389	Touch lightly Nature's sweet Guitar	147
	请轻触大自然美妙的吉他	148
1390	These held their Wick above the West—	148
	这些举着他们的灯芯在西方天上——	148
1391	They might not need me—yet they might—	149
	他们也许不需要我——但也许需要——	149
1392	Hope is a strange invention—	149
	希望是一个奇怪的发明——	149
1393	Lay this Laurel on the One	150
	把这月桂戴给	150
1394	Whose Pink career may have a close	151
	谁粉红色的生涯会截止	151
1395	After all Birds have been investigated and laid aside—	151
	把所有鸟儿检查一遍并放置一边——	152
1396	She laid her docile Crescent down	152
	她把她温顺的新月放下	152
1397	It sounded as if the Streets were running	153
	听起来好像街道在奔跑	153
1398	I have no Life but this—	154
	我只有这条生命——	154
1399	Perhaps they do not go so far	154
	也许他们并未走那么远	155
1400	What mystery pervades a well!	155
	一口井充满奥秘！	156
1401	To own a Susan of my own	157
	拥有我自己的苏珊	157
1402	To the stanch Dust	158

	我们安全地把你交付 ………………………………………………………	158
1403	My Maker—let me be …………………………………………………	158
	我的创造者——让我对你 ………………………………………………	158
1404	March is the Month of Expectation. ………………………………	159
	三月是充满希冀的月份。……………………………………………………	159
1405	Bees are Black, with Gilt Surcingles— ………………………………	159
	黑压压一群蜜蜂，个个扎着金色腰带—— ………………………………	160
1406	No Passenger was known to flee— …………………………………	160
	从没听说有旅客逃离—— ……………………………………………………	160
1407	A Field of Stubble, lying sere ………………………………………	160
	一地的残茬，枯黄 ……………………………………………………………	161
1408	The Fact that Earth is Heaven— ……………………………………	161
	事实是地球即天堂—— ………………………………………………………	161
1409	Could mortal lip divine ……………………………………………	162
	假如凡人的唇可以预测 ………………………………………………………	162
1410	I shall not murmur if at last …………………………………………	162
	我不会絮叨如果最终 …………………………………………………………	163
1411	Of Paradise' existence ……………………………………………	163
	对于天堂的存在 ………………………………………………………………	163
1412	Shame is the shawl of Pink …………………………………………	164
	羞愧是条粉红的围巾 …………………………………………………………	164
1413	Sweet Skepticism of the Heart— …………………………………	164
	心有温馨的疑虑—— …………………………………………………………	165
1414	Unworthy of her Breast ………………………………………………	165
	她的胸部无那价值 ……………………………………………………………	165
1415	A wild Blue sky abreast of Winds …………………………………	165
	狂野的蓝天与威胁它的风 …………………………………………………	166
1416	Crisis is sweet and yet the Heart ……………………………………	166
	危机是甜蜜的然而心 …………………………………………………………	167
1417	How Human Nature dotes ……………………………………………	168
	人性多么溺爱 ……………………………………………………………………	169
1418	How lonesome the Wind must feel Nights— ……………………	169
	风一定觉得夜晚多么凄凉—— ……………………………………………	170
1419	It was a quiet seeming Day— ………………………………………	170

	这是一个貌似宁静的日子——	171
1420	One Joy of so much anguish	171
	如此深重痛苦中的一丝欢愉—	171
1421	Such are the inlets of the mind—	172
	这些就是心灵的入口——	172
1422	Summer has two Beginnings—	172
	夏季两度开启——	173
1423	The fairest Home I ever knew	173
	我所知的最美家园	174
1424	The Gentian has a parched Corolla—	174
	龙胆有一个焦枯的花冠——	174
1425	The inundation of the Spring	175
	春季的泛滥	175
1426	The pretty Rain from those sweet Eaves	176
	可爱的雨来自那些甜美的屋檐	176
1427	To earn it by disdaining it	176
	以蔑视它来赢取	177
1428	Water makes many Beds	177
	水给那些反感睡眠的人	177
1429	We shun because we prize her Face	178
	我们回避因为珍视她的面目	178
1430	Who never wanted—maddest Joy	178
	从无需要的人——对狂欢	178
1431	With Pinions of Disdain	179
	用轻蔑的翅翼	179
1432	Spurn the temerity—	180
	踢开那无礼——	180
1433	How brittle are the Piers	180
	这些桥墩多么脆弱	181
1434	Go not too near a House of Rose—	181
	别太靠近玫瑰花房——	181
1435	Not that he goes—we love him more	182
	不是他走了——我们才更爱他	182
1436	Than Heaven more remote,	182

	比天堂更渺远无际， ………………………………………	183
1437	A Dew sufficed itself— ……………………………………	184
	一颗露珠有自足感—— ……………………………………	184
1438	Behold this little Bane— …………………………………	185
	看这小小的灾星—— ………………………………………	185
1439	How ruthless are the gentle— ……………………………	185
	温柔多么绝情—— …………………………………………	186
1440	The healed Heart shows its shallow scar ………………	186
	愈合的心显露浅浅的疤痕 …………………………………	186
1441	These Fevered Days—to take them to the Forest ……	186
	这些炙热的日子——该送它们到森林里 …………………	187
1442	To mend each tattered Faith ……………………………	187
	每一个残破信仰的修补 ……………………………………	187
1443	A chilly Peace infests the Grass ………………………	187
	草丛中弥漫清寒的寂静 ……………………………………	188
1444	A little Snow was here and there ………………………	188
	四处是小小的雪花 …………………………………………	188
1445	Death is the supple Suitor ………………………………	189
	死神是个灵活的追求者 ……………………………………	189
1446	His Mind like Fabrics of the East ………………………	190
	他的思想像东方的锦缎 ……………………………………	190
1447	How good his Lava Bed, …………………………………	190
	他的熔岩床有多棒， ………………………………………	190
1448	How soft a Caterpillar steps— …………………………	191
	毛毛虫的步履多么轻盈—— ………………………………	191
1449	I thought the Train would never come— ………………	191
	我原以为火车决不会来—— ………………………………	192
1450	The Road was lit with Moon and star— ………………	192
	道路被星月照亮—— ………………………………………	192
1451	Whoever disenchants ……………………………………	193
	谁去警醒 ……………………………………………………	193
1452	Your thoughts dont have words every day ……………	194
	你的思想不会每天都有文字 ………………………………	194
1453	A Counterfeit—a Plated Person— ……………………	194

	一个仿冒者——是一个镀金的人——	195
1454	Those not live yet	195
	那些质疑复活的人	196
1455	Opinion is a flitting thing,	196
	舆论是飞逝之物，	196
1456	So gay a Flower	197
	一朵花如此欢愉	197
1457	It stole along so stealthy	197
	它如此悄悄潜行	197
1458	Time's wily Chargers will not wait	197
	时间狡猾的快马只会等候	198
1459	Belshazzar had a Letter—	198
	伯沙撒有一封信——	198
1460	His Cheek is his Biographer—	199
	他的脸颊是他的传记作者——	199
1461	"Heavenly Father" —take to thee	199
	"天上的父"——给你带去	200
1462	We knew not that we were to live—	200
	我们本不知我们会活下来——	200
1463	A Route of Evanescence	201
	一条倏然消逝的路上	201
1464	One thing of it we borrow	202
	我们向它借的一样东西	202
1465	Before you thought of Spring	203
	在你想到春天之前	203
1466	One of the ones that Midas touched	204
	迈达斯触到了其中一位	205
1467	A little overflowing word	206
	一个娇小洋溢的字眼	207
1468	A winged spark doth soar about—	207
	一粒带翅的火花四处飞扬——	207
1469	If wrecked upon the Shoal of Thought	208
	如果在思想的浅滩也失事	208
1470	The Sweets of Pillage, can be known	208

	对掠夺的甜头，有所认识	208
1471	Their Barricade against the Sky	208
	他们对抗天空的路障	209
1472	To see the Summer Sky	209
	凝望夏日的天空	209
1473	We talked with each other about each other	210
	我们相互谈论彼此	210
1474	Estranged from Beauty—none can be—	210
	疏远美——没人能如愿——	211
1475	Fame is the one that does not stay—	211
	名声这东西可不会驻停——	211
1476	His voice decrepit was with Joy—	211
	他衰朽的声音透出欢欣——	212
1477	How destitute is he	212
	他多么贫寒	212
1478	Look back on Time, with kindly eyes—	213
	回望时光，双眼慈祥——	213
1479	The Devil—had he fidelity	213
	魔鬼——假如他忠贞	213
1480	The fascinating chill that music leaves	214
	这音乐留下的迷人寒意	214
1481	The way Hope builds his House	214
	希望筑造他的房	215
1482	'Tis whiter than an Indian Pipe—	215
	它的白胜过水晶兰——	216
1483	The Robin is a Gabriel	216
	知更鸟是加百列天使	217
1484	We shall find the Cube of the Rainbow.	218
	我们会找出彩虹的立方体。	218
1485	Love is done when Love's begun,	218
	爱一开始就意味着截止，	218
1486	Her spirit rose to such a height	219
	她的情绪如此高涨	219
1487	The Savior must have been	219

	救世主肯定是 ···	220
1488	Birthday of but a single pang ·····························	220
	仅是一次剧痛的生日 ·································	220
1489	A Dimple in the Tomb ·······································	220
	坟墓中的一个笑靥 ···································	221
1490	The Face in evanescence lain ································	221
	那张逐渐消失的脸 ···································	221
1491	The Road to Paradise is plain, ·····························	222
	到天堂的路很平坦，·································	222
1492	"And with what body do they come?"— ·················	222
	"他们带什么身体前来?"—— ·························	223
1493	Could that sweet Darkness where they dwell ···········	223
	如若他们寓居的那片甜美黑暗 ·······················	224
1494	The competitions of the sky ································	224
	天空中的种种竞争 ···································	224
1495	The Thrill came slowly like a Boon for ···············	224
	颤栗缓缓袭来像一种恩赐 ···························	225
1496	All that I do ···	225
	我所做的全部 ·······································	226
1497	Facts by our side are never sudden ·····················	226
	我们身边的事实从不突然 ···························	226
1498	Glass was the Street—in tinsel Peril ·················	227
	街道是玻璃——危险又明亮 ·························	227
1499	How firm Eternity must look ······························	228
	永恒看起来多么稳固 ·································	228
1500	It came his turn to beg— ··································	228
	轮到他来乞求—— ···································	229

附录 1955年集注版与1960年阅读版词汇和标点差异一览表 ······ 230

1201

So I pull my Stockings off
Wading in the Water
For the Disobedience' Sake
Boy that lived for "Ought to"①

Went to Heaven perhaps at Death
And perhaps he did'nt
Moses was'nt fairly used—
Ananias was'nt—

1201

我因此脱去长袜
在水中向前踩
因为不愿服从
按"应该"而活的男孩

或许死后上天堂
或许也没去
摩西②未受公平对待——
亚拿尼亚③也是——

---

① "Ought to"在1960年阅读版中为"or'ter"。
② 摩西（Moses）：据《圣经·旧约·申命记》第34章第4~5节记载，摩西遵奉上帝，经历千辛万苦把以色列人带往迦南福地，那是上帝应许给以色列人的居所（promised land），但上帝却让摩西在到达目的地之前死去："And the LORD said unto him, This is the land which I sware unto Abraham, unto Isaac, and unto Jacob, saying, I will give it unto thy seed: I have caused thee to see it with thine eyes, but thou shalt not go over thither. So Moses the servant of the LORD died there in the land of Moab, according to the word of the LORD."（Deuteronomy 34: 4-5）。
③ 亚拿尼亚（Ananias）：据《圣经·新约·使徒行传》第5章第1~6节记载，亚拿尼亚把自己的田产卖掉，把钱献给大家，但私自留了几份，便因欺哄圣灵而死："But a certain man named Ananias, with Sapphira his wife, sold a possession, and kept back part of the price, ... and laid it at the apostles' feet. But Peter said, Ananias, why hath Satan filled thine heart to lie to the Holy Ghost, and to keep back part of the price of the land? ... thou hast not lied unto men, but unto God. And Ananias hearing these words fell down, and gave up the ghost...And the young men arose, wound him up, and carried him out, and buried him."（Acts 5: 1-6）。诗作者或因此认为亚拿尼亚未受上帝公平对待。

1202

The Frost was never seen—
If met, too rapid passed,
Or in too unsubstantial Team—
The Flowers notice first

A Stranger hovering round
A Symptom of alarm
In Villages remotely set
But search effaces him

Till some retrieveless Night
Our Vigilance at waste
The Garden gets the only shot
That never could be traced.

Unproved is much we know—
Unknown the worst we fear—
Of Strangers is the Earth the Inn
Of Secrets is the Air—

To analyze perhaps
A Philip would prefer
But Labor vaster than myself
I find it to infer.

1202

寒霜从不让人看到——
即使遇见，也是稍纵即逝
或以缥缈无形的团队——
被花儿首先探知

有位陌生人在周围出没
一种恐慌情绪

在偏僻的村庄弥漫
但却寻不到他的踪迹

直到某个回想不起的夜里
我们都丧失了警惕
花园遭受了一次袭击
却怎么也找不出痕迹。

我们所知的大多无法证实——
我们最恐惧的又不得而知——
地球旅馆到处是陌生人
空气中充满秘密——

或许腓力①更愿意
对此进行分析
但工作量超乎我能力
如果要去推理。

1203

The Past is such a curious Creature
To look her in the Face
A Transport may receipt us
Or a Disgrace—

Unarmed if any meet her
I charge him fly
Her faded Ammunition
Might yet reply.

---

① 腓力（Philip）：据《圣经·新约·约翰福音》第14章第6～10节记载，腓力不信耶稣的话，要耶稣拿出证据来："Jesus saith unto him, I am the way, the truth, and the life: no man cometh unto the Father, but by me...Philip saith unto him, Lord, show us the Father, and it sufficeth us. Jesus saith unto him, Have I been so long time with you, and yet hast thou not known me, Philip? he that hath seen me hath seen the Father; and how sayest thou then, Show us the Father? Believest thou not that I am in the Father, and the Father in me?"（John 14: 6 - 10）。

1203

过去是个如此奇特的生灵
盯着看她的脸
迎接我们的或是欢欣
或觉得有失颜面——

谁见她时毫无防备
我会催他赶紧飞逸①
她褪色的②炮弹
说不定还会回击。

1204

Whatever it is—she has tried it—
Awful Father of Love—
Is not Ours the chastising—
Do not chastise the Dove—

Not for Ourselves, petition—
Nothing is left to pray—
When a subject is finished—
Words are handed away—

Only lest she be lonely
In thy beautiful House
Give her for her Transgression
License to think of us—

1204③

不管怎样——她已尝试——

---

① 飞逸（fly）：诗作者提供的另一个可选词是"flee"（逃逸），本诗用"fly"强调飞一般的逃逸，突出速度，彰显紧急。

② 褪色的（faded）：诗作者提供的另一个可选词是"Rusty"（锈迹斑斑的），或许作者认为用"faded"更能形象地体现鲜活的现在和褪色的过去之对比。

③ 艾米莉·狄金森的儿时友伴、表妹伊莱扎（Eliza Maria Coleman Dudley, 1832—1871）于1871年6月3日因肺结核去世，时年39岁。本诗写于1871年，目前尚不清楚本诗的写作是否与此事件有关。

爱的严父——
该责罚的不是我们——
也别对那鸽子惩处——

并非为我们，祈愿——
也没什么需要求助——
当一位子民生命结束——
语言也已交出——

惟愿她不感孤独
在你美丽的屋宅
她既已越界
请允她把我们缅怀——

1205

Immortal is an ample word
When what we need is by
But when it leaves us for a time
'Tis a necessity.

Of Heaven above the firmest proof
We fundamental know
Except for it's marauding Hand
It had been Heaven below.

1205①

永生只是一个堂皇的字眼
当我们所需的都伸手可及

---

① 艾米莉·狄金森把本诗第二节作为她1872年3月12日写给文学导师托马斯·希金森（Thomas Wentworth Higginson，1823—1911）的一封短信的结尾。希金森的哥哥弗兰西斯·希金森（Francis John Higginson，1806—1872）于3月9日去世，艾米莉·狄金森在报纸上看到讣告后给希金森写了这封慰问短信。诗节之前的信写道："I am sorry your Brother is dead. / I fear he was dear to you. / I should be glad to know you were painlessly grieved—"（L371）。

但当它离开我们一段时间
它就成为必需。

上界的天堂确凿无疑
我们基本了解
若非它那只掠劫的手
天堂早已落户下界。

1206

The Show is not the Show
But they that go—
Menagerie to me
My Neighbor be—
Fair Play—
Both went to see—

1206①

演出就不是演出
若无他们加入——
我的邻居对我而言
就是动物马戏团——
迷人的戏——
两者都曾去看——

---

① 这首写赠他人的诗写于1872年,其中第3~4行也是艾米莉·狄金森于1872年12月写给文学导师希金森的一封信的结尾:"Thank you for having been to Amherst. Could you come again that would be far better—though the finest wish is the futile one. When I saw you last, it was Mighty Summer—Now the Grass is Glass and the Meadow Stucco... Thank you for the 'Lesson.' I will study it though hitherto/ Menagerie to me/ My Neighbor be."(L381)。信中提到感谢希金森到访阿默斯特(Amherst),指希金森1870年8月16日到阿默斯特对艾米莉·狄金森的首次拜访。当时希金森曾问她是否感觉自己与社会缺乏接触,她答道:"I never thought of conceiving that I could ever have the slightest approach to such a want in all future time."(L342a)希金森或许有建议艾米莉·狄金森到纽波特回访自己。希金森当年6月刚搬到罗德岛的纽波特(Newport, Rhode Island)居住。美国作家凯特·菲尔德[即Mary Katherine(Kate)Field, 1838—1896]曾在1864年9月14日马萨诸塞州汉普登县斯普林菲尔德(春田)镇(Springfield, Hampden County)出版的报纸 Springfield Daily Republican 上化名 Straws, Jr., 以"A Human Menagerie"为题详述纽波特的热闹情景。本诗大意:纽波特再热闹得像个动物马戏团,若无游客加入,也热闹不了;我的邻居也像马戏团,我每日均可观看。两者都是人间的迷人大戏,我确曾观赏。

1207

He preached upon "Breadth" till it argued him narrow—
The Broad are too broad to define
And of "Truth" until it proclaimed him a Liar—
The Truth never flaunted a Sign—

Simplicity fled from his counterfeit presence
As Gold the Pyrites would shun—
What confusion would cover the innocent Jesus
To meet so enabled a Man!

1207①

他鼓吹"大度"直至它反驳他为狭隘——
宽广太宽难以定义
也鼓吹"真理"直至它宣称他是撒谎者——
真理从不用名号夸示——

单纯逃离他虚假的外表
正如金子不会与黄铁矿相混——
有多少混乱令无辜的耶稣迷惑
面见如此一个能人！

1208

Our own possessions—though our own—
'Tis well to hoard anew—
Remembering the Dimensions
Of Possibility.

---

① 第1207、1209和1210首是艾米莉·狄金森于1872年12月写给文学导师希金森的一封信（L381）中随附的3首诗。

1208①

我们的财物——虽已属于我们——
重新贮藏一次有好处——
记住可能性的
各种维度。

1209

To disappear enhances—
The Man that runs away
Is tinctured for an instant
With Immortality

But yesterday a Vagrant—
Today in Memory lain
With superstitious value
We tamper with "Again"

But "Never" far as Honor
Withdraws the Worthless thing
And impotent to cherish
We hasten to adorn—

Of Death the sternest function
That just as we discern
The Excellence defies us—
Securest gathered then

The Fruit perverse to plucking,

---

① 本诗是第1206首诗题注中提到的艾米莉·狄金森于1872年12月写给文学导师希金森的一封信的一部分，信的开头是："To live is so startling, it leaves but little room for other occupations though Friends are if possible an event more fair. I am happy you have the Travel you so long desire and chastened—that my Master met neither Accident nor Death."（L381），之后紧接本诗。本诗大意：能够再次拥有自己的所有，是好事一桩，要时刻记住人生有各种可能性，尤其是各种变故（Accident）或死亡（Death）。

But leaning to the Sight
With the ecstatic limit
Of unobtained Delight—

1209
消失平添魅力——
人一旦跑开
顿时染上
不朽的色彩

但昨日在世上漂泊——
今日就躺在记忆里
焕发迷信的价值
我们贿赂"再次"

但"永不"远似荣誉
把无用之物藏起
却无力去珍惜
我们匆匆粉饰的现世——

死亡最残酷的作用
是当我们能分辨时
各种褒誉却对我们藐视——
虽可最稳妥地采集

那果实不宜采摘,
却吸引人的眼睛
迷狂至极地期待
那无法获得的欢欣——

1210
The Sea said "Come" to the Brook—
The Brook said "Let me grow" —
The Sea said "Then you will be a Sea—

I want a Brook—Come now"!

The Sea said "Go" to the Sea—
The Sea said "I am he
You cherished" — "Learned Waters—
Wisdom is stale—to Me"

1210

大海对小溪说"来吧"——
小溪答道"等我长大"——
大海说"那时你就变成海了——
我要的是小溪——现在就来吧"！

大海对大海说"走开"——
大海答道"我就是往昔
你曾喜爱的小溪呀"——"渊博的溪水呀——
你的智慧——对我已过时"

1211

A Sparrow took a Slice of Twig
And thought it very nice
I think, because his empty Plate
Was handed Nature twice—

Invigorated, waded
In all the deepest Sky
Until his little Figure
Was forfeited away—

1211

一只麻雀衔起一截细枝
就自觉满意
我想，是因为他空空的碟子
已被呈给自然两次——

他满心欢喜,奋力翻飞
在无限深邃的天空
直到他小小的身躯
没入苍茫中——

1212

A word is dead
When it is said,
Some say.
I say it just
Begins to live
That day.

1212①

一个字会死亡
一经开口讲,
这是一些人的意见。
我说它才
开始有生命
在那一天。

1213

We like March.
His Shoes are Purple—
He is new and high—
Makes he Mud for Dog and Peddler,
Makes he Forests dry.
Knows the Adder Tongue his coming
And presents her Spot—
Stands the Sun so close and mighty

---

① 题注:这是艾米莉·狄金森1872年写赠给表妹路易丝·诺克罗斯(Louise Norcross, 1842—1896)的诗,诗前写道:"Thank you dear for the passage. How long to live the truth is."(L374)。

That our Minds are hot.

News is he of all the others—
Bold it were to die
With the Blue Birds exercising
On his British Sky.

Version of 1872

We like March—his shoes are Purple.
He is new and high—
Makes he Mud for Dog and Peddler—
Makes he Forests Dry—
Knows the Adders① Tongue his coming
And begets her spot—
Stands the Sun so close and mighty—
That our Minds are hot.
News is he of all the others—
Bold it were to die
With the Blue Birds buccaneering
On his British sky—

Version of 1878

1213
我们喜爱三月。
他穿着紫色的鞋——
清新又高挑——
他给狗和小贩制造泥泞,
他让森林变干燥。
赤莲知道他驾临
尽力展示她的斑斓——
低低的太阳威力无比

---

① "Adders" 在1960年阅读版中为 "Adder's"。

我们的心思快要晒出火焰。

他会带来其他一切的消息①——
此时连死去都显得无礼
正当成群的蓝鸫操练
在他不列颠的空域。

（1872 年版）

我们喜爱三月——他穿着紫色的鞋。
清新又高挑——
他给狗和小贩制造泥泞——
他让森林变干燥——
赤莲知道他驾临
尽力长出她的斑斓——
低低的太阳威力无比——
我们的心思快要晒出火焰。
他会带来其他一切的消息——
此时连死去都显得无礼
正当成群的蓝鸫掳掠
在他不列颠的空域——

（1878 年版）

1214

We introduce ourselves
To Planets and to Flowers
But with ourselves
Have etiquettes
Embarrassments
And awes

---

① 他会带来其他一切的消息：三月之后，其他的月份或季节等会接踵而至。艾米莉·狄金森曾称三月为"宣告之月"["that month of Proclamation"（L976）]，她在另外 13 首诗中也提及三月，即第 136、634、736、812、844、1137、1177、1320、1395、1404、1471、1690、1764 首。

1214

我们介绍自己
给行星和花朵
但对我们自己
彬彬有礼
既局促
又畏惧

1215

I bet with every Wind that blew
Till Nature in chagrin
Employed a Fact to visit me
And scuttle my Balloon—

1215

我与吹过的每一阵风都打赌
直至大自然气不过
雇请一位事实来看我
把我的气球戳破——

1216

A Deed knocks first at Thought
And then—it knocks at Will—
That is the manufacturing spot
And Will at Home and well

It then goes out an Act
Or is entombed so still
That only to the ear of God
It's Doom is audible—

1216

一个行动先敲击想法
接着——敲击意志——

那是生发之地
而意志自在又闲适

随后它发出一个行为
或者被静静埋葬
唯有上帝的耳朵
能听到它的灭亡——

1217
Fortitude incarnate
Here is laid away
In the swift Partitions
Of the awful Sea—

Babble of the Happy
Cavil of the Bold
Hoary the Fruition
But the Sea is old

Edifice of Ocean
Thy tumultuous Rooms
Suit me at a venture
Better than the Tombs

1217
坚毅的体现
在此被置于
可怕的大海
迅疾的分区——

快乐者的絮语
大胆者的挑剔
成就镀上灰白
但大海已老去

海洋的大厦
你喧嚣的房间
适合我去冒险
胜过坟墓之便

1218

Let my first Knowing be of thee
With morning's warming Light—
And my first Fearing, lest Unknowns
Engulf thee in the night—

1218

愿我最先感知的是你
在温暖的晨光里——
而我最初的恐惧,是唯恐未知
在暗夜将你吞噬——

1219

Now I knew I lost her—
Not that she was gone—
But Remoteness travelled
On her Face and Tongue.

Alien, though adjoining
As a Foreign Race—
Traversed she though pausing
Latitudeless Place.

Elements Unaltered—
Universe the same
But Love's transmigration—
Somehow this had come—

Henceforth to remember

Nature took the Day
I had paid so much for—
His is Penury
Not who toils for Freedom
Or for Family
But the Restitution
Of Idolatry.

1219

如今我知道失去了她——
非因她已不见——
而是遥远
行过她的舌头和脸。

虽毗邻，却陌生
如异国的族裔——
她虽犹疑却已穿越
无纬度之地。

万物均未改变——
宇宙一如从前
但爱的迁移——
恐怕已经实现——

此后要切记
我劳心费力的那一天
已被大自然攫取——
他就是一贫如洗
既不为自由奋斗
也不为家庭出力
只想把偶像崇拜
恢复如过去。

1220

Of Nature I shall have enough

When I have entered these
Entitled to a Bumble bee's
Familiarities.

1220
我对大自然的拥有已足够
当我走进这些
一只大黄蜂熟悉的
一切。

1221
Some we see no more, Tenements of Wonder
Occupy to us though perhaps to them
Simpler are the Days than the Supposition
Their removing Manners
Leave us to presume

That oblique Belief which we call Conjecture
Grapples with a Theme stubborn as Sublime
Able as the Dust to equip it's feature
Adequate as Drums
To enlist the Tomb.

1221
有些人我们不会再见，那些奇妙的房屋
永驻我们心间或许也让他们梦绕魂牵
那些日子比设想的简单
它们迁移的风采
让我们浮想联翩

我们称为猜想的那种倾斜信念
与一个坚定似崇高的主题纠缠
能干如尘土修饰自己的外观

如大鼓
足以征召坟墓。

1222

The Riddle we can guess
We speedily despise—
Not anything is stale so long
As Yesterday's surprise—

1222①

我们能猜出的谜
我们很快便瞧不起——
没什么东西能长久陈腐
如昨日的惊奇——

1223

Who goes to dine must take his Feast
Or find the Banquet mean—
The Table is not laid without
Till it is laid within.

For Pattern is the Mind bestowed
That imitating her
Our most ignoble Services
Exhibit worthier.

1223

去赴宴的人要么欢享美餐

---

① 本诗是艾米莉·狄金森1870年10月写给文学导师希金森的一封信的开头，紧接诗歌之后的是这几句："The Risks of Immortality are perhaps it's charm—A secure Delight suffers in enchantment—"（L353）。

要么发现筵席低档——
餐桌不会摆在外面
除非里面已经开张。

因为总体安排由思想赋予
模拟她的心思
我们最不光彩的服务
显得更有价值。

1224

Like Trains of Cars on Tracks of Plush
I hear the level Bee—
A Jar across the Flowers goes
Their Velvet Masonry

Withstands until the sweet Assault.
Their Chivalry consumes—
While He, victorious tilts away
To vanquish other Blooms.

1224

像长毛绒轨道上的一列列车厢
我听见平稳的蜜蜂嗡唱——
一阵刺耳声穿越花丛
它们天鹅绒的屋房

抵挡着直至那甜蜜的攻击
令它们的骑士气概尽失——
而他,大摇大摆地离开
去征服其他花枝。

1225

It's Hour with itself
The Spirit never shows.

What Terror would enthrall the Street
Could Countenance disclose

The Subterranean Freight
The Cellars of the Soul—
Thank God the loudest Place he made
Is licensed to be still.

1225
它自在自省的时间
精神从不公布。
什么恐惧会将街道迷住
愿面容能透露

那地下的货物
那灵魂的地窖——
感谢上帝他创造的最喧嚣之所
获准保持静悄悄。

1226
The Popular Heart is a Cannon first—
Subsequent a Drum—
Bells for an Auxiliary
And an Afterward of Rum—

Not a Tomorrow to know it's name
Nor a Past to stare—
Ditches for Realms and a Trip to Jail
For a Souvenir

1226
大众倾心的首先是一门大炮——
随后是一面鼓——
响钟作为辅助

跟在后的是朗姆①——

既不知明日的名字
也不对过去查看——
通往王国的沟渠还是去往牢狱之旅
都为纪念

1227

My Triumph lasted till the Drums
Had left the Dead alone
And then I dropped my Victory
And chastened stole along
To where the finished Faces
Conclusion turned on me
And then I hated Glory
And wished myself were They.

What is to be is best descried
When it has also been—
Could Prospect taste of Retrospect
The tyrannies of Men
Were Tenderer—diviner
The Transitive toward.
A Bayonet's contrition
Is nothing to the Dead.

1227

我获胜的感觉持续
直至锣鼓将死者遗弃
我随即抛下胜利
心怀愧疚偷偷摸回去

---

① 朗姆（Rum）：指朗姆酒。

走近那些已了断的脸庞
它们向我展示了结论
我于是感到对荣耀的憎恨
甘愿换我作他们。

那即将到来的极易辨别
当它曾经发生——
如果未来能对过去有所了解
人类的暴政
会更温和——更神圣
对于过渡人物。
刺刀的悔悟
对死者毫无帮助。

1228

So much of Heaven has gone from Earth
That there must be a Heaven
If only to enclose the Saints
To Affidavit given.

The Missionary to the Mole
Must prove there is a Sky
Location doubtless he would plead
But what excuse have I?

Too much of Proof affronts Belief
The Turtle will not try
Unless you leave him—then return
And he has hauled away.

1228

如此多的天堂已离开人间
那就肯定有一个天堂
但愿其中包含圣徒

还有宣誓书奉上。

传教士要向鼹鼠证明
肯定有一个天庭
他无疑会反问地点
我用什么理由回应？

过多证据会损害信念
海龟不会尝试
除非你置之不理——又回返
才发现他已姗姗远去。

1229

Because He loves Her
We will pry and see if she is fair
What difference is on her Face
From Features others wear.

It will not harm her magic pace
That we so far behind—
Her Distances propitiate
As Forests touch the Wind

Not hoping for his notice vast
But nearer to adore
'Tis Glory's far sufficiency
That makes our trying poor.

1229

因为他爱她
我们会去打听她是否美丽
她脸上特征有何差异
与他人的相比。

我们远远跟在后面

不会影响她幻妙脚步——
她远远的距离给人慰藉
仿佛森林对风的轻抚

不寄望他巨大关注
只愿能更近前去敬拜
正是荣耀杳远的丰足
使我们的努力变得无奈。①

1230

It came at last but prompter Death
Had occupied the House—
His pallid Furniture arranged
And his metallic Peace—

Oh faithful Frost that kept the Date
Had Love as punctual been
Delight had aggrandized the Gate
And blocked the coming in.

1230

它终于来临但更迅捷的死神
已霸占了整个房屋——
摆好他苍白的家具
显出他金属般的静穆——

啊，忠实的寒霜如期而至
假如爱也如此准时

---

① 正是荣耀杳远的丰足/ 使我们的努力变得无奈：原文 "'Tis Glory's far sufficiency/ That makes our trying poor." 两行与第 122 首诗题注提及的相似，也出现在艾米莉·狄金森 1870 年 10 月写给文学导师希金森的信中。这两行诗之前写道："the fear is mine, dear friend, and the power your's—"（L353）。艾米莉·狄金森给 "sufficiency" 提供的另一个可选词是 "overtakelessness"，给 "trying" 提供的另一个可选词是 "running"，结合本诗前文语境，"sufficiency" 前的 "far" 应意指距离，即 "遥远的，杳远的"。

欢乐早已给大门升级
把闯入阻止。

1231

Somewhere upon the general Earth
Itself exist Today—
The Magic passive but extant
That consecrated me—

Indifferent Seasons doubtless play
Where I for right to be—
Would pay each Atom that I am
But Immortality—

Reserving that but just to prove
Another Date of Thee—
Oh God of Width, do not for us
Curtail Eternity!

1231

在大地上的某处
今天它依然发生——
那消极但确实存在的魔力
它使我变得神圣——

冷淡的四季毫无疑虑地运行
为有权存在其中——
我会付出我每一颗微粒
除了永生——

坚持如此就为证明
与你的另一次约会尚存——
啊宽广的上帝,别为我们
削减永恒!

1232

The Clover's simple Fame
Remembered of the Cow—
Is better than enameled Realms
Of notability.
Renown perceives itself
And that degrades the Flower—
The Daisy that has looked behind
Has compromised it's power—

1232

红花草简朴的名声
能被母牛记起——
胜过在光耀的声名场
有闪亮的名气。
出名而能自知
那就把花儿贬低——
回头看的雏菊
减损了自身的魅力——

1233

Had I not seen the Sun
I could have borne the shade
But Light a newer Wilderness
My Wilderness has made—

1233

假如我没看到太阳
我还能忍受荫凉
但光明把我的旷野
变成一片更新的荒原——

1234

If my Bark sink

'Tis to another sea—
Mortality's Ground Floor
Is Immortality—

1234
如果我的小船沉没
那是去另一片海——
在死亡的底层
是永生的所在——

1235
Like Rain it sounded till it curved
And then I knew 'twas Wind—
It walked as wet as any Wave
But swept as dry as sand—
When it had pushed itself away
To some remotest Plain
A coming as of Hosts was heard
That was indeed the Rain—
It filled the Wells, it pleased the Pools
It warbled in the Road—
It pulled the spigot from the Hills
And let the Floods abroad—
It loosened acres, lifted seas
The sites of Centres stirred
Then like Elijah rode away
Upon a Wheel of Cloud.

1235
它听起来像雨直到它拐弯
我才知道那是风在嚎——
它行走如波浪般潮湿
但掠过像沙一样干燥——
当它推动自己前去

到某块最偏僻的平原地
就能听到仿佛千军万马冲锋
那真的就是雨——
它令水井涨溢,池塘快意
它在路面上响叮当——
它拔出山间水龙头的塞子
让洪水奔涌泛滥——
土地松动,海面升高
中心各处①人心惶惶
然后驾着一轮乌云离去
像以利亚②一样。

1236

Like Time's insidious wrinkle
On a beloved Face
We clutch the Grace the tighter
Though we resent the crease

The Frost himself so comely
Dishevels every prime
Asserting from his Prism
That none can punish him

1236

像时光隐隐的痕印
在亲爱的人脸上浮现
我们把恩典攥得更紧
虽然对皱纹感到讨厌

---

① 中心各处(sites of Centres):可能指人类各聚居点。
② 以利亚(Elijah):据《圣经·旧约·列王纪(下)》第2章第11节记载,希伯来先知以利亚乘马车升天:"And it came to pass, as they still went on, and talked, that, behold, there appeared a chariot of fire, and horses of fire, and parted them both asunder; and Elijah went up by a whirlwind into heaven."(2 Kings 2:11)。

寒霜本人如此秀丽
却扰弄每一个花期
从他的晶棱发出声明
说没人可以对他惩治

1237

My Heart ran so to thee
It would not wait for me
And I affronted grew
And drew away
For whatsoe'er my pace
He first achieve thy Face
How general a Grace
Allotted two—

Not in malignity
Mentioned I this to thee—
Had he obliquity
Soonest to share
But for the Greed of him—
Boasting my Premium—
Basking in Bethleem
Ere I be there—

1237

我的心急奔向你
也不等我跟他一起
我因此感到气愤
兀自走开去
不论我步伐如何调换
还是他先抵达你的脸
多慷慨的一份恩典
竟可以分出两份——

并非出于恶意
我把这向你提及——
若非他有歪心思
早已拿来分半
但他出于贪婪——
他吹嘘要占我的分量——
在伯利恒①晒太阳
在我抵达之前——

1238

Power is a familiar growth—
Not foreign—not to be—
Beside us like a bland Abyss
In every company—
Escape it—there is but a chance—
When consciousness and clay
Lean forward for a final glance—
Disprove that and you may—

1238

权力是一种常见的生长物——
不陌生——也非未来之属——
就在我们身边像平淡的深渊
在每一群人里面——
逃离它——机会只有一次——
当意识和肉体
前倾去看最后一眼——
你须驳斥然后才可以——

---

① 伯利恒（Bethleem）：原文"Bethleem"可指"Bethlehem"（伯利恒），巴勒斯坦中部城镇，耶稣的降生地。"Bethleem"更可能指新罕布什尔州白山（the White Mountains of New Hampshire）上的度假胜地。艾米莉·狄金森的朋友、诗人、小说家海伦·亨特太太（Mrs. Helen Hunt, 即 Helen Fiske Hunt Jackson, 1830—1885）曾去度假的小镇。

1239

Risk is the Hair that holds the Tun
Seductive in the Air—
That Tun is hollow—but the Tun—
With Hundred Weights—to spare—
Too ponderous to suspect the snare
Espies that fickle chair
And seats itself to be let go
By that perfidious Hair—

The "foolish Tun" the Critics say—
While that delusive Hair
Persuasive as Perdition,
Decoys it's Traveller

1239

冒险是那头发悬着大桶
在空中散发诱魅——
桶是空的——但桶——
有上百重量的——空位——
太笨拙难以怀疑其中有鬼
瞅见那张椅子晃悠
就坐下去以被
那不忠的头发推走——

"愚笨的桶"评论家们说道——
而那骗人的头发
像毁灭一样有说服力,
继续诱骗旅人信它

1240

The Beggar at the Door for Fame
Were easily supplied
But Bread is that Diviner thing
Disclosed to be denied

1240

在门口讨要声名的乞丐
很容易获得供应
但面包是更神圣的东西
显示然后就被否定

1241

The Lilac is an ancient shrub
But ancienter than that
The Firmamental Lilac
Upon the Hill tonight—
The Sun subsiding on his Course
Bequeaths this final Plant
To Contemplation—not to Touch—
The Flower of Occident.
Of one Corolla is the West—
The Calyx is the Earth—
The Capsules burnished Seeds the Stars—
The Scientist of Faith
His research has but just begun—
Above his synthesis
The Flora unimpeachable
To Time's Analysis—
"Eye hath not seen" may possibly
Be current with the Blind
But let not Revelation
By theses be detained—

1241

紫丁香是一种古老的灌木
但更古老的是
天空中的紫丁香
在今夜的山岗——
太阳沿它的航道沉落

遗下这最后的植物
给沉思——而非让人触摸——
这西隅的花朵。
花冠是西方——
花萼是地球——
荚膜里磨亮的种子是星星——
信仰的科学家
他的研究才刚开始——
但超出了他综合法的能力
这株植物无可置疑
经得起时间的分析——
"有眼看不见"① 或许
对于盲人很平常
但别让启示
被论文阻挡——

1242

To flee from memory

Had we the Wings

Many would fly

Inured to slower things

Birds with surprise

Would scan the cowering Van

Of men escaping

From the mind of man

1242

逃离记忆

如果我们有翅翼

很多人一定会飞逸

---

① 有眼看不见（Eye hath not seen）：据《圣经·新约·哥林多前书》第 2 章第 9 节记载："But as it is written, Eye hath not seen, nor ear heard, neither have entered into the heart of man, the things which God hath prepared for them that love him." (1 Corinthians 2：9)。

习惯了慢吞吞的东西
惊愕的鸟
定会对这群畏缩的先锋目不转睛
看一群人在逃跑
离开人类的心灵

1243

Safe Despair it is that raves—
Agony is frugal.
Puts itself severe away
For it's own perusal.

Garrisoned no Soul can be
In the Front of Trouble—
Love is one, not aggregate—
Nor is Dying double—

1243

喊叫的绝望往往安然无恙——
痛苦一向吝于外露。
剧痛将自己移至别处
只让自己细读。

没有灵魂可以防卫
面对麻烦的穷追——
爱是一,不是集合体——
死也不会翻倍——

1244

The Butterfly's Assumption Gown
In Chrysoprase Apartments hung
This afternoon put on—

How condescending to descend
And be of Buttercups the friend
In a New England Town—

1244

蝴蝶那假想的长袍
悬挂在绿玉髓的公寓
被午后披上身——

多么骄傲的屈就
成为金凤花的朋友
在一个新英格兰小镇——

1245

The Suburbs of a Secret
A Strategist should keep,
Better than on a Dream intrude
To scrutinize the Sleep.

1245

一个秘密的郊区
应由一位战略家守关,
与其侵入梦里
不如细查睡眠。

1246

The Butterfly in honored Dust
Assuredly will lie
But none will pass the Catacomb
So chastened as the Fly—

1246

蝴蝶在荣耀的尘里
定会躺倒
但没有谁经过那墓穴
有如苍蝇那么心焦——

1247

To pile like Thunder to it's close
Then crumble grand away
While Everything created hid
This—would be Poetry—

Or Love—the two coeval come—
We both and neither prove—
Experience either and consume—
For None see God and live—

1247

似天雷般高高堆积
然后轰然溃逝
一切创造物全隐匿
这——就是诗——

或爱——两者同时而至——
我们都能也都不能证实——
体验其一就会死——
因为没人能活着去见上帝——

1248

The incidents of love
Are more than it's Events—
Investment's best Expositor
Is the minute Per Cents—

1248

爱的琐事
多于它的大事——
投资的最佳说明人
是那微小的百分比——

1249

The Stars are old, that stood for me—
The West a little worn—
Yet newer glows the only Gold
I ever cared to earn—
Presuming on that lone result
Her infinite disdain
But vanquished her with my defeat
'Twas Victory was slain.

1249①

群星已衰老,那代表我自己——
西方有些破败——
但我唯一想拥有的那粒金子
焕发出更新的光彩——
仰赖于那唯一的结局
她对我无限鄙弃
但我用我的失败将她征服
被杀害的是胜利。

1250

White as an Indian Pipe
Red as a Cardinal Flower
Fabulous as a Moon at Noon
February Hour—

1250②

白如一株水晶兰

---

① 这是艾米莉·狄金森写赠给嫂子苏珊的诗,写于 1873 年末或 1874 年初。最后四行也出现在艾米莉·狄金森 1874 年 1 月写给文学导师希金森的一封信中,但其中倒数第三行的"Her"改成了"his",倒数第二行的"her"改成了"him"。信中诗前写道:"Meeting a Bird this Morning, I begun to flee—He saw it and sung."(L405)。

② 艾米莉·狄金森曾在信中称二月为"February, that Month of fleetest sweetness." (L971)。

红似红花半边莲
神奇像正午的月亮
那二月的时光——

1251

Silence is all we dread.
There's Ransom in a Voice—
But Silence is Infinity.
Himself have not a face.

1251①

寂静是我们所惧。
声音里含有赎金——
但寂静是无限。
他自己没有脸。

1252

Like Brooms of Steel
The Snow and Wind
Had swept the Winter Street—
The House was hooked
The Sun sent out
Faint Deputies of Heat—
Where rode the Bird
The Silence tied
His ample—plodding Steed
The Apple in the Cellar snug
Was all the one that played.

1252

像无数钢制的扫帚

---

① 本诗是艾米莉·狄金森1873年秋天写给嫂子苏珊的一封信（L397）的结尾。当时苏珊正带着孩子在纽约的日内瓦（Geneva, New York）探望自己的姐姐。

那风和雪
扫过冬日的大街——
房屋被钩住
太阳派出
一批虚弱的热量代理——
在鸟儿驰骋之地
寂静拴系
他硕大——迟缓的马匹
蜷缩在地窖里的苹果
是唯一还在嬉戏。

1253

Had this one Day not been.
Or could it cease to be
How smitten, how superfluous,
Were every other Day!

Lest Love should value less
What Loss would value more
Had it the stricken privilege,
It cherishes before.

1253

假如没有这一天。
或它可以消失
多么苦恼,多么多余,
那其余的每个日子!

为免损失重视
而爱却贬低
假如那受打击的有权利
它定会将以往珍惜。

1254

Elijah's Wagon knew no thill

Was innocent of Wheel
Elijah's horses as unique
As was his vehicle—

Elijah's journey to portray
Expire with him the skill
Who justified Elijah
In feats inscrutable—

1254①
以利亚的马车没有车把
也没有轮子
以利亚的马匹也很独特
一如他的车子——

对以利亚旅程的描绘
那技巧已随他一起终止
他确证了以利亚
取得不可思议的伟绩——

1255
Longing is like the Seed
That wrestles in the Ground,
Believing if it intercede
It shall at length be found.

The Hour, and the Clime—
Each Circumstance unknown,
What Constancy must be achieved
Before it see the Sun!

---

① 见第1235首注释②。

1255

渴望就像种子
在地里煎熬,
相信假如它求情
终将会被看到。

时间,和天气——
每一样都不熟悉,
需有什么样的坚持
才能与太阳相遇!

1256

Not any higher stands the Grave
For Heroes than for Men—
Not any nearer for the Child
Than numb Three Score and Ten—

This latest Leisure equal lulls
The Beggar and his Queen
Propitiate this Democrat
A Summer's Afternoon—

1256

坟墓并没有更高
英雄的和平民的相比——
那孩子也并未更接近
比那麻木的七十——

最近的闲暇同样催人昏沉
那乞丐与他的王后
抚慰这位民主党人
一个夏日的午后——

1257

Dominion lasts until obtained—

Possession just as long—
But these—endowing as they flit
Eternally belong.

How everlasting are the Lips
Known only to the Dew—
These are the Brides of permanence
Supplanting me and you

1257
控制会持续直至完全得到——
占有也同样长久——
但这些——他们掠过时所献赠
则永远属其所有。

这些唇会留存多久
唯有露珠知悉——
它们是永恒的新娘
替代了我和你

1258
Who were "the Father and the Son"
We pondered when a child,
And what had they to do with us
And when portentous told

With inference appalling
By Childhood fortified
We thought, at least they are no worse
Than they have been described.

Who are "the Father and the Son"
Did we demand Today
"The Father and the Son" himself

Would doubtless specify—

But had they the felicity
When we desired to know,
We better Friends had been, perhaps,
Than time ensue to be—

We start—to learn that we believe
But once—entirely—
Belief, it does not fit so well
When altered frequently—

We blush, that Heaven if we achieve—
Event ineffable—
We shall have shunned until ashamed
To own the Miracle—

1258①
谁是"圣父与圣子"
我们儿时这么沉思,
他们和我们有何关系
当被煞有介事地告知

用骇人的推论
凭孩提以来的坚不可摧
我们想,至少他们没有更糟

---

① 艾米莉·狄金森在1862年4月25日写给文学导师希金森的一封信(L261)中提到自己和家里人的宗教态度:"They are religious—except me—and address an Eclipse, every morning—whom they call their 'Father.'"。艾米莉·狄金森的朋友霍兰医生(Dr. Holland, 即 Josiah Gilbert Holland, 1819—1881) 1881年10月12日去世,艾米莉·狄金森在1881年10月写给霍兰夫人(Mrs. J. G. Holland, 即 Elizabeth Luna Chapin Holland, 1823—1896)的一封慰问信里提到她对上帝的看法: "I shall never forget the Doctor's prayer, my first morning with you—so simple, so believing. That God must be a friend—that was a different God—and I almost felt warmer myself, in the midst of a tie so sunshiny." (L731)。

比起原先对他们的描绘。

谁是"圣父与圣子"
假如我们今天还询问
"圣父与圣子"自己
肯定会亲自现身——

但假如一开始我们想知道
他们就乐意作答,
或许,我们的朋友关系,
不会比如今的差——

我们开始——了解我们所信
只有一次——不折不扣——
信念,不那么适合
当它经常改变的时候——

我们羞愧,假如我们抵达天堂——
这件难以言喻之事——
我们该尽量回避直至
惶恐地等到了奇迹——

1259

A Wind that rose
Though not a Leaf
In any Forest stirred
But with itself did cold engage
Beyond the Realm of Bird—
A Wind that woke a lone Delight
Like Separation's Swell
Restored in Arctic Confidence
To the Invisible—

1259①

一阵风刮起
虽未曾搅动
森林中一张叶片
却带来了寒意
自飞鸟王国以远——
一阵风催醒孤寂的欢欣
如别离的起伏心情
以极寒的信心
又重返无形——

1260

Because that you are going
And never coming back
And I, however absolute
May overlook your Track—

Because that Death is final,
However first it be
This instant be suspended
Above Mortality—

Significance that each has lived
The other to detect
Discovery not God himself
Could now annihilate

Eternity, Presumption

---

① 本诗（除最后4行外）是艾米莉·狄金森约1874年（富兰克林版全集认为是1871年初）写给嫂子苏珊的一封信的结尾，诗之前的信写道："It is sweet you are better—I am greedy to see you. Your Note was like the Wind. The Bible chooses that you know to define the Spirit."（L407）。艾米莉·狄金森还将本诗最后4行作为1874年1月写给文学导师希金森的一封信的结尾（L405），该信表达了对希金森的新年牵挂的感谢。

The instant I perceive
That you, who were Existence
Yourself forgot to live—

The "Life that is" will then have been
A thing I never knew—
As Paradise fictitious
Until the Realm of you—

The "Life that is to be," to me,
A Residence too plain
Unless in my Redeemer's Face
I recognize your own—

Of Immortality who doubts
He may exchange with me
Curtailed by your obscuring Face
Of everything but He—

Of Heaven and Hell I also yield
The Right to reprehend
To whoso would commute this Face
For his less priceless Friend.

If "God is Love" as he admits
We think that he must be
Because he is a "jealous God"
He tells us certainly

If "All is possible with" him
As he besides concedes
He will refund us finally
Our confiscated Gods—

1260
因为你将要离去
再也不会返回
我,不论多么绝对
也会对你的踪迹不再理会——

因为死是最终阶段,
不论起初是怎样
这一刻将定格
在死亡上——

重要的是各自曾活过
并察觉了对方
这一发现如今上帝自己
也无法将它消亡

永恒,是一种假定
在那一刻我发觉
作为存在的,你
却将生活忘却——

那时"现有的生活"就是
我从未知悉的事物——
如天堂般虚幻
直至它是你的国度——

那"将来的生活",对于我,
是过于简朴的居住点
除非在我救赎者的脸上
我认出你的容颜——

怀疑永生的人
可与我交换
你朦胧的脸
夺走了一切除了他——

我也可出让
对天堂和地狱的申斥权
给某人想用这张脸
换他不那么珍贵的友伴。

倘若如他所承认"上帝就是爱"
那我们认为他一定就是
因为他是个"爱嫉妒的"上帝
他明确向我们告知

倘若他"一切皆有可能"
一如他另外所承认
那他终会向我们退回
我们被没收去的诸神——

1261

A Word dropped careless on a Page
May stimulate an eye
When folded in perpetual seam
The Wrinkled Maker lie

Infection in the sentence breeds
We may inhale Despair
At distances of Centuries
From the Malaria—

1261①

一个字无意中掉落纸页
会令眼睛受刺激
一旦折叠这满身皱纹的制造者
就躺在永久的褶缝里

句子中的感染滋生
我们可能吸入绝望
在距离疟疾
几世纪的地方——

1262

I cannot see my soul but know 'tis there
Nor ever saw his house nor furniture,
Who has invited me with him to dwell;
But a confiding guest consult as well,
What raiment honor him the most,
That I be adequately dressed,
For he insures to none
Lest men specified adorn
Procuring him perpetual drest
By dating it a sudden feast.

1262②

我看不见我的灵魂但知道它就在那里

---

① 本诗第1节是艾米莉·狄金森1872年末写给表妹路易丝·诺克罗斯（Louise Norcross, 1842—1896）的一封信的结尾，但"stimulate"改成了"consecrate"，"Maker"改成了"Author"。诗之前写道："If I should see your face no more it will be your portrait, and if I should, more vivid than your mortal face. We must be careful what we say. No bird resumes its egg."（L379）。
② 本诗是艾米莉·狄金森1873年冬天写给弗朗西斯·诺克罗斯（Frances Norcross, 1847—1919）和路易丝·诺克罗斯两位表妹的一封信的一部分，诗之前的信这样写道："I know I love my friends—I feel it far in here where neither blue nor black eye goes, and fingers cannot reach. I know 'tis love for them that sets the blister in my throat, many time a day, when winds go sweeter than their wont, or a different cloud puts my brain from home."（L382）。

也不曾见过他的房子和家具，
他邀请我与他同住；
但一位推心置腹的客人总要问清楚，
什么衣服最能表示对他的敬意，
我总该着装得体，
因他从不保证喜欢哪一款
以免人们刻意打扮
为他准备永久的衣装
标明为突如其来的盛宴而穿。

1263

There is no Frigate like a Book
To take us Lands away
Nor any Coursers like a Page
Of prancing Poetry—
This Travel① may the poorest take
Without offence② of Toll—
How frugal is the Chariot
That bears the Human soul.

1263③

没有一艘快艇比得上一本书
把我们带向远方
也没有一匹骏马比得上一页
跳跃的诗章——
赤贫者也能踏上这旅程
无须担心通行费——
承载人类灵魂的马车
多么实惠。

---

① "Travel" 在1960年阅读版中为 "Traverse"。
② "offence" 在1960年阅读版中为 "oppress"。
③ 本诗是艾米莉·狄金森1873年写给弗朗西斯·诺克罗斯和路易丝·诺克罗斯两位表妹的一封信（L400）的结尾部分。

1264

This is the place they hoped before,
Where I am hoping now.
The seed of disappointment grew
Within a capsule gay,
Too distant to arrest the feet
That walk this plank of balm—
Before them lies escapeless sea—
The way is closed they came.

1264①

此地是他们从前的期待,
现在是我所青睐。
失望的种子逐渐长大
在一个欢乐的荚里,
太遥远无法将
走在这块香膏板上的脚阻击——
他们面前是毫无退意的海——
他们的来路已封闭。

1265

The most triumphant Bird I ever knew or met
Embarked upon a twig today
And till Dominion set
I famish to behold so eminent a sight
And sang for nothing scrutable
But intimate Delight.
Retired, and resumed his transitive Estate—
To what delicious Accident
Does finest Glory fit!

---

① 本诗是艾米莉·狄金森1873年5月下旬写给表妹弗朗西斯·诺克罗斯的一封信的一部分,诗之前写道:"Thank you, dear, for the love. I am progressing timidly. Experiment has a stimulus which withers its fear."(L390)。

1265①

我认识或见过的最得意的鸟
今天站上一根细枝
等到领地确立
我渴望看到引人注目的景致
他放声歌唱并无具体原因
而是发自内心的欢愉。
隐逸，然后再次回荡在他的移动庄园——
哪个美妙的事件
适配这最绚烂的光艳！

1266

When Memory is full
Put on the perfect Lid—
This Morning's finest syllable
Presumptuous Evening said—

1266②

当记忆满涨
盖上那完美的盖子——
今晨最美的声响
冒昧的夜晚表示——

1267

I saw that the Flake was on it
But plotted with Time to dispute—

---

① 本诗是艾米莉·狄金森1873年4月写给弗朗西斯·诺克罗斯和路易丝·诺克罗斯两位表妹的一封信的结尾部分，诗之前写道："so with a few spring touches, nature remains unchanged."（L388），诗中的"famish"被改成"perish"，"eminent"被改成"competent"，"intimate"被改成"impudent"。她也把本诗加入其在1873年夏天写给霍兰夫人的一封信里，诗之前写道："Eden, always eligible, is peculiarly so this noon. It would please you to see how intimate the Meadows are with Sun—Besides—"（L391）。

② 本诗写于1873年或1874年初，写于一张字条上，随附在一封艾米莉·狄金森写给霍兰夫人的信里。

"Unchanged" I urged with a candor
That cost me my honest Heart—

But "you" —she returned with valor
Sagacious of my mistake
"Have altered—Accept the pillage
For the progress' sake" —

1267①

我看见雪片覆在上面
但仍与时间密谋争执——
"未曾改变"我急切直言
这使我失去我心的诚实——

但"你"——她勇敢回击
明了我的错误
"已经改变——请接受劫掠
为了进步"——

1268

Confirming All who analyze
In the Opinion fair
That Eloquence is when the Heart
Has not a Voice to spare—

1268

所有在民意市集
作分析的人都确认

---

① 题解：时间时刻行掠夺青春、生命之事，"我"看到头发覆雪，仍想与时间合谋掩盖事实，强说未有改变，但对方了然于心，勇敢揭露，说"我"其实已有改变，敬请接受青春年华被劫掠的事实，这样人生才能继续前行。本诗约写于1873年，或与艾米莉·狄金森的儿时好友艾比（Abby Maria Wood，即 Ms. Daniel Bliss，1830—1915）当时到阿默斯特拜访艾米莉·狄金森有关联。

雄辩出现
当心不发声——

1269

I worked for chaff and earning Wheat
Was haughty and betrayed.
What right had Fields to arbitrate
In matters ratified?

I tasted Wheat and hated Chaff
And thanked the ample friend—
Wisdom is more becoming viewed
At distance than at hand.

1269

我找寻麦麸却得到麦粒
既高傲又觉受到背叛。
田地有什么权利干预
已被批准的事项?

我品尝麦粒但憎恨麦麸
感谢那位浩瀚的友伴——
智慧更受重视
远处胜过近旁。

1270

Is Heaven a Physician?
They say that He can heal—
But Medicine Posthumous
Is unavailable—
Is Heaven an Exchequer?
They speak of what we owe—
But that negotiation
I'm not a Party to—

1270

天堂是个医生么?
他们说他会治病——
但人死后才开的药
肯定得不到——
天堂是财政部么?
他们在谈我们欠的账——
但那个讨论
没我参与的份——

1271

September's Baccalaureate
A combination is
Of Crickets—Crows—and Retrospects
And a dissembling Breeze

That hints without assuming—
An Innuendo sear
That makes the Heart put up it's Fun
And turn Philosopher.

1271

九月的告别演讲
融汇了种种
包括蟋蟀——乌鸦——和回想
还有一阵欲盖弥彰的轻风

暗示而非假设——
一种枯乏的射影含沙
让心收起了玩乐
变成哲学家。

1272

So proud she was to die

It made us all ashamed
That what we cherished, so unknown
To her desire seemed—
So satisfied to go
Where none of us should be
Immediately—that Anguish stooped
Almost to Jealousy—

1272

她如此骄傲地赴死
让我们都心含愧疚
我们所珍视的，好似
从不是她追求——
如此心满意足离去
我们谁都无法抵达那里
顷刻——极大的痛苦
几乎降为妒忌——

1273

That sacred Closet when you sweep—
Entitled "Memory" —
Select a reverential Broom—
And do it silently.

'Twill be a Labor of surprise—
Besides Identity
Of other Interlocutors
A probability—

August the Dust of that Domain—
Unchallenged—let it lie—
You cannot supersede itself
But it can silence you—

1273

当你打扫那个神圣的密室——
名为"记忆"——
请用一把恭敬的扫帚——
别弄出声息。

这工作会令人惊奇——
还要分清
其他交谈者的身份
有这种可能性——

八月是那里的一粒尘——
别去触碰——就让它这么躺着——
你无法将它扫除
它却可以让你陷入沉默——

1274

The Bone that has no Marrow,
What Ultimate for that?
It is not fit for Table
For Beggar or for Cat.

A Bone has obligations—
A Being has the same—
A Marrowless Assembly
Is culpabler than shame.

But how shall finished Creatures
A function fresh obtain?
Old Nicodemus' Phantom
Confronting us again!

1274

没有骨髓的骨头,

最终有谁需要?
它不宜上餐桌
也不宜给乞丐或小猫。

一根骨头有义务——
一个生命亦如此——
一副无骨髓的肉身
其罪过大于羞耻。

但已了断的生灵
如何重获运转?
老尼哥底母①的魅影
我们再次撞见!

1275

The Spider as an Artist
Has never been employed—
Though his surpassing Merit
Is freely certified

By every Broom and Bridget
Throughout a Christian Land—
Neglected Son of Genius
I take thee by the Hand—

---

① 尼哥底母(Nicodemus):据《圣经·新约·约翰福音》第3章1~9节记载尼哥底母对耶稣关于人死后重生的说法产生疑问:"There was a man of the Pharisees, named Nicodemus, a ruler of the Jews: The same came to Jesus by night, and said unto him, Rabbi, we know that thou art a teacher come from God: ...Jesus answered and said unto him, Verily, verily, I say unto thee, Except a man be born again, he cannot see the kingdom of God. Nicodemus saith unto him, How can a man be born when he is old? can he enter the second time into his mother's womb, and be born? Jesus answered, Verily, verily, I say unto thee, Except a man be born of water and of the Spirit, he cannot enter into the kingdom of God. ...Marvel not that I said unto thee, Ye must be born again... Nicodemus answered and said unto him, How can these things be?" (John 3: 1-9)。

1275

蜘蛛作为艺术家
从未被选聘——
虽然它超群的技艺
可轻易得到证明

通过扫帚和主妇①
在基督教的大地——
被埋没的天才之子
我用手抓住了你——

1276

'Twas later when the summer went
Than when the Cricket came—
And yet we knew that gentle Clock
Meant nought but Going Home—
'Twas sooner when the Cricket went
Than when the Winter came
Yet that pathetic Pendulum
Keeps esoteric Time

1276

夏日的离去
比蟋蟀到来晚一步——
但我们知道那温和的钟声
无非是归家的催促——
蟋蟀的离去
比冬日到来早一点
但那哀婉的钟摆
却摆出玄奥的时间

---

① 主妇（Bridget）：原文"Bridget"可指异教徒的谷物女神（pagan grain goddess）、爱尔兰的圣女（holy woman in Ireland）、北欧的女圣徒（female saint in northern Europe）；也喻指"maid, housemaid, housekeeper, housewife, female household servant"，即家庭主妇或女仆之类。

1277

While we were fearing it, it came—
But came with less of fear
Because that fearing it so long
Had almost made it fair—

There is a Fitting—a Dismay—
A Fitting—a Despair—
'Tis harder knowing it is Due
Than knowing it is Here.

They Trying on the Utmost
The Morning it is new
Is Terribler than wearing it
A whole existence through.

1277

我们害怕它,它就出现——
但并没这么恐惧
因为长久的害怕
几乎使它显得美丽——

有一种恰如其分的——沮丧——
一种恰如其分的——绝望——
知道它要来比知道它已在
更令人紧张。

不断尝试惊惧的极限
在新的早晨
比直接将它全部承受
更加吓人。

1278

The Mountains stood in Haze—
The Valleys stopped below
And went or waited as they liked
The River and the Sky.

At leisure was the Sun—
His interests of Fire
A little from remark withdrawn—
The Twilight spoke the Spire,

So soft upon the Scene
The Act of evening fell
We felt how neighborly a Thing
Was the Invisible.

1278

山峦在暮霭中屹立——
山谷在山下静止
随意离去或等候
那天空和河流。

太阳闲来无事——
对火饶有兴趣
隐约听见了几句——
暮光对塔尖的细语,

如此温和恬静
那夜幕的降临
我们感觉那无形
与我们如此贴近。

1279

The Way to know the Bobolink

From every other Bird
Precisely as the Joy of him—
Obliged to be inferred.

Of impudent Habiliment
Attired to defy,
Impertinence subordinate
At times to Majesty.

Of Sentiments seditious
Amenable to Law—
As Heresies of Transport
Or Puck's Apostacy.

Extrinsic to Attention
Too intimate with Joy—
He compliments existence
Until allured away

By Seasons or his Children—
Adult and urgent grown—
Or unforeseen aggrandizement
Or, happily, Renown—

By Contrast certifying
The Bird of Birds is gone—
How nullified the Meadow—
Her Sorcerer withdrawn!

1279
了解食米鸟的方式
通过其他的鸟只
与得知他的快乐完全一致——
必须得靠推理。

穿着奇装异服
是为表示反对,
再傲慢的行为
有时为显权威。

再具煽动的情绪
也有可循的规律——
一如极端的冲动
或帕克①的背弃。

不在乎外人关注
只沉溺于欢愉——
他恭维造物
直至被诱而去

被四季或他的孩子——
已成年又急迫——
或未曾预见的高贵
或,幸运地,声名远播——

通过对比证实
众鸟之鸟不知去向——
草地多么空荡——
她的巫师已退场!

1280

The harm of Years is on him—
The infamy of Time—
Depose him like a Fashion
And give Dominion room.

---

① 帕克(Puck):莎士比亚戏剧《仲夏夜之梦》(*A Midsummer Night's Dream*)中爱惹祸、喜恶作剧但又不负责任、淘气和变化多端的精灵。

Forget his Morning Forces—
The Glory of Decay
Is a minuter Pageant
Than least Vitality.

1280

岁月对他的伤害——
让时间丢脸——
废黜他像时尚频换
给统治腾出空间。

忘记他清晨的力量——
那衰败的荣耀
它的盛典
比最小的活力还微小。

1281

A stagnant pleasure like a Pool
That lets it's Rushes grow
Until they heedless tumble in
And make the Water slow

Impeding navigation bright
Of Shadows going down
Yet even this shall rouse itself
When freshets come along.

1281

迟钝的欢愉像个水池
任由灯芯草长出
直至他们贸然闯入
使水流减速

妨碍航行的顺畅

令水波①不兴
但即使这样它也会激荡
当洪水行经。

1282

Art thou the thing I wanted?
Begone—my Tooth has grown—
Supply the minor Palate
That has not starved so long—
I tell thee while I waited
The mystery of Food
Increased till I abjured it
And dine without Like God—

rough draft I

Art thou the thing I wanted?
Begone—my Tooth has grown—
Affront a minor palate
Thou did'st② not goad so long—

I tell thee while I waited—
The mystery of Food
Increased till I abjured it
Subsisting now like God—

rough draft II

1282

你是我曾需要的东西？
走开——我的牙已长出——

---

① 水波（Shadows）：艾米莉·狄金森提供的另一个可选词是"Ripples"（涟漪）。这里的原文"Shadows"指水波或涟漪在水面形成的阴影。

② "did'st"在1960年阅读版中为"could'st"。

可以供给那小嘴①
它尚未挨饿多久——
我告诉你在我等待时
食物的神秘升级
直至我声明放弃
无须吃喝像上帝——

（草稿1）

你是我曾需要的东西？
走开——我的牙已长出——
冒犯一张小嘴
你刺激太久——

我告诉你在我等待时——
食物的神秘升级
直至我声明放弃
如今存活似上帝——

（草稿2）

1283

Could Hope inspect her Basis
Her Craft were done—
Has a fictitious Charter
Or it has none—

Balked in the vastest instance
But to renew—
Felled by but one assassin—
Prosperity—

----

① 嘴（Palate）：原文"Palate"指上颚，在诗中喻指嘴。

1283

假如希望能检视她的基础
就知她的手艺已落后——
要么有张虚构的特许证
要么啥也没有——

在最重大事情上犹豫
只为更新自己——
被刺客击倒一次——
随后就一切顺利——

1284

Had we our senses
But perhaps 'tis well they're not at Home
So intimate with Madness
He's liable with them

Had we the eyes within our Head—
How well that we are Blind—
We could not look upon the Earth—
So utterly unmoved—

1284

假如我们有理智
但或许他们不在也没关系
他们与疯癫关系紧密
他也乐意与他们在一起

假如我们的眼长在头里边——
我们就可以什么都看不见——
不用再看到地球——
如此铁心冷面——

1285

I know Suspense—it steps so terse

And turns so weak away—
Besides—Suspense is neighborly
When I am riding by—

Is always at the Window
Though lately I descry
And mention to my Horses
The need is not of me—

1285
我知道悬念——它举步若轻
消逝时无比盈弱——
而且——悬念就在附近
当我打马经过——

它总待在窗边
虽然我后来才发现
还对我的马儿说
它要找的不是我——

1286
I thought that nature was enough
Till Human nature came
But that the other did absorb
As Parallax a Flame—

Of Human nature just aware
There added the Divine
Brief struggle for capacity
The power to contain

Is always as the contents

But give a Giant room
And you will lodge a Giant
And not a smaller man

1286
我以为大自然已足够
直到人性出现
但另一个会吸纳
如视差吸纳火焰——

刚意识到人性
又增加了神性
短暂地争抢空间
那包含的能力

总与内容一致
只要给个大房
你会让巨人入住
而非一个矮汉

1287
In this short Life
That only lasts an hour
How much—how little—is
Within our power

1287
这个短暂的生命
只持续了一小时
有这么多——这么少——属于
我们控制

1288

Lain in Nature—so suffice us
The enchantless Pod
When we advertise existence
For the missing Seed—

Maddest Heart that God created
Cannot move a sod
Pasted by the simple summer
On the Longed for Dead

1288

对我们已足够——安置于大自然
将那朴实无华的荚
此时我们昭告天下
为那颗丢失的种子——

上帝创造的最狂热的心
也无法移动一块草片
它被天真的夏日
粘上对死者的思念

1289

Left in immortal Youth
On that low Plain
That hath nor Retrospection
Nor Again—
Ransomed from years—
Sequestered from Decay
Canceled like Dawn
In comprehensive Day—

1289①

遗留在不朽的青春里
在那低低的平原
既无往昔的追忆
也不会再次出现——
从岁月里赎出——
隔绝了腐朽
像黎明一样淡去
于巍巍②降临的白昼——

1290

The most pathetic thing I do
Is play I hear from you—
I make believe until my Heart
Almost believes it too
But when I break it with the news
You knew it was not true
I wish I had not broken it—
Goliah—so would you—

1290

我做的最令人伤感的事
是假装我收到了你的消息——
我让自己相信直到我的心
也几乎不去怀疑
但当我用消息将它揭穿
原来你早知它并非真实

---

① 题解：一位青年死在平原上，定格于不朽的青春，既不会有对往昔的追忆，也永不会再出现。他已经从岁月中被赎出，岁月不再记录他的生老病死，从此与物质肉身的腐朽隔绝，在黎明消逝、白昼降临时，他步入永恒。

② 巍巍（comprehensive）：原文"comprehensive"的字面义是"包容（inclusive）、总（total）、包罗万象（all-encompassing）"，这里取形象义。

真希望我没揭穿它——
歌利亚①——但愿你也是——

1291

Until the Desert knows
That Water grows
His Sands suffice
But let him once suspect
That Caspian Fact
Sahara dies

Utmost is relative—
Have not or Have
Adjacent sums
Enough—the first Abode
On the familiar Road
Galloped in Dreams—

1291

直至沙漠得知
水位的涨势
他的沙子一直足够量
但令他一度怀疑
那里海的事实
撒哈拉会消亡

---

① 歌利亚（Goliah）：原文"Goliah"即"Goliath"。据《圣经·旧约·撒母耳记（上）》第17章4和48~50节记载，非利士人和以色列人打仗，非利士巨人歌利亚被以色列少年大卫用弹弓射亡："And there went out a champion out of the camp of the Philistines, named Goliath, of Gath, whose height was six cubits and a span. …And it came to pass, when the Philistine arose, and came, and drew nigh to meet David, that David hastened, and ran toward the army to meet the Philistine. And David put his hand in his bag, and took thence a stone, and slang it, and smote the Philistine in his forehead, that the stone sunk into his forehead; and he fell upon his face to the earth. So David prevailed over the Philistine with a sling and with a stone, and smote the Philistine, and slew him; but there was no sword in the hand of David."（1 Samuel 17: 4, 48-50）。艾米莉·狄金森在第540首诗和书信（L154）中也曾提到歌利亚。

终极是相对而言——
无和有之间
数量相差无几
足够——是第一个居处
在熟悉的道路
在梦里奋蹄——

1292

Yesterday is History,
'Tis so far away—
Yesterday is Poetry—
'Tis Philosophy—
Yesterday is mystery—
Where it is Today
While we shrewdly speculate
Flutter both away

1292

昨日已成历史,
相距遥远无比——
昨日是一首诗——
它引发哲思——
昨日是一个谜——
那里孕育了今日
当我们苦想冥思
两者就拍翅消逝

1293

The things we thought that we should do
We other things have done
But those peculiar industries
Have never been begun—

The Lands we thought that we should seek

When large enough to run
By Speculation ceded
To Speculation's Son—

The Heaven, in which we hoped to pause
When Discipline was done
Untenable to Logic
But possibly the one—

1293①
我们认为该去做的事情
我们完成的却是其他事
但那些特别的劳作
却从无开始之日——

我们认为该去追寻的远方
当我们长大足以去闯荡
却被向往转给
向往的儿子手上——

天堂，我们希望驻足
当所有磨炼已完成
虽不合逻辑
但或许就这个成真——

1294
Of Life to own—
From Life to draw—
But never touch the reservoir—

---

① 本诗是 1876 年春天艾米莉·狄金森写给文学导师希金森的一封信（L368）及另一封信（L459）的内容之一。

1294①

把生命拥有——
从生命里汲取——
但别去碰那储存库——

1295

Two Lengths has every Day—
It's absolute extent
And Area superior
By Hope or Horror lent—

Eternity will be
Velocity or Pause
At Fundamental Signals
From Fundamental Laws.

To die is not to go—
On Doom's consummate Chart
No Territory new is staked—
Remain thou as thou art.

1295②

每一天都有两个长度——
它的绝对范围
和优越区域
由希望或恐惧借给——

---

① 本诗是1874年5月下旬艾米莉·狄金森写给文学导师希金森的一封信（L413）的内容之一。该信开头是艾米莉·狄金森对希金森的一首诗"Decoration"的看法，紧接着就是本诗。关于艾米莉·狄金森与希金森的诗"Decoration"的渊源，可参见Loeffelholz, Mary. "Dickinson's 'Decoration'." ELH, 2005, 72, 3: 663-689. 另，第1393首诗的题注再次提到"Decoration"。

② 题解：每一天都有两个长度，恐惧的一天度日如年，快乐的一天倏忽结束。永恒或是一种一直高速的状态或是停歇状态，这要根据自然法则显示的自然征兆来定。死亡并非离开，因为并无一张末日安置表，为死者标出新的安置点，构成死者一生的所有一切依然在原来的世界里原样留存。

永恒就是
要么疾驰要么停脚
面对源自基本法则的
基本信号。

死亡并非离去——
在末日的完美图表上
并未标出一块新疆域——
你仍保持如原样。

1296

Death's Waylaying not the sharpest
Of the thefts of Time—
There Marauds a sorer Robber,
Silence—is his name—
No Assault, nor any Menace
Doth betoken him.
But from Life's consummate Cluster—
He supplants the Balm.

1296①

死亡的拦截对时间的窃取
并非最令人心伤的方式——
有位更凶残的劫匪在抢劫,
沉默——是他的名字——
没有攻击,或任何威胁

---

① 艾米莉·狄金森的父亲爱德华(Edward Dickinson, 1803—1874)的妹妹凯瑟琳(Catherine Dickinson, 1814—1895)1835 年嫁给约瑟夫(Joseph A. Sweetser)。1874 年 1 月 21 日,约瑟夫从纽约市的家里走出后就再未返回,所有报纸都刊登了事情经过,但未接获任何相关线索,从此杳无音信。本诗是艾米莉·狄金森约在 1874 年 1 月底或 2 月写给凯蒂姑姑(Aunt Katie)的一封信的主要内容,除了本诗,信的内容还包括本诗前的一句话:"Saying Nothing, My Aunt Katie, sometimes says the most." (L408)。

将他预示。
但从生命的完美集群里——
他取代了慰藉的香脂。

1297

Go slow, my soul, to feed thyself
Upon his rare approach—
Go rapid, lest Competing Death
Prevail upon the Coach—
Go timid, should his final eye
Determine thee amiss—
Go boldly—for thou paid'st his price
Redemption—for a Kiss—

1297①

慢些走,我的灵魂,去获取滋养
他难得来这——
快点走,以免争抢的死神
挤满了马车——
小心走,以免他最后一眼
确认是你的错误——
大胆走——因为你付了他开的价
付一个吻——换救赎——

1298

The Mushroom is the Elf of Plants—
At Evening, it is not—
At Morning, in a Truffled Hut
It stop upon a Spot

---

① 本诗是艾米莉·狄金森 1874 年 3 月写给弗朗西斯·诺克罗斯和路易丝·诺克罗斯两位表妹的一封信的一部分,诗之前写道:"Infinite March is here, and I 'hered' a blue-bird. Of course I am standing on my head!"(L410)。本诗中的"他"可能指三月。

As if it tarried always
And yet it's whole Career
Is shorter than a Snake's Delay
And fleeter than a Tare—

'Tis Vegetation's Juggler—
The Germ of Alibi—
Doth like a Bubble antedate
And like a Bubble, hie—

I feel as if the Grass was pleased
To have it intermit—
This surreptitious scion
Of Summer's circumspect.

Had Nature any supple Face
Or could she one contemn—
Had Nature an Apostate—
That Mushroom—it is Him!

1298①

蘑菇是植物的精灵——
夜晚,尚无它的消息——
清晨,一个菌棚里
它在一个角落挺立

仿佛它一直待在那
其实它一生的全部
比一条蛇迟到的时间还短暂
比一株杂草的生长还迅速——

---

① 本诗第4节是1874年5月下旬艾米莉·狄金森写给文学导师希金森的一封信的内容之一。诗节之前写道:"You kindly ask for my Blossoms and Books—I have read but a little recently—Existence has overpowered Books. Today, I slew a Mushroom—"(L413)。

它是植物界的魔法师——
置身局外的菌子——
像个水泡提前来到
又像个水泡，闪逝——

我感觉草丛似乎乐意
让它暂时消失——
由谨小慎微的夏日
暗里催生的孩子。

假如自然中有一张脸柔腴
或有一样是她所蔑视——
假如自然中有个叛逆——
那蘑菇——他就是！

1299

Delight's Despair at setting
Is that Delight is less
Than the sufficing Longing
That so impoverish.

Enchantment's Perihelion
Mistaken oft has been
For the Authentic orbit
Of it's Anterior Sun.

1299①

欢乐消退时的绝望
是指欢乐不比

---

① 题解：向往和想象比现实更美好。当欢乐消退，会发现欢乐不如之前满心向往时的快乐，虽然那时还只是向往，完全没有得到欢乐。那充满魅力令人渴望的近日点，也被错误地认为是先前头脑中想象的太阳轨道，以为想象中的才是真正足够有魅力的。

满怀向往时那么多
虽然向往也一贫如洗。

魅力的近日点
时常被误报
是先前的太阳
可靠的轨道。

1300

From his slim Palace in the Dust
He relegates the Realm,
More loyal for the exody
That has befallen him.

1300①

自他尘土中的狭长宫殿
他将那个王国降级,
对降临他头上的放逐
更忠贞不渝。

1301

I cannot want it more—
I cannot want it less—
My Human Nature's fullest force
Expends itself on this.

And yet it nothing is
To him who easy owns—
Is Worth itself or Distance
He fathoms who obtains.

---

① 本诗约写于1874年,可能是艾米莉·狄金森为纪念于1874年6月16日去世的父亲爱德华而作。另参见第1312首诗。

1301
我无法想要更多——
也不能想要更少——
我天性的全部精力
都已在这上面消耗。

但它一点也不重要
如果轻易就能得到——
要显出价值或距离
必须求索方能获取。

1302
I think that the Root of the Wind is Water—
It would not sound so deep
Were it a Firmamental Product—
Airs no Oceans keep—
Mediterranean intonations—
To a Current's Ear—
There is a maritime conviction
In the Atmosphere—

1302
我认为风植根于水——
它听来不会那么深
如果它是往来苍穹之物——
天空也不会把海洋留存——
地中海的声调——
在流水的耳朵听来——
犹如一种海的信念
在大气中传开——

1303
Not One by Heaven defrauded stay—
Although he seem to steal
He restitutes in some sweet way
Secreted in his will—

1303

并非受天堂蒙骗的就会留下——
虽然他看似已偷偷行动
他以某种甜蜜的方式复原
隐藏在他的遗愿中——

1304

Not with a Club, the Heart is broken
Nor with a Stone—
A Whip so small you could not see it
I've known

To lash the Magic Creature
Till it fell,
Yet that Whip's Name
Too noble then to tell.

Magnanimous as Bird
By Boy descried—
Singing unto the Stone
Of which it died—

Shame need not crouch
In such an Earth as Our's—
Shame—stand erect—
The Universe is your's.

1304①

心碎,不是因为棍棒

---

① 本诗写于 1874 年。其主题可参证艾米莉·狄金森 1861 年写给她心目中的"主人"(Master)的一封信的开头:"If you saw a bullet hit a Bird—and he told you he was'nt shot—you might weep at his courtesy, but you would certainly doubt his word—"(L233)。

也不是因为石子——
是一根鞭子小得你无法看见
我早已知悉

鞭打那神奇的生灵
直至它倒地，
而那鞭子的名字
高贵得无法提及。

像鸟儿般大度
小男孩看见——
向置它死命的石子
歌唱——

耻辱无须蜷曲
在我们这样的世界里——
耻辱——挺立——
宇宙就属于你。

1305

Recollect the Face of me
When in thy Felicity,
Due in Paradise today
Guest of mine assuredly—

Other Courtesies have been—
Other Courtesy may be—
We commend ourselves to thee
Paragon of Chivalry.

1305①

请想起我的脸庞
当你幸福满盈,
今天就到天堂
我的客人肯定——

其他的礼仪已成现实——
另一个礼仪或可实现——
我们把自己举荐给你
骑士精神的典范。

1306

Surprise is like a thrilling—pungent—
Upon a tasteless meat
Alone—too acrid—but combined
An edible Delight.

1306②

惊奇像一阵战栗——那么刺激——
当面对一块无味的肉
单个——太辛辣——但混在一起
有一种吃的享受。

1307

That short—potential stir

---

① 本诗第1节与第1180首诗第1节语境相似。据《圣经·新约·路加福音》第23章42~43节记载,被钉在十字架上的耶稣临死前与旁边同样被钉在十字架上的两个犯人中的一个对话:"And he said unto Jesus, Lord, remember me when thou comest into thy kingdom. And Jesus said unto him, Verily I say unto thee, Today shalt thou be with me in paradise."(Luke 23: 42-43)。本诗第1节隐现圣经中耶稣对待犯人宽宏大度的礼仪,即答应犯人和自己一起上天堂。第2节说耶稣对其他人显示了其宽宏的礼仪(other courtesies),实现了让他们上天堂的允诺;那对另一个人(或指诗作者自己)或许也可能同样施行其宽宏的礼仪(other courtesy),为此,诗中的说话人将自己举荐给耶稣,并赞美耶稣是骑士精神的完美典范。

② 题解:惊奇和一块索然无味的肉,单个均不美味,但两者混在一起品尝,就有一种享受的愉悦。

That each can make but once—
That Bustle so illustrious
'Tis almost Consequence—

Is the eclat of Death—
Oh, thou unknown Renown
That not a Beggar would accept
Had he the power to spurn—

1307①
那短暂——潜在的轰动
每人只能制造一次——
那喧闹如此显赫
几乎就是大事——

这是死亡的荣耀——
啊,你这无名的声誉
没一个乞丐愿接受
如果他有能力摈弃——

1308
The Day she goes
Or Day she stays
Are equally supreme—
Existence has a stated width
Departed, or at Home—

1308
她离开的日子
或逗留的时光
都同样至高无比——

---

① 题解:人生只有一次葬礼,它显赫喧闹得如大事件,但没人想要这样的荣耀。

存在有固定的宽度
不论住家，或离去——

1309

The Infinite a sudden Guest
Has been assumed to be—
But how can that stupendous come
Which never went away?

1309

无限是一位不速之客
一直被这么假设——
但那种浩瀚怎能到来
因它从未离开？

1310

The Notice that is called the Spring
Is but a month from here—
Put up my Heart thy Hoary work
And take a Rosy Chair.

Not any House the Flowers keep—
The Birds enamor Care—
Our salary the longest Day
Is nothing but a Bier.

1310①

那被称为春天的通告
离此地只一个月的距离——
我的心啊放下你灰白的操劳

---

① 题解：距离春天只有一个月的时间，赶紧放下冬天的工作（灰白的操劳），坐在玫瑰红椅上歇一歇，不必每日都那么操劳。花儿用心操持的花房或花丛，也不见鸟儿倾心体察。人生如最漫长的一日，操劳到头得到的报酬，不过是一副停尸用的棺架。

坐上玫瑰红椅。

没有一所花儿操持的房子——
有鸟儿去倾心体察——
最长一日的薪资
不过是一副棺架。

1311

This dirty—little—Heart
Is freely mine.
I won it with a Bun—
A Freckled shrine—

But eligibly fair
To him who sees
The Visage of the Soul
And not the knees.

1311①

这颗肮脏——小小的——心
完全属于我。
我用一个圆面包赢得了它——
一个带斑点的神座——

但对他已算公平
他仅目睹
灵魂的面容
而非膝部。

1312

To break so vast a Heart

---

① 题解：用一个圆面包，赢得了一个脏兮兮小孩子的欢心。

Required a Blow as vast—
No Zephyr felled this Cedar straight—
'Twas undeserved Blast—

1312①
让如此巨大的一颗心破碎
也需要一次巨大的打击——
没有轻风会将这棵笔直的雪松刮倒——
这是不该有的暴力——

1313
Warm in her Hand these accents lie
While faithful and afar
The Grace so awkward for her sake
It's fond subjection wear—

1313
这些话语暖暖地躺在她手里
而在谦谦的远方
那天恩因她而手足无措
显出一贯的敬服模样——

1314
When a Lover is a Beggar
Abject is his Knee—
When a Lover is an Owner
Different is he—

What he begged is then the Beggar—
Oh disparity—
Bread of Heaven resents bestowal
Like an obloquy—

---

① 本诗约写于1874年，可能是艾米莉·狄金森为纪念于1874年6月16日去世的父亲爱德华而作。另参见第1300首诗。

1314①

当恋人是个乞丐
卑屈的是他的膝——
当恋人是个物主
他就今非昔比——

他所曾讨要的此时成了乞丐②——
啊,差别如此大——
天堂的面包反感白送
视之如同责骂——

1315

Which is the best—the Moon or the Crescent?
Neither—said the Moon—
That is best which is not—Achieve it—
You efface the Sheen.

Not of detention is Fruition—
Shudder to attain.
Transport's decomposition follows—
He is Prism born.

1315

哪个最好——满月还是弦月?
都不是——月亮回答——
没到最好才是最好———旦达到——
你就失去了光华。

---

① 题解:当跪膝讨要爱的恋人得到了爱,成为了拥有爱的物主,情势就会发生反转,他曾向之乞求的对方此时成为向自己讨要爱的乞丐。天堂的面包(真爱)很反感这种讨要才赠予的做法,并视之为责骂。爱应是平等奉献,不是互相卑躬屈膝。

② 他所曾讨要的此时成了乞丐:原文实际是指"他"所曾向之讨要的对方此时成了乞丐。

停滞并非理想的结果——
达到时战栗不停。
之后便是狂喜的解体——
他天生是棱镜。

1316

Winter is good—his Hoar Delights
Italic flavor yield—
To Intellects inebriate
With Summer, or the World—

Generic as a Quarry
And hearty—as a Rose—
Invited with Asperity
But welcome when he goes.

1316

冬天挺好——他灰白的欢愉
散发的风味浓烈——
给那些头脑沉醉于
夏天,或整个世界——

像采石场一样普通
像玫瑰一样——热情——
以粗暴的语言邀请
但他走时也欢迎。

1317

Abraham to kill him
Was distinctly told—
Isaac was an Urchin—
Abraham was old—

Not a hesitation—
Abraham complied—
Flattered by Obeisance
Tyranny demurred—

Isaac—to his children
Lived to tell the tale—
Moral—with a Mastiff
Manners may prevail.

1317
亚伯拉罕要杀他①
已被明确要求——
以撒是个顽童——
亚伯拉罕已老朽——

没有丝毫犹豫——
亚伯拉罕就遵从——
出于对恭敬的满意
暴政提出反对——

以撒——活了下来
把故事告诉他的后裔——
道德——傍着恶犬
其做派尽人皆知。

---

① 亚伯拉罕要杀他：据《圣经·旧约·创世纪》第 22 章第 1～18 节记载，神要考验亚伯拉罕，要亚伯拉罕杀掉自己的独生子以撒用以敬神，在亚伯拉罕将要杀以撒的刹那，神阻止了亚伯拉罕："And he said, Take now thy son, thine only son Isaac, whom thou lovest, and get thee into the land of Moriah; and offer him there for a burnt offering upon one of the mountains which I will tell thee of. ...And Abraham stretched forth his hand, and took the knife to slay his son. And the angel of the LORD called unto him out of heaven, and said, Abraham, Abraham: and he said, Here am I. And he said, Lay not thine hand upon the lad, neither do thou any thing unto him: for now I know that thou fearest God, seeing thou hast not withheld thy son, thine only son from me."（Genesis 22: 2, 10-12）。

1318

Frigid and sweet Her parting Face—
Frigid and fleet my Feet—
Alien and vain whatever Clime
Acrid whatever Fate.

Given to me without the Suit
Riches and Name and Realm—
Who was She to withhold from me
Penury and Home?

1318

寒冷又甜蜜是她离别的脸——
寒冷又迅疾是我的双足——
什么气候都陌生与徒然
什么命运都严酷。

还未追求就给了我
财富、名望和无边疆域——
她到底是谁竟不给我
贫穷和家园?

1319

How News must feel when travelling
If News have any Heart
Alighting at the Dwelling
'Twill enter like a Dart!

What News must think when pondering
If News have any Thought
Concerning the stupendousness
Of it's perceiveless freight!

What News will do when every Man

Shall comprehend as one
And not in all the Universe
A thing to tell remain?

1319
如果消息有心
消息有何感受当旅行期间
停靠在人居处
它定会像支短箭闯入！

如果消息有思想
消息有何想法当考虑
有关它察觉不到的
货物之巨！

消息会如何应对当人人
如一人一样理解了一切
整个宇宙已没什么
需要讲解？

1320
Dear March—Come in—
How glad I am—
I hoped for you before—
Put down your Hat—
You must have walked—
How out of Breath you are—
Dear March, how are you, and the Rest—
Did you leave Nature well—
Oh March, Come right up the stairs with me—
I have so much to tell—

I got your Letter, and the Birds—
The Maples never knew that you were coming—till I called

I declare—how Red their Faces grew—
But March, forgive me—and
All those Hills you left for me to Hue—
There was no Purple suitable—
You took it all with you—

Who knocks? That April.
Lock the Door—
I will not be pursued—
He stayed away a Year to call
When I am occupied—
But trifles look so trivial
As soon as you have come

That Blame is just as dear as Praise
And Praise as mere as Blame—

1320
亲爱的三月——请进——
我多么高兴——
我早就盼着你来——
请脱下帽子——
你一定是走着来的——
看你气喘吁吁的样子——
亲爱的三月,你还好么,还有其他人呢——
你走时大自然怎么样——
啊三月,赶紧和我上楼——
我有很多话要对你讲——

我收到了你的信,还有那些鸟儿——
枫叶一直不知道你要来——直到我呼喊
我大声地说——他们的脸变得多红啊——
但是三月,也请你原谅我——还有
你留下来给我染色的群山——

一直没有合适的紫色——
你全都带走了——

是谁在敲门？肯定是四月。
快把门锁紧——
我不想被他追缠——
他离开了一年杳无音信
正当我忙碌不堪——
但那些琐事变得多么微不足道
只要你一来到

责怪就像夸奖一样亲切
夸奖像责怪一样不值一提——

1321①

Elizabeth told Essex
That she could not forgive
The clemency of Deity
However—might survive—
That secondary succor
We trust that she partook
When suing—like her Essex
For a reprieving Look—

1321

伊丽莎白告诉埃塞克斯
说她不能原谅②
神的仁慈

---

① 题解：在现实中，伊丽莎白女王不能原谅埃塞克斯伯爵，但相信女王会愿意担当第二次的救援者，向上帝求告缓刑，当看到她的埃塞克斯伯爵恳求缓死的目光。

② 伊丽莎白女王（Queen Elizabeth I, 1533—1603）1601年下令将自己心爱的宠臣埃塞克斯伯爵（Robert Devereux, 2nd Earl of Essex, 1565—1601）斩首。她虽深爱对方，但不能原谅对方发动叛乱反对自己。

不论——存在多长——
那二次救援者
我们相信她会担当
当恳求——如她的埃塞克斯
一个缓死的目光——

1322

Floss won't save you from an Abyss
But a Rope will—
Notwithstanding a Rope for a Souvenir
Is not beautiful—

But I tell you every step is a Trough—
And every stop a Well—
Now will you have the Rope or the Floss?
Prices reasonable—

1322

丝线不会救你出深渊
绳索却可以——
尽管把绳索当作纪念
不算得美丽——

但我告诉你每一步都是一条沟槽——
每一站都是一口井——
现在你选绳索还是丝线?
价格都合理合情——

1323

I never hear that one is dead
Without the chance of Life
Afresh annihilating me
That mightiest Belief,

Too mighty for the Daily mind
That tilling it's abyss,
Had Madness, had it once or twice
The yawning Consciousness,

Beliefs are Bandaged, like the Tongue
When Terror were it told
In any Tone commensurate
Would strike us instant Dead

I do not know the man so bold
He dare in lonely Place
That awful stranger Consciousness
Deliberately face—

1323
我从未听说一个人死了
不再有机会存活
那个最强大的信念
再次击溃了我，

太过强大对日常的头脑
在它深渊里耕地，
会令人疯狂，只要它①有一两次
有那昏昏的意识，

信念被包扎，像舌头
假如它讲述恐惧
以任何相称的语气
会立即置我们于死地

---

① 它：本行和上一行的"它"指"日常的头脑"（the Daily mind），下一行的"昏昏的意识"（yawning Consciousness）指对死亡的意识。

我不知那人如此胆大
他敢闯孤寂之地
故意去面对
那可怕陌生人的意识——

1324

I send you a decrepit flower
That nature sent to me
At parting—she was going south
And I designed to stay—

Her motive for the souvenir
If sentiment for me
Or circumstances prudential
Withheld invincibly—

1324

我寄你一枝枯萎的花
那是大自然寄给我的
临别——她去往南方
而我打算留下——

她送纪念品的动机
是出于对我的情谊
抑或各情境的周全考虑
已不得而知——

1325

Knock with tremor—
These are Caesars—
Should they be at Home
Flee as if you trod unthinking
On the Foot of Doom—

These receded to accostal
Centuries ago—
Should they rend you with "How are you"
What have you to show?

1325①

战战兢兢地敲门——
这些都是凯撒——
假如他们在家
你赶紧逃离仿佛是你无意
将厄运的脚踩踏——

这些人早已不理召唤
在几世纪之前——
假如他们对你开口说"你好吗"
你该如何表现?

1326

Our little secrets slink away—
Beside God's shall not tell—
He kept his word a Trillion years
And might we not as well—
But for the niggardly delight
To make each other stare
Is there no sweet beneath the sun
With this that may compare—

1326

我们的小秘密已逃潜——
上帝的秘密也不会说出——

---

① 本诗约写于1874年,写在一张字条的背面,上面还写有这几个字:"Dear Father—Emily",本诗所写或许与艾米莉·狄金森的父亲爱德华有关,爱德华于1874年6月16日去世。

他信守诺言一万亿年
我们也许也不会透露——
除非为那吝啬的快乐
让彼此面面相觑
天底下没有甜蜜之事
能与此相比——

1327

The Symptom of the Gale—
The Second of Dismay—
Between it's Rumor and it's Face—
Is almost Revelry—

The Houses firmer root—
The Heavens cannot be found—
The Upper Surfaces of things
Take covert in the Ground—

The Mem'ry of the Sun
Not Any can recall—
Although by Nature's sterling Watch
So scant an interval—

And when the Noise is caught
And Nature looks around—
"We dreamed it"? She interrogates—
"Good Morning" —We propound?

1327

大风的征兆——
惊愕的瞬间——
在风的传言和它的脸面之间——
几乎就是欢宴——

房屋立得更稳——
天空无法被发现——
万物上层的表面
都往地里潜——

对太阳的记忆
已回想不起半点——
虽然据大自然精确的手表
仅仅间隔了很短——

当喧声能听到
大自然环顾四望——
"是我们在做梦？"她问道——
"早安"——我们该这么讲？

1328

The vastest earthly Day
Is shrunken small
By one Defaulting Face
Behind a Pall—

1328

尘世最宏大的一天
向缩小演变
被一张不出现的脸
在一件棺罩后面——

1329

Whether they have forgotten
Or are forgetting now
Or never remembered—
Safer not to know—

Miseries of conjecture

Are a softer woe
Than a Fact of Iron
Hardened with I know—

1329
不论他们已忘记
或正把记忆擦去
或从未记起——
最好别知悉——

猜测带来的苦恼
是更柔软的疼
超过那铁的事实
由"我知"确证——

1330
Without a smile—Without a Throe
A Summer's soft Assemblies go
To their entrancing end
Unknown—for all the times we met—
Estranged, however intimate—
What a dissembling Friend—

1330
没有欢笑——没有苦痛
一场夏日温柔的聚众
走到了迷人的尽头
不相识——尽管我们一直相遇——
也疏远,不论多亲密——
好一位装模作样的朋友——

1331
Wonder—is not precisely Knowing
And not precisely Knowing not—

A beautiful but bleak condition
He has not lived who has not felt—

Suspense—is his maturer Sister—
Whether Adult Delight is Pain
Or of itself a new misgiving—
This is the Gnat that mangles men—

1331
疑惑——既非全部了解
也非完全不知——
这是美妙但遗憾的状态
没体验过的人不算存活在世——

悬念——是他更成熟的姐妹——
不论成年的快乐是痛苦
抑或它本身就是一种新的疑虑——
这等小事总令人茫然无主——

1332
Pink—small—and punctual—
Aromatic—low—
Covert—in April—
Candid—in May—
Dear to the Moss—
Known to the Knoll—
Next to the Robin
In every human Soul—
Bold little Beauty
Bedecked with thee
Nature forswears
Antiquity—

1332①

粉红——小巧——准时——
芳香——缕缕——
在四月——隐蔽——
在五月——开放——
苔藓见了惬意——
山丘也有所知悉——
跟在知更鸟之后
深入每个人心里——
这娇小夺目的美丽
装扮有你
大自然就摆脱
老气——

1333

A little Madness in the Spring
Is wholesome even for the King,
But God be with the Clown—
Who ponders this tremendous scene—
This whole Experiment of Green—
As if it were his own!

1333

春天里的一点疯狂
甚至也有益于国王,
但愿上帝和小丑在一起——
小丑琢磨这宏大的场面——
这整个绿色的实验——
仿佛都属于他自己!

---

① 这是艾米莉·狄金森送给自己嫂子苏珊的一首诗,描写的是野草莓树(arbutus)。该诗在1890年出版的第一本诗选集中被赋予标题"May—Flower"。在1886年早春写给乔治牧师(Rev. George Sherwood Dickerman, 1843—1937)的妻子伊丽莎白(Elizabeth Mansfiled Street, 1843—1926)的一封信开头,艾米莉·狄金森曾写道:"Daphne always seems to me a more civic Arbutus, though the sweet Barbarian will forgive me if the suggestion is invidious, for are not both as beautiful as Delight can make them?"(L1037)。

1334

How soft this Prison is
How sweet these sullen bars
No Despot but the King of Down
Invented this repose

Of Fate if this is All
Has he no added Realm
A Dungeon but a Kinsman is
Incarceration—Home.

1334①

这座牢狱多安宁
这些阴郁的栅栏多迷人
除了地狱之王没有哪个暴君
营造这种静谧沉沉

如果这一切都是命运
假如他不另有疆域
地牢只不过是位亲戚
监禁——就是家居。

1335

Let me not mar that perfect Dream
By an Auroral stain
But so adjust my daily Night
That it will come again.

Not when we know, the Power accosts—

---

① 本诗第 1 节是艾米莉·狄金森 1875 年 1 月写给霍兰夫人的一封信中的部分内容,在诗节之前写道:"Mother is Asleep in the Library—Vinnie—in the Dining Room—Father—in the Masked Bed—in the Marl House."(L432)。艾米莉·狄金森的父亲爱德华于 1874 年 6 月 16 日去世。

The Garment of Surprise
Was all our timid Mother wore
At Home—in Paradise.

1335

我还是别玷污那完美的梦
用晨曦的斑点
而是据此调整我平常的夜晚
这样它肯定还会出现。

我们不知何时,那股力量来搭讪——
那件令人惊奇的衣裳①
就是我们胆小的母亲所穿
在家中——在天堂。

1336

Nature assigns the Sun—
That—is Astronomy—
Nature cannot enact a Friend—
That—is Astrology.

1336②

大自然指派太阳——

---

① 令人惊奇的衣裳(Garment of Surprise):或可参证《圣经·旧约·创世纪》第2章第25节至第3章第7节中记述,亚当和夏娃起初赤身裸体,偷吃禁果后有了智慧,才知自身并无遮挡,乃取无花果的叶子编裙子:"And the eyes of them both were opened, and they knew that they were naked; and they sewed fig leaves together, and made themselves aprons."(Genesis 3:7)。

② 题注:本诗是艾米莉·狄金森1875年写给朋友霍兰夫人的一封信的结尾,诗之前写道:"I have the little Book and am twice triumphant—Once for itself, and once for Those who enabled me—The embarrassment of the Psalmist who knew not what to render his friend—is peculiarly mine—Though he has canceled his consternations, while my own remain—Thank you with all my strength—and Doctor [Holland] as yourself—And again yourself for the sweet note."(L439)。信中提到的诗篇作者对上帝的感激之情,见于《圣经·旧约·诗篇》第116章第12节的记述:"What shall I render unto the LORD for all his benefits toward me?"(Psalm 116:12)。本诗是讲大自然可以指派太阳,因为太阳是自然的一部分,那是天文学领域的事情;但大自然并不能给"我"送来一位朋友,因为那是星相学的事情,换言之,那是靠运气或命运的。而"我"如今有你这一位朋友,"我"无比感激,无比幸运。

那就叫——天文学——
大自然无法扮成一位朋友——
那就叫——星相学。

1337

Upon a Lilac Sea
To toss incessantly
His Plush Alarm
Who fleeing from the Spring
The Spring avenging fling
To Dooms of Balm—

1337①

在一片紫丁香的海域
持续不断地抛起
他长毛绒绒的惊惧
他刚自春天逃跑
却被春天报复性地一抛
投入芬芳的绝地——

1338

What tenements of clover
Are fitting for the bee,
What edifices azure
For butterflies and me—

---

① 本诗写于 1875 年。1875 年 10 月底,艾米莉·狄金森把本诗最后三行寄给朋友、诗人、小说家海伦(原 Mrs. Helen Hunt, 1875 年后成为 Helen Fiske Hunt Jackson, 原名 Helen Maria Fiske, 1830—1885),三行诗前只有一句话:"Have I a word but Joy?"(L444)。艾米莉·狄金森寄这封信时正值海伦第二次结婚,她 1875 年 10 月 22 日嫁给威廉(William Sharpless Jackson, 1836—1919),她的首任丈夫爱德华(Edward Bissell Hunt, 1822—1863)死于 1863 年。海伦婚后住在丈夫的家乡科罗拉多斯普林斯(Colorado Springs,属科罗拉多州埃尔帕索县)。1876 年 3 月 20 日她从科罗拉多斯普林斯给艾米莉·狄金森回信,表示不解诗中之意:"I do wish I knew just what 'dooms' you meant, though!"(L444a)。本诗中的 spring 既喻指婚姻,也与现实地名耦合。

What residences nimble
Arise and evanesce
Without a rhythmic rumor
Or an assaulting guess.

1338①
哪些红花草的公寓
适合蜜蜂生活,
哪些蔚蓝的大厦
适合蝴蝶和我——
哪些轻灵的住所
出现又消弭
既不招引断续的谣言
也无攻击性的猜疑。

1339

A Bee his burnished Carriage
Drove boldly to a Rose—
Combinedly alighting—
Himself—his Carriage was—
The Rose received his visit
With frank tranquility②
Withholding not a Crescent
To his Cupidity—
Their Moment consummated—
Remained for him—to flee—
Remained for her—of rapture
But the humility.

---

① 艾米莉·狄金森把本诗寄给了当地阿默斯特学院(Amherst College)的院长威廉(William Augustus Stearns, 1805—1876)的夫人丽贝卡(Rebecca Alden Frazar, 1803—1855)。威廉自1854年起担任阿默斯特学院院长直至1876年去世。
② "tranquility"在1960年阅读版中为"tranquillity"。

1339①

一只蜜蜂乘它锃亮的车驾
径直驶向一朵玫瑰花——
双双停下——
他自己——就是他的车驾——
玫瑰迎接它
诚恳而淡然
连一弯叶片也不保留
以满足他的贪婪——
欢乐的时刻过后——
就是他的——逃离——
就是她的——神迷
但含着卑屈。

1340

A Rat surrendered here
A brief career of Cheer
And Fraud and Fear.

Of Ignominy's due
Let all addicted to
Beware.

The most obliging Trap
It's tendency to snap
Cannot resist—

Temptation is the Friend
Repugnantly resigned
At last.

---

① 艾米莉·狄金森把本诗写在一张字条上,字条上没写抬头称呼,也无落款签名,不知她想寄给谁,但也许从未寄出。字条上除了本诗,还有诗之前的一句话:"Sweet is it as Life, with it's enhancing Shadow of Death."(L446)。

1340
一只耗子在此屈服于
一阵短暂的欢愉
还有欺骗和恐惧。

对丑行所应得
愿所有沉迷者
警醒。

最诱人的陷阱
它噬啮成性
无法抗拒——

诱惑是这样一位朋友
令人反感地退走
最后。

1341
Unto the Whole—how add?
Has "All" a further realm—
Or Utmost an Ulterior?
Oh, Subsidy of Balm!

1341
往全部里——怎能再加?
难道"所有"之外还另有空间——
极限之外还有更远?
啊,香膏①的补添!

---

① 香膏(Balm):艾米莉·狄金森在诗中使用 balm 一共 19 次,在书信中使用 18 次,有指安慰(物)、有助缓解的东西之意,一如《圣经·旧约·耶利米书》第 8 章第 22 节记述:"Is there no balm in Gilead; is there no physician there? why then is not the health of the daughter of my people recovered?"(Jeremiah 8:22)。有指涂抹于死者身上的油,一如《圣经·旧约·创世纪》第 37 章第 25 节中记述的乳香(香油、香膏):"And they sat down to eat bread: and they lifted up their eyes and looked, and, behold, a company of Ishmeelites came from Gilead with their camels bearing spicery and balm and myrrh, going to carry it down to Egypt."(Genesis 37:25)。一般情况下指起治疗或安慰、缓解、解除作用之物,包括实物,如作为药品的香膏,也包括精神性的东西,如安慰。

1342

"Was not" was all the Statement.
The Unpretension stuns—
Perhaps—the Comprehension—
They wore no Lexicons—

But lest our Speculation
In inanition die
Because "God took him" mention—
That was Philology—

1342①

"不在世"就是全部所记。
这种朴实无华令人震撼——
或许——是理解的问题——
他们没有字典——

但为防我们的猜测
在虚空里消解
因为"神将他取去"有所指涉——
那就是文献学——

1343

A single Clover Plank

---

① 题注：以诺（Enoch）是亚当的后代，活了 365 岁。"以诺与神同行，神将他取去，他就不在世了"，《圣经·旧约·创世纪》第 5 章第 24 节如此记述："And Enoch walked with God: and he was not; for God took him."（Genesis 5：24）。《圣经·旧约·创世纪》第 5 章第 3~23 节记述了以诺和亚当的血缘关系："And Adam lived an hundred and thirty years, and begat a son in his own likeness, after his image; and called his name Seth...And Seth lived an hundred and five years, and begat Enos...And Enos lived ninety years, and begat Cainan...And Cainan lived seventy years, and begat Mahalaleel...And Mahalaleel lived sixty and five years, and begat Jared...And Jared lived an hundred sixty and two years, and he begat Enoch...And all the days of Enoch were three hundred sixty and five years. And Enoch walked with God: and he was not; for God took him."（Genesis 5：3-24）。本诗可能写于艾米莉·狄金森的父亲去世一周年之时，其父亲爱德华于 1874 年 6 月 16 日去世。

Was all that saved a Bee
A Bee I personally knew
From sinking in the sky—

Twixt① Firmament above
And Firmament below
The Billows of Circumference
Were sweeping him away—

The idly swaying Plank
Responsible to nought
A sudden Freight of Wind assumed
And Bumble Bee was not—

This harrowing event
Transpiring in the Grass
Did not so much as wring from him
A wandering "Alas" —

1343
是一根红花草的茎条
救了一只蜜蜂
我亲眼看到蜜蜂
坠落自天空——

就在高空
和低空之间
普天翻腾的巨浪
正将他席卷——

那兀自摇摆的茎条

---

① "Twixt" 在 1960 年的阅读版中为 " 'Twixt "。

正在百无聊赖中
原想承载疾风的货物
而不是一只大黄蜂——

这一惨痛的事件
发生在草丛间
恍惚间他都挤不出
"哎呀，我的天"——

1344

Not any more to be lacked—
Not any more to be known—
Denizen of Significance
For a span so worn—

Even Nature herself
Has forgot it is there—
Sedulous of her Multitudes
Notwithstanding Despair—

Of the Ones that pursued it
Suing it not to go
Some have solaced the longing
To accompany—

Some—rescinded the Wrench—
Others—Shall I say
Plated the residue of Adz
With Monotony.

1344

不再为人所需——
不再被人所知——
举足轻重的居民

一段如此疲惫的时期——

甚至大自然自己
已忘记它在那里——
牵念她的众生
尽管绝望丧气——

想得到它的那些
请求它别离场
有些已缓解
陪伴的渴望——

有些——撤回了扳手——
其他的——按我的说道
则给扁斧的残余
镀上单调。

1345

An antiquated Grace
Becomes that cherished Face
As well as prime
Enjoining us to part
We and our pouting Heart
Good friends with time

1345

一种古雅的恩典
成就了那令人珍爱的脸
犹如最美的光阴
告诫我们各自前行
我们和我们郁闷的心
都与时间友好亲近

1346

As Summer into Autumn slips
And yet we sooner say
"The Summer" than "the Autumn," lest
We turn the sun away,

And almost count it an Affront
The presence to concede
Of one however lovely, not
The one that we have loved—

So we evade the charge of Years
On one attempting shy
The Circumvention of the Shaft
Of Life's Declivity.

1346①

正如夏天溜进了秋天
但我们宁愿称之为
"夏天"而非"秋天"，以免
把太阳吓退，

且几乎当它是一种冒犯
等于对当前让退
那无论多可爱的，并非
我们所曾爱的那位——

因此我们避开岁月的摧残
对那位羞怯的企图

---

① 题注：本诗可能写于艾米莉·狄金森的父亲去世（1874年6月16日）一周年之时。艾米莉·狄金森约在1874年10月将本诗寄给朋友鲍尔斯（Samuel Bowles, 1826—1878），在诗之前写道："The Paper wanders so I cannot write my name on it, so I give you Father's Portrait instead."（L420）。

绕开生命的衰退
射出的箭簇。

1347

Escape is such a thankful Word
I often in the Night
Consider it unto myself
No spectacle in sight

Escape—it is the Basket
In which the Heart is caught
When down some awful Battlement
The rest of Life is dropt—

'Tis not to sight the savior—
It is to be the saved—
And that is why I lay my Head
Upon this trusty word—

1347

逃跑是个令人感激的词
我时常在夜间
我独自对它沉思
没任何奇观在眼前

逃跑——是一个篮
心在里面被困
当被扔下某个可怕的城垛
那生命的其余部分——

不是要看看拯救者——
而是做个得救者——
那便是为何我要将我头
靠上这可信词语的一侧——

1348

Lift it—with the Feathers
Not alone we fly—
Launch it—the aquatic
Not the only sea—
Advocate the Azure
To the lower Eyes—
He has obligation
Who has Paradise—

1348

提起它——与羽毛一起
我们并非独自飞翔——
起航它——那水域
并非唯一的海洋——
倡导那蔚蓝
给更低微的目光——
他就有责任
他若有天堂——

1349

I'd rather recollect a setting
Than own a rising sun
Though one is beautiful forgetting—
And true the other one.

Because in going is a Drama
Staying cannot confer
To die divinely once a Twilight—
Than wane is easier—

1349

我宁愿回忆夕阳场景
也不愿拥有升起的朝日

虽然一个是美丽的幻影——
另一个是真实。

因为行进是一出戏
停留无法给予
在一个静穆的黄昏死去——
比慢慢地消蚀容易——

1350

Luck is not chance—
It's Toil—
Fortune's expensive smile
Is earned—
The Father of the Mine
Is that old-fashioned Coin
We spurned—

1350

幸运并非偶然——
要付出辛劳——
运气昂贵的笑脸
需努力才得到——
矿藏之父相当于
那枚老式硬币
我们拒绝要——

1351

You cannot take itself
From any Human soul—
That indestructible estate
Enable him to dwell—
Impregnable as Light
That every man behold
But take away as difficult
As undiscovered Gold—

1351

从任何人的心灵
你都无法将它攫取——
那坚不可摧的宅地
使他得以安居——
如稳固的光线
每个人都看见
却如未发现的金矿
拿不走半点——

1352

To his simplicity
To die—was little Fate—
If Duty live—contented
But her Confederate.

1352①

对于他单纯的想法
死去——是命运微小的工作——
假如职责还活着——甚感满意
那也只是她的同伙。

1353

The last of Summer is Delight—

---

① 这是艾米莉·狄金森1876年1月写给文学导师希金森的一封信的结尾诗,诗前面的引言是:"Mr. Bowles lent me flowers twice, for my Father's Grave."(L449)。艾米莉·狄金森还将本诗寄给了詹金斯牧师(Rev. Jonathan. Leavitt. Jenkins, 1830—1913)或他的家人。詹金斯牧师于1867年起担任艾米莉·狄金森家乡阿默斯特(Amherst)镇第一公理会教堂(First Congregationalist Church)执行牧师(acting pastor),直至1877年离职,前往匹兹菲尔德(Pittsfield, Massachusetts)任职。詹金斯牧师深受狄金森一家所敬重,艾米莉·狄金森1886年去世后的葬礼就是由詹金斯牧师与阿默斯特教堂当时的在任牧师迪克曼(Rev. George S. Dickerman)共同主持的。本诗或意指"他"认为死是命中注定的事,并无遗憾,假如还有什么职责的话,那也会配合命运的需要去做的。

Deterred by Retrospect.
'Tis Ecstasy's revealed Review—
Enchantment's Syndicate.

To meet it—nameless as it is—
Without celestial Mail—
Audacious as without a Knock
To walk within the Vail①.

1353②
夏季最后的日子属于欢乐——
受到回忆的阻拦。
它是狂喜流露出的怀想——
魅力的共同宣言。

要见它——它无名无姓——
也无天上来信——
需大胆无畏如行在帐内
不敲出一丝声音。

1354
The Heart is the Capital of the Mind—
The Mind is a single State—
The Heart and the Mind together make
A single Continent—

---

① "Vail" 在1960年的阅读版全集中为 "Veil"。据《圣经·旧约·出埃及记》第26章第33节记述："And thou shalt hang up the vail under the taches, that thou mayest bring in thither within the vail the ark of the testimony: and the vail shall divide unto you between the holy place and the most holy." (Exodus 26: 33)。"vail" 可以有 "priesthood garment" 之意；"walk within the Vail" 可以有 "enter the most holy place; go into the presence God" 之意。本诗中的 "vai" 可指 "帐幔"。

② 本诗和第1354、1355、1356、1357首诗一起，随附于艾米莉·狄金森1876年1月写给文学导师希金森的一封信（L449）中。

One—is the Population—
Numerous enough—
This ecstatic Nation
Seek—it is Yourself.

1354

头脑自成一国——
心是头脑的首府——
心和头脑合体
自成一块大陆——

人口有——一——
数量足矣——
这个沸腾的国度
查查看——它是你自己。

1355

The Mind lives on the Heart
Like any Parasite—
If that is full of Meat
The Mind is fat.

But if the Heart omit
Emaciate the Wit—
The Aliment of it
So absolute.

1355

头脑依靠心而活
像任何寄生虫一样——
如果天天吃肉
头脑就会肥胖。

但如果心一时忘记

智力就会消瘦下去——
它对营养品的急需
不容置疑。

1356

The Rat is the concisest Tenant.
He pays no Rent.
Repudiates the Obligation—
On Schemes intent

Balking our Wit
To sound or circumvent—
Hate cannot harm
A Foe so reticent—
Neither Decree prohibit him—
Lawful as Equilibrium.

1356

耗子是最简便的租户。
他不交房租。
不履行义务——
还有计划地企图

阻止我们的机智
去探测或回避——
憎恨无法伤害
如此沉默的仇敌——
法令也不能制止他——
像平衡一样合法。

1357

"Faithful to the end" Amended
From the Heavenly Clause—
Constancy with a Proviso

Constancy abhors—

"Crowns of Life" are servile Prizes
To the stately Heart,
Given for the Giving, solely,
No Emolument.

$(version\ I\ )$

- - - - - - - - -

"Faithful to the end" Amended
From the Heavenly clause—
Lucrative indeed the offer
But the Heart withdraws—

"I will give" the base Proviso—
Spare Your "Crown of Life" —
Those it fits, too fair to wear it—
Try it on Yourself—

$(version\ II\ )$

1357①
"忠心至终"修改
自天堂的条款——
坚贞有附加条件
令坚贞憎厌——

"生命的冠冕"是卑屈的奖品

---

① 本诗第一个版本和第 1353、1354、1355、1356 首一起，随附于艾米莉·狄金森 1876 年 1 月写给文学导师希金森的一封信（L449）中。本诗中的直接引语，参见《圣经·新约·启示录》第 2 章第 10 节记述："Fear none of those things which thou shalt suffer: behold, the devil shall cast some of you into prison, that ye may be tried; and ye shall have tribulation ten days: be thou faithful unto death, and I will give thee a crown of life."（你将要受的苦你不用怕。魔鬼要把你们中间几个人下在监狱里，叫你们被试炼。你们必受患难十日。你务要至死忠心，我就赐给你那生命的冠冕。）(Revelation 2: 10)。

对于庄严的心,
为给予而给予,仅仅,
没有酬金。

(第1个版本)

"忠心至终"修改
自天堂的条款——
这规定有利可图
但心极力避免——

"我就赐给"这卑劣的附加条件——
不必你"生命的冠冕"——
那些适合戴的,太高洁无须戴它——
你可自戴额前——

(第2个版本)

1358

The Treason of an accent
Might Ecstasy transfer—
Of her effacing Fathom
Is no Recoverer—

(version I)

The Treason of an Accent
Might vilify the Joy—
To breathe—corrode the rapture
Of Sanctity to be—

(version II)

1358①

对口音的背离
会转移狂喜——
她莫测的深度
无法恢复如昔——

（第 1 个版本）

对口音的背离
会诋毁欢愉——
呼吸——会腐蚀狂喜
它圣洁无比——

（第 2 个版本）

1359

The long sigh of the Frog
Upon a Summer's Day
Enacts intoxication
Upon the Revery—
But his receding Swell
Substantiates a Peace
That makes the Ear inordinate
For corporal release—

1359②

青蛙长长地叹息
在一个夏日
令人沉迷

---

① 本诗第一个版本是艾米莉·狄金森于1876年2月写给文学导师希金森的一封信的部分内容。信的开头写道："There is so much that is tenderly profane in even the sacredest Human Life—that perhaps it is instinct and not design, that dissuades—us from it."（L450）。

② 本诗是艾米莉·狄金森于1876年春天写给文学导师希金森的一封信的结尾，诗之前写道："I was always told that conjecture surpassed Discovery, but it must have been spoken in caricature, for it is not true—"（L459）。信中把本诗中的"Revery"的改成了"Passer by"。

在幻想里——
但逐渐退去的蛙潮
使宁静沉落
耳朵一时不知所措
对于肉体的解脱——

1360

I sued the News—yet feared—the News
That such a Realm could be—
"The House not made with Hands" it was—
Thrown open wide to me—

1360①

我既渴求那消息——又害怕——那消息
会是这样一个王国所在——
即"不是人手所造的房子"② ——
向我敞开——

1361

The Flake the Wind exasperate
More eloquently lie
Than if escorted to it's Down
By Arm of Chivalry.

---

① 本诗是艾米莉·狄金森于1876年春天写给文学导师希金森的一封信的部分内容。诗之前写道:" Your thought is so serious and captivating, that it leaves one stronger and weaker too, … It is still as distinct as Paradise—the opening your first Book—It was Mansions—Nations—Kinsmen—too—to me—"(L458)。艾米莉·狄金森这封信的主旨是赞美希金森1863年出版的书 *Out-Door Papers*,因此诗中提及的"消息"应是指这本书。

② 不是人手所造的房子:原文"The House not made with Hands"参见《圣经·新约·哥林多后书》第5章第1节记述:"For we know that if our earthly house of this tabernacle were dissolved, we have a building of God, an house not made with hands, eternal in the heavens."(我们原知道,我们这地上的帐篷若拆毁了,必得神所造,不是人手所造,在天上永存的房屋。)(2 Corinthians 5:1)。

1361①

风惹怒的雪花
更潇洒地躺
赛过由骑士的臂膀
护送至其羽绒床。

1362

Of their peculiar light
I keep one ray
To clarify the Sight
To seek them by—

1362②

对于他们独特的光
我只需一束
以照亮现场
将他们找出——

1363

Summer laid her simple Hat
On it's boundless Shelf—
Unobserved—a Ribin③ slipt,
Snatch it for yourself.

---

① 本诗是艾米莉·狄金森于1876年夏末写给文学导师希金森的夫人玛丽（Mary Elizabeth Channing, 1820—1877）的一封慰问信的部分内容，信中对玛丽的父亲瓦尔特（Walter Channing, 1786—1876）在1876年7月27日的离世表示慰问。信的开头写道："The 'Happiness' without a cause, is the best Happiness, for Glee intuitive and lasting is the gift of God. I fear we have all sorrow, though of different forms—but with Life so very sweet at the Crisp, what must it be unfrozen! I hope you may sometime be so strong as to smile at now—That is our Hope's criterion, for things that are—are ephemeral, but those to come—long—and besides."（L472）。

② 本诗是艾米莉·狄金森于1876年8月写给文学导师希金森的一封信的结尾。艾米莉·狄金森在信中对希金森夫人玛丽的父亲瓦尔特在1876年7月27日的离世表示安慰，信中也提到自己父亲的去世给自己带来的孤独。信的开头写道："I hope Mrs Higginson is no more ill. I am glad if I did not disturb her. Loneliness for my own Father made me think of her."（L470）。诗中的"他们"，可能指两位去世的父亲。

③ Ribin 在1960年阅读版中为"Ribbon"。

Summer laid her supple Glove
In it's sylvan Drawer—
Wheresoe'er, or was she—
The demand of Awe?

1363①
夏日将她朴素的帽子
置于无边的帽架——
无人觉察———条丝带滑落，
为你将它抢下。

夏日将她柔软的手套
置于丛林的抽屉——
究竟在哪里，或者是她——
出于畏惧？

1364
How know it from a Summer's Day?
It's Fervors are as firm—
And nothing in the Countenance
But scintillates the same—
Yet Birds examine it and flee—
And Vans without a name
Inspect the Admonition
And sunder as they came—

1364②
从一个夏日如何得知？

---

① 本诗第 2 节是艾米莉·狄金森于 1876 年 10 月末写给文学导师希金森的一封信（L477）的结尾。

② 本诗约写于 1876 年，约 10 月底 11 月初在秋老虎（Indian summer）过后不久，被艾米莉·狄金森邮寄给文学导师希金森的夫人玛丽，可能是作为季节性的问候。玛丽于 1877 年 9 月 2 日病逝。本诗写的可能就是深秋初冬时段气温返热如夏的秋老虎天气特征。

它的炽热还一样稳定——
脸面上无处不是
亮闪依旧不停——
但鸟儿考察后已逃离——
还有无名的一群群
审视了这警告
在来路上已散开无影——

1365

Take all away—
The only thing worth larceny
Is left—the Immortality—

1365①

一切已拿去——
唯一值得偷窃的东西
永生——得以留取——

1366

Brother of Ingots—Ah Peru—
Empty the Hearts that purchased you—

1366②

金锭的兄弟——啊,秘鲁——
把心清空若将你购入——

---

① 本诗是艾米莉·狄金森1876年春写给文学导师希金森的一封信的部分内容。诗之前写道:"I am glad 'Immortality' pleased you. I believed it would. I suppose even God himself could not withhold that now—When I think of my Father's lonely Life and his lonelier Death, there is this redress—"(L457)。本诗的意旨应与艾米莉·狄金森的父亲爱德华于1874年6月16日的去世有关。在1876年8月写给弗朗西斯·诺克罗斯和路易丝·诺克罗斯两位表妹的一封信中,艾米莉·狄金森写道:"I dream about father every night, always a different dream, and forget what I am doing daytimes, wondering where he is. Without any body, I keep thinking. What can that be?"(L471)。

② 艾米莉·狄金森写了3首有关友谊和爱情主题的相似短诗,其一赠给嫂子苏珊(见L581);其二赠给朋友爱德华·塔克曼(Edward Tuckermam,1817—1886)的夫人莎拉(Sara Eliza Sigourney Cushing,1832—1915)(见L677),以安慰她因自己的朋友、阿默斯特学院35岁的数学和自然哲学教授伊莱休(Elihu Root,1845—1880)1880年12月3日之死引起的悲伤。本诗是第3首,约写于1876年。约翰逊1960年的阅读版全集把另外两首(1366B、1366C)也列印了出来。

1367①

"Tomorrow"—whose location
The Wise deceives
Though it's hallucination
Is last that leaves—
Tomorrow—thou Retriever
Of every tare—
Of Alibi art thou
Or ownest where?

1367

"明天"——它的所在
由智者掩盖
虽然关于它的幻觉
最后才离开——
明天——你重又带回
每一棵荒草杂芜——
你有不出现的理由
或者竟在何处?

1368

Love's stricken "why"
Is all that love can speak—
Built of but just a syllable
The hugest hearts that break.

---

① 本诗被艾米莉·狄金森于1877年初寄给霍兰夫人,诗前的引言是"Austin will come tomorrow."(L490),之所以有此引言是霍兰夫妇此前曾邀请艾米莉·狄金森的哥哥奥斯汀到家做客,但奥斯汀未回复。艾米莉·狄金森信中此言纯粹是逗弄霍兰夫人,她在给霍兰夫人的下一封信中为此做了解释并请求谅解:"Will my little Sister excuse me? ... I am ashamed and sorry. I meant hypothetic tomorrows—though are there any other? I deserve to be punished. I am—in regret. Austin said he should write you, and that Sue w'd too—but he is too overcharged with care, and Sue with scintillation, and I fear they have not—Austin was pleased and surprised, that you wished for him, and still hopes he may go, but not now—"(L491)。

1368①

爱重伤后的一声"为何"
是爱能说出的一切——
构成只需一个音节②
就可让最大的心碎裂。

1369

Trusty as the stars

Who quit their shining working

Prompt as when I lit them

In Genesis' new house,

Durable as dawn

Whose antiquated blossom

Makes a world's suspense

Perish and rejoice.

1369③

像群星一样可信
停止了它们的闪光
迅捷如当初我将它们点亮
在创世的新房,
持久如拂晓
它古老的花朵
令一个世界的悬念
消亡又狂欢。

---

① 艾米莉·狄金森1876年6月8日把本诗（L463）寄给了当地阿默斯特学院的院长威廉的夫人丽贝卡。威廉自1854年起担任阿默斯特学院院长直至1876年6月8日去世。
② 一个音节：英文中"why"只有一个音节。
③ 本诗是艾米莉·狄金森1876年11月写给弗朗西斯·诺克罗斯和路易丝·诺克罗斯两位表妹的一封信（L479）中的结尾部分。

1370

Gathered into the Earth,
And out of story—
Gathered so that strange Fame—
That lonesome Glory
That hath no omen here—but Awe—

1370

汇聚到地里去，
还从记叙里——
如此聚集那奇异的声名——
那寂寞的荣誉
这里没有预示——只有敬畏——

1371

How fits his Umber Coat
The Tailor of the Nut?
Combined without a seam
Like Raiment of a Dream—

Who spun the Auburn Cloth?
Computed how the girth?
The Chestnut aged grows
In those primeval Clothes—

We know that we are wise—
Accomplished in Surprise—
Yet by this Countryman—
This nature—how undone!

1371

他赭色的外套有多合身
坚果的裁缝？
这了无缝痕的衣装

像梦的霓裳——

谁织这红褐色的衣服?
腰围如何算出?
栗子渐渐成熟
穿着这身原始的行头——

我们自认为聪明无比——
可以造就奇迹——
但对比这位同人——
这位大自然——简直一事无成!

1372

The Sun is one—and on the Tare
He doth as punctual call
As on the conscientious Flower
And estimates them all—

1372

太阳就一个——而对莠草
他准时去拜见
一如对那尽职的花朵
并把他们评价一遍——

1373

The worthlessness of Earthly things
The Ditty is that Nature Sings—
And then—enforces their delight
Till Synods are inordinate—

1373

世间一切毫无价值
大自然唱起了那小曲——
接着——就强调它们的欢愉
直至宗教会议混乱无序——

1374

A Saucer holds a Cup
In sordid human Life
But in a Squirrel's estimate
A Saucer hold a Loaf.

A Table of a Tree
Demands the little King
And every Breeze that run along
His Dining Room do swing.

His Cutlery—he keeps
Within his Russet Lips—
To see it flashing when he dines
Do Birmingham eclipse—

Convicted—could we be
Of our Minutiae
The smallest Citizen that flies
Is heartier than we—

1374

在污秽的人类生活里
茶托用来放茶杯
但按松鼠的估计
茶托为盛面包而备。

一棵树的餐桌旁
需要那位小小的王
每一阵冲过来的轻风
都在他餐厅里来回闯。

他含着——餐具
在他黄褐色的唇间——
它在他就餐时闪亮
令伯明翰的餐具黯淡——

假如我们——相信
我们过度沉迷于琐碎
那位飞翔的娇小公民
都比我们开心——

1375

Death warrants are supposed to be
An enginery of equity
A merciful mistake
A pencil in an Idol's Hand
A Devotee has oft consigned
To Crucifix or Block

1375

死刑令被看作是
一个公正的机制
一个仁慈的错误
一支偶像手中的铅笔
时常把信徒托付
给十字架或行刑柱

1376

Dreams are the subtle Dower
That make us rich an Hour—
Then fling us poor
Out of the purple Door
Into the Precinct raw
Possessed before—

1376

梦是上天的赠予
能使我们暂时富裕——
随后又变成穷人
被推出紫色的大门
陷入贫寒的境地
一如往昔——

1377

Forbidden Fruit a flavor has
That lawful Orchards mocks—
How luscious lies within the Pod
The Pea that Duty locks—

1377①

禁果有一种滋味
不为正规的果园接受——
躺在豆荚里多美啊
那受缚于职责的豌豆——

1378

His Heart was darker than the starless night
For that there is a morn
But in this black Receptacle
Can be no Bode of Dawn

1378

他的心比无星光的夜晚还暗
不过拂晓总会来到

---

① 本诗写于1876年。艾米莉·狄金森于1883年写给侄子爱德华(奈德) [Edward (Ned) Dickinson, 1861—1898] 的信这样写道:"We have all heard of the Boy whose Constitution required stolen fruit, though his Father's Orchard was loaded—There was something in the unlawfulness that give it a saving flavor—"(L851)。

但在这黑暗的容器里
可没有一点黎明的征兆

1379

His Mansion in the Pool
The Frog forsakes—
He rises on a Log
And statements makes—
His Auditors two Worlds
Deducting me—
The Orator of April
Is hoarse Today—
His Mittens at his Feet
No Hand hath he—
His eloquence a Bubble
As Fame should be—
Applaud him to discover
To your chagrin
Demosthenes has vanished
In Waters Green—

1379

青蛙遗弃
池塘中的大宅——
站上一根圆木头
开始叙说精彩——
它的听众来自两个世界
但没有我——
这四月的演说家
今天有点嘶哑——
他的手套戴在脚上
他没有手——
他的雄辩是一个水泡
如声名一样不长久——

为他鼓掌
会让你恼怒
德摩斯梯尼①早已消失
在碧波深处——

1380

How much the present moment means
To those who've nothing more—
The Fop—the Carp—the Atheist—
Stake an entire store
Upon a Moment's shallow Rim
While their commuted Feet
The Torrents of Eternity
Do all but inundate—

1380

此刻还有多大意义
对那些已一无所有的人——
花花公子——吹毛求疵的人——无神论者——
把全部的贮存
都押在瞬间窄窄的边际
而他们来回走动的双脚
那永恒的洪流
唯独未将它们淹掉——

1381

I suppose the time will come
Aid it in the coming

---

① 德摩斯梯尼（Demosthenes）：德摩斯梯尼（前384—前322）是公元前4世纪时期古希腊雅典雄辩家、民主派政治家。极力反对马其顿入侵希腊，发表《反腓力辞》等演说，谴责马其顿王腓力二世（Philip Ⅱ of Macedon）的扩张野心。后因反马其顿运动失败而自杀。希腊哲学家普鲁塔克（Plutarch, 46—120）在他的《传记集》（*Parallel Lives*）中，以罗马第一演说家西塞罗（Marcus Tullius Cicero, 前106—前43）来对照德摩斯梯尼。

When the Bird will crowd the Tree
And the Bee be booming.

I suppose the time will come
Hinder it a little
When the Corn in Silk will dress
And in Chintz the Apple

I believe the Day will be
When the Jay will giggle
At his new white House the Earth
That, too, halt a little—

1381
我猜那个时候会来到
它来时请帮一帮
那时鸟儿挤满林中
蜂儿忙着嗡唱。

我猜那个时候会来到
请挡它一挡
玉米要穿上丝装
苹果披印花衣裳

我相信会有那么一天
那时松鸦咯咯笑
在大地他崭新的白房前
那,也得,少安毋躁——

1382
In many and reportless places
We feel a Joy—
Reportless, also, but sincere as Nature
Or Deity—

It comes, without a consternation—
Dissolves—the same—
But leaves a sumptuous Destitution—
Without a Name—

Profane it by a search—we cannot
It has no home—
Nor we who having once inhaled it—
Thereafter roam.

1382

在许多难以言明之地
我们感到一种欢愉——
同样，难以言传，但真挚如自然
或神意——

它来时，毫不令人惊异——
消逝——也如此——
但留下一种丰盛的贫瘠——
没有名字——

找寻而亵渎它——我们做不到
它没有固定住处——
我们曾将它吸入——
从此无法悠然漫步。

1383

Long Years apart—can make no
Breach a second cannot fill—
The absence of the Witch does not
Invalidate the spell—

The embers of a Thousand Years
Uncovered by the Hand

That fondled them when they were Fire
Will stir and understand

1383①
常年的分离——不会造成
无法立刻弥补的隔阂——
巫师的缺席不会
令咒语失效——

千年的余烬
曾被手侍弄烟火不灭
如今被手撩开
还会骚动且理解

1384
Praise it—'tis dead—
It cannot glow—
Warm this inclement Ear
With the encomium it earned
Since it was gathered here—
Invest this alabaster Zest
In the Delights of Dust—
Remitted—since it flitted it
In recusance august.

1384
赞美它吧——它已死亡——
无法再发微光——
温暖这只历经风雨的耳朵
就用它获得的赞扬
它既已被召集到这里——
就让这份雪白的热忱
怀着尘土的欢愉——

---

① 类似主题可参见第 1132 首诗。

已放弃——既然它已迁离它
以威严的抗拒。

1385

"Secrets" is a daily word
Yet does not exist—
Muffled—it remits surmise—
Murmured—it has ceased—
Dungeoned in the Human Breast
Doubtless secrets lie—
But that Grate inviolate—
Goes nor comes away
Nothing with a Tongue or Ear—
Secrets stapled there
Will emerge but once—and dumb—
To the Sepulchre—

1385

"秘密"是一个日常词语
但它并不存在——
若被包住——无从猜疑——
若被念起——不再是秘密——
在人类的心牢里
肯定隐藏着秘密——
但那栅栏结实无比——
不能出来也不能进去
凡有舌有耳的东西——
秘密不会驻扎那里
它只出现一次——然后无声无息——
直至坟墓里——

1386

[stanza 1]

Summer—we all have seen—
A few of us—believed—

A few—the more aspiring
Unquestionably loved—

[**stanza 2**]
But Summer does not care—
She takes her gracious way   She goes her sylvan way—
    goes   spacious   her ample way—
          subtle—   perfect
          simple—
          mighty—
          gallant—
As eligible as the moon
As unperverted as the moon   ~~as undiverted as the Moon—~~
                                             As eligible as the Moon—
                                                 unavailing
To the Temerity—   ~~from her Divinity~~
    a   to our extremity—
    our   adversity—
                                             By our obliquity.

[**stanza 3**]
Deputed to adore—   Created to adore—
~~Contented~~
The ~~Lot~~ to be adored
  Doom

                                             The Affluence evolved—
                                                 conferred—
                                                 bestowed—
                                                 involved—

Unknown as to an Ecstasy
The Embryo endowed—

1386①

[第 1 节]
夏天——我们都曾见过——
我们有几个人——相信它——
几个——胸怀抱负的人
毫不含糊地热爱它——

[第 2 节]
但夏天并不在意——
她走她舒适的路　　　　　　　她走她的林荫路——
　走　**宽敞的**　　　　　　　　　昂首阔步——
　　　精妙的——　　　　　　　　　完美的
　　　简单的——
　　　显赫的——
　　　雄伟的——
像月亮一样适合
像月亮一样无邪　　　　　　　像月亮一样专注——
　　　　　　　　　　　　　　像月一样胜任——
　　　　　　　　　　　　　　　　徒劳

那种唐突——　　　　　　　　自她的神性里
一种　　　　　　　　　　　　走向我们的绝境——
对我们的　　　　　　　　　　　逆境——
　　　　　　　　　　　　　　用我们的拐弯抹角。

[第 3 节]
被委派以敬慕——　　　　　　创造出来以敬慕——
乐于
那该敬慕的命运——
　　　劫数

　　　　　　　　　　　　　　那衍生的富裕——

---

① 这是艾米莉·狄金森诗歌原稿中最杂乱的一首草稿,显示了修改和斟酌的痕迹。译文中黑体的字为译者所标,以显示这是约翰逊 1960 年的阅读版中选用的版本。为展现原文完整样貌,译者未改动原文字体。

被授予的——
被赠予的——
相关的——

不为人知犹如
胎儿不知自发的狂喜——

1387

The Butterfly's Numidian Gown
With spots of Burnish roasted on
Is proof against the Sun
Yet prone to shut it's spotted Fan
And panting on a Clover lean
As if it were undone—

1387

在蝴蝶努米底亚式的①长衣上面
镶着许多闪亮的斑点
能抵挡炎炎烈日
但容易闭合它斑斓的羽扇
倚着一株红花草喘息奄奄
仿佛已疲惫不堪——

1388

Those cattle smaller than a Bee
That herd upon the eye—
Whose tillage is the passing Crumb—
Those Cattle are the Fly—
Of Barns for Winter—blameless—
Extemporaneous stalls
They found to our objection—

---

① 努米底亚式的（Numidian）：原文"Numidian"源自"Numidia"，指努米底亚，北非古国，位于今阿尔及利亚北部。本诗中的"Numidian"意指"奇异的（exotic）、色彩斑斓的（colorful）"。

On eligible walls—
Reserving the presumption
To suddenly descend
And gallop on the Furniture—
Or odiouser offend—
Of their peculiar calling
Unqualified to judge
To Nature we remand them
To justify or scourge—

1388

那些牛比蜜蜂还小
成群在眼睛上停——
其耕地就是途经的碎面包——
那些牛就是苍蝇——
过冬用的牛仓——无可指责——
只是临时的兽栏
它们知道我们反感——
设立在适宜的墙上——
足以这样假想
突然落下来
在家具上驰骋——
或做更令人厌恶的祸害——
对它们奇特的行径
没资格判罚
我们将它们还押给自然
去嘉许或鞭打——

1389

Touch lightly Nature's sweet Guitar
Unless thou know'st the Tune
Or every Bird will point at thee
Because a Bard too soon—

1389

请轻触大自然美妙的吉他
除非你了解曲调
否则每只鸟都会指着你
因为一位行吟诗人来得太早——

1390

These held their Wick above the West—
Till when the Red declined—
Or how the Amber aided it—
Defied to be defined—

Then waned without disparagement
In a dissembling Hue
That would not let the Eye decide
Did it abide or no—

1390①

这些举着他们的灯芯在西方天上——
直至红色逐渐消退——
或琥珀黄如何出来帮忙——
难以仔细描绘——

接着毫不感到轻贬
淡化成一种欲盖弥彰的色彩
让肉眼无法分辨
它到底还在或已离开——

---

① 本诗第 2 节是艾米莉·狄金森于 1877 年 11 月寄给文学导师希金森的一封信的部分内容，紧接诗节后写道："is Sunset's, perhaps—only."（L486），表明这一诗节是描写落日的。艾米莉·狄金森还把整首诗写入 1878 年初寄给霍兰医生的一封信中，在诗之前这样写道："We hope that you are happy as far as Peace is possible, to Mortal and immortal Life—...But I intrude on Sunset, and Father and Mr Bowles."（L544），说明本诗既写落日，也暗喻她 1874 年 6 月 16 日去世的父亲爱德华，以及 1878 年 1 月 16 日逝世的朋友鲍尔斯。

1391

They might not need me—yet they might—
I'll let my Heart be just in sight—
A smile so small as mine might be
Precisely their necessity—

1391①

他们也许不需要我——但也许需要——
我会敞开心扉让他们刚好看到——
一个微笑如我般纤小或许
正是他们所需——

1392

Hope is a strange invention—
A Patent of the Heart—
In unremitting action
Yet never wearing out—

Of this electric Adjunct
Not anything is known
But it's unique momentum
Embellish all we own—

1392②

希望是一个奇怪的发明——

---

① 本诗是艾米莉·狄金森1877年春天寄给文学导师希金森夫人玛丽的一封信的结尾，诗之前写道："Forgive me if I come too much—the time to live is frugal—and good as is a better earth, it will not quite be this. How could I find the way to you and Mr Higginson without a Vane, or any Road？"（L498）。玛丽已生病几年，并于1877年9月2日逝世。艾米莉·狄金森时常在给希金森的信中问候玛丽，并至少4次亲自写问候信给玛丽。艾米莉·狄金森还将本诗寄给了詹金斯牧师的夫人。

② 本诗第2节是艾米莉·狄金森1877年春天寄给文学导师希金森夫人玛丽的一封信（L498）的部分内容，但最后一行的"Embellish all we own—"改成了"inebriate of our own"；倒数第二行中的"But"改成了"Thought"。

属于心的专利——
它永不停歇地进行
永远不会泄气——

这令人激动的附属品
人们并无了解
但它独特的冲劲
美化我们拥有的一切——

1393

Lay this Laurel on the One
Too intrinsic for Renown—
Laurel—veil your deathless tree—
Him you chasten, that is He!

1393①

把这月桂戴给

---

① 艾米莉·狄金森于1877年6月中旬，可能是16日，即她父亲爱德华去世3周年之际，给文学导师希金森写信，本诗和第1394首诗同是这封信的部分内容。信写得较为哀婉，信中本诗之前写道："Summer is so kind I had hoped you might come. Since my Father's dying, everything sacred enlarged so—it was dim to own—When a few years old—I was taken to a Funeral which I now know was of peculiar distress, and the Clergyman asked, 'Is the Arm of the Lord shortened that it cannot save?' He italicized the 'cannot.' I mistook the accent for a doubt of Immortality and not daring to ask, it besets me still, though we know that the mind of the Heart must live if it's clerical part do not. Would you explain it to me? I was told you were once a Clergyman. It comforts an instinct if another have felt it too. I was rereading your 'Decoration.' You may have forgotten it."（L503）。作者在信中首次将希金森当作被委任的牧师来请教永生问题，信中还提到去世的父亲以及读过的希金森的诗"Decoration"。该诗是希金森1874年6月投稿到 *Scribner's Monthly* 的一首悼念阵亡战士的28行诗歌。对于艾米莉·狄金森因为读了自己的诗受到激发而写了本诗（第1393、1394首），希金森过后对两首诗作了比较评价，认为艾米莉·狄金森的这首4行诗比他那首28行的诗要更凝练："It is the condensed essence of that and so far finer."（参见：Loeffelholz, Mary. "Dickinson's 'Decoration'." *ELH*, 2005, 72, 3: 663–689.）。另，第1294首诗的注释也提到"Decoration"。

自带名望而不求显赫的那一位——
月桂——把你不死之树遮蔽——
他是你要惩戒的人,是他无疑!

1394

Whose Pink career may have a close
Portentous as our own, who knows?
To imitate these Neighbors fleet
In awe and innocence, were meet.

1394①

谁粉红色的生涯会截止
像我们的一样可怖,有谁知?
要学这些邻居一样飞逝
在敬畏和天真中,倒也适宜。

1395

After all Birds have been investigated and laid aside—
Nature imparts the little Blue-Bird—assured
Her conscientious Voice will soar unmoved
Above ostensible Vicissitude.

First at the March—competing with the Wind—
Her panting note exalts us—like a friend—
Last to adhere when Summer cleaves away—
Elegy of Integrity.

---

① 艾米莉·狄金森于1877年6月中旬,可能是16日,也即她父亲爱德华去世3周年之际,给文学导师希金森写信,本诗和第1393首诗同是这封信(L503)的部分内容。信的开头写道:"I find you with Dusk—for Day is tired, and lays her antediluvian cheek to the Hill like a child. Nature confides now—I hope you are joyful frequently, these beloved Days. And the health of your friend bolder. I remember her with my Blossoms and wish they were her's.",紧接着就是本诗,诗之后是这样的话:"Summer is so kind I had hoped you might come. Since my Father's dying."。

1395①

把所有鸟儿检查一遍并放置一边——
大自然才向小蓝鸫透露——自信满满
她认真的声音会稳稳窜上天
高于万物表面的变迁。

先是在行进时——与风竞技——
她喘吁吁的歌声令我们激荡——像位朋友——
最后当夏日劈路而去时依然坚持——
那正直的挽歌。

1396

She laid her docile Crescent down
And this confiding Stone
Still states to Dates that have forgot
The News that she is gone—

So constant to it's stolid trust,
The Shaft that never knew—
It shames the Constancy that fled
Before it's emblem flew—

1396②

她把她温顺的新月放下

---

① 艾米莉·狄金森1877年8月寄给文学导师希金森一封信,并随附了本诗和第1396～1398首诗。在信的结尾她写道:"I send you a Gale, and an Epitaph—and a Word to a Friend, and a Blue Bird, for Mrs Higginson. Excuse them if they are untrue—Since you cease to teach me, how could I improve?"(L513),其中提到的 "a Gale" 指第1397首诗,"an Epitaph" 指第1396首诗,"a Word to a Friend" 指第1398首诗,"a Blue Bird" 就是指本诗(第1395首)。信中提到的希金森的夫人玛丽,不久后于1877年9月2日病逝。1877年12月3日,她的朋友鲍尔斯中风,几周以后逝世,她写给他的最后一封信里也引用了本诗最后两行,但其中的"cleaves"改成了"swerve"。

② 参见第1395首注释。此外,艾米莉·狄金森也把本诗寄给霍兰夫人,但把诗第2行中的"confiding"改成了"mechanic"。寄给霍兰夫人的诗,其纸张上方贴了两张剪报,左边那张是一颗星星和一弯新月,右边那张是互相斜靠着的几块墓碑,这些墓碑图是从家乡阿默斯特本地出版的周报,即1856年12月的《罕布什尔和富兰克林快报》(*Hampshire and Franklin Express*)上剪下来的。

而这块石头推心置腹
还在向忘记了她已离去
这一消息的日期陈述——

如此坚持它不动声色的信赖，
连墓碑都从未知悉——
它使坚贞蒙羞而逃开
先于它徽章的飘起——

1397

It sounded as if the Streets were running
And then—the Streets stood still—
Eclipse—was all we could see at the Window
And Awe—was all we could feel.

By and by—the boldest stole out of his Covert
To see if Time was there—
Nature was in an Opal Apron,
Mixing fresher Air.

1397①

听起来好像街道在奔跑
随后——街道站定不走——
晦暗一片——是我们在窗边所见
敬畏——是我们全部感受。

渐渐地——那最大胆的悄悄溜出藏身处
去看时间是否还在那里——

---

① 参见第1395首注释。第1134首诗主题与本诗相似，艾米莉·狄金森的书信中也有类似的描写，如1881年春季写给弗朗西斯·诺克罗斯和路易丝·诺克罗斯两位表妹的一封信："We have had two hurricanes within as many hours, one of which came near enough to untie my apron—but this moment the sun shines, Maggie's hens are warbling, and a man of anonymous wits is making a garden in the lane to set out slips of bluebird."（L690）。

大自然穿着蛋白石围裙,
正在搅拌更清新的空气。

1398
I have no Life but this—
To lead it here—
Nor any Death—but lest
Dispelled from there—

Nor tie to Earths to come—
Nor Action new—
Except through this extent—
The Realm of you—

1398①
我只有这条生命——
在这里捱度——
我也没有死亡——只唯恐
被从那里驱逐——

没有对未来尘世的牵系——
也没有任何新举措——
除了穿越这片天地——
你的王国——

1399
Perhaps they do not go so far
As we who stay, suppose—
Perhaps come closer, for the lapse
Of their corporeal clothes—

---

① 参见第1395首注释。本诗也被艾米莉·狄金森写入1877年寄给朋友鲍尔斯的一封信的结尾部分,紧接本诗的就是信的最后一行:"It is strange that the most intangible thing is the most adhesive."(L515)。

It may be know so certainly
How short we have to fear
That comprehension antedates
And estimates us there—

1399①
也许他们并未走那么远
非如留下的我们，所设想——
也许还更近些，依据他们
身穿的衣物消逝的时长——

或许可以很确定知道
我们的恐惧有多短暂
以至理解抢了先
在那边对我们做了估算——

1400
What mystery pervades a well!
That water lives so far—
A neighbor from another world
Residing in a jar

Whose limit none have ever seen,
But just his lid of glass—
Like looking every time you please

---

① 艾米莉·狄金森1877年9月将本诗第1节寄给文学导师希金森，以对希金森夫人玛丽于1877年9月2日的病逝向希金森表示慰问。诗节前有一句引言："If I could help you?"，诗节后附这样的文字："Did she know she was leaving you? The Wilderness is new—to you. Master, let me lead you."（L517）。诗中的"they"和"their"分别改为"she"和"her"。艾米莉·狄金森也在1877年（一说1876年）把本诗寄给表哥威廉（William Cooper Dickinson, 1827—1899）的两个妹妹，哈丽特（Harriet Austin Dickinson, 1835—1913）和玛莎（Martha Maria Dickinson, 1829—?），诗之前的引言是："You are very kind to have wished for me, and I think it sweet, but accustomed to all, through Father, they remind me too deeply of him for Peace. You, too, have been lessened. Let us remember together."（L518）。

In an abyss's face!

The grass does not appear afraid,
I often wonder he
Can stand so close and look so bold
At what is awe to me.

Related somehow they may be,
The sedge stands next the sea—
Where he is floorless
And does no timidity betray

But nature is a stranger yet;
The ones that cite her most
Have never passed her haunted house,
Nor simplified her ghost.

To pity those that know her not
Is helped by the regret
That those who know her, know her less
The nearer her they get.

1400①
一口井充满奥秘！
水位如此低——
从另一世界来的一位邻居
就安身在一口缸里

缸底无人能见，

---

① 艾米莉·狄金森 1877 年把本诗最后两节（L530）寄给了嫂子苏珊，把其中的"nature"改成了"Susan"，把"passed"改成了"scaled"，把"simplified"改成了"compromised"。

只看到它的玻璃盖面——
每次当你有心探看
都晃似一张深渊的脸!

小草并不显得惊慌,
我时常觉得稀奇
他竟能如此大胆近前探望
使我敬畏的东西。

他们或有某种联系,
莎草傍着大海屹立——
在那里他触不到底
却丝毫不露怯意

不过自然仍是个陌生人;
最常谈起她的人
从未经过她的鬼屋,
也无从简述她的鬼魂。

对不了解她的人的同情
被一个遗憾打消
即那些了解她的人,离她越近
知道得越少。

1401

To own a Susan of my own
Is of itself a Bliss—
Whatever Realm I forfeit, Lord,
Continue me in this!

1401①

拥有我自己的苏珊

---

① 艾米莉·狄金森于 1877 年把本诗(L531)寄给了嫂子苏珊。

本身就是一种极乐——
不管失去什么王国，主啊，
请让我坚持不舍！

1402

To the stanch Dust
We safe commit thee—
Tongue if it hath,
Inviolate to thee—
Silence—denote—
And Sanctity—enforce thee—
Passenger—of Infinity—

1402

我们安全地把你交付
给坚实的尘土——
如果它有舌头，
不会对你亵渎——
沉默——就是表示——
神圣——助你威赫——
无限的——乘客——

1403

My Maker—let me be
Enamored most of thee—
But nearer this
I more should miss—

1403

我的创造者——让我对你
无比痴迷——
但越接近这么做
我错过的就会越多——

1404

March is the Month of Expectation.
The things we do not know—
The Persons of prognostication
Are coming now—
We try to show becoming firmness—
But pompous Joy
Betrays us, as his first Betrothal
Betrays a Boy.

1404①

三月是充满希冀的月份。
我们未知的事——
那些预言的人
都将姗然而至——
我们努力表现得矜持——
但盛大的欢乐
使我们无法自已,就像首次订婚
让一个男孩喜形于色。

1405

Bees are Black, with Gilt Surcingles—
Buccaneers of Buzz.
Ride abroad in ostentation
And subsist on Fuzz.

Fuzz ordained—not Fuzz contingent—
Marrows of the Hill.
Jugs—a Universe's fracture
Could not jar or spill.

---

① 关于三月的诗,还可参见第1213首和第1320首。

1405①

黑压压一群蜜蜂,个个扎着金色腰带——
这些乱哄哄的海盗。
在外面四处招摇
花粉是它们存活的依靠。

是神定的花粉——而非偶然的出现——
那是山的精华。
这些坛坛罐罐——一个宇宙的裂口
无法晃动或泼洒。

1406

No Passenger was known to flee—
That lodged a night in memory—
That wily—subterranean Inn
Contrives that none go out again—

1406②

从没听说有旅客逃离——
只要住了一夜在记忆里——
那狡诈的——地下客栈
成功阻止任何人再露面——

1407

A Field of Stubble, lying sere
Beneath the second Sun—
It's Toils to Brindled People thrust—
It's Triumphs—to the Bin—
Accosted by a timid Bird

---

① 本诗是艾米莉·狄金森1877年5月写给霍兰夫人的一封信的部分内容。诗之前的文字这样写道:"I must just show you a Bee, that is eating a Lilac at the Window. There—there—he is gone! How glad his family will be to see him!"(L502)。

② 艾米莉·狄金森把本诗赠给了朋友霍兰医生。

Irresolute of Alms—
Is often seen—but seldom felt,
On our New England Farms—

1407①

一地的残茬，枯黄
在二次太阳下躺——
它的辛劳推给汗渍斑斑的人——
它的胜利——推给谷仓——
一只胆怯的鸟儿前去搭讪
施予的优柔寡断——
时常看见——但少有感受，
在我们新英格兰农庄——

1408

The Fact that Earth is Heaven—
Whether Heaven is Heaven or not
If not an Affidavit
Of that specific Spot
Not only must confirm us
That it is not for us
But that it would affront us
To dwell in such a place—

1408②

事实是地球即天堂——
不论天堂是否天堂

---

① 本诗是艾米莉·狄金森 1877 年 3 月写给侄子爱德华（奈德）的一封信的部分内容，当时奈德正处于病后初愈的状态。信的开头写道："I send you a Portrait of the Parish, and the first Sugar—Dont bite the Parish, by mistake, though you may be tempted—"，诗之后是信的结尾："I rejoice you are better—Grandma's fervent love—"（L493）。

② 艾米莉·狄金森把本诗写赠给了哥哥奥斯汀，抬头称呼对方为"奥利弗"（Oliver），这是艾米莉·狄金森自 19 世纪 50 年代起对奥斯汀使用的昵称。

若无一个书面证明
确认那个具体地点
不仅会使我们相信
它并非为我们而创
且是对我们的冒犯
住在那样一个地方——

1409

Could mortal lip divine
The undeveloped Freight
Of a delivered syllable
'Twould crumble with the weight.

1409①

假如凡人的唇可以预测
发出的音节
未曾显露的货物
它会因沉重而碎裂。

1410

I shall not murmur if at last
The ones I loved below
Permission have to understand
For what I shunned them so—
Divulging it would rest my Heart
But it would ravage their's—
Why, Katie, Treason has a Voice—
But mine—dispels—in Tears.

---

① 探索文字作用的诗还可参见第 1261 首诗等。

1410①

我不会絮叨如果最终
我挚爱的下界的人
允许体谅
为何我如此躲避他们——
泄密会让我心安
却会令他们愤怒——
啊,凯蒂,背叛可以出声——
而我的——却是在泪水里——消除。

1411

Of Paradise' existence
All we know
Is the uncertain certainty—
But it's vicinity infer,
By it's Bisecting
Messenger—

1411

对于天堂的存在

---

① 本诗写于 1877 年,可能从未被赠予他人。在诗稿第 4 页,艾米莉·狄金森还另写下了三行诗:"We shun because we prize her Face/ Lest sight's ineffable disgrace/ Our Adoration stain"(即第 1429 首诗)。诗中的"Katie"可能指凯特·安东(Kate Anthon,即 Kate Scott Turner,1831—1917),她是艾米莉·狄金森的嫂子苏珊的好友,她的丈夫特纳(Campbell Ladd Turner,1831—1857)也与艾米莉·狄金森相识。她与艾米莉·狄金森于 1859 年首次见面,在 1877 年到访过艾米莉·狄金森居住的阿默斯特镇。艾米莉·狄金森认识的另外 4 位名为"凯特(蒂)"的人,其一是凯蒂姑姑(Aunt Katie),即艾米莉·狄金森的父亲爱德华的妹妹凯瑟琳(Catherine Dickinson,1814—1895),她 1835 年嫁给约瑟夫(Joseph A. Sweetser);其二是孩提友伴凯特·希区柯克(Kate Hitchcock,即 Katherine Hitchcock,1826—1895),其父爱德华·希区柯克(Edward Hitchcock,1793—1864)是阿默斯特学院的化学教授,1845—1854 年任学院院长;其三是凯特·纽曼(Kate Newman),很早就过世了;其四是凯特·霍兰(Kate Holland,1853—1936),也即霍兰医生的女儿,她于 1882 年 9 月 27 日与布利克(Bleeker Van Wagenen,1847—1921)结婚。艾米莉·狄金森曾在 1883 年初给霍兰夫人的信中提到两人结婚的事:"it must have been a bleak Holiday for your loved Kate—Would it be chivalrous to say, we rejoice it was 'Bleeker'? …We hope "Mr-Bridegroom" is better, as Gilbert calls those sacred ones."(L801),还在 1883 年 3 月寄给霍兰夫人的另一封信(L806)中提及"Mrs Van Wagenen"。

我们所知的一切
是不确定的确定——
但可推测它在邻近地带,
据它那一分为二的
信差——

1412

Shame is the shawl of Pink
In which we wrap the Soul
To keep it from infesting Eyes—
The elemental Veil
Which helpless Nature drops
When pushed upon a scene
Repugnant to her probity—
Shame is the tint divine.

1412

羞愧是条粉红的围巾
我们用它把灵魂包紧
免受众目的侵扰——
这原始的面罩
由无助的天性降下
当它被推到
有违于她正直的场景——
羞愧是圣洁的色调。

1413

Sweet Skepticism of the Heart—
That knows—and does not know—
And tosses like a Fleet of Balm—
Affronted by the snow—
Invites and then retards the Truth
Lest Certainty be sere
Compared with the delicious throe
Of transport thrilled with Fear—

1413

心有温馨的疑虑——
有所知——也有所不知——
忐忑如一队香脂——
受到冰雪的打击——
既欢迎又阻挠真理
以免确定变枯萎无力
比之与甜美的阵痛
狂喜中怀着恐惧——

1414

Unworthy of her Breast
Though by that scathing test
What Soul survive?
By her exacting light
How counterfeit the white
We chiefly have!

1414

她的胸部无那价值
虽然以那样严苛的测试
什么灵魂能幸免?
经她苛刻的光照射
我们主要拥有的白色
竟以假冒显现!

1415

A wild Blue sky abreast of Winds
That threatened it—did run
And crouched behind his Yellow Door
Was the defiant sun—
Some conflict with those upper friends

So genial in the main
That we deplore peculiarly
Their arrogant campaign—

1415
狂野的蓝天与威胁它的风
齐头并进——忙着奔突
桀骜不驯的太阳
在他黄色的门后蹲伏——
与这些上层朋友的某种纷争
大体而言非常友善
以致我们深感遗憾
他们的阵仗如此傲慢——

1416
[**stanza one**]
Crisis is sweet and yet the Heart
Upon the hither side
Has Dowers of Prospective
Surrendered by the Tried—
Witheld to the arrived—
　　　　　Debarred—
　　　　　　denied
To Denizens denied

[**stanza two**]
Inquire of the proudest Rose
　　　　fullest
　　　　　closing
Which *rapture* —she preferred
　　triump[h]
　　　　Hour—
　　　　　moment
And she would tell you sighing—

```
                              answer
                    will point undoubtedlly
        And she will point you fondly—
                              longingly
                                sighing
        The transport of the Bud—
                   rapture
        To her surrendered Bud.
                  rescinded
        The Hour of her Bud—
                session of
        To her rescinded Bud
                     receding
                     Departed—
                     Receipted Bud
                     Expended
```

1416①

[第1节]
危机是甜蜜的然而心
在这一边
有憧憬的禀赋
由那受煎熬的给予——
不给抵达的人——
　　被阻止的——
　　不被承认的
不给外来人员

[第2节]
询问最骄傲的玫瑰
　　最绚烂的

---

① 这是艾米莉·狄金森诗歌的草稿，显示了修改和斟酌的痕迹。译文中黑体字为译者所标，以显示这是约翰逊1960年的阅读版全集中选用的版本。为展现原文完整样貌，译者未改动原文字体。

  正闭合的
  哪一狂喜——**它更欢喜**
    胜利
    时辰——
    一刻
  它会叹息着告诉你——
     回答
   无疑会指给你
  她会深情地指给你——
    渴望地
   叹息地
  花蕾的沉迷——
    狂喜
  她颓唐的花蕾。
   已消褪的
  她的花期——
    花季
  它已消褪的花蕾
   正褪去的
   已离去的——
   已签收的花蕾
   已褪尽的

1417

How Human Nature dotes
On what it cant detect.
The moment that a Plot is plumbed
It's meaning is extinct—①

Prospective is the friend
Reserved for us to know
When Constancy is clarified

---

① "It's meaning is extinct—" 在 1960 年的阅读版中为 "Prospective is extinct—"。

Of Curiosity—

Of subjects that resist
Redoubtablest is this
Where go we—
Go we anywhere
Creation after this?

1417

人性多么溺爱
它无法探知的一切。
一个密谋被探出的那一刻
其意义也随之湮灭——

前景是一位朋友
专门留给我们认识
当恒心被澄清
原来只是好奇——

那些抗拒被揭开的事物
最可敬畏的就在于
我们所往之探求——
那里是否也有个造物
在这个之后?

1418

How lonesome the Wind must feel Nights—
When people have put out the Lights
And everything that has an Inn
Closes the shutter and goes in—

How pompous the Wind must feel Noons
Stepping to incorporeal Tunes
Correcting errors of the sky

And clarifying scenery

How mighty the Wind must feel Morns
Encamping on a thousand dawns
Espousing each and spurning all
Then soaring to his Temple Tall—

1418

风一定觉得夜晚多么凄凉——
当人们熄灭了灯光
凡有居处的万物
纷纷合上百叶窗然后进屋——

风一定觉得正午多么华丽
踏着缥缈的乐曲
纠正天空的错误
擦亮世间景物

风一定觉得清晨多么威仪
驻扎在无数的黎明里
逐个接纳又弃之一旁
然后飞上他高高的庙堂——

1419

It was a quiet seeming Day—
There was no harm in earth or sky—
Till with the closing sun
There strayed an accidental Red
A Strolling Hue, one would have said
To westward of the Town—

But when the Earth began to jar
And Houses vanished with a roar
And Human Nature hid

We comprehended by the Awe
As those that Dissolution saw
The Poppy in the Cloud

1419

这是一个貌似宁静的日子——
天上地下都没有伤心事——
直至太阳落山
偶然逸出一缕红光
一缕漫游的色调，有人会这么讲
朝向小镇的西边——

但当地面开始震动不止
房屋轰然消失
人性全都隐藏
我们因敬畏而领悟
一如那些人注目
那红罂粟在云中消亡

1420

One Joy of so much anguish
Sweet nature has for me
I shun it as I do Despair
Or dear iniquity—
Why Birds, a Summer morning
Before the Quick of Day
Should stab my ravished spirit
With Dirks of Melody
Is part of an inquiry
That will receive reply
When Flesh and Spirit sunder
In Death's Immediately—

1420

如此深重痛苦中的一丝欢愉

对我而言具有甜蜜的特性
我一直躲避像躲避绝望
或严重的邪恶行径——
为何鸟儿们,在夏日清晨
白昼倏至之前
会戳刺我沉醉的心灵
用旋律的短剑
这一点需探个究竟
一定会得到回答
当灵与肉分离
在死亡的刹那——

1421

Such are the inlets of the mind—
His outlets—would you see
Ascend with me the eminence
Of immortality—

1421

这些就是心灵的入口——
而他的出口——假如你想看见
请和我一起攀升
至永生之巅——

1422

Summer has two Beginnings—
Beginning once in June—
Beginning in October
Affectingly again—

Without, perhaps, the Riot

But graphicer① for Grace—
As finer is a going
Than a remaining Face—

Departing then—forever—
Forever—until May—
Forever is deciduous—
Except to those who die—

1422
夏季两度开启——
一次始于六月——
十月再次开启
无比真切——

或许，没有，骚动
但其优雅更清晰——
因为一张动态的脸
比静止的脸更显精细——

然后就离去——永远——
永远——直至五月——
永远只是短暂——
除了对那些死者——

1423
The fairest Home I ever knew
Was founded in an Hour
By Parties also that I knew
A spider and a Flower—
A manse of mechlin and of Floss—

---

① "graphicer" 在 1960 年的阅读版中为 "graphicker"。

1423

我所知的最美家园
一个小时就筑起
当事方我也认识
花儿一朵和蜘蛛一只——
一座梅希林花边和丝线①的宅第——

1424

The Gentian has a parched Corolla—
Like azure dried
'Tis Nature's buoyant juices
Beatified—
Without a vaunt or sheen
As casual as Rain
And as benign—

When most is part—it comes—
Nor isolate it seems
It's Bond it's Friend—
To fill it's Fringed career
And aid an aged Year
Abundant end—

It's lot—were it forgot—
This Truth endear—
Fidelity is gain
Creation is o'er—

1424②

龙胆有一个焦枯的花冠——
像晒干的蓝天

---

① 关于梅希林花边和丝线，分别在第274和第1322首诗中也有提及。
② 提及龙胆的诗还有第18、20、331、342、442首。

它是自然旺盛的叶汁
得到了祝福的圣言——
既不炫耀也无光彩
像雨一般随意
也同样和蔼——

当大多数已离开——它才到来——
它看来并非孤立无奈
有至亲有朋友——
填满它边缘化的生涯
帮助老迈的年华
有结尾的丰收——

它的命运——假如它被忘记——
更凸显这一真理的价值——
即忠诚就是收获
创造已停止——

1425

The inundation of the Spring
Enlarges every soul—
It sweeps the tenement away
But leaves the Water whole—

In which the soul at first estranged—
Seeks faintly for it's shore
But acclimated—pines no more
For that Peninsula—

1425

春季的泛滥
令每一个灵魂膨胀——
它卷走了屋房
却留下一片汪洋——

水中的灵魂起初感到疏离——
无力地把岸边寻找
可一旦适应——就不再苦盼
苦盼那个半岛——

1426

The pretty Rain from those sweet Eaves
Her unintending Eyes—
Took her own Heart, including ours,
By innocent Surprise—

The wrestle in her simple Throat
To hold the feeling down
That vanquished her—defeated Feat—
Was Fervor's sudden Crown—

1426

可爱的雨来自那些甜美的屋檐
她无心无意的双眼——
迷住了她的，和我们的心，
以其天真无邪的惊羡——

她单纯的喉咙竭力
把情感镇在下面
那征服了她——令行动失败的——
是激情突如其来的冠冕——

1427

To earn it by disdaining it
Is Fame's consummate Fee—
He loves what spurns him—
Look behind—He is pursuing thee.

So let us gather—every Day—

The Aggregate of
Life's Bouquet
Be Honor and not shame—

1427

以蔑视它来赢取
这就是功名高昂的付费——
他喜欢那唾弃他的东西——
看你身后——他紧紧追随。

所以让我们收集——每一天——
积攒
生活的花束
是荣耀而非耻辱——

1428

Water makes many Beds
For those averse to sleep—
It's awful chamber open stands—
It's Curtains blandly sweep—
Abhorrent is the Rest
In undulating Rooms
Whose Amplitude no end invades—
Whose Axis never comes.

1428

水给那些反感睡眠的人
造了许多床——
它可怕的房间敞开着——
它的窗帘恹恹飘荡——
令人憎恶的是歇息
在这些起伏的房间
它们的广袤没有尽头侵入——
它们的中心轴永不出现。

1429

We shun because we prize her Face
Lest sight's ineffable disgrace
Our Adoration stain

1429①

我们回避因为珍视她的面目
以免目睹那难以形容的耻辱
玷污我们的爱慕

1430

Who never wanted—maddest Joy
Remains to him unknown—
The Banquet of Abstemiousness
Defaces that of Wine—

Within it's reach, though yet ungrasped
Desire's perfect Goal—
No nearer—lest the Actual—
Should disenthrall thy soul—

1430

从无需要的人——对狂欢
肯定一无所知——
节制的盛宴
损毁美酒的面子——

触手可及，虽未能抓取
就是欲望完美的目标——
不能更近——以免现实——
将你灵魂的痴迷取消——

---

① 参见第1410首诗的题注。

1431

With Pinions of Disdain
The soul can farther fly
Than any feather specified
in Ornithology—
It wafts this sordid Flesh
Beyond it's dull—control
And during it's electric gale—
The body is a soul—
instructing by the same—
How little work it be—
To put off filaments like this
for immortality—

1431

用轻蔑的翅翼
灵魂能飞得更远
胜过标出的任何毛羽
在鸟类学里面——
它使这肮脏的肉体飘扬
摆脱自身无聊的——管控
而在它风驰电掣的疾风中——
肉身就化作了灵魂——
借助同样的指导——
这工作多么微小——
像这样将丝丝羁绊脱掉
为永生的目标——

1432[①]

Spurn the temerity—
Rashness of Calvary—
Gay were Gethsemane
Knew we of Thee—

1432

踢开那无礼——
髑髅地[②]的冒失——
客西马尼[③]会充满欢愉
如果我们认识你——

1433

How brittle are the Piers
On which our Faith doth tread—
No Bridge below doth totter so—
Yet none hath such a Crowd.

It is as old as God—
Indeed—'twas built by him—
He sent his Son to test the Plank,
And he pronounced it firm.

---

① 这是艾米莉·狄金森约1879年4月寄给朋友、诗人、小说家海伦（原Mrs. Helen Hunt，1875年后成为Helen Fiske Hunt Jackson，原名Helen Maria Fiske，1830—1885）的一首诗（L601），但本诗约写于1878年底。海伦曾于1878年秋天拜访艾米莉·狄金森的居住地阿默斯特镇，应该是她回家（科罗拉多斯普林斯）后才收到了艾米莉·狄金森寄来的这首诗。她随后把本诗转寄给了艾米莉·狄金森的文学导师希金森，并在诗稿下方写了这样的评语："Wonderful twelve words!——"。艾米莉·狄金森曾在1878年11月底给希金森的一封信中提及她与海伦的交往："I had a sweet Forenoon with Mrs Jackson recently, who brought her Husband to me for the first time—"（L574）。

② 髑髅地（Calvary）：即耶稣受难地，指耶稣被钉上十字架的地方，位于耶路撒冷以西的一座山上。参见《圣经·新约·路加福音》第23章第33节记载："And when they were come to the place, which is called Calvary, there they crucified him, and the malefactors, one on the right hand, and the other on the left."（Luke 23：33）。

③ 客西马尼（Gethsemane）：耶路撒冷附近橄榄山下的一个花园，即耶稣被犹大出卖而被捕处，蒙难地。参见《圣经·新约·马太福音》第26章第36节："Then cometh Jesus with them unto a place called Gethsemane, and saith unto the disciples, Sit ye here, while I go and pray yonder."（Matthew 26：36）。

1433①

这些桥墩多么脆弱
我们的信仰就在上面踏过——
天底下没有哪座桥如此摇晃——
也没有哪座桥上的人如此多。

它像上帝一样古老——
确实——就是他造——
他派儿子来测试桥板,
他宣称桥很牢靠。

1434

Go not too near a House of Rose—
The depredation of a Breeze
Or inundation of a Dew
Alarms it's walls away—
Nor try to tie the Butterfly,
Nor climb the Bars of Ecstasy,
In insecurity to lie
Is Joy's insuring quality.

1434②

别太靠近玫瑰花房——

---

① 这是艾米莉·狄金森约 1878 年 6 月寄给文学导师希金森的一封信中的部分内容,诗之前写道:"I have thought of you often since the Darkness—though we cannot assist another's Night—I have hoped you were saved—That those have immortality with whom we talked about it, makes it no more mighty—but perhaps more sudden—"(L553)。此时距希金森的夫人玛丽病逝的日子 1877 年 9 月 2 日已有约 9 个月。关于信仰的比喻,可参见第 185、915 首诗。

② 这是艾米莉·狄金森 1878 年 7 月寄给朋友爱德华·塔克曼(Edward Tuckermam, 1817—1886)的夫人莎拉(Sara Eliza Sigourney Cushing, 1832—1915)的一首诗,诗之前有这样的附言:"Would it be prudent to subject an apparitional interview to a grosser test? the Bible portentously says 'that which is Spirit is Spirit.'"(L558)。莎拉可能之前提议过两人见面而非仅仅通信,故艾米莉·狄金森回复此诗,暗示两人不要太靠近,欢乐具有躁动不定的特点,一旦会面,一切确定、明晰和具体,欢乐恐不再。艾米莉·狄金森随后在 1878 年 8 月给对方的另一封信里说相见远不如猜测那样充满魔力:"To see is perhaps never quite the sorcery that it is to surmise"(L565)。信中所提圣经所言,参见《圣经·新约·约翰福音》第 3 章第 1~6 节记载耶稣对尼哥底母的怀疑所作的回答:"There was a man of the Pharisees, named Nicodemus, a ruler of the Jews…That which is born of the flesh is flesh; and that which is born of the Spirit is spirit."(John 3:1-6)。

清风的掠劫
露水的泛滥
惊得它壁残垣缺——
也别试着牵住蝴蝶,
或爬上狂喜的栏杆,
终日躁动不歇
正是欢乐保险的特点。

1435

Not that he goes—we love him more
Who led us while he stayed.
Beyond earth's trafficking frontier,
For what he moved, he made.

1435①

不是他走了——我们才更爱他
他在时也一直将我们引导。
在地球交通的边界以外,
他所搬走的,都是他造。

1436

Than Heaven more remote,
For Heaven is the root,
But these the flitted seed.
More flown indeed
Than ones that never were,
Or those that hide, and are.

What madness, by their side,

---

① 艾米莉·狄金森的朋友鲍尔斯于 1878 年 1 月 16 日去世。本诗是艾米莉·狄金森约 1878 年 1 月下旬寄给鲍尔斯夫人玛丽的一封慰问信的部分内容,诗之前写道:"Dear 'Mr. Sam' is very near, these midwinter days. When purples come on Pelham, in the afternoon we say 'Mr. Bowles's colors.' I spoke to him once of his Gem chapter, and the beautiful eyes rose till they were out of reach of mine, in some hallowed fathom." (L536)。其中提及的"Gem chapter"指《圣经·新约·启示录》第 21 章。

A vision to provide
Of future days
They cannot praise.

My soul, to find them, come,
They cannot call, they're dumb,
Nor prove, nor woo,
But that they have abode
Is absolute as God,
And instant, too.

1436①

比天堂更渺远无际,
因为天堂是根基,
但这些飞逝的种子。
飞得更远,确实
比从未飞翔过的那些,
或现在隐藏,和存活的那些。

多么疯狂,以他们的力量,
提供一幅景象
关于未来的日子
他们已无法美誉。

我的灵魂,来,去将他们发现,
他们已无法喊叫,哑口无言,
既不能证实,也不能求助,
但他们有住址
这一点既像上帝一样真实,
也,飘忽。

---

① 玛利亚(Maria Whitney of Northampton, 1830—1909)是艾米莉·狄金森的朋友鲍尔斯的夫人玛丽的亲戚。鲍尔斯去世也令玛利亚深感悲痛。本诗是艾米莉·狄金森写赠给玛利亚的,表示慰问。艾米莉·狄金森在 1878 年初在写给玛利亚的一封信里也提到过鲍尔斯:"That he has received Immortality who so often conferred it, invests it with a more sudden charm."(L537)。

1437

A Dew sufficed itself—
And satisfied a Leaf
And felt "how vast a destiny"—
"How trivial is Life!"

The Sun went out to work—
The Day went out to play
And not again that Dew be seen
By Physiognomy

Whether by Day Abducted
Or emptied by the Sun
Into the Sea in passing
Eternally unknown

Attested to this Day
That awful Tragedy
By Transport's instability
And Doom's celerity.

1437

一颗露珠有自足感——
也令一片叶子满意
感叹"天命多么浩瀚"——
"生命多么琐细!"

太阳外出工作——
白昼外出游玩
那颗露珠无人再见
露其容颜

是否被白昼拐跑
或被太阳倾倒
到流经的海里
永远无人知晓

这一天确实是
可怕的悲剧
因狂喜的变异
和厄运的迅疾。

1438
Behold this little Bane—
The Boon of all alive—
As common as it is unknown
The name of it is Love—

To lack of it is Woe—
To own of it is Wound—
Not elsewhere—if in Paradise
It's Tantamount be found—

1438
看这小小的灾星——
受所有人垂青——
既普通又默默无闻
它的名字叫爱情——

缺少它令人断肠——
拥有它让人心伤——
无法在别处——假使在天堂
能看到与它等同的模样——

1439
How ruthless are the gentle—

How cruel are the kind—
God broke his contract to his Lamb
To qualify the Wind—

1439

温柔多么绝情——
仁慈多么残酷——
上帝撕毁与他的羔羊的契约
好让风不受约束——

1440

The healed Heart shows it's shallow scar
With confidential moan—
Not mended by Mortality
Are Fabrics truly torn—
To go its convalescent way
So shameless is to see
More genuine were Perfidy
Than such Fidelity.

1440

愈合的心显露浅浅的疤痕
发出隐秘的呻吟——
凡人无力修补
严重撕裂的组织——
它正走向康复
见此也毫不觉丢人
背信更显真诚
比起忠贞。

1441

These Fevered Days—to take them to the Forest
Where Waters cool around the mosses crawl—
And shade is all that devastates the stillness
Seems it sometimes this would be all—

1441

这些炙热的日子——该送它们到森林里
那里流水的清凉在苔藓四周匍匐——
只有阴影打破宁静
有时仿佛这就是全部——

1442

To mend each tattered Faith
There is a needle fair
Though no appearance indicate—
'Tis threaded in the Air—

And though it do not wear
As if it never Tore
'Tis very comfortable indeed
And spacious as before—

1442

每一个残破信仰的修补
都有一根针无比灵巧
虽然没有迹象表明——
空中有针线操劳——

尽管它并未残旧
仿佛从未磨破
它确实非常舒适
和以前一样宽绰——

1443

A chilly Peace infests the Grass
The Sun respectful lies—
Not any Trance of industry
These shadows scrutinize—

Whose Allies go no more astray
For service or for Glee—
But all mankind deliver here
From whatsoever sea—

1443①

草丛中弥漫清寒的寂静
太阳恭敬地躺下——
没有一丝劳作的迷离神情
让这些阴影逐个细查——

它的同类从此不再迷途
不论是劳苦还是欢喜——
但全人类都输送至此处
不论从哪一片海里——

1444

A little Snow was here and there
Disseminated in her Hair—
Since she and I had met and played
Decade had gathered to Decade—

But Time had added not obtained
Impregnable the Rose
For summer too indelible
Too obdurate for Snows—

1444②

四处是小小的雪花

---

① 题解：描绘落日时分墓园的情形。
② 本诗可能与艾米莉·狄金森的朋友海伦 1878 年秋天拜访艾米莉·狄金森的居住地阿默斯特镇有关。

撒落于她的纤发——
自我与她相遇嬉玩
十年匆匆复又十年——

但时间递增却无所获
玫瑰依然无懈可击
夏季难以将它抹去
对雪而言顽固无比——

1445

Death is the supple Suitor
That wins at last—
It is a stealthy Wooing
Conducted first
By pallid innuendoes
And dim approach
But brave at last with Bugles
And a bisected Coach
It bears away in triumph
To Troth unknown
And Kinsmen as divulgeless
As throngs of Down—①

1445

死神是个灵活的追求者
最终将胜利赢取——
一种偷偷摸摸的求爱
首先开始
通过苍白的暗示
接着暗暗接近
但最后大胆吹起冲锋号

---

① "And Kinsmen as divulgeless/As throngs of Down—" 在 1960 年的阅读版中为 " And Kindred as responsive/As Porcelain."。

一辆一分为二的马车上阵
得意洋洋地开向
无人知晓的姻缘
亲戚秘不可宣
如绒毛蜂拥向前——

1446

His Mind like Fabrics of the East
Displayed to the despair
Of everyone but here and there
An humble Purchaser—
For though his price was not of Gold—
More arduous there is—
That one should comprehend the worth
Was all the price there was—

1446

他的思想像东方的锦缎
没人看到它显现
因为寻常所见
都是清贫的买家——
虽然它贵不如金子——
却更难得到它——
因为认识它的价值
才是要付出的代价——

1447

How good his Lava Bed,
To this laborious Boy—
Who must be up to call the World
And dress the sleepy Day—

1447

他的熔岩床有多棒,

对这辛劳的男孩来讲——
他得起身叫醒世界
为困倦的白昼梳妆——

1448

How soft a Caterpillar steps—
I find one on my Hand
From such a velvet world it comes
Such plushes at command
It's soundless travels just arrest
My slow—terrestrial eye
Intent upon it's own career
What use has it for me—

1448

毛毛虫的步履多么轻盈——
我看见一只在我手边
它从毛绒绒的世界而来
长绒舞翩跹
它无声的穿行正好引起
我迟缓——世俗的眼睛注意
专注它自己的事业
这对我有何意义——

1449

I thought the Train would never come—
How slow the whistle sang—
I dont① believe a peevish Bird
So whimpered for the Spring—
I taught my Heart a hundred times
Precisely what to say—

---

① "dont" 在1960年的阅读版中为 "don't"。

Provoking Lover, when you came
It's Treatise flew away
To hide my strategy too late
To wiser be too soon—
For miseries so halcyon
The happiness atone—

1449

我原以为火车决不会来——
你听那汽笛多么低——
我不信一只暴躁的鸟
会因春天而抽泣——
我已告诉我心一百遍
把要说的话反复背——
惹人烦的爱人,当你到来时
它的讲稿就不翼而飞
隐藏我的心思已太迟
理智也来不及恢复——
如此平静的悲惨
幸福才能弥补——

1450

The Road was lit with Moon and star—
The Trees were bright and still—
Descried I—by the distant Light
A Traveller on a Hill—
To magic Perpendiculars
Ascending, though Terrene—
Unknown his shimmering ultimate—
But he indorsed the sheen—

1450

道路被星月照亮——

林木明朗而安详——
我发现——借助远远的光
一位旅人在一座山上——
向那些魔力的峭壁
攀登,虽还在尘世——
尚不明他闪光的终极——
但他认可那清辉熠熠——

1451

Whoever disenchants
A single Human soul
By failure of irreverence
Is guilty of the whole.

As guileless as a Bird
As graphic as a star
Till the suggestion sinister
Things are not what they are—

1451

谁去警醒
一颗人类的心灵
用无端的不敬
就该负疚整件事情。

像鸟儿一样率直
像星星一样分明
直至出现不详的暗示
说事情并非如此情形——

1452

Your thoughts dont[①] have words every day
They come a single time
Like signal esoteric sips
Of the communion Wine
Which while you taste so native seems
So easy so to be
You cannot comprehend it's price
Nor it's infrequency

1452

你的思想不会每天都有文字
它们只出现一次
像啜饮圣餐酒
那种玄秘的暗示
虽然你尝起来像本地口味
也能轻易酿产
你就是不理解它的价值
也不明白它为何很少出现

1453

A Counterfeit—a Plated Person—
I would not be—
Whatever strata of Iniquity
My Nature underlie—
Truth is good Health—and Safety, and the Sky.
How meagre, what an Exile—is a Lie,
And Vocal—when we die—

---

① "dont" 在1960年的阅读版中为"don't"。

1453①

一个仿冒者——是一个镀金的人——
我不会是——
不论有什么邪恶层
潜藏在我天性里——
真理就是健康——安全,以及天宇。
谎言——多么贫瘠,游无定居,
会发声——当我们死去——

1454

Those not live yet
Who doubt to live again—
"Again" is of a twice
But this—is one—
The Ship beneath the Draw
Aground—is he?
Death—so—the Hyphen of the Sea—
Deep is the Schedule
Of the Disk to be—
Costumeless Consciousness—
That is he—

---

① 本诗约写于 1879 年,可能寄给了哥哥奥斯汀。诗原稿抬头是"机密——"(In petto—),附有奥斯汀的女儿比安琪太太(Ms. Martha Gilbert Dickinson Bianchi [Mattie], 1866—1943)的批注,说阿默斯特镇当地一位牧师洛思罗普(Rev. C. D. Lothrop)的女儿离家向邻居求助,指控父亲虐待她。几位邻居,包括奥斯汀,一起设法帮助私了此事。但后来牧师的女儿重新提出指控,闹得满城风雨。马萨诸塞州汉普登县斯普林菲尔德(春田)镇(Springfield, Hampden County)出版的报纸《春田共和报》(Springfield Republican)作了详细报道。洛思罗普牧师为此于 1879 年 4 月 17 日控告报社诽谤。为防止当地法院偏袒,案件移交到埃塞克斯县(Essex County)审理,最后判决洛思罗普败诉。《春田共和报》是由鲍尔斯二世(Samuel Bowles II, 1797—1851)于 1824 年创办的周报,1844 年改为日报,对美国共和党的创立(1854 年)有重要影响。鲍尔斯的儿子鲍尔斯三世接替父亲出版该报直至去世,后又由他的儿子鲍尔斯四世(Samuel Bowles IV, 1851—1915)接任成为该报出版人和总编。该报在鲍尔斯(鲍尔斯三世是艾米莉·狄金森的好友,除非特殊说明,书信和注释中所称鲍尔斯均指鲍尔斯三世)执掌的 19 世纪中后期曾是新英格兰地区发行量最大的日报,具有全国影响力。2017 年美国大报排名中,该报排第 69 名。

1454①

那些质疑复活的人
没有真正活过——
"复"意味两次
但这个——是一次——
吊桥下的船
难道他算——搁浅?
因此——死——只是大海的连接线——
深邃的是那即将到来的
圆盘的计划——
那无遮无掩的意识——
那就是他——

1455

Opinion is a flitting thing,
But Truth, outlasts the Sun—
If then we cannot own them both—
Possess the oldest one—

1455②

舆论是飞逝之物,
但真理,比太阳长久——
如若我们不能二者兼得——
就选最古老的拥有——

---

① 本诗约写于1879年,原稿上落款为"复活节"("Easter—"),可能是艾米莉·狄金森写赠给嫂子苏珊的。本诗可能指生前与死后是一体,死是连接两者的连接线,所以质疑死后生活的人没有真正活过。因为如果生前和死后是一体,那没有死后的生活,也就没有生前的生活。一艘船通过吊桥,吊桥前后都属于船的一次航行,而非两截航行。真正深邃的是那计划,即圆盘(圆满)何时到来,那无遮无掩、没有隔断、连为一体的意识,那就是生前和死后的一生,那就是永生。"Disk"(Disc)在艾米莉·狄金森的诗中有多种含义,可以指王国、领地、脸盘、圆盘、圆满、圆轮等。

② 本诗约写于1879年,写在艾米莉·狄金森写赠给嫂子苏珊的一张字条上,字条开头写道:"Emily is sorry for Susan's Day—/ To be singular under plural circumstances, is a becoming heroism—"(L625),然后紧接本诗。

1456

So gay a Flower
Bereaves the Mind
As if it were a Woe—
Is Beauty an Affliction—then?
Tradition ought to know—

1456①

一朵花如此欢愉
令头脑失去了自己
仿佛它是一种苦恼——
难道——美丽是一种滋扰？
传统应该知道——

1457

It stole along so stealthy
Suspicion it was done
Was dim as to the wealthy
Beginning not to own—

1457②

它如此悄悄潜行
疑虑已停止
朦胧得仿佛对于富人
并未拥有开始——

1458

Time's wily Chargers will not wait
At any Gate but Woe's—
But there—so gloat to hesitate
They will not stir for blows—

---

① 本诗约写于 1879 年，可能是艾米莉·狄金森写赠给嫂子苏珊的，并随附了一朵花。
② 本诗可能是艾米莉·狄金森写赠给嫂子苏珊的。

1458①

时间狡猾的快马只会等候
在悲伤的大门——
但在那里——得意地思前想后
连打个响鼻也不会动弹半分——

1459

Belshazzar had a Letter—
He never had but one—
Belshazzar's Correspondent
Concluded and begun
In that immortal Copy
The Conscience of us all
Can read without it's Glasses
On Revelation's Wall—

1459②

伯沙撒③有一封信——
他从来只有一封——

---

① 本诗写于1879年,艾米莉·狄金森把诗寄给侄子奈德,抬头是"奈德",结尾署名是"迪克—吉姆"("Dick—Jim"),这可能是奈德的两匹马的名字。此前两匹马曾有过脱缰奔逃的情况。

② 这是艾米莉·狄金森写赠给侄子奈德的一首诗,约写于1879年,诗下面落款为"根据我们邻居的建议"("Suggested by our Neighbor")以及作者的签名。因此本诗可能是因1879年4月结案的洛思罗普(Rev. C. D. Lothrop)案而作的又一首诗。参见第1453首诗题注。

③ 伯沙撒(Belshazzar):巴比伦最后一位国王,他设宴款待贵族宾朋,做出了亵渎神灵的行为,忽然间一只神秘的隐形大手出现,在宫殿墙壁上写下一些人们看不懂的文字,只有但以理(Daniel)能读懂,他告诉伯沙撒王说他已被神降罪,他在位的日子不多了。《圣经·旧约·但以理书》第5章有记述:"Belshazzar the king made a great feast to a thousand of his lords, and drank wine before the thousand.... In the same hour came forth fingers of a man's hand, and wrote over against the candlestick upon the plaister of the wall of the king's palace: and the king saw the part of the hand that wrote.... Then came in all the king's wise men: but they could not read the writing, nor make known to the king the interpretation thereof.... Then Daniel answered and said before the king, Let thy gifts be to thyself, and give thy rewards to another; yet I will read the writing unto the king, and make known to him the interpretation.... And this is the writing that was written, MENE, MENE, TEKEL, UPHARSIN. This is the interpretation of the thing: MENE; God hath numbered thy kingdom, and finished it. TEKEL; Thou art weighed in the balances, and art found wanting. PERES; Thy kingdom is divided, and given to the Medes and Persians.... In that night was Belshazzar the king of the Chaldeans slain."(Daniel 5: 1, 5, 8, 17, 25 – 28, 30)。

伯沙撒的写信人
在那不朽的抄本中
结束又开始
我们所有人的良知
不戴眼镜也能读到
在神启的墙上显示——

1460

His Cheek is his Biographer—
As long as he can blush
Perdition is Opprobrium—
Past that, he sins in peace—

1460①

他的脸颊是他的传记作者——
只要他还会脸红
毁灭是一种谴责——
过了那个阶段,他犯错也从容——

1461

"Heavenly Father" —take to thee
The supreme iniquity
Fashioned by thy candid Hand
In a moment contraband—
Though to trust us—seems to us
More respectful— "We are Dust" —
We apologize to thee
For thine own Duplicity—

---

① 本诗落款为"贼——"("Thief—"),写于1879年,可能寄给了艾米莉·狄金森的侄子奈德,当时约18岁的他被人们发现偷吃糖果和一张馅饼。艾米莉·狄金森在此前(1878年)写给奈德的一封信里就写道:"Dear Ned, You know that Pie you stole—well, this is that Pie's Brother—"(L571)。本诗可能意指人做错会脸红,等于自我揭示了自我行为。如果脸红的情况消失,是值得谴责的。过了脸红的阶段,人再犯错,就变得从容,不再脸红也就不再有负罪感了。

1461①

"天上的父"——给你带去

这最大的不义

由你公正的手造就

在一个不该的时候——

虽然信任我们——似乎是对我们

更尊重——"我们是尘"——

我们还是向你赔礼

为你自己的表里不一——

1462

We knew not that we were to live—

Nor when—we are to die—

Our ignorance—our cuirass is—

We wear Mortality

As lightly as an Option Gown

Till asked to take it off—

By his intrusion, God is known—

It is the same with Life—

1462②

我们本不知我们会活下来——

也不知何时——会死去——

我们的无知——是我们的胸甲——

我们披戴死期

---

① 这是艾米莉·狄金森写赠给侄子奈德的诗，在诗稿背后写有"奈德——。"（"Ned—."）。这是作者向侄子分享自己对上帝的看法。类似的对宗教逆反的诗也可见于第1479首等。

② 这是1878年12月份艾米莉·狄金森写给文学导师希金森的一封信的结尾，该信祝贺了希金森新近与玛丽订婚，诗之前的引言是："Till it has loved—no man or woman can become itself—Of our first Creation we are unconscious—"（L575）。本诗同时也是稍后的1879年初（富兰克林全集版为1878年12月）艾米莉·狄金森写给玛利亚（Maria Whitney of Northampton, 1830—1909）的一封信（L591）的结尾。本诗意为：我们本不知会有生，也不知何时死，是上帝决定我们死和生，也因为他干预我们的存在，才被我们所知。

轻如自选的长袍
直至被要求脱去——
通过他的闯入,上帝才被知道——
这与生命无异——

1463

A Route of Evanescence
With a revolving Wheel—
A Resonance of Emerald—
A Rush of Cochineal—
And every Blossom on the Bush
Adjusts it's tumbled Head—
The mail from Tunis①, probably,
An easy Morning's Ride—

1463②

一条倏然消逝的路上
有个轮子飞速转动——

---

① "Tunis"一词的语源,参见:Davidson, Frank. "A Note on Emily Dickinson's Use of Shakespeare." *New England Quarterly*, XVIII (1945): 407 - 408. 该文认为"Tunis"源自莎士比亚戏剧《暴风雨》(*The Tempest*),显见莎士比亚对艾米莉·狄金森的影响,参见:"She that is queen of Tunis; she that dwells/ Ten leagues beyond man's life; she that from Naples/ Can have no note, unless the sun were post—" (*The Tempest*, II, i, 246 - 248). 对本诗中意象的讨论,参阅 Smith, Grover. "Dickinson's A Route of Evanescence," *Explicator*, Vol. 7, Issue 7 (May 1949), item 54: 106 - 109.

② 这是艾米莉·狄金森的名诗之一,可能写于 1879 年,艾米莉·狄金森曾 6 次将它寄给亲友,每次略有小改动,有时会在信中直接告诉对方本诗是写"蜂鸟"("Humming Bird"或"A Humming Bird")。艾米莉·狄金森另一首写蜂鸟的诗是第 500 首。本版诗是艾米莉·狄金森 1880 年初寄给朋友爱德华·塔克曼的夫人莎拉的一封信的结尾,诗前的引言写道:"I send you only a Humming Bird—Will you let me add a few Jasmin in a few Days?" (L627);其二,1879 年,艾米莉·狄金森将本诗寄给朋友海伦,诗前引言是:"To the Oriole you suggested I add a Humming Bird and hope they are not untrue—" (L602);其三,1880 年 11 月,艾米莉·狄金森在写给文学导师希金森的一封信 (L675) 里附寄了 4 首诗,本诗是其中之一;其四,1882 年 10 月,艾米莉·狄金森将本诗寄给哥哥奥斯汀的情人托德夫人 (Ms. Mabel Loomis Todd, 1856—1932),诗前引言是:"I cannot make an Indian Pipe but please accept a Humming Bird." (L770);其五,艾米莉·狄金森还在 1883 年 4 月写给朋友耐尔斯 (Thomas Niles, 1825—1894) 的一封信 (L814) 里附寄了 3 首诗,本诗是其中之一;其六,大约也是 1883 年 4 月,艾米莉·狄金森还将本诗寄给弗朗西斯·诺克罗斯和路易丝·诺克罗斯两位表妹,信的落款是"Humming bird"。

一阵祖母绿的反响——
一抹胭脂红的匆匆——
灌木上的每一朵花
都将歪倒的头抬起——
来自突尼斯的邮件,或许,
一上午的轻松之旅——

1464

One thing of it we borrow
And promise to return—
The Booty and the Sorrow
It's Sweetness to have known—
One thing of it we covet—
The power to forget—
The Anguish of the Avarice
Defrays the Dross of it—

1464①

我们向它借的一样东西
并且答应一定归还的——
是战利品和悲戚
我们欣悉——
我们贪求它的一样东西——
是遗忘的能力——
贪欲的苦闷
已偿付了它的渣滓——

---

① 本诗是艾米莉·狄金森在1879年12月圣诞节过后没多久写给文学导师希金森的一封信的部分内容,该信向希金森表示谢意,感谢他送的礼物——《美国作家简论》(*Short Studies of American Authors*)一书。信中本诗前写道:"Remorse for the brevity of a Book is a rare emotion, though fair as Lowell's 'Sweet Despair' in the Slipper Hymn—",诗之后紧跟这样的话:"Had I tried before reading your Gift, to thank you, it had perhaps been possible, but I waited and now it disables my Lips—"(L622)。本诗可能指读了该书之后既有收获的喜悦也有感到自己技不如人的难过,所以渴望得到一种能力,能够忘记自己的劣势和他人的优势带来的难过,而那种贪婪般的渴望导致的苦闷好歹令自己的难过缓解了一些。

1465

Before you thought of Spring
Except as a Surmise
You see—God bless his suddenness—
A Fellow in the Skies
Of independent Hues
A little weather worn
Inspiriting habiliments
Of Indigo and Brown—
With specimens of Song
As if for you to choose—
Discretion in the interval
With gay delays he goes
To some superior Tree
Without a single Leaf
And shouts for joy to Nobody
But his seraphic self—

1465①

在你想到春天之前
除了猜度
你会看见——上帝保佑它突如其来——
天空中一位小伙
自放光彩
携带些许季节的光芒
它令人振奋的衣装
棕褐中夹着靛蓝——

---

① 本诗描写的是北美的蓝知更鸟，也称蓝鹎（blue bird）。艾米莉·狄金森约在1879年早春将本诗寄给朋友爱德华·塔克曼的夫人莎拉，也寄给了朋友海伦。海伦在1879年5月12日回信说道："I know your 'Blue bird' by heart—and that is more than I do of any of my own verses. —I also want your permission to send it to Col. Higginson to read. These two things are my testimonial to its merit. We have blue birds here—I might have had the sense to write something about one myself, but I never did; and now I never can. For which I am inclined to envy, and perhaps hate you."（L601a）。

唱着特定的几首歌
仿佛专为你而选——
在歌声间歇它自在思量
怀着姗姗的欢愉跃上
某根巍巍的树枝
没有一片叶子
它欢呼雀跃不向他人
只向天使般的自己——

1466

One of the ones that Midas touched
Who failed to touch us all
Was that confiding Prodigal
The reeling Oriole—

So drunk he disavows it
With badinage divine—
So dazzling we mistake him
For an alighting Mine—

A Pleader—a Dissembler—
An Epicure—a Thief—
Betimes an Oratorio—
An Ecstasy in chief—

The Jesuit of Orchards
He cheats as he enchants
Of an entire Attar
For his decamping wants—

The splendor of a Burmah
The Meteor of Birds,
Departing like a Pageant
Of Ballads and of Bards—

I never thought that Jason sought
For any Golden Fleece
But then I am a rural man
With thoughts that make for Peace—

But if there were a Jason,
Tradition bear with me
Behold his lost Aggrandizement
Upon the Apple Tree—

1466①
迈达斯②触到了其中一位
未能将我们全部触及
那一位就是轻信的浪子
那摇摇晃晃的金黄鹂——

他醉醺醺地否认
用神圣的戏谑之词——
如此炫目我们误以为他是
一块飞落的金矿石——

一位狡辩者——伪君子——
享乐者——贼盗——
适时唱一出神圣剧——
让人迷狂是其主调——

---

① 朋友海伦曾提议艾米莉·狄金森写一首关于金黄鹂的诗，艾米莉·狄金森随后写了一首关于蜂鸟的诗（第1463首）寄给了海伦，在信中她对海伦写道："To the Oriole you suggested I add a Humming Bird and hope they are not untrue—"（L602）。艾米莉·狄金森也把描写金黄鹂的这首诗寄给了海伦。

② 迈达斯（Midas）：希腊神话传说中贪婪的弗里吉亚国王（King of Phrygia），获得酒神狄俄尼索斯（Dionysus）赋予的一种能力——凡他触摸到的一切都变成金子。

这果园中的耶稣会士
一边施魔一边骗取
一整个玫瑰花油
以为他潜逃时所需——

一只金莺①的璀璨
众鸟眼中的流星,
像歌谣和吟游诗人的盛会
他离去时的场景——

我从没想过伊阿宋②
去寻找什么金羊毛
但毕竟我是个乡下人
求和平的想法充满大脑——

但假如真有个伊阿宋
传统会对我宽谅
看他遗失的宝物③
在那棵苹果树上——

1467

A little overflowing word
That any, hearing, had inferred
For Ardor or for Tears,
Though Generations pass away,
Traditions ripen and decay,
As eloquent appears—

---

① 金莺(Burmah):原文"Burmah"指上文的"Oriole",与上文提到的金黄鹂是同一只鸟。"Burmah"也可引申指东南亚国家缅甸(Burma),鸟类资源丰富。
② 伊阿宋(Jason):古希腊神话中率领阿尔戈英雄们(the Argonauts)寻找金羊毛的英雄,是神话中科尔喀斯(Colchis)国王厄忒斯(King Aeëtes)之女美狄亚(Medea)的丈夫。擅长巫术的美狄亚协助伊阿宋从她父亲手里夺取金羊毛。
③ 宝物(Aggrandizement):原文"Aggrandizement"实际指金羊毛,以呼应上文提到的伊阿宋。延伸义指荣誉、地位、权利、奖品、财富。

1467

一个娇小洋溢的字眼
任何人,听见,就能推断
是代表热情或泪水涟涟,
尽管一代一代已逝去,
传统成熟又萎地,
依然显现似雄辩——

1468

A winged spark doth soar about—
I never met it near
For Lightning it is oft mistook
When nights are hot and sere—

It's twinkling Travels it pursues
Above the Haunts of men—
A speck of Rapture—first perceived
By feeling it is gone—
Rekindled by some action quaint

1468

一粒带翅的火花四处飞扬——
我从未在附近碰到
它时常被误认是闪电
当夜晚炎热又寂寥——

它追寻的是闪烁的旅程
在人类的魂牵梦绕之上——
一点狂喜——才有所感
就在感觉中消散——
又重被某个奇异的举动点燃①

---

① 又重被某个奇异的举动点燃:在富兰克林编辑版的艾米莉·狄金森诗歌全集中没有这一行。在诗歌原稿中本行离诗歌主体部分较远,约翰逊认为它可能是第 5 行的备选句。

1469

If wrecked upon the Shoal of Thought
How is it with the Sea?
The only Vessel that is shunned
Is safe—Simplicity—

1469

如果在思想的浅滩也失事
到了海上怎么办？
那被避开的唯一船只
就是安全的——简单——

1470

The Sweets of Pillage, can be known
To no one but the Thief—
Compassion for Integrity
Is his divinest Grief—

1470

对掠夺的甜头，有所认识
没有谁只有小偷——
对正直的同情
是他最神圣的哀愁——

1471

Their Barricade against the Sky
The martial Trees withdraw
And with a Flag at every turn
Their Armies are no more.

What Russet Halts in Nature's March
They indicate or cause
An inference of Mexico
Effaces the Surmise—

Recurrent to the After Mind
That Massacre of Air—
The Wound that was not Wound nor Scar
But Holidays of War—

1471①
他们对抗天空的路障
好战的树木纷纷撤去
每个拐角有一面旗帜
他们的大军已全无踪迹。

他们暗示或导致
什么红褐②停步于自然的行军里
对墨西哥③的推理
消除了猜疑——

反复出现在事后脑海里
是那空气的大屠杀——
伤口既非伤口也非伤疤
而是战争的嘉年华——

1472
To see the Summer Sky
Is Poetry, though never in a Book it lie—
True Poems flee—

1472
凝望夏日的天空

---

① 题解：本诗描绘秋天叶落的情景。
② 红褐（Russet）：原文"Russet"可指红褐色、黄褐色，或指秋天成熟的表皮粗糙的红褐色苹果。
③ 墨西哥（Mexico）：可能喻指美国和墨西哥在 1846 年 4 月至 1848 年 2 月间爆发的关于领土控制权的美墨战争（Mexican-American War）。作为战胜方的美国兼并了得克萨斯州，使其成为美国的第 28 个州。

那就是诗,尽管从未现于书中——
真正的诗飞逝——

1473

We talked with each other about each other
Though neither of us spoke—
We were listening to the seconds① Races
And the Hoofs of the Clock—
Pausing in Front of our Palsied Faces
Time compassion took—
Arks of Reprieve he offered to us—
Ararats—we took—

1473

我们相互谈论彼此
虽然谁也没说一个字——
我们倾听秒针的匆匆步履
时钟的蹄子——
在我们麻痹的脸前歇息
满怀怜悯的时间——
他给我们暂时避难的方舟——
我们接受了——亚拉腊山②——

1474

Estranged from Beauty—none can be—
For Beauty is Infinity—
And power to be finite ceased
Before Identity was creased③.

---

① "seconds" 在 1960 年阅读版中为 "seconds'"。
② 亚拉腊山(Ararat):位于土耳其东部,据《圣经·旧约·创世纪》第 8 章第 4 节记述,大洪水过后,诺亚方舟停靠于亚拉腊山:"And the ark rested in the seventh month, on the seventeenth day of the month, upon the mountains of Ararat." (Genesis 8:4)。
③ "creased" 在 1960 年阅读版中为 "leased"。

1474
疏远美——没人能如愿——
因为美就是无限——
那成为有限的力已成乌有
先于身份起皱。

1475
Fame is the one that does not stay—
It's occupant must die
Or out of sight of estimate
Ascend incessantly—
Or be that most insolvent thing
A Lightning in the Germ—
Electrical the embryo
But we demand the Flame

1475
名声这东西可不会驻停——
它的占有者都会死去
或者无法预计前景
会上升一直持续——
或者是那最资不抵债的东西
胚芽中的闪电——
是胚胎带上了电
但我们仍渴求那火焰

1476
His voice decrepit was with Joy—
Her words did totter so
How old the News of Love must be
To make Lips elderly
That purled a moment since with Glee—
Is it Delight or Woe—
Or Terror—that do decorate
This livid interview—

1476

他衰朽的声音透出欢欣——
他吐出的言词飘忽不定
这爱的消息得有多古老
能让嘴唇变得年事已高
竟因一时的欢喜而絮叨——
是快乐或是悲伤——
或是惊惧——这样装扮
这铅灰色的会面——

1477

How destitute is he
Whose Gold is firm
Who finds it every time
The small stale Sum—
When Love with but a Pence
Will so display
As is a disrespect
To India.

1477①

他多么贫寒
他的金子稳稳当当
他每次总发现
还是那一小份陈旧份量——
当爱只用一个便士

---

① 题解：有钱不花，总嫌钱少，其钱数目总不变，这样的人无异于穷人；哪怕只有一便士，但花出去了，便显出同等大的价值，简直可以不屑于印度的富庶。据《圣经·新约·马太福音》第25章第30节记述，耶稣惩罚那拿了一千银子去埋在地下，既不生财也损财的人，将他抛入野外黑暗中："And cast ye the unprofitable servant into outer darkness: there shall be weeping and gnashing of teeth."（Matthew 25：30）。

便可显示同样的价值
不啻是对印度
一种轻视。

1478

Look back on Time, with kindly eyes—
He doubtless did his best—
How softly sinks that trembling sun
In Human Nature's West—

1478

回望时光,双眼慈祥——
他的确已倾尽力量——
看颤抖的太阳如何轻柔地沉降
在人性的西方——

1479

The Devil—had he fidelity
Would be the best friend—
Because he has ability—
But Devils cannot mend—
Perfidy is the virtue
That would but he resign
The Devil—without question
Were thoroughly divine

1479①

魔鬼——假如他忠贞
会是最好的朋友——
因为他有能力——
但魔鬼没法补救——

---

① 题解:类似的对宗教逆反的诗也可见于第1461首等。

背信弃义就是美德
假如他肯一直放任
魔鬼——毫无疑问
是彻头彻尾的神圣

1480

The fascinating chill that music leaves

Is Earth's corroboration

Of Ecstasy's impediment—

'Tis Rapture's germination

In timid and tumultuous soil

A fine—estranging creature—

To something upper wooing us

But not to our Creator—

1480①

这音乐留下的迷人寒意

是大地证实

对迷狂的遏制——

这是狂喜的肇始

在羞怯又骚动的土里

一种精妙——疏远的生物——

把我们诱向某种上界的东西

但不是去往我们的造物主——

1481

The way Hope builds his House

It is not with a sill—

Nor Rafter—has that Edifice

---

① 本诗约写于1879年。艾米莉·狄金森曾在1872年末写给文学导师希金森的一封信中提到，季节轮替导致的大地变化所带来的伤害如音乐一般："When I saw you last, it was Mighty Summer—Now the Grass is Glass and the Meadow Stucco, and 'Still Waters' in the Pool where the Frog drinks. These Behaviors of the Year hurt almost like Music—"（L381）。

But only Pinnacle—

Abode in as supreme
This superficies
As if it were of Ledges smit
Or mortised with the Laws—

1481①
希望筑造他的房
与基石无关——
那大厦——也没有椽子
只有塔尖——

安居其内同样极高级
这种外貌
仿佛是用岩脊凿造
或用法则打榫接牢——

1482
'Tis whiter than an Indian Pipe—
'Tis dimmer than a Lace—
No stature has it, like a Fog
When you approach the place—
Nor any voice imply it here
Or intimate it there
A spirit—how doth it accost—
What function hath the Air?
This limitless Hyperbole
Each one of us shall be—
'Tis Drama—if Hypothesis
It be not Tragedy—

---

① 描写希望主题的诗还可参见第254、1392、1547首等。

1482①

它的白胜过水晶兰——
它暗淡赛过花边——
它无固定形状,像一团雾烟
当你走近那地方——
无一丝声响暗示它在此
或意指它在彼
一个幽灵——它如何搭讪——
空气有何效力?
我们每人都将是
这无限制的夸大——
这是一出戏——如果假设
它不是悲剧的话——

1483

The Robin is a Gabriel
In humble circumstances—
His Dress denotes him socially,
Of Transport's Working Classes—
He has the punctuality
Of the New England Farmer—
The same oblique integrity,
A Vista vastly warmer—

A small but sturdy Residence,
A self denying Household,
The Guests of Perspicacity
Are all that cross his Threshold—
As covert as a Fugitive,
Cajoling Consternation
By Ditties to the Enemy
And Sylvan Punctuation—

---

① 第1250首诗提到二月是"White as an Indian Pipe."。

1483①

知更鸟是加百列天使②

处于卑微的境地——

他的衣着表明他社会地位,

是运输业的工人阶级——

他严格守时

像新英格兰农民——

同样有不易明瞭的正直,

一幅温馨得多的场景——

---

① 描写知更鸟的诗还有第634、828首等。第285首诗提到:"The Robin's my Criterion for Tune—"。

② 加百列天使(Gabriel):大天使之一,是报喜天使。据《圣经·新约·路加福音》第1章记述,加百列奉神旨向童女玛丽亚预报耶稣将降生:"And in the sixth month the angel Gabriel was sent from God unto a city of Galilee, named Nazareth, To a virgin espoused to a man whose name was Joseph, of the house of David; and the virgin's name was Mary. And the angel came in unto her, and said, Hail, thou that art highly favoured, the Lord is with thee: blessed art thou among women.... And the angel said unto her, Fear not, Mary: for thou hast found favour with God. And, behold, thou shalt conceive in thy womb, and bring forth a son, and shalt call his name JESUS." (Luke 1: 26 - 28, 30 - 31)。据《圣经·旧约·但以理书》记载,加百列也曾现身于但以理面前传话:"And I heard a man's voice between the banks of Ulai, which called, and said, Gabriel, make this man to understand the vision. So he came near where I stood: and when he came, I was afraid, and fell upon my face: but he said unto me, Understand, O son of man: for at the time of the end shall be the vision. Now as he was speaking with me, I was in a deep sleep on my face toward the ground: but he touched me, and set me upright. And he said, Behold, I will make thee know what shall be in the last end of the indignation: for at the time appointed the end shall be. The ram which thou sawest having two horns are the kings of Media and Persia. And the rough goat is the king of Grecia: and the great horn that is between his eyes is the first king. Now that being broken, whereas four stood up for it, four kingdoms shall stand up out of the nation, but not in his power. And in the latter time of their kingdom, when the transgressors are come to the full, a king of fierce countenance, and understanding dark sentences, shall stand up. And his power shall be mighty, but not by his own power: and he shall destroy wonderfully, and shall prosper, and practise, and shall destroy the mighty and the holy people. And through his policy also he shall cause craft to prosper in his hand; and he shall magnify himself in his heart, and by peace shall destroy many: he shall also stand up against the Prince of princes; but he shall be broken without hand. And the vision of the evening and the morning which was told is true: wherefore shut thou up the vision; for it shall be for many days." (Daniel 8: 16 - 26)。

一处小而坚固的居所，
一个自我隐蔽的家园，
唯有观察敏锐的宾客
才能跨过他门槛——
像逃犯一样隐蔽，
用小曲在敌人心中
勾起惊惧
以及林中时隐时现的行踪——

1484

We shall find the Cube of the Rainbow.
Of that, there is no doubt.
But the Arc of a Lover's conjecture
Eludes the finding out.

1484①

我们会找出彩虹的立方体。
这一点，毋庸置疑。
但一个恋人臆测的弧线
总将发现躲避。

1485

Love is done when Love's begun,
Sages say,
But have Sages known?
Truth adjourn your Boon
Without Day.

1485②

爱一开始就意味着截止，

---

① 本诗是艾米莉·狄金森1880年1月寄给朋友爱德华·塔克曼的夫人莎拉的一封信的结尾，诗之前的信写道："I read your little Letter—it had like Bliss—the minute length—It were dearer had you protracted it, but the Sparrow must not propound his Crumb—"（L628）。

② 艾米莉·狄金森把本诗寄给了朋友爱德华·塔克曼的夫人莎拉。

智者明言,
但智者可知?
真理暂缓你的恩赐
没有期限。

1486

Her spirit rose to such a height
Her countenance it did inflate
Like one that fed on awe.
More prudent to assault the dawn
Than merit the ethereal scorn
That effervesced from her.

1486①

她的情绪如此高涨
她的面容确实膨胀
像个以敬畏为食的人。
攻击黎明更显明智
胜于赞美缕缕蔑视
从她身上外渗。

1487

The Savior must have been
A docile Gentleman—
To come so far so cold a Day
For little Fellowmen—

The Road to Bethlehem
Since He and I were Boys
Was leveled, but for that 'twould be
A rugged billion Miles—

---

① 艾米莉·狄金森曾把本诗最后三行寄给自己的嫂子苏珊。

1487①
救世主肯定是
一位温良的绅士——
这么冷的天里迢迢而至
就为了卑微的人子——

去往伯利恒的路
自我和他孩提起
就被整平,若非如此
定有崎岖十亿英里——

1488

Birthday of but a single pang
That there are less to come—
Afflictive is the Adjective
But affluent the doom—

1488②
仅是一次剧痛的生日
未来会越过越少——
令人苦恼的是那形容词
但厄运足够富饶——

1489

A Dimple in the Tomb
Makes that ferocious Room
A Home—

---

① 艾米莉·狄金森于1880年11月(一说1881年春天)寄给文学导师希金森的一封信里随附了4首诗,本诗是其中一首。信中给4首诗分别起了标题,本诗的标题是"Christ's Day",信中对4首诗标题的提示如下:"They are Christ's Birthday—Cupid's Sermon—A Humming-Bird—and My Country's Wardrobe—."(L675)。

② 这是艾米莉·狄金森写赠给嫂子苏珊并祝贺她50岁生日的诗。苏珊40岁生日时艾米莉·狄金森也写了一首诗祝贺(见第1156首)。诗大意是:生日过一次痛一次,且过一次少一次,最令人苦恼的是那个形容词"single",但是厄运却从来都不会少,从来都不是"single"。

1489①

坟墓中的一个笑靥
让那个残暴的房间
成为家园——

1490

The Face in evanescence lain
Is more distinct than ours—
And ours surrendered for it's sake
As Capsules are for Flower's—
Or is it the confiding sheen
Dissenting to be won
Descending to enamor us
Of Detriment divine?

1490②

那张逐渐消失的脸
比我们的更为鲜明——
我们的因此而枯萎
像蒴果为花朵消形——
或竟是那信任的光彩
不同意被赢取
下来令我们醉心于
那神圣的伤害？

---

① 这是艾米莉·狄金森1880年3月底或4月初写给文学导师希金森的一封慰问信的结尾诗，诗之前的信写道："Most of our Moments are Moments of Preface—'Seven Weeks' is a long Life—if it is all lived—The little Memoir was very touching. I am sorry she was not willing to stay—…The flight of such a fraction takes all our Numbers Home—'Room for one more' was a plea for Heaven—…The route of your little Fugitive must be a tender wonder—and yet"（L641）。此前不久的1880年3月，希金森1880年1月26日出生的女儿路易莎（Louisa）不幸夭折，去世时才7周大。

② 艾米莉·狄金森从报纸上得知，文学导师希金森的女儿路易莎在1880年3月不幸夭折，去世时才7周大，于是在1880年3月给希金森寄去了本诗，诗之前只有一句引言："I was very sorry for what the Paper told me—I hoped it was not true—"（L630）。

1491

The Road to Paradise is plain,
And holds scarce one.
Not that it is not firm
But we presume
A Dimpled Road
Is more preferred.
The Belles of Paradise are few—
Not me—nor you—
But unsuspected things—
Mines have no Wings.

1491①

到天堂的路很平坦,
但路上人影稀罕。
并非它不坚实
而是我们预计
凹凸不平的路
更让人爱慕。
天堂的美女寥寥无几——
非我——非你——
而是些不曾意想的东西——
宝矿可没有翅翼。

1492

"And with what body do they come?" —
Then they *do* come—Rejoice!
What Door—What Hour—Run—run—My Soul!
Illuminate the House!

---

① 本诗是艾米莉·狄金森1880年7月4日写给霍兰夫人的一封信的部分内容,诗前引言写道: "The Weather is like Africa and the Flowers like Asia and the Numidian Heart of your 'Little Friend' neither slow nor chill—" (L650)。

"Body!" Then real—a Face and Eyes—
To know that it is them! —
Paul knew the Man that knew the News—
He passed through Bethlehem—

1492①
"他们带什么身体前来?"② ——
那么他们*真的*来了——令人欢喜!
进什么门——在什么时辰——快跑——快跑——我的灵魂!
照亮那房子!

"身体!"那是真的——有脸有眼——
可知那就是他们! ——
保罗认识了解消息的那个人③——
他曾路过伯利恒——

1493
Could that sweet Darkness where they dwell
Be once disclosed to us
The clamor for their loveliness
Would burst the Loneliness—

---

① 本诗是艾米莉·狄金森 1880 年 10 月写给马萨诸塞州威尔斯利公理会教堂(Congregational Church in Wellesley, Massachusetts) 的牧师佩雷斯 (Perez Dickinson Cowan, 1843—1923) 的 一封信 (L671) 的部分内容。佩雷斯是她的表弟,他年幼的女儿玛格丽特 (Margaret McClung Cowan, 1876—1879) 于 1879 年 11 月 8 日去世。不久,他寄给艾米莉·狄金森一本回顾女儿短暂一生的纪念册。艾米莉·狄金森回信确认收到了纪念册。信内的本诗,半是诗歌半像散文,是献给佩雷斯女儿的挽歌。

② 他们带什么身体前来: 此句出自《圣经·新约·哥林多前书 1》第 15 章第 35 节圣保罗 (St. Paul) 的问话: "But some man will say, How are the dead raised up? and with what body do they come?"(或有人问,死人怎样复活。带着什么身体来呢?) (1 Corinthians 15: 35)。圣保罗还对人生前的身体和死后复活的身体作了辨析: "It is sown a natural body; it is raised a spiritual body. There is a natural body, and there is a spiritual body." (所种的是血气的身体,复活的是灵性的身体。若有血气的身体,也必有灵性的身体。) (1 Corinthians 15: 44)。

③ 那个人: 这里指耶稣 (Jesus)。

1493①

如若他们寓居的那片甜美黑暗
一旦向我们透露
对他们的美好发出的欢呼
定会冲破孤独——

1494

The competitions of the sky
Corrodeless ply.

1494②

天空中的种种竞争
无腐蚀的发生③。

1495

The Thrill came slowly like a Boon for
Centuries delayed
It's fitness growing like the Flood

---

① 玛利亚（Maria Whitney, 1830—1909）是艾米莉·狄金森的朋友鲍尔斯的夫人玛丽的亲戚。本诗是艾米莉·狄金森约 1880 年 6 月写给玛利亚的一封信的部分内容，信中本诗之前写道："I shall miss saying to Vinnie when we hear the Northampton Bell—as in subtle states of the West we do—'Miss Whitney is going to Church'—though must not everywhere be Church to Hearts that have or have had—a Friend？"（L643）。玛利亚从执教的北安普顿斯密斯学院（Smith College in Northampton）离职，并可能离开那里，但未知去往何处。对艾米莉·狄金森来说仍是"甜美黑暗"，但一旦能向她透露，那么，如信中所言，北安普顿教堂大钟（Northampton Bell）的欢声，定能解艾米莉·狄金森心中的寂寥孤独。

② 本诗是艾米莉·狄金森约 1880 年写给弗朗西斯·诺克罗斯和路易丝·诺克罗斯两位表妹的一封信的开头部分，诗之前有一行引言："Did the 'stars differ' from each other in anything but 'glory,' there would be often envy."（L669）。信中的引言源自《圣经·新约·哥林多前书》第 15 章第 41 节圣保罗（St. Paul）所言："There is one glory of the sun, and another glory of the moon, and another glory of the stars: for one star differeth from another star in glory."（日有日的荣光，月有月的荣光，星有星的荣光。这星和那星的荣光，也有区别。）（1 Corinthians 15: 41）

③ 发生（ply）：据 Emily Dickinson Lexicon，原文 "ply" 意指 "occur; happen; take place; proceed; continue"。

In sumptuous solitude—
The desolation only missed
While Rapture changed it's Dress
And stood amazed before the Change
In ravished Holiness—

1495①

颤栗缓缓袭来像一种恩赐
迟到了几个世纪
它的畅意增涨像洪水漫溢
渗入丰盈的孤寂——
荒芜会思念不已
唯当狂喜更换其华衣
并惊讶面对这种变异
陷入一种神圣的沉迷——

1496

All that I do
Is in review
To his enamored mind
I know his eye
Where e'er I ply
Is pushing close behind

Not any Port
Nor any flight
But he doth there preside
What omnipresence lies in wait
For her to be a Bride

---

① 题解：狂喜带来的颤栗像一种恩赐，虽迟来了很久，但它引起的畅意像洪水上涨，漫溢进我内心的孤寂，顿时觉得丰盈豪奢，不再似从前内心充满荒芜凄凉之感。只有当狂喜变换了衣装，激情不再，内心才会恢复荒芜凄凉，才会再次思念那狂喜的颤栗，面对眼前这种变化，仍陷入对神圣狂喜的沉迷中。

1496

我所做的全部
就是回顾
他迷恋的心灵
我知道他的目光
不论我徜徉何方
都紧跟身后随行

不是什么口岸
不是什么飞翔
但他确在那里主掌
怎样的无处不在埋伏着等待
等待她成为新娘

1497

Facts by our side are never sudden
Until they look around
And then they scare us like a spectre
Protruding from the Ground—

The height of our portentous Neighbor
We never know—
Till summoned to his recognition
By an Adieu—

Adieu for whence
The sage cannot conjecture
The bravest die
As ignorant of their resumption
As you or I—

1497

我们身边的事实从不突然
直至他们环顾

然后惊吓我们像一个幽灵
从地下冒出——

我们不祥邻居的高度
我们从不了解——
直至被召去对他辨识
用一次告别——

告别前往何处
智者也猜不出
最勇敢的人死去
对他们复活的无知
一如我或你——

1498

Glass was the Street—in tinsel Peril
Tree and Traveller stood—
Filled was the Air with merry venture
Hearty with Boys the Road—

Shot the lithe Sleds like shod vibrations
Emphasized and gone
It is the Past's supreme italic
Makes this Present mean—

1498①

街道是玻璃——危险又明亮
树木和旅人站在上面——
空气充满快乐的冒险
路上嬉闹的男孩随处可见——

---

① 题解：或描写冬季结冰的街道上的场景。

柔韧雪橇射出去像穿着鞋在摇摆
始而清晰继而消弭
是过去的辉煌存在①
使这眼前平淡无奇——

1499

How firm Eternity must look
To crumbling men like me
The only Adamant Estate
In all Identity—

How mighty to the insecure
Thy Physiognomy
To whom not any Face cohere—
Unless concealed in thee

1499

永恒看起来多么稳固
对如我般摇摇欲坠的人
那是唯一坚实的庄园
不论从哪方面确认——

对于颠沛的人多么显赫
你那容颜
没有一张脸能与之贴合——
除非隐匿在你里面

1500

It came his turn to beg—
The begging for the life

---

① 辉煌存在（supreme italic）："italic" 一词在艾米莉·狄金森的诗中使用4次，在本诗中意指 "grandeur; magnificence"，原文 "supreme italic" 相当于双重凸显或强调了过去的辉煌存在。

Is different from another Alms
'Tis Penury in Chief—

I scanned his narrow realm
I gave him leave to live
Lest Gratitude revive the snake
Though smuggled his reprieve

1500
轮到他来乞求——
乞求要生命
不同于另一种施舍
它主要是赤贫——

我扫视他狭窄的王国
我准许他活命
以免感激会让蛇复活
虽然偷带了他的缓刑

附录 1955年集注版与1960年阅读版词汇和标点差异一览表

序号	1955年集注版	1960年阅读版	诗序号
1	Ought to	or'ter	1201
2	did'nt	didn't	1201
3	was'nt	wasn't	1201
4	it's	its	1205、1216、1221、1225、1226、1232、1239、1243、1247、1248、1271、1281、1295、1298、1313、1319、1323、1327、1340、1361、1363、1364、1367、1387、1392、1396、1407、1411、1424、1425、1428、1430、1431、1434、1438、1440、1448、1449、1452、1459、1463、1464、1468、1475、1490、1495
5	Adders Tongue	Adder's Tongue	1213（1878年版）
6	hot.	hot	1213
7	Tomb.	Tomb	1221
8	For a Souvenir	For a Souvenir—	1226
9	2个诗节	3个诗节	1239
10	Traveller	Traveller.	1239
11	Seeds the Stars—	Seeds the Stars	1241
12	me and you	me and you.	1257
13	absolute	absolute,	1260
14	first it be	first it be,	1260
15	Travel	Traverse	1263
16	offence	oppress	1263
17	esoteric Time	esoteric Time.	1276
18	come along.	come along	1281

续表

序号	1955年集注版	1960年阅读版	诗序号
19	did'st	could'st	1282
20	Our's	Ours	1304
21	your's	yours	1304
22	tranquility	tranquillity	1339
23	Twixt	'Twixt	1343
24	Vail	Veil	1353
25	Ribin	Ribbon	1363
26	understand	understand—	1383
27	their's	theirs	1410
28	*To her rescinded Bud*	To her rescinded Bud.	1416
29	It's meaning is extinct—	Prospective is extinct—	1417
30	cant	can't	1417
31	graphicer	graphicker	1422
32	for immortality—	for immortality	1431
33	And Kinsmen as divulgeless / As throngs of Down—	And Kindred as responsive/ As Porcelain.	1445
34	dont	don't	1449、1452
35	seconds	seconds'	1473
36	creased	leased	1474

本书获中央高校基本科研业务费专项资金资助（项目编号：CBZZ202303）

The Poems of Emily Dickinson

艾米莉·狄金森诗选 ③

1501~1775首

[美]艾米莉·狄金森 著　　周建新 译

华南理工大学出版社

·广州·

图书在版编目（CIP）数据

艾米莉·狄金森诗选.3，1501～1775首：英汉对照/（美）艾米莉·狄金森（Emily Dickinson）著；周建新译. —广州：华南理工大学出版社，2024.12

ISBN 978-7-5623-7443-5

Ⅰ.①艾… Ⅱ.①艾… ②周… Ⅲ.①诗集-美国-近代-英、汉 Ⅳ.①I712.24

中国国家版本馆CIP数据核字（2023）第209446号

艾米莉·狄金森诗选.3（1501～1775首）
（美）艾米莉·狄金森（Emily Dickinson）著　周建新　译

出 版 人：房俊东
出版发行：华南理工大学出版社
　　　　　（广州五山华南理工大学17号楼，邮编510640）
　　　　　http://hg.cb.scut.edu.cn　　　E-mail：scutc13@scut.edu.cn
　　　　　营销部电话：020-87113487　87111048（传真）
策划编辑：吴翠微
责任编辑：陈　蓉
责任校对：梁樱雯
印 刷 者：广州小明数码印刷有限公司
开　　本：787mm×1092mm　1/20　印张：11.3　字数：245千
版　　次：2024年12月第1版　印次：2024年12月第1次印刷
定　　价：168.00元（全三册）

版权所有　盗版必究　印装差错　负责调换

译者前言

　　本书一如前五个选译本,是从约翰逊编辑的 1955 年集注版《艾米莉·狄金森诗歌全集》中按顺序选取第 1501～1775 首诗,译为中文,仍取英汉对照体例。约翰逊编的 1955 年集注版与其编的 1960 年阅读版在文本上有些许不同,包括字词、标点等。字词、标点方面的差异已在附录的对照表中列出,读者可自行查阅。本书对一些难读、难懂之处提供了题解或注释,比之前五本选译本提供的量要多一些,但远未涵盖全部。

　　本书收录的第 1501～1648 首诗整理自艾米莉·狄金森诗歌原稿,写作年代是 1880 年至艾米莉·狄金森去世的 1886 年,这 148 首诗大多表面平静,但其下涌动着情感,每一首诗都有沉甸甸的内涵,表明此时的诗作者虽仍为人生悲欢无奈缠绕,但总体上也能平静看淡,体现了虽仍被触痛但也能超脱的心态,这恐怕是艾米莉·狄金森生命晚期的心态,而此时的她才刚步入 50 岁的人生年龄段,不免令人感到悲凉。

　　第 1649～1709 首诗是由艾米莉·狄金森的嫂子苏珊按艾米莉·狄金森诗歌原稿誊抄而来,原稿已遗失,因此无法知晓这些诗歌的创作年份。这 61 首誊抄版诗歌完全没有了艾米莉·狄金森诗歌的形式风格,其标点、节奏、韵律、字词关系等,具有大众诗歌的特征,具有符合大众审美诗歌的流畅性、音乐性、易解性等特点,读起来很有熟悉感,表明这些诗歌不是严格意义上的艾米莉·狄金森诗歌,而是经苏珊之手,改变成了流行的大众诗歌样式的苏珊式诗歌。苏珊是才女,尤擅散文,具有较好的文学素养,这些诗歌体现了其在诗歌方面的大众化品位。

　　艾米莉·狄金森去世后,其妹妹维尼(Vinnie,即 Lavinia Norcross Dickinson,1833—1899)首先找到苏珊,希望苏珊可以帮忙整理艾米莉·狄金森的诗稿,但由于苏珊工作效率不高,一拖再拖,维尼转而请哥哥奥斯汀的情人托德夫人帮忙整理。本书第 1710～1775 首诗是由托德夫人按艾米莉·狄金森诗歌原稿誊抄而来,原稿也已遗失,也无法知晓这些诗歌的创作年份。这 66 首誊抄版诗歌表面看似具有明显的艾米莉·狄金森诗歌的形式特征,实则这些形式特征赋予诗歌的表述风格与艾米莉·狄金森诗歌的表述风格大异其趣。如果说苏珊式的诗歌仍具有大众诗歌的特征，这66首托德夫人式的诗歌则既无大众诗歌的品位，也无艾米莉·狄金森诗歌的内涵品质。托德夫人十分仰慕艾米莉·狄金森的诗歌才华，她劳心劳力，积极编辑出版最初几本艾米莉·狄金森诗歌和书信选集，但囿于自身文学素养和诗歌感受性的不足，她虽努力从诗歌原稿中搜寻、还原艾米莉·狄金森诗歌原貌，但终未捕得原诗灵魂，从而使其誊抄版成为一种扭曲、怪异的诗歌版本。译者翻译苏珊式的诗歌时，起初无法下手，尔后落笔别扭、生疏，而译托德夫人式的诗歌之初，则惶惶无措，被迫停笔几周。因艾米莉·狄金森表达的语气、语调、态度、节奏、快慢、长短等，译者已了然于心，其形象已栩栩如生多年，如今要跳出艾米莉·狄金森模式，进入托德夫人式的诗歌，以另外的然而却未知的模式进行表达，一时竟无所适从。

约翰逊版全集共1775首诗，本书是第六本诗歌选译集，也是最后一本。本书译文之不足在所难免，请读者诸君不吝批评指正。由于艾米莉·狄金森的诗歌一般都没有标题，本书目录中取每首诗第一行作为标题，书中诗歌的序号均按约翰逊版中的序号。题解或注释中所引《圣经》原文均来自 King James 版。提及艾米莉·狄金森书信全集中的某一封信时，以"L"开头，后接信的序号。以上提到的约翰逊两个全集本以及狄金森书信全集是指：

Dickinson, Emily. *The Poems of Emily Dickinson: Including Variant Readings Critically Compared with All Known Manuscripts*. Ed. Thomas H. Johnson. 3 vols. Cambridge, MA: Belknap Press of Harvard University. Press, 1955.

Dickinson, Emily. *The Letters of Emily Dickinson*. Eds. Thomas H. Johnson, Theodora Van Wagenen Ward. 3 vols. Cambridge, MA: Belknap Press of Harvard University. Press, 1958.

Dickinson, Emily. *The Complete Poems of Emily Dickinson*. Ed. Thomas H. Johnson. Boston: Little, Brown and Company, 1960.

译者
2024年9月

目 录

1501	It's little Ether Hood ·················	1
	它以太的小兜套·················	1
1502	I saw the wind within her ·············	1
	我看见风在她内部·················	3
1503	More than the Grave is closed to me— ···	4
	不仅坟墓对我闭门—— ·············	4
1504	Of whom so dear ····················	5
	谁的如此可爱 ·····················	5
1505	She could not live upon the Past ········	5
	她无法靠过去生活 ·················	5
1506	Summer is shorter than any one— ······	5
	夏季短过任何季节—— ·············	6
1507	The Pile of Years is not so high ········	6
	岁月的堆积并无多高·················	6
1508	You cannot make Remembrance grow ····	7
	你无法让记忆生长·················	7
1509	Mine Enemy is growing old— ··········	8
	我的敌人正在苍老—— ·············	8
1510	How happy is the little Stone ··········	8
	多么快乐的小石头·················	9
1511	My country need not change her gown, ··	9
	我的国家不必更换她的外衣,·········	10
1512	All things swept sole away ············	10
	万物一扫而尽 ·····················	10
1513	"Go travelling with us!" ·············	11
	"去和我们出游!" ·················	11
1514	An Antiquated Tree ·················	11

	一棵古老的树 ·································	11
1515	The Things that never can come back, are several— ········	12
	一去再不复返的事物，只是少数—— ·················	12
1516	No Autumn's intercepting Chill ···················	13
	秋季拦截的寒意 ·····························	13
1517	How much of Source escapes with thee— ············	13
	有多少源泉随你逃之夭夭—— ····················	14
1518	Not seeing, still we know— ·····················	14
	没看见，我们也知晓—— ·······················	14
1519	The Dandelion's pallid tube ·····················	15
	蒲公英苍白的茎管 ···························	15
1520	The stem of a departed Flower ···················	15
	花朵已谢的茎枝 ·····························	16
1521	The Butterfly upon the Sky, ····················	16
	天空的蝴蝶, ·······························	16
1522	His little Hearse like Figure ····················	17
	它小灵车般的身型 ···························	17
1523	We never know we go when we are going— ·········	18
	我们走时毫不意识到要走—— ····················	18
1524	A faded Boy—in sallow Clothes ··················	18
	一个憔悴的男孩——身穿灰黄衣裳 ················	19
1525	He lived the Life of Ambush ····················	19
	他过着隐伏的生活 ···························	19
1526	His oriental heresies ···························	20
	他的东方邪说 ·······························	20
1527	Oh give it Motion—deck it sweet ·················	20
	啊，让它动起来——把它打扮得可爱 ··············	21
1528	The Moon upon her fluent Route ··················	21
	康庄大道上的月亮 ···························	21
1529	'Tis Seasons since the Dimpled War ················	22
	那次酒窝大战以来已过去几季 ····················	22
1530	A Pang is more conspicuous in Spring ···············	22

	一阵剧痛在春天更引人注目 ……………………… 23
1531	Above Oblivion's Tide there is a Pier ……………… 23
	遗忘的潮水之上一个码头屹立 ……………………… 23
1532	From all the Jails the Boys and Girls …………… 24
	自所有牢房里男孩和女孩们 ………………………… 24
1533	On that specific Pillow …………………………… 24
	在那特定的枕头上 …………………………………… 25
1534	Society for me my misery ………………………… 25
	社交对我而言是痛苦 ………………………………… 25
1535	The Life that tied too tight escapes …………… 25
	束缚太紧的生命一旦逃逸 …………………………… 26
1536	There comes a warning like a spy ……………… 26
	像密探发出的一个警示 ……………………………… 26
1537	Candor—my tepid friend— ……………………… 26
	率直——我不温不火的朋友—— …………………… 27
1538	Follow wise Orion ………………………………… 27
	跟随智慧的猎户座 …………………………………… 27
1539	Now I lay thee down to Sleep— ………………… 27
	如今我安放你入睡—— ……………………………… 28
1540	As imperceptibly as Grief ………………………… 28
	像忧伤一样难以察觉 ………………………………… 28
1541	No matter where the Saints abide, ……………… 29
	不论圣徒们停驻何处, ……………………………… 29
1542	Come show thy Durham Breast …………………… 29
	来把你达拉谟牛般的胸脯 …………………………… 30
1543	Obtaining but our own Extent …………………… 30
	只需获得我们自己的空间 …………………………… 31
1544	Who has not found the Heaven—below— ……… 31
	谁没发现天堂——在下界—— …………………… 31
1545	The Bible is an antique Volume— ……………… 31
	圣经是一卷古书—— ………………………………… 32
1546	Sweet Pirate of the heart, ……………………… 33

	心灵温柔的海盗，	33
1547	Hope is a subtle Glutton—	33
	希望是个狡猾的贪食者——	34
1548	Meeting by Accident,	34
	在意外中邂逅，	34
1549	My Wars are laid away in Books—	35
	我的战争都写进了书里——	35
1550	The pattern of the sun	36
	太阳的式样	36
1551	Those—dying then,	36
	那些——从前在弥留时候，	36
1552	Within thy Grave!	37
	在你坟墓里！	37
1553	Bliss is the plaything of the child—	37
	幸福是孩童的玩具——	37
1554	"Go tell it"—What a Message—	37
	"去说出来"——是什么信息——	38
1555	I groped for him before I knew	39
	我不知不觉将他搜寻	39
1556	Image of Light, Adieu—	39
	光的形象，再见——	39
1557	Lives he in any other world	40
	他活在其他任何世界	40
1558	Of Death I try to think like this—	40
	对于死亡我试着这么想——	40
1559	Tried always and Condemned by thee	41
	一向由你审判和定罪	41
1560	To be forgot by thee	42
	被你忘记	42
1561	No Brigadier throughout the Year	43
	一年中没有哪位准将	43
1562	Her Losses make our Gains ashamed—	44

		她的损失使我们的收获蒙羞——	45
1563	By homely gift and hindered Words	45
	家常的礼物和支吾的话语	45
1564	Pass to thy Rendezvous of Light,	46
	去到你光的约会地，	46
1565	Some Arrows slay but whom they strike—	46
	有些箭只能杀死被射中的人——	46
1566	Climbing to reach the costly Hearts	47
	努力攀抵那些昂贵的心	47
1567	The Heart has many Doors—	47
	心有许多门扉——	48
1568	To see her is a Picture—	48
	眼见她是一幅画——	48
1569	The Clock strikes one that just struck two—	49
	曾敲两次的钟只敲了一次——	49
1570	Forever honored be the Tree	49
	那棵树永为人称道	50
1571	How slow the Wind—	50
	风真慢——	51
1572	We wear our sober Dresses when we die,	51
	我们死时穿着素衣，	51
1573	To the bright east she flies,	51
	她飞向明亮的东方，	52
1574	No ladder needs the bird but skies	53
	鸟儿需要天空而非梯子	53
1575	The Bat is dun, with wrinkled Wings—	53
	蝙蝠暗褐，翅膀皱褶——	54
1576	The Spirit lasts—but in what mode—	55
	灵魂一直延续——但以什么方式——	56
1577	Morning is due to all—	56
	清晨莅临所有人——	57
1578	Blossoms will run away,	57

	花儿终会凋残，	57
1579	It would not know if it were spurned,	57
	它不知道它会否被拒，	58
1580	We shun it ere it comes,	58
	它还没来我们就躲避，	59
1581	The farthest Thunder that I heard	59
	我听到的最远的雷声	60
1582	Where Roses would not dare to go,	61
	玫瑰不敢去的地方，	61
1583	Witchcraft was hung, in History,	61
	巫术已被绞死，在历史里，	61
1584	Expanse cannot be lost—	61
	浩瀚不可能失去——	62
1585	The Bird her punctual music brings	63
	鸟儿带来她准时的音乐	63
1586	To her derided Home	63
	来到她受嘲笑的家	64
1587	He ate and drank the precious Words—	64
	他饮食珍贵的文字——	65
1588	This Me—that walks and works—must die,	65
	这个我——行走和工作——必须死，	65
1589	Cosmopolites without a plea	66
	世界公民没有请求	66
1590	Not at Home to Callers	66
	对来访者无人在家	67
1591	The Bobolink is gone—the Rowdy of the Meadow—	67
	食米鸟已离去——那草地的喧闹者——	68
1592	The Lassitudes of Contemplation	68
	沉思的困倦	69
1593	There came a Wind like a Bugle—	69
	一阵风吹来像号角——	69
1594	Immured in Heaven!	70

	监禁在天堂！ ……………………………………………	70
1595	Declaiming Waters none may dread— ………………	71
	滔滔之水无人惧怕—— ……………………………………	71
1596	Few, yet enough, …………………………………………	71
	少，也已足够， ……………………………………………	71
1597	'Tis not the swaying frame we miss, …………………	72
	我们怀念的不是摇晃的身影， ……………………………	72
1598	Who is it seeks my Pillow Nights— …………………	72
	是谁找寻我安枕的夜晚—— ………………………………	73
1599	Though the great Waters sleep, ………………………	73
	尽管浩瀚之水已安睡， ……………………………………	74
1600	Upon his Saddle sprung a Bird ………………………	74
	一只鸟跳上他马鞍 …………………………………………	75
1601	Of God we ask one favor, ………………………………	75
	我们求上帝一个恩惠， ……………………………………	76
1602	Pursuing you in your transitions, ……………………	76
	在你过渡时期追寻你， ……………………………………	76
1603	The going from a world we know ……………………	76
	从我们了解的世界 …………………………………………	77
1604	We send the Wave to find the Wave— ………………	77
	我们派波浪去找波浪—— …………………………………	78
1605	Each that we lose takes part of us; …………………	78
	每一次丧失都带走我们的一部分； ………………………	78
1606	Quite empty, quite at rest, ……………………………	78
	空荡荡，静悄悄， …………………………………………	79
1607	Within that little Hive …………………………………	79
	在那小小蜂巢里 ……………………………………………	80
1608	The ecstasy to guess ……………………………………	80
	揣测的狂喜 …………………………………………………	80
1609	Sunset that screens, reveals— ………………………	80
	遮蔽的落日，显露—— ……………………………………	80
1610	Morning that comes but once, ………………………	81

	只出现一次的清晨， …………	81
1611	Their dappled importunity …………	81
	对他们的胡搅蛮缠 …………	81
1612	The Auctioneer of Parting …………	81
	别离的拍卖师 …………	82
1613	Not Sickness stains the Brave, …………	82
	不是疾病玷污了勇士， …………	82
1614	Parting with Thee reluctantly, …………	83
	与你别离依依， …………	83
1615	Oh what a Grace is this, …………	83
	啊这是何等的恩典， …………	83
1616	Who abdicated Ambush …………	84
	谁放弃了隐伏 …………	84
1617	To try to speak, and miss the way …………	84
	想要开口，却不知所以 …………	85
1618	There are two Mays …………	85
	有两个可以 …………	85
1619	Not knowing when the Dawn will come, …………	86
	不知黎明何时来到， …………	86
1620	Circumference thou Bride of Awe …………	86
	寰宇你这敬畏的新娘 …………	86
1621	A Flower will not trouble her, it has so small a Foot, …………	87
	一朵花不会将她打扰，它的脚这么小巧， …………	87
1622	A Sloop of Amber slips away …………	87
	一艘琥珀单桅船悄悄驶离 …………	87
1623	A World made penniless by that departure …………	87
	因那次别离而一文不名的世界 …………	88
1624	Apparently with no surprise …………	88
	显然不感到惊讶 …………	88
1625	Back from the cordial Grave I drag thee …………	89
	从亲切的坟墓里我拽回你 …………	89
1626	No Life can pompless pass away— …………	89

	没有生命可以平淡无奇地逝去——	89
1627	The pedigree of Honey	90
	蜜的谱系	90
1628	A Drunkard cannot meet a Cork	91
	醉汉不可能见到瓶塞	91
1629	Arrows enamored of his Heart—	91
	箭簇迷恋他的心——	92
1630	As from the earth the light Balloon	92
	就像轻气球从地面	92
1631	Oh Future! thou secreted peace	92
	啊未来！你隐匿的宁静	93
1632	So give me back to Death—	93
	那么请把我交还给死亡——	93
1633	Still own thee—still thou art	94
	依然拥有你——你依然活着	94
1634	Talk not to me of Summer Trees	94
	别跟我谈夏天的树木	95
1635	The Jay his Castanet has struck	95
	松鸦已敲起他的响板	95
1636	The Sun in reigning to the West	96
	驶向西方的太阳	96
1637	Is it too late to touch you, Dear?	96
	是不是太迟赶不上你了，亲爱的？	96
1638	Go thy great way!	96
	走你的大道！	97
1639	A Letter is a joy of Earth—	97
	信是人间一种欢愉——	97
1640	Take all away from me, but leave me Ecstasy,	97
	把我的一切带走，但给我留下狂喜，	98
1641	Betrothed to Righteousness might be	98
	许配于正义或许	98
1642	"Red Sea," indeed! Talk not to me	99

	"红海,"确实！别跟我讲	99
1643	Extol thee—could I—Then I will	99
	赞美你——如果可以——我会努力	100
1644	Some one prepared this mighty show	100
	有人准备了这场盛大表演	101
1645	The Ditch is dear to the Drunken man	101
	水沟是醉汉的挚爱	102
1646	Why should we hurry—why indeed	102
	我们为何匆忙——为何这样	103
1647	Of Glory not a Beam is left	103
	一束荣光也没留下	103
1648	The immortality she gave	103
	她永生的献出	104
1649	A Cap of Lead across the sky	104
	一顶铅帽跨过苍天	104
1650	A lane of Yellow led the eye	105
	一条黄色小径把目光带进	105
1651	A Word made Flesh is seldom	105
	有血有肉的字很少	106
1652	Advance is Life's condition	107
	前进是生命的前提	107
1653	As we pass Houses musing slow	107
	正如我们经过一座座房慢慢思量	108
1654	Beauty crowds me till I die	108
	美拥挤我直至我死去	108
1655	Conferring with myself	108
	我正与自己商议	108
1656	Down Time's quaint stream	109
	驶入时光奇异的河流	109
1657	Eden is that old-fashioned House	109
	伊甸园是那所老式房屋	110
1658	Endanger it, and the Demand	110

	危害它，然后索要	111
1659	Fame is a fickle food	111
	声名是无常的食物	111
1660	Glory is that bright tragic thing	112
	荣耀是那光鲜可悲的东西	112
1661	Guest am I to have	112
	我愿有客人	113
1662	He went by sleep that drowsy route	113
	他趁安眠沿那条困倦之道	113
1663	His mind of man, a secret makes	113
	他的人类思想，由一个秘密造就	114
1664	I did not reach Thee	114
	我尚未抵达你	115
1665	I know of people in the Grave	117
	我认识墓中的人们	117
1666	I see thee clearer for the Grave	117
	我看你更清楚因那坟墓	118
1667	I watcher her face to see which way	118
	我盯着她的脸想看从哪个渠道	118
1668	If I could tell how glad I was	119
	如果我能说出我有多高兴	119
1669	In snow thou comest	119
	你在风雪中来到	120
1670	In Winter in my Room	120
	在冬季我的房间里	122
1671	Judgment is justest	123
	审判最显正义	123
1672	Lightly stepped a yellow star	124
	一颗黄色的星轻轻迈步	124
1673	Nature can do no more	124
	大自然不能再做什么	125
1674	Not any sunny tone	125

	没有任何阳光的乐曲 …………………………………………	125
1675	Of this is Day composed …………………………………	126
	一天是这样构成 …………………………………………	126
1676	Of Yellow was the outer Sky ……………………………	126
	那黄色的是外太空 ………………………………………	127
1677	On my volcano grows the Grass ………………………	127
	我的火山上长着青草 ……………………………………	127
1678	Peril as a Possession ……………………………………	127
	危险已是个人财物 ………………………………………	128
1679	Rather arid delight ………………………………………	128
	相当乏味的欢愉 …………………………………………	128
1680	Sometimes with the Heart ………………………………	129
	有时用心 …………………………………………………	129
1681	Speech is one symptom of Affection …………………	129
	言语是爱的一种表示 ……………………………………	129
1682	Summer begins to have the look ………………………	130
	夏季开始有一种神色 ……………………………………	131
1683	That she forgot me was the least ………………………	131
	她把我忘记最不值一提 …………………………………	132
1684	The Blunder is in estimate ……………………………	132
	错误是在估计方面 ………………………………………	132
1685	The butterfly obtains ……………………………………	133
	蝴蝶所获取的 ……………………………………………	133
1686	The event was directly behind Him ……………………	134
	事件就在他身后 …………………………………………	134
1687	The gleam of an heroic Act ……………………………	134
	英雄行为的光芒 …………………………………………	135
1688	The Hills erect their Purple Heads ……………………	135
	群山昂起紫色的头 ………………………………………	135
1689	The look of thee, what is it like ………………………	135
	你的样子，像什么 ………………………………………	136
1690	The ones that disappeared are back …………………	136

	那消失的回来了 …………………………………	136
1691	The overtakelessness of those …………………	137
	那些人的无法超越 ……………………………	137
1692	The right to perish might be tho't ……………	137
	死的权利或许被认为是 ………………………	138
1693	The Sun retired to a cloud ………………………	138
	太阳退入一片云 ………………………………	138
1694	The wind drew off ………………………………	139
	风撤离 …………………………………………	139
1695	There is a solitude of space ……………………	140
	有一种空间的孤寂 ……………………………	140
1696	These are the days that Reindeer love ………	140
	这是驯鹿喜爱的时光 …………………………	141
1697	They talk as slow as Legends grow ……………	141
	他们交谈缓慢如传奇的生长 …………………	141
1698	T'is easier to pity those when dead ……………	142
	对死者惋惜很容易 ……………………………	142
1699	To do a magnanimous thing ……………………	142
	做高尚的事情 …………………………………	142
1700	To tell the Beauty would decrease ……………	143
	说出美会减低 …………………………………	143
1701	To their apartment deep ………………………	143
	他们深处的公寓 ………………………………	144
1702	To-day or this noon ……………………………	144
	今日或今日下午 ………………………………	144
1703	T'was comfort in her Dying Room ……………	144
	这是一种慰藉在她临终的房间 ………………	145
1704	Unto a broken heart ……………………………	145
	走进一颗破碎的心 ……………………………	145
1705	Volcanoes be in Sicily …………………………	146
	火山在西西里 …………………………………	146
1706	When we have ceased to care …………………	146

	我们已不在乎时 …………………………………… 147
1707	Winter under cultivation …………………… 147
	培育中的冬天 ………………………………… 147
1708	Witchcraft has not a Pedigree ……………… 147
	巫术并无家谱 ………………………………… 147
1709	With sweetness unabated …………………… 148
	怀着未减的甜蜜 ……………………………… 148
1710	A curious Cloud surprised the Sky, ……… 149
	一片奇特的云让天空惊叹, …………………… 149
1711	A face devoid of love or grace, …………… 149
	一张缺乏爱或优雅的脸, ……………………… 150
1712	A Pit—but Heaven over it— ……………… 150
	一个深渊——但苍天在上—— ………………… 151
1713	As subtle as tomorrow ……………………… 151
	像明天一样飘渺 ……………………………… 151
1714	By a departing light ………………………… 152
	借助一束离去的光线 ………………………… 152
1715	Consulting summer's clock, ………………… 152
	查验了夏日时钟, ……………………………… 152
1716	Death is like the insect …………………… 153
	死亡就像昆虫 ………………………………… 153
1717	Did life's penurious length ………………… 154
	是否生命贫瘠的长度 ………………………… 154
1718	Drowning is not so pitiful ………………… 154
	溺亡并没那么可怜 …………………………… 155
1719	God is indeed a jealous God— …………… 155
	上帝的确是个爱嫉妒的上帝—— ……………… 155
1720	Had I known that the first was the last … 155
	假如我知道第一杯是最后一杯 ……………… 156
1721	He was my host—he was my guest, ……… 156
	他是我的主人——他是我的客人, …………… 156
1722	Her face was in a bed of hair, …………… 157

	她的脸在一丛毛发间，	157
1723	High from the earth I heard a bird;	157
	在离地的高处我听到一只鸟叫；	158
1724	How dare the robins sing,	159
	知更鸟竟敢歌唱，	159
1725	I took one Draught of Life—	160
	我啜饮一口生命的玉液——	160
1726	If all the griefs I am to have	160
	如果我应有的全部悲伤	161
1727	If ever the lid gets off my head	161
	假如盖子从我头上掉下	161
1728	Is Immortality a bane	162
	难道永生是个灾祸	162
1729	I've got an arrow here.	162
	我有一支箭在这里。	162
1730	"Lethe" in my flower,	163
	"忘川水"在我花里，	163
1731	Love can do all but raise the Dead	163
	爱无所不能除了不能复活死人	164
1732	My life closed twice before its close;	164
	我的生命结束前已结束过两次；	164
1733	No man saw awe, nor to his house	165
	没人见过敬畏，他也不许任何人	165
1734	Oh, honey of an hour,	166
	啊，一小时的甜言蜜语，	167
1735	One crown that no one seeks	167
	一顶王冠没人求取	167
1736	Proud of my broken heart, since thou didst break it,	168
	为我破碎的心自豪，既然你将它打碎，	169
1737	Rearrange a "Wife's" affection!	169
	重新调整一位"妻子"的爱!	170
1738	Softened by Time's consummate plush,	171

	被时间完美的毛绒软化，	171
1739	Some say goodnight—at night—	171
	有人道晚安——在夜晚——	172
1740	Sweet is the swamp with its secrets,	172
	充满秘密的湿地很美丽，	172
1741	That it will never come again	173
	正是它一去不返	173
1742	The distance that the dead have gone	173
	死者已走的距离	174
1743	The grave my little cottage is,	174
	坟墓是我的小屋，	174
1744	The joy that has no stem no core,	175
	无茎无核的欢乐，	175
1745	The mob within the heart	175
	内心深处的暴徒	176
1746	The most important population	176
	最重要的居民	176
1747	The parasol is the umbrella's daughter,	177
	阳伞是伞的女儿，	177
1748	The reticent volcano keeps	177
	沉默寡言的火山坚持	178
1749	The waters chased him as he fled,	178
	他逃跑时大水紧追不舍，	179
1750	The words the happy say	179
	愉快说出的话语	179
1751	There comes an hour when begging stops,	180
	有一个时辰恳求止声，	180
1752	This docile one inter	180
	请将这温良的一位埋葬	180
1753	Through those old Grounds of memory,	181
	沿那些记忆的故地，	181
1754	To lose thee—sweeter than to gain	182

	失去你——其甜蜜胜过获取	182
1755	To make a prairie it takes a clover and one bee,	182
	造一片草原需一棵红花草和一只蜜蜂,	183
1756	'Twas here my summer paused	183
	我的夏季就在此暂停	183
1757	Upon the gallows hung a wretch,	184
	绞刑架上吊着一个卑鄙的人,	184
1758	Where every bird is bold to go	184
	那里每只鸟儿都敢去	184
1759	Which misses most,	185
	哪一个思念最深,	185
1760	Elysium is as far as to	185
	极乐世界之远	186
1761	A train went through a burial gate,	186
	一行人穿过墓地大门口,	186
1762	Were nature mortal lady	187
	假如自然是个凡间女子	187
1763	Fame is a bee.	188
	声名是一只蜂。	188
1764	The saddest noise, the sweetest noise,	188
	最悲伤的聒噪,最甜美的聒噪,	189
1765	That Love is all there is,	190
	爱就是现有的一切,	190
1766	Those final Creatures, —who they are—	190
	那些最后的生灵,——他们是谁——	190
1767	Sweet hours have perished here;	191
	甜美的时光在此消逝;	191
1768	Lad of Athens, faithful be	191
	雅典的小伙,要忠实	191
1769	The longest day that God appoints	191
	上帝指定的最长的一天	192
1770	Experiment escorts us last—	192

	实验护送我们到最后—— …………………………………… 192
1771	How fleet—how indiscreet an one— …………………… 192
	多迅疾——多轻率的一次—— ………………………… 193
1772	Let me not thirst with this Hock at my Lip, ………… 193
	别让我口含霍克酒依然干渴, ……………………… 193
1773	The Summer that we did not prize, ………………… 193
	我们不曾珍视的夏季, ……………………………… 194
1774	Too happy Time dissolves itself …………………… 194
	过于欢乐的时光自行消散 ………………………… 194
1775	The earth has many keys. ………………………… 194
	地球有许多曲调。 ………………………………… 195

附录 1955 年集注版与 1960 年阅读版词汇和标点差异一览表 …… 196

后记 ……………………………………………………………… 203

1501
It's little Ether Hood
Doth sit upon it's Head—
The millinery supple
Of the sagacious God—

Till when it slip away
A nothing at a time—
And Dandelion's Drama
Expires in a stem.

1501
它以太的小兜套
就在它头上罩——
这是睿智的上帝
柔顺的软帽——

直至它悄悄滑落
每次一点虚无——
蒲公英的戏剧
就在一根茎上谢幕。

1502
I saw the wind within her   [scrap 1
I knew it blew for me—   recto]
But she must buy my shelter
I asked Humility
      - - - - - - - - - -
I watched the fluttering spirit
bought   vanquished
That would not intercede
Gibraltar could surrender
But not this little maid—
      my

Precisely how it ended
~~Precisely is it known~~
~~How~~   Principally
Redemption is the one
Of whom the explanation
Is hitherto unknown
            exposition   [scrap 1
is prudently unknown   verso]

The saved have no remembrance
            left
The saved have no remembrance
In our competing Days
Tis still is an assistance
It
But their's forget in praise

It is a timid Bulwark
            Bulwark
Superfluous in theirs—
The Universe was needy
but not my little maid

Nor have the saved remembrance   [scrap 2]

I watched the precious Beggar   [scrap 3]
            Subtle Beggar
But she must pay for succor
    my price
        Humility
Of whom the exposition
Not one of us will own

1502①
我看见风在她内部　　　　　　［碎片 1，正面］
我知它因我而起——
但她需得到我庇护
我谦卑地请求她同意

我看着这翻飞的心灵
得到　　被征服的
它不会求情
直布罗陀可能会屈服
但这少女不会让步——
　我的

它到底会怎样结束
它到底是否为人所知
如何　　　突出的
其一是获得救赎
但对此如何解释
至今未知内幕
　　　　显露　　　　　　　　［碎片 1，反面］
谨慎地未揭内幕

得救者未存丝毫记忆
　　　　留
得救者未存丝毫记忆
在我们纷争的日子里
这依然是一种助益

---

① 原稿是 3 张草稿碎片，约写于 1880 年，诗节间似有联系，但难以拼成完整的一首诗。约翰逊 1960 年的阅读版只选辑了第 1 节（前 4 行），富兰克林版全集则选辑了前 4 节。

它
但他们的则在赞誉中忘记

这是一种差强人意的佑庇
　　　　　　　佑庇
对他们显得多余——
全世界都急需
只除了我这位少女

得救者也没有记忆　　　　　　［碎片2］

我看着那稀罕的乞讨者　　　　［碎片3］
　　　不露声色的乞讨者
但她需偿付拯救者
　我的努力
　谦卑
他显露的丝毫
我们谁也得不到

1503
More than the Grave is closed to me—
The Grave and that Eternity
To which the Grave adheres—
I cling to nowhere till I fall—
The Crash of nothing, yet of all—
How similar appears—

1503
不仅坟墓对我闭门——
除了坟墓还有永恒
那是坟墓所紧依——
我无处攀附直至我坠落——

什么都没碎裂,但又都已打破——
两者看来何其相似——

1504

Of whom so dear
The name to hear
Illumines with a Glow
As intimate—as fugitive
As Sunset on the snow—

1504

谁的如此可爱
那名字听起来
闪耀着微光
私密——似逃亡
似雪地上的夕阳——

1505

She could not live upon the Past
The Present did not know her
And so she sought this sweet at last
And nature gently owned her
The mother that has not a knell
for either Duke or Robin

1505

她无法靠过去生活
现在又不认识她
所以最后她寻找这位也不错
大自然温柔地收留了她
不论对公爵还是知更鸟
这位母亲丧钟都没敲一下

1506

Summer is shorter than any one—

Life is shorter than Summer—
Seventy Years is spent as quick
As an only Dollar—

Sorrow—now—is polite—and stays—
See how well we spurn him—
Equally to abhor Delight—
Equally retain him—

1506
夏季短过任何季节——
生命更比夏季短促——
七十年的光阴流泻
像花一张美元那样快速——

悲伤——如今——彬彬有礼——挥之不去——
看我们如何唾弃他——
既憎恶欢乐——
又挽留他——

1507
The Pile of Years is not so high
As when you came before
But it is rising every Day
From recollection's Floor
And while by stepping① on my Heart
I still can reach the top
Efface the burden② with your face
And catch me ere I drop

1507
岁月的堆积并无多高

---

① "stepping" 在1960年阅读版中为 "standing"。
② "burden" 在1960年阅读版中为 "mountain"。

不似你从前来时
但它每天都在上升
自回忆的地面升起
脚踩在我的心上
我还能触到它顶部
请用你的脸庞抹去那重物
并在我掉落前将我抓住

1508

You cannot make Remembrance grow
When it has lost it's Root—
The tightening the Soil around
And setting it upright
Deceives perhaps the Universe
But not retrieves the Plant—
Real Memory, like Cedar Feet
Is shod with Adamant—
Nor can you cut Remembrance down
When it shall once have grown—
It's Iron Buds will sprout anew
However overthrown—

1508

你无法让记忆生长
当它失去了根基——
把周围的泥土压实
并将它竖起
或许可以骗过宇宙
但无法挽回那棵植物——
真正的记忆，如雪松之足
穿的鞋无比坚固——
你也无法将记忆砍倒
一旦它已长出——
它的铁芽会重新萌发

无论被怎样颠覆——

1509

Mine Enemy is growing old—
I have at last Revenge—
The Palate of the Hate departs—
If any would avenge

Let him be quick—the Viand flits—
It is a faded Meat—
Anger as soon as fed is dead—
'Tis starving makes it fat—

1509①

我的敌人正在苍老——
我终于可以复仇——
恨的上颚②离去——
如果谁想报仇

请他快一点——佳肴转瞬即逝——
这块肉已褪色晦暗——
怒气一经喂饱就消失——
是饥饿使它肥胖——

1510

How happy is the little Stone
That rambles in the Road alone,
And does'nt care about Careers

---

① 本诗是 1880 年 11 月艾米莉·狄金森写给文学导师希金森的一封信中随附的 4 首诗之一。艾米莉·狄金森在信中给本诗取的标题是"丘比特的布道"（Cupid's Sermon）："I enclose those you allow, adding a fourth, lest one of them you might think profane—They are Christ's Birthday—Cupid's Sermon—A Humming-Bird—and My Country's Wardrobe—"（L675）。

② 上颚（Palate）：喻指感觉（味觉）、食欲、渴望。

And Exigencies never fears—
Whose Coat of elemental Brown
A passing Universe put on,
And independent as the Sun
Associates or glows alone,
Fulfilling absolute Decree
In casual simplicity—

1510①
多么快乐的小石头
它独自在路上漫游,
不为事业操劳
不受急务烦扰——
它朴素的褐色外衣
是路过的宇宙给它披,
它独立自主如太阳
结伴或独自发光,
顺应绝对的天理
以单纯的随意——

1511
My country need not change her gown,
Her triple suit as sweet
As when 'twas cut at Lexington,
And first pronounced "a fit."

Great Britain disapproves, "the stars";
Disparagement discreet, —

---

① 艾米莉·狄金森1881年把本诗寄给自己的嫂子苏珊,并在诗后附言:"Heaven the Balm of a Surly Technicality!"(L744)。1882年夏天,她又把本诗写在她给文学导师希金森的一封信里,信中本诗之后,相隔一行还写了另外4行诗(即第1543首):"Obtaining but our own Extent/In whatsoever Realm—/'Twas Christ's own personal Expanse/That bore him from the Tomb—"(L767),参见第1543首诗注释。

There's something in their attitude
That taunts her bayonet.

1511①

我的国家不必更换她的外衣，
她的三件套依然美丽
一如它在莱克星顿②剪裁时，
首次被认为"适宜"。

大不列颠不同意，"那些星星"；
带着谨慎的轻蔑，——
他们态度里的某种含义
奚落了她的刺刀。

1512

All things swept sole away
This—is immensity—

1512③

万物一扫而尽
这——就是浩瀚——

---

① 本诗是1880年11月艾米莉·狄金森写给文学导师希金森的一封信中随附的4首诗之一，艾米莉·狄金森在信中给本诗取的标题是"我国家的衣橱"（My Country's Wardrobe）："I enclose those you allow, adding a fourth, lest one of them you might think profane—They are Christ's Birthday—Cupid's Sermon—A Humming-Bird—and My Country's Wardrobe—"（L675）。本诗似是为纪念美国独立日而写，她似乎把本诗也寄给了嫂子苏珊，还附了一面旗："a flag of her own making—three bits of braid, red, white, and blue, pinned together with a thorn!" [参见：Chadwick, John White. "Poems of Emily Dickinson." Christian Register 70 (Dec. 31, 1891): 868-869. 或 Leyda, Jay. The Years and Hours of Emily Dickinson. Archon Books, 1970. vol. I, 379; vol. II, 349]。

② 莱克星顿（Lexington）：美国马萨诸塞州东北部城镇，美国独立战争的第一枪在此地打响。

③ 本诗是大约1881年艾米莉·狄金森写给文学导师希金森的一封信的结尾两行诗，诗之前的信这样写道："It is solemn to remember that Vastness—is but the Shadow of the Brain which casts it—"（L735）。

1513

"Go travelling with us!"
Her travels daily be
By routes of ecstasy
To Evening's Sea—

1513①

"去和我们出游！"
她 每日都在旅途
沿狂喜之路
往夜海深处——

1514

An Antiquated Tree
Is cherished of the Crow
Because that Junior Foliage is disrespectful now
To venerable Birds
Whose Corporation Coat
Would decorate Oblivion's
Remotest Consulate.

1514②

一棵古老的树
为乌鸦钟爱
因为那嫩叶如今慢待

---

① 艾米莉·狄金森的文学导师希金森的女儿玛格丽特（Margaret Waldo Higginson, 1881—1910）出生于1881年7月25日，艾米莉·狄金森随后（约在秋天）给希金森写了一封贺信，本诗是该信的结尾，诗之前的信这样写道："I am very glad of the Little Life, and hope it may make no farther flight than it's Father's Arms—Home and Roam in one—I know but little of Little Ones, but love them very softly—"（L728）。诗中的"Her"应是指玛格丽特。本诗第一句是对玛格丽特说的话。

② 本诗是1881年3月末艾米莉·狄金森写给霍兰夫人（Mrs. J. G. Holland, 即 Elizabeth Luna Chapin Holland, 1823—1896）的一封信的部分内容，信的开头写道："Spring, and not a Blue Bird, but I have seen a Crow—'in his own Body on the Tree', almost as prima facie—They love such outlawed Trees—"（L689），随后紧接本诗。

那些年长可敬的鸟儿
它们集体的外衣
可以装饰遗忘
最偏远的官邸。

1515

The Things that never can come back, are several—
Childhood—some forms of Hope—the Dead—
Though Joys—like Men—may sometimes make a Journey—
And still abide—
We do not mourn for Traveler, or Sailor,
Their Routes are fair—
But think enlarged of all that they will tell us
Returning here—
"Here!" There are typic "Heres"—
Foretold Locations—
The Spirit does not stand—
Himself—at whatsoever Fathom
His Native Land—

1515①

一去再不复返的事物,只是少数——
童年——某些形式的希望——还有死者——
虽然欢乐——像人类——有时会去周游——
但仍会留驻——

---

① 霍兰医生(Dr. Holland,即 Josiah Gilbert Holland,1819—1881)因心脏病发作于 1881 年 10 月 12 日去世,艾米莉·狄金森即在当月写了 4 封信(即 L729～L732)给霍兰夫人,本诗是第 5 封信,写于 1881 年末,月份不能确定,信内除了本诗,还有信末语:"Emily, with love."(L733)。本诗结尾部分指死者肉体虽埋在土中,但灵魂不会滞留在土里,它终会上天堂。霍兰医生 1844 年毕业于马萨诸塞州的伯克希尔医学院(Berkshire Medical College),之后从医 4 年,1848 年转行,分别在弗吉尼亚州和密西西比州的学校教书,1850 年转至新闻行业,与鲍尔斯三世(Samuel Bowles Ⅲ,1826—1878)一同编辑由鲍尔斯父亲鲍尔斯二世(Samuel Bowles Ⅱ,1797—1851)于 1824 年在马萨诸塞州汉普登县斯普林菲尔德(春田)镇(Springfield, Hampden County)创办的周报《春田共和报》(Springfield Republican,1844 年改为日报),此后开始撰写新闻评论以及进行诗歌和小说创作,当时人们惯称他为"Dr. Holland"。

我们并不哀悼旅人，或水手，
他们的线路是坦途——
只是海阔天空地想他们将给我们的叙述
当他们返回此处——
"此处！"多少个特别的"此处"——
都是已预知的地点——
灵魂不会停驻——
他自己——不论在什么深度
在他的故土——

1516

No Autumn's intercepting Chill
Appalls this Tropic Breast—
But African Exuberance
And Asiatic rest.

1516①

秋季拦截的寒意
不会令这热带的心胸震惊——
除非是非洲的繁茂
和亚洲的宁静。

1517

How much of Source escapes with thee—
How chief thy sessions be—
For thou hast borne a universe
Entirely away.

---

① 本诗是艾米莉·狄金森1881年11月底写给霍兰夫人的一封信的结尾。该信是对霍兰医生的怀念，诗之前提到，艾米莉·狄金森在昨夜几近凌晨时，在房间里再看到报告霍兰先生去世噩耗的电报，恍惚间就看到自己在11月几近凌晨时分向霍兰先生道晚安时，霍兰先生将两只手分别放在她和妹妹维尼（Vinnie，即Lavinia Norcross Dickinson，1833—1899）的头上，说他会永远记住那阳光和场景："He put one Hand on Vinnie's Head and the other on mine, and his Heart on your's, as we both knew, and said that the sunshine and the scene he should always remember."（L738）。艾米莉·狄金森在1881年底也把本诗寄给了嫂子苏珊。

1517①

有多少源泉随你逃之夭夭——
有你在的日子多么重要——
因你已把宇宙
整个带走。

1518

Not seeing, still we know—
Not knowing, guess—
Not guessing, smile and hide
And half caress—

And quake—and turn away,
Seraphic fear—
Is Eden's innuendo
"If you dare"?

1518②

没看见,我们也知晓——
不知晓,也能猜到——
猜不到,就隐藏和微笑
半拥半抱——

颤抖着——转身离去,

---

① 本诗是艾米莉·狄金森1881年圣诞节前写给霍兰夫人的一封信的结尾。该信表达了节日的祝福,也安慰对方,同时缅怀霍兰医生:"Dare we wish the brave sister a sweet Christmas, who remembered us punctually in sorrow as in peace? ...Shall we wish a triumphant Christmas to the brother withdrawn? Certainly he possesses it."(L742)。

② 这是艾米莉·狄金森1881年底寄给爱德华·塔克曼(Edward Tuckermam, 1817—1886)的夫人莎拉(Sara Eliza Sigourney Cushing, 1832—1915)的一首诗,诗前有这样的留言:"Vinnie asked me if I had any Message for you, and while I was picking it, you ran away."(L741)。看似莎拉到访时,妹妹维尼问艾米莉·狄金森有什么话捎给莎拉,艾米莉·狄金森尚未想好,莎拉就走了。本诗首节指不见面也能知道或猜到双方对对方的情意,如果猜不到,就隐藏起来笑对;第二节指不敢见人的恐惧,和当初伊甸园中亚当和夏娃所受的诱惑类似,即在于敢不敢去尝试。

天使般的恐惧——
是那伊甸园的暗示
"你敢不敢去"?

1519

The Dandelion's pallid tube
Astonishes the Grass,
And Winter instantly becomes
An infinite Alas—
The tube uplifts a signal Bud
And then a shouting Flower, —
The Proclamation of the Suns
That sepulture is o'er.

1519①

蒲公英苍白的茎管
令小草惊讶,
冬季顷刻变成
一声无尽的哎呀——
茎管擎起一个显眼的蓓蕾
随后变为呐喊的花朵,——
这是阳光的宣告
说蛰伏期已过。

1520

The stem of a departed Flower

---

① 本诗写于1881年。艾米莉·狄金森1881年11月8日把本诗寄给了朋友爱德华·塔克曼的夫人莎拉,诗后附言:"Vinnie told me, dear friend, you were speaking of Mr. Root—"(L739)。艾米莉·狄金森的哥哥奥斯汀的情人托德夫人称,随附本诗的还有一枝压扁了的、绑着红丝带的蒲公英:"The following little poem-note contained a pressed dandelion tied with scarlet ribbon."附言中所提到的"Mr. Root",可参见第1366首诗注释。艾米莉·狄金森曾于1880年12月初给爱德华·塔克曼的夫人莎拉写信(见L677),以安慰她因自己朋友、阿默斯特学院(Amherst College)数学和自然哲学教授、35岁的伊莱休(Elihu Root, 1845—1880)于1880年12月3日之死引起的悲伤。

Has still a silent rank.
The Bearer from an Emerald Court
Of a Despatch of Pink.

1520①
花朵已谢的茎枝
仍有一种沉寂的名分。
这来自翠绿庭院的搬运工
送来了桃红。

1521
The Butterfly upon the Sky,
That does'nt② know its Name
And has'nt③ any tax to pay
And has'nt any Home
Is just as high as you and I,
And higher, I believe,
So soar away and never sigh
And that's the way to grieve—

1521④
天空的蝴蝶，

---

① 艾米莉·狄金森1881年1月1日把本诗寄给了朋友爱德华·塔克曼的夫人莎拉作为新年祝福，诗之前写道："My Bird—Who is 'Today'? 'Yesterday' was a Year ago—and yet," (L684)，随后紧接本诗。
② "does'nt"在1960年阅读版中为"doesn't"。
③ "has'nt"在1960年阅读版中为"hasn't"，下一行的has'nt同。
④ 本诗写于1881年，艾米莉·狄金森1881年8月将它寄给朋友莎莉（Sally, 即 Sarah Jenkins）和侄女玛莎（Martha Gilbert Dickinson, 1866—1943, 昵称 Mattie），抬头是："'Little Women—'"（L718）。当时可能是玛莎正在匹兹菲尔德（Pittsfield, Massachusetts）看望莎莉，或者是莎莉到艾默斯特拜访玛莎。玛莎是艾米莉·狄金森哥哥奥斯汀及其妻子苏珊的女儿，后成为比安琪太太（Ms. Martha Gilbert Dickinson Bianchi）。莎莉是詹金斯牧师（Rev. Jonathan Leavitt Jenkins, 1830—1913）及其妻子莎拉的女儿，玛莎的好友。詹金斯牧师于1867年起担任艾米莉·狄金森家乡阿默斯特镇第一公理会教堂（First Congregationalist Church）执行牧师（acting pastor），直至1877年离职，前往匹兹菲尔德任职。詹金斯牧师深受狄金森一家所敬重，艾米莉·狄金森1886年去世后的葬礼就是由詹金斯牧师与阿默斯特教堂时任牧师迪克曼（Rev. George Sherwood Dickerman, 1843—1937）共同主持。

不知姓甚名谁

无税可交

无家可归

其高恰如我和你，

甚至更高，我认为，

所以远走高飞吧别叹息

那才是伤心应有的作为——

1522

His little Hearse like Figure

Unto itself a Dirge

To a delusive Lilac

The vanity divulge

Of Industry and Morals

And every righteous thing

For the divine Perdition

Of Idleness and Spring—

1522①

它小灵车般的身型

---

① 本诗写于1881年，艾米莉·狄金森当年将它寄给6岁的侄子吉尔伯特（吉布）(Thomas Gilbert [Gib] Dickinson, 1875—1883)，取标题为"The Bumble Bee's Religion"，诗前写道："For Gilbert to carry to his Teacher—"，诗后留言："'All Liars shall have their part'—Jonathan Edwards—'And let him that is athirst come'—Jesus—"（L712），据说还附了一只死了的蜜蜂。这是假定给吉布的老师看的诗，意请老师不要让吉布太辛劳，如诗所言，辛勤的蜜蜂最后会累死，自己成为自己的挽歌。对于迷惑蜜蜂的紫丁香而言，揭示了勤勉、德行以及每一件所谓正当事情的虚荣和空无，相对于懒散和春天的神圣的毁灭。诗后留言的意思是请老师不要向吉布说谎，说勤勉努力是正道，而应勉励他做他渴望做之事，原文见《圣经·新约·启示录》第21章第6节和第8节："I will give unto him that is athirst of the fountain of the water of life freely...But the fearful, and unbelieving, and the abominable, and murderers, and whoremongers, and sorcerers, and idolaters, and all liars, shall have their part in the lake which burneth with fire and brimstone: which is the second death."（Revelation 21: 6, 8），以及第22章第17节耶稣所言："And the Spirit and the bride say, Come. And let him that heareth say, Come. And let him that is athirst come. And whosoever will, let him take the water of life freely."（Revelation 22: 17）。第1598首诗中则直接引用第21章第8节原文（参见第1598首诗注释）。本诗表达的观点在艾米莉·狄金森1878年初给霍兰夫人的一封信中也有透露："Give my love to him [Dr. Holland], and tell him the 'Bee' is a reckless Guide. Dear Mr Bowles found out too late, that Vitality costs itself."（L542）。

自身是挽歌一首
对虚妄的紫丁香
把虚荣泄露
有关勤勉和德行
以及正当事情的每一件
相对于那神圣的毁灭
有关懒散和春天——

1523

We never know we go when we are going—
We jest and shut the Door—
Fate—following—behind us bolts it—
And we accost no more—

1523①

我们走时毫不意识到要走——
我们说笑着把门关——
命运——跟在我们身后——插上门拴——
从此我们再无搭讪——

1524

A faded Boy—in sallow Clothes
Who drove a lonesome Cow
To pastures of Oblivion—
A statesman's Embryo—

The Boys that whistled are extinct—
The Cows that fed and thanked

---

① 本诗写于1881年。艾米莉·狄金森以它作为1881年4月中旬写给弗朗西斯·诺克罗斯（Frances Norcross, 1847—1919）和路易丝·诺克罗斯（Louise Norcross, 1842—1896）两位表妹的一封信的结尾，信中诗之前写道："It is startling to think that the lips, which are keepers of thoughts so magical, yet at any moment are subject to the seclusion of death."（L691）。本诗表明，我们随时都可能在毫不察觉的情况下离世，再无与亲人朋友见面攀谈的机会。

Remanded to a Ballad's Barn
Or Clover's Retrospect—

1524
一个憔悴的男孩——身穿灰黄衣裳
赶一头落寞的母牛
到遗忘的牧场——
一名政治家的胚子——

那些吹哨的男孩已灭亡——
喂饱的牛群心怀感激
被押回歌谣的谷仓
或红花草的追忆里——

1525
He lived the Life of Ambush
And went the way of Dusk
And now against his subtle name
There stands an Asterisk
As confident of him as we—
Impregnable we are—
The whole of Immortality intrenched
Within a star—

1525①
他过着隐伏的生活
出没在黄昏里
如今在他敏感的名字旁边
打上了一个星形标记
如我们一般对他充满信心——
我们坚信不移——

---

① 本诗与第 1616 首诗只有第 1 行和最后两行不同。

永生的全部已得以构筑
在一颗星里——

1526

His oriental heresies
Exhilarate the Bee,
And filling all the Earth and Air
With gay apostasy

Fatigued at last, a Clover plain
Allures his jaded eye
That lowly Breast where Butterflies
Have felt it meet to die—

1526

他的东方邪说
令蜜蜂振奋无比,
令大地和空气
充斥叛教的欢愉

终于力竭,一棵平凡的红花草
诱惑他疲惫的眼
那低低的隆起蝴蝶曾在那里
感受与死亡谋面——

1527

Oh give it Motion—deck it sweet
With Artery and Vein—
Upon it's fastened Lips lay words—
Affiance it again
To that Pink stranger we call Dust—
Acquainted more with that
Than with this horizontal one
That will not lift it's Hat—

1527①

啊，让它动起来——把它打扮得可爱
用动脉和静脉——
在它紧闭的唇上施加言词——
让它再来
与那我们称为尘土的粉红陌客联姻——
与那一位更熟识
而非平躺的这一位
它不会举起帽子——

1528

The Moon upon her fluent Route
Defiant of a Road—
The Star's Etruscan Argument
Substantiate a God—

If Aims impel these Astral Ones
The ones allowed to know
Know that which makes them as forgot
As Dawn forgets them—now—

1528②

康庄大道上的月亮
对道路表示蔑视——
星星伊特鲁里亚般的③论点

---

① 题解：面对即将入土成为陌生人的死者，真希望其能再活过来，再可爱地动起来，而非眼前这样躺着一动不动。

② 本诗写于1881年末。另一版本写于1882年末或1883年初，是已经或准备寄赠给某人的，其第2节完全不同，富兰克林版取本版，其第2节为："How archly spared the Heaven 'to come'—/If such prospective be—/By superseding Destiny/And dwelling there today—"。

③ 伊特鲁里亚般的（Etruscan）：伊特鲁里亚（Etruria）是意大利中西部古国，位于现今意大利的托斯卡纳区（Tuscany），后被罗马人吞并。伊特鲁里亚文明对古罗马有深远影响。迄今考古学界和历史学界尚无法确证伊特鲁里亚人起源于何处，他们也没有留下任何文学、宗教和哲学的书面记录。

证明了神的真实——

假如是目的驱使这些星体
那些获准了解的就明白
是什么令它们被忘记
一如黎明忘记它们——现在——

1529

'Tis Seasons since the Dimpled War
In which we each were Conqueror
And each of us were slain
And Centuries 'twill be and more
Another Massacre before
So modest and so vain—
Without a Formula we fought
Each was to each the Pink Redoubt—

1529

那次酒窝大战①以来已过去几季
那时我们各自取得了胜利
又各自被杀掉
需几世纪或更迟
另一场杀戮再发生时
如此谦逊如此徒劳——
我们战斗不循定规
各自是对方的粉红堡垒——

1530

A Pang is more conspicuous in Spring

---

① 酒窝大战（Dimpled War）：按 *Emily Dickinson Lexicon* 解释，"Dimpled"有"粗糙（厉）的、蓬头垢面的、空洞（虚）的"（rough, coarse, disheveled, empty, hollow）之义，但据本诗内容，极可能指两位女性之间的一次大争斗或狂欢，两位女性可能指艾米莉·狄金森本人以及与她有亲密（暧昧）关系的嫂子苏珊。

In contrast with the things that sing
Not Birds entirely—but Minds—
Minute Effulgencies and Winds—
When what they sung for is undone
Who cares about a Blue Bird's Tune—
Why, Resurrection had to wait
Till they had moved a Stone—

1530
一阵剧痛在春天更引人注目
比起那些歌唱的事物
不全是鸟儿——还有思想——
细小的光芒和轻风飞扬——
如果他们歌颂的对象已消弭
谁还在意一只蓝鹊的乐曲——
不管怎样，要复活也得等待
等他们把一块石头移开——

1531
Above Oblivion's Tide there is a Pier
And an effaceless "Few" are lifted there—
Nay—lift themselves—Fame has no Arms—
And but one smile—that meagres Balms—

─────
　　　　　　　are scattered there.
Scattered—I say—To place them side by side
Enough will not be found when all have died.

1531①
遗忘的潮水之上一个码头屹立
一个冲刷不掉的"少数"被高举在那里——

---

① 本诗原稿处于草稿状态，应是一首尚未全部完成的两个诗节的诗。约翰逊 1960 年阅读版只取前 4 行。

不——是他们自举——声名可没有手臂——
只有一个微笑——那微薄的抚慰剂——

$-----$

被散置那里。
散置——我说——以将他们并排摆放
不可能够数如果一切已消亡。

1532

From all the Jails the Boys and Girls
Ecstatically leap—
Beloved only Afternoon
That Prison doesn't keep

They storm the Earth and stun the Air,
A Mob of solid Bliss—
Alas—that Frowns should lie in wait
For such a Foe as this—

1532[①]

自所有牢房里男孩和女孩们
欣喜若狂地跳出——
只有下午才令人爱
那时监狱无人看护

他们冲击大地震撼空气,
一群暴民欢天喜地——
哎——即使不满也只能静待
面对这样的仇敌——

1533

On that specific Pillow

---

① 本诗约写于1881年,1892年和1896年发表时曾分别被编辑冠于标题"Saturday"和"Saturday Afternoon"。本诗应是描述学校下午放学时孩子们疯狂涌出学校的情形。

Our projects flit away—
The Night's tremendous Morrow
And whether sleep will stay
Or usher us—a stranger—
To situations new
The effort to comprise it
Is all the soul can do.

1533①
在那特定的枕头上
我们的计划飞走——
那黑夜巨大的翌日
以及睡眠会否驻留
或引导我们———一位陌生客——
到新的场景
努力包容它
便是灵魂能做的一切。

1534
Society for me my misery
Since Gift of Thee—

1534②
社交对我而言是痛苦
自从有你的礼物——

1535
The Life that tied too tight escapes

---

① 题解：躺在死亡之床那特定的枕头上，人生的计划飞逝了，想想那黑夜过后巨大无边的翌日，以及今夜的睡眠是否还是正常的睡眠，抑或就引导我们这样的陌生客到一个新的世界，对于这些以及这个新世界的新场景，我们所能做的，只有努力包容和接受它，因为没有别的选择。

② 题解：自从有了你的礼物，我就只愿与你的礼物和你的爱在一起，不愿进入社会人群中与人交往。

Will ever after run
With a prudential look behind
And spectres of the Rein—
The Horse that scents the living Grass
And sees the Pastures smile
Will be retaken with a shot
If he is caught at all—

1535
束缚太紧的生命一旦逃逸
会一直奔跑不停
一边谨慎向后看去
还有缰绳的幽灵——
嗅到丰草的马匹
望见牧场露笑
用枪弹才能重新抢回
假如真要把他抓到——

1536
There comes a warning like a spy
A shorter breath of Day
A stealing that is not a stealth
And Summers are away—

1536
像密探发出的一个警示
白昼一次更短促的呼吸
一种悄然的行为但并非鬼祟
夏日就这样远去——

1537
Candor—my tepid friend—
Come not to play with me—
The Myrrhs, and Mochas, of the Mind

Are it's iniquity—

1537①

率直——我不温不火的朋友——
别来与我玩乐——
心灵中的没药和摩卡
都是它的罪恶——

1538

Follow wise Orion
Till you waste your Eye—
Dazzlingly decamping
He is just as high—

1538②

跟随智慧的猎户座
直至你枉费眼光——
在迷离光辉中隐没
它依然高高在上——

1539

Now I lay thee down to Sleep—
I pray the Lord thy Dust to keep—
And if thou live before thou wake—
I pray the Lord thy Soul to make—

---

① 艾米莉·狄金森1882年把本诗寄给嫂子苏珊,诗前引言写道:"How inspiriting to the clandestine Mind those Words of Scripture, 'We thank thee that thou hast hid these things'—"(L853)。其中的引语源自《圣经·新约·马太福音》第11章第25节:"At that time Jesus answered and said, I thank thee, O Father, Lord of heaven and earth, because thou hast hid these things from the wise and prudent, and hast revealed them unto babes."(*Matthew* 11:25)。

② 艾米莉·狄金森1882年把本诗寄给嫂子苏珊,诗前引言写道:"A 'Pear' to the Wise is sufficient—"(L758)。本诗原稿较为潦草,约翰逊1955年版和1960年版全集均取原稿4行,富兰克林版全集则取原稿8行。

1539①
如今我安放你入睡——
我愿上主守护你的尘灰——
假如你苏醒前重获生命——
我愿上主赋予你魂灵——

1540
As imperceptibly as Grief
The Summer lapsed away—
Too imperceptible at last
To seem like Perfidy—
A Quietness distilled
As Twilight long begun,
Or Nature spending with herself
Sequestered Afternoon—
The Dusk drew earlier in—
The Morning foreign shone—
A courteous, yet harrowing Grace,
As Guest, that would be gone—
And thus, without a Wing
Or service of a Keel
Our Summer made her light escape
Into the Beautiful.

1540②
像忧伤一样难以察觉

---

① 本诗写于 1882 年,是对大众熟悉的以下睡前祷告语的戏拟:"Now I lay me down to sleep/I pray my Lord my soul to keep./Should I die before I wake,/I pray the Lord my soul to take."(参见:Ford, Paul Leicester, ed. *The New England Primer*, New York: Dodd, Mead and Company, 1897: 46.)艾米莉·狄金森可能把本诗寄给了嫂子苏珊。

② 本诗写于 1882 年末,是本诗 4 个版本中最新的一版。最早的一版写于 1865 年,比随后的 1866 年修订版和寄赠希金森版以及 1882 年版均多了 16 行。后 3 个版本之间只有少数文字差异。艾米莉·狄金森 1866 年 6 月 9 日把本诗与另外 3 首诗 (即 "Blazing in Gold" "Maple make this Bed" "To undertake is to achieve") 一起,随附在一封寄给文学导师希金森的信中(L319)。希金森 1891 年在《大西洋月刊》发表《艾米莉·狄金森书信》一文,介绍他与艾米莉·狄金森的交往,以本诗作为该文的结尾 [参见: Higginson, Thomas Wentworth. "Emily Dickinson's Letters," *Atlantic Monthly* 68, 4 (October 1891): 444 - 456.]。

夏日悄然远去——
太过隐秘
不像背信弃义——
一种宁谧渗出
仿佛早已日暮,
或大自然消磨自己
在幽寂的下午——
黄昏早早降临——
晨光已然陌生——
一种殷勤、却恼人的风度,
像意欲离去的,客人——
就这样,无须翅翼
或劳烦舟楫
我们的夏日飘然逃逸
进入美的境地。

1541

No matter where the Saints abide,
They make their Circuit fair
Behold how great a Firmament
Accompanies a Star.

1541

不论圣徒们停驻何处,
总令他们的巡游绚烂
看苍穹多么浩瀚
有一颗星星陪伴。

1542

Come show thy Durham Breast
To her who loves thee best,
Delicious Robin—
And if it be not me

At least within my Tree

Do the avowing—

Thy Nuptial so minute

Perhaps is more astute

Than vaster suing—

For so to soar away

Is our propensity

The Day ensuing—

1542①

来把你达拉谟牛般的胸脯

给挚爱你的她一睹,

美妙的知更鸟——

假如我不是那个对象

至少可在我的树上

进行表白——

你的婚礼如此微型

或许这更英明

比起更浩大的求爱——

因为就此腾飞离场

确是我们的倾向

当随后的那天到来——

1543

Obtaining but our own Extent

In whatsoever Realm—

'Twas Christ's own personal Expanse

That bore him from the Tomb—

---

① 本诗前6行诗是艾米莉·狄金森1882年夏天写给文学导师希金森的一封信（L767）的部分内容。

1543①

只需获得我们自己的空间
不论在什么国度——
正是基督自身个人的浩瀚
将他载出了坟墓——

1544

Who has not found the Heaven—below—
Will fail of it above—
For Angels rent the House next our's②,
Wherever we remove—

1544③

谁没发现天堂——在下界——
在上界也难寻它踪迹——
因为天使就租住我们隔壁,
不论我们搬到哪里——

1545

The Bible is an antique Volume—
Written by faded men
At the suggestion of Holy Spectres—

---

① 本诗是艾米莉·狄金森1882年夏天写给文学导师希金森的一封信（L767）的结尾,在信中本诗之前隔一空行,是第1510首诗（参见第1510首注释）。本诗也是艾米莉·狄金森1882年底写给朋友詹姆斯·克拉克（James Dickinson Clark, 1828—1883）的一封信的部分内容,但诗第1行中的"our"改成了"his"。艾米莉·狄金森的"尘世间最亲爱的朋友"（dearest earthly friend）、她心仪的牧师沃兹华斯（Charles Wadsworth, 1814—1882）于1882年4月1日逝世,而詹姆斯·克拉克也是沃兹华斯的挚友。艾米莉·狄金森在信中忆念沃兹华斯:"I am glad you loved him and please to thank your Brother for prizing him so much. He was a Dusk Gem, born of troubled Waters, astray in any Crest below. Heaven might give him Peace, it could not give him Grandeur, for that he carried with himself to whatever scene—"（L776）。信中提及的"Brother"指詹姆斯·克拉克的弟弟查尔斯·克拉克（Charles Henry Clark, 1833—?）。

② our's: 在约翰逊1960年的阅读版中为"ours"。

③ 这是艾米莉·狄金森1883年写给朋友莎莉和侄女玛莎的一封信的结尾诗。当时玛莎正在匹兹菲尔德拜访詹金斯一家,信中写道:"I hope you are having superb times, and am sure you are, for I hear your voices, mad and sweet—as a Mob of Bobolinks."（L845）。

Subjects—Bethlehem—
Eden—the ancient Homestead—
Satan—the Brigadier—
Judas—the Great Defaulter—
David—the Troubador—
Sin—a distinguished Precipice
Others must resist—
Boys that "believe" are very lonesome—
Other Boys are "lost"—
Had but the Tale a warbling Teller—
All the Boys would come—
Orpheus' Sermon captivated—
It did not condemn—

1545①
圣经是一卷古书——
由先人写成
依照神圣幽灵②的建议——
主题——伯利恒——
伊甸园——古老的家宅——
撒旦——准将——
犹大——大叛徒——
大卫——行吟诗人——
原罪——一个闻名的绝壁
其他的必须抵抗——
"相信的"男孩非常孤独——
其他的男孩感到"迷惘"——
只要这故事能有婉转的讲述——

---

① 本诗写于1882年,艾米莉·狄金森将它寄给因病在家休养的侄子奈德(Edward [Ned] Dickinson, 1861—1898), 21岁的奈德当时是阿默斯特学院(Amherst College)的本科生。" 'Sanctuary Privileges' for Ned, as he is unable to attend—" (L753)是信的开头,接着便是本诗。本诗最早的草稿写于1879年,其时,本诗中的"warbling"一词原为"thrilling",作者为"thrilling"提供了13个备选词,其中包括"warbling"。

② 神圣幽灵(Holy Spectres):注意此词与"圣灵"(Holy Spirit)的含义不同。

所有男孩都会前来领受——
俄尔甫斯①的布道迷人——
因为它没有诅咒——

1546

Sweet Pirate of the heart,
Not Pirate of the Sea,
What wrecketh thee?
Some spice's Mutiny—
Some Attar's perfidy?
Confide in me.

1546②

心灵温柔的海盗,
而非海上的海盗,
是什么令你的船失事?
某次香料的起义——
某次玫瑰油的背弃?
请向我倾吐秘密。

1547

Hope is a subtle Glutton—
He feeds upon the Fair—
And yet—inspected closely
What Abstinence is there—

---

① 俄尔甫斯（Orpheus）:希腊神话中的诗人、音乐家,其歌声能迷住神、人、野兽,使山林、岩石等无生命的物体移动。他的妻子欧律狄刻（Eurydice）死后,他去冥府向冥王哈迪斯（Hades）求情,想让妻子重回阳间,但终因他刚一到阳间就忍不住回头看了一眼妻子而功亏一篑,因彼时其妻尚未跨过阴阳分界线,未到阳间。

② 这是艾米莉·狄金森1882年1月写给爱德华·塔克曼的夫人莎拉的一封信的结尾诗,诗之前写道:"The Gray Afternoon—the sweet knock, and the ebbing voice of the Boys are a pictorial Memory—and then the Little Bins and the Purple Kernels—'twas like the Larder of a Doll—To the inditing Heart we wish no sigh had come—"（L745）。艾米莉·狄金森的信对莎拉带孩子们来访以及送来水果礼品表达谢意。

His is the Halcyon Table—
That never seats but One—
And whatsoever is consumed
The same amount remain—

1547
希望是个狡猾的贪食者——
他专挑美食吃——
但——也会仔细检视
看有什么禁食——

它的餐桌是太平桌——
从来只有一人就座——
不论吃掉了什么
总还剩那么多——

1548
Meeting by Accident,
We hovered by design—
As often as a Century
An error so divine
Is ratified by Destiny,
But Destiny is old
And economical of Bliss
As Midas is of Gold—

1548
在意外中邂逅，
我们有意踌躇——
一世纪才一次
有如此神圣的错误
得到命运的准许，
但年迈的命运

它吝惜福气
像米达斯①吝惜黄金——

1549

My Wars are laid away in Books—
I have one Battle more—
A Foe whom I have never seen
But oft has scanned me o'er—
And hesitated me between
And others at my side,
But chose the best—Neglecting me—till
All the rest, have died—
How sweet if I am not forgot
By Chums that passed away—
Since Playmates at threescore and ten
Are such a scarcity—

1549②

我的战争都写进了书里——
还剩一场战役——
一个我素未谋面的仇敌
却时常将我审视——
在我和周遭的人里
举棋犹豫,
但取了最佳人选——而将我忽视——直至
周遭的人,皆已死去——
若谢世的老友们未将我忘记
该多美好——

---

① 米达斯（Midas）：希腊神话传说中贪婪的弗里吉亚国王（King of Phrygia），获得酒神狄俄尼索斯（Dionysus）赋予的一种能力，即凡他触摸到的一切都变成金子。
② 题解：我一生的奋斗都记录在我的书（诗歌）里，只剩最后一个与死神（仇敌）的战斗。我从未见过它，它总在上下审视我，在我和我周围的人之间欲舍欲取，选择对手，渐渐地把他们一个个都带走了，就剩我一个70岁的老人面对死神了，若那些死去的老友们还能惦记我，那该多好，只因人生七十古来稀，玩伴寥寥。

只因人生七十
玩伴稀少——

1550

The pattern of the sun
Can fit but him alone
For sheen must have a Disk
To be a sun—

1550

太阳的式样
只能对他恰当
因为光辉总需一个圆盘
才能叫太阳——

1551

Those—dying then,
Knew where they went—
They went to God's Right Hand—
That Hand is amputated now
And God cannot be found—

The abdication of Belief
Makes the Behavior small—
Better an ignis fatuus
Than no illume at all—

1551

那些——从前在弥留时候,
知道将往哪里走——
他们去往上帝的右手——
那只手如今已被砍掉
上帝也已找不到——

信仰的退位
让行动渺小——
一星磷火
总胜过毫无光照——

1552

Within thy Grave!
Oh no, but on some other flight—
Thou only camest to mankind
To rend it with Good night—

1552①

在你坟墓里!
啊不,是在进行其他某种高飞——
你只是来到人间
用晚安将它撕碎——

1553

Bliss is the plaything of the child—
The secret of the man
The sacred stealth of Boy and Girl
Rebuke it if we can

1553

幸福是孩童的玩具——
成人心中的秘密
少男少女圣洁的私情
我们一有可能就训斥

1554

"Go tell it"—What a Message—

---

① 题解:人死后看着是被葬入了坟墓,但实际是飞升入了天堂。人来到人间成为人类,最终只是以告别的晚安,将人类(人间)的心撕碎。

To whom—is specified—
Not murmur—not endearment—
But simply—we—obeyed—
Obeyed—a Lure—a Longing?
Oh Nature—none of this—
To Law—said sweet Thermopylae
I give my dying Kiss—

1554
"去说出来"① ——是什么信息——
谁是——指定的听众——
无须低语——不必亲昵——
只简单说——我们——服从——
服从——诱惑——欲望?
啊,大自然——不是这些——
是服从律法——温柔的塞莫皮莱②说
我献上临终的吻别——

---

① 去说出来（Go tell it）：纪念公元前 480 年温泉关战役纪念碑上的铭文，由希腊历史学家希罗多德（Herodotus, c. 484 BC—c. 425 BC）所写：" go tell it to the Spartan strangers passing by, that here, obedient to their laws we lie"。铭文出自其著作《历史》（*Histories*, c. 425BC），原文为希腊文（见 T. E. Page 编 *Herodotus*, 1938：545, book Ⅶ, no. 228. 2），由于译者理解的原因，英语译文不止一种。原文作者常被误认为是古希腊抒情诗人西蒙尼德斯（Simonides of Ceos, c. 556BC - 468BC），这误读恐源于拜占庭时代的帕拉廷文集（*Palatine Anthology*）（见 W. R. Paton 编 *The Greek Anthology*, 1917：139. no. 249），以及公元前 1 世纪的罗马政治家西塞罗（Marcus Tullius Cicero, 106BC - 43BC）的《图斯库兰争论》（*Tusculanae Disputationes*, Chapt. 1 Sect. 101）中的记载。后世的编者如希勒（Eduardus Hiller, 1818—1891）的《抒情诗集》（*Anthologia Lyrica*, 1904：251. no. 78）、迪尔（Ernestvs Diehl, 1874—1947）的《希腊抒情诗选》（*Anthologia Lyrica Graeca*, 1922：92）、埃德蒙兹（John Maxwell Edmonds, 1875—1958）的《希腊抒情诗》（*Lyra Graeca*, 1924：353. no. 119）、坎贝尔（David A. Campbell, 1927— ）的《希腊抒情诗》（*Greek Lyric Poetry*, 1967：98. no. 92D）等均被误导而采用了这一说法，不过佩奇（Denys Lionel Page, 1908—1978）在其编的《希腊警句》（*Epigrammata Graeca*, 1975：18, no. XXⅡ [b]）中对此意见有所保留。

② 塞莫皮莱（Thermopylae）："Thermopylae" 意为 "热的入口、炽热的门"，通俗译为 "温泉关"，古时曾是一山口，现今是希腊东部一多岩石平原。公元前 480 年的温泉关战役（Battle of Thermopylae）在此打响，一支几千人的希腊部队（包括著名的斯巴达 300 勇士）在此迎战数量远大于他们的波斯大军，双方在此战斗了 2 天。另见第 1613 首诗注释。

1555

I groped for him before I knew
With solemn nameless need
All other bounty sudden chaff
For this foreshadowed Food
Which others taste and spurn and sneer—
Though I within suppose
That consecrated it could be
The only Food that grows

1555

我不知不觉将他搜寻
怀着庄严莫名之需
所有其他慷慨瞬时变为打趣
因这预示性的美食
别人品尝后讥笑和鄙弃——
尽管我内心认定
它可被圣化为
唯一生长的食品

1556

Image of Light, Adieu—
Thanks for the interview—
So long—so short—
Preceptor of the whole—
Coeval Cardinal—
Impart—Depart—

1556

光的形象,再见——
感谢这场会面——
如此漫长——如此短暂——
全体的导师——
同时代的红衣主教——
赋予——离去——

1557

Lives he in any other world
My faith cannot reply
Before it was imperative
'Twas all distinct to me—

1557

他活在其他任何世界
我的信仰无法答复
在它成为亟需之前
我的感受非常清楚——

1558

Of Death I try to think like this—
The Well in which they lay us
Is but the Likeness of the Brook
That menaced not to slay us,
But to invite by that Dismay
Which is the Zest of sweetness
To the same Flower Hesperian,
Decoying but to greet us—

I do remember when a Child
With bolder Playmates straying
To where a Brook that seemed a Sea
Withheld us by it's roaring
From just the Purple Flower beyond
Until constrained to clutch it
If Doom itself were the result,
The boldest leaped, and clutched it—

1558

对于死亡我试着这么想——
他们把我们放入的那口井

只不过像条小溪
不是威胁要我们的命,
而是用惊惶表示邀请
那是甜蜜的热忱
邀请至同一朵如西方之花,
以诱惑表示问候我们——

我还记得孩提时
和更大胆的玩伴游荡
遇到仿佛大海的小溪
激流咆哮将我们阻挡
够不到对面那朵紫色花
直至不得不抓住它
即使下场是死亡,
最大胆的人仍会跃起,抓住它——

1559

Tried always and Condemned by thee
Permit me this reprieve
That dying I may earn the look
For which I cease to live—

1559①

一向由你审判和定罪
这一次请许我缓刑
临终的我或蒙那个眼神的垂青
我为此放弃了生命——

---

① 本诗写于 1882 年。艾米莉·狄金森 1878 年写给她爱恋的洛德法官（Judge Otis Phillips Lord, 1812—1884）的一封信（L559）的内容或有参考意义："I confess that I love him—rejoice that I love him—I thank the maker of Heaven and Earth—that gave him me to love—the exultation floods me. I cannot find my channel—the Creek turns Sea—at thought of thee—Will you punish me?"

1560

To be forgot by thee
Surpasses Memory
Of other minds
The Heart cannot forget
Unless it contemplate
What it declines
I was regarded then
Raised from oblivion
A single time
To be remembered what—
Worthy to be forgot
Is my renown

1560①

被你忘记
胜过铭记
被其他人物
心无法遗忘
除非它思量
要把什么疏忽
那我就被注意
从遗忘里升起
就那么一次
被记起何以——
值得忘记
是我的声誉

---

① 本诗写于1883年，大意指：被你忘记，胜过被其他人铭记，只因我爱你。忘记并非随意之举，心首先翻检记忆库，思量储存的内容中哪些值得忘记，那是我最后一次被记起。艾米莉·狄金森1883年4月10日将本诗最后3行寄给了好友海伦（原Mrs. Helen Hunt，1875年后成为Helen Fiske Hunt Jackson，原名Helen Maria Fiske，1830—1885），并随附一朵花，但有几处改动："To be remembered what? Worthy to be forgot, is their renown—"。

1561

No Brigadier throughout the Year
So civic as the Jay—
A Neighbor and a Warrior too
With shrill felicity
Pursuing Winds that censure us
A February Day,
The Brother of the Universe
Was never blown away—
The Snow and he are intimate—
I've often seem them play
When Heaven looked upon us all
With such severity
I felt apology were due
To an insulted sky
Whose pompous frown was Nutriment
To their Temerity—
The Pillow of this daring Head
Is pungent Evergreens—
His Larder—terse and Militant—
Unknown—refreshing things—
His Character—a Tonic—
His future—a Dispute—
Unfair an Immortality
That leaves this Neighbor out—

1561[①]
一年中没有哪位准将
比松鸦更像平民百姓——

---

① 这是艾米莉·狄金森1883年4月底写给文学导师希金森的一封信（L819）时随附的一首诗，也是艾米莉·狄金森给希金森写信时最后一次随信附诗，据猜测，艾米莉·狄金森给希金森寄赠本诗，是因她认为本诗体现了她诗艺的完美。本诗可能也被寄赠给艾米莉·狄金森的嫂子苏珊。第1177首诗也将松鸦比拟为准将。

是邻居也是武士
快乐的尖叫不停
追逐指责我们的风
在一个二月的天高,
这宇宙的兄弟
从未被吹跑——
白雪和他是密友——
我常见他们嬉闹
当苍天注视我们全体
如此严厉
我觉得应表歉意
向被辱的天宇
它自大的蹙额是一种营养
助长他们的忤逆——
这颗鲁莽脑袋的枕头
是馥郁的常青树——
他的食橱——简洁而威武——
未知的——令人振奋的食物——
他的性格——一种补药——
他的未来——一场争议——
永生很不公道
若将这位邻居排挤——

1562

Her Losses make our Gains ashamed—
She bore Life's empty Pack
As gallantly as if the East
Were swinging at her Back.
Life's empty Pack is heaviest,
As every Porter knows—
In vain to punish Honey—
It only sweeter grows.

1562①

她的损失使我们的收获蒙羞——
她勇敢背负生活的空袋
仿佛东方
在她背上摇摆。
生活的空袋最沉,
一如每个脚夫所知——
惩罚蜂蜜徒劳无益——
只会令它更加甜蜜。

1563

By homely gift and hindered Words
The human heart is told
Of Nothing—
"Nothing" is the force
That renovates the World—

1563②

家常的礼物和支吾的词语
使人心告知以
虚无——
"虚无"就是那种力

---

① 本诗是艾米莉·狄金森1883年4月寄给Roberts Brothers出版社编辑耐尔斯(Thomas Niles, 1825—1894)的一封信的结尾,诗之前她提到随信附诗3首给耐尔斯,以及已读完耐尔斯寄给她的刚出版的布兰德(Mathilde Blinde)所著英国小说家艾略特(George Eliot为笔名,原名Mary Ann Evans, 1819—1880,她自称Mary Ann或Marian Evans)的传记:"a Thunderstorm—a Humming Bird, and a Country Burial. *The Life of Marian Evans* had much I never knew—a Doom of Fruit without the Bloom, like the Niger Fig."(L814),接着就是本诗。本诗也被寄给嫂子苏珊,但诗内的"Her"和"She"改成了"His"和"He"。1883年5月15日,艾米莉·狄金森最喜爱的威利堂弟(Cousin Willie,即William Hawley Dickinson, 1832—1883)在萨拉托加(Saratoga Springs, Saratoga County, New York)去世,给苏珊寄诗的日期可能是在此日之后。威利堂弟的父亲威廉(William Dickinson, 1804—1887)是艾米莉·狄金森的父亲爱德华(Edward Dickinson, 1803—1874)的弟弟。本诗是献给艾略特的,艾米莉·狄金森对艾略特的喜爱可见于她给弗朗西斯·诺克罗斯和路易丝·诺克罗斯两位表妹的书信中(如L389、L710)。

② 本诗写于1883年,艾米莉·狄金森将它寄赠嫂子苏珊。

让世界翻天覆地——

1564

Pass to thy Rendezvous of Light,
Pangless except for us—
Who slowly ford the Mystery
Which thou hast leaped across!

1564①

去到你光的约会地,
没有痛苦除了我们——
还缓缓蹚过那个神秘
而你已一跃完成!

1565

Some Arrows slay but whom they strike—
But this slew all *but* him—
Who so appareled his Escape—
Too trackless for a Tomb—

1565②

有些箭只能杀死被射中的人——

---

① 本诗是为纪念艾米莉·狄金森的侄子吉尔伯特而作。吉尔伯特于1883年10月5日因伤寒症去世,妹妹维尼在写给朋友的信中透露了艾米莉·狄金森因此所受的打击:"Emily received a nervous shock the night Gilbert died & was alarmingly ill for weeks—…Emily was devoted to Gilbert & was there the night of his death—"(见 Sewall, Richard B. *The life of Emily Dickinson*. 2 vols. New York: Farra, Straus and Giroux, 1994.)艾米莉·狄金森1883年10月初将本诗作为一封寄给嫂子苏珊的慰问信(L868)的结尾。1885年2月,她又将本诗写在给文学导师希金森的一封信(L972)中,作为该信的结尾。她曾请求希金森允许她送给他一本克罗斯(J. W. Cross)著的《书信和日记讲述的乔治·艾略特传记》(*George Eliot's Life Related in Her Letters and Journals*)。1885年初,该书出版,她随即寄给希金森,并随附这封包含本诗的信件,信中本诗所指的对象就变为艾略特。

② 本诗是为纪念侄子吉尔伯特而作,艾米莉·狄金森1884年10月将它寄赠嫂子苏珊,诗之前这样写道:"Twice, when I had Red Flowers out, Gilbert knocked, raised his sweet Hat, and asked if he might touch them—Yes, and take them too, I said, but Chivalry forbade him—Besides, he gathered Hearts, not Flowers—"(L938)。

但这一支杀死了全部*唯独* 他无虞——
他如此乔装逃逸——
坟墓追不到他的踪迹——

1566

Climbing to reach the costly Hearts
To which he gave the worth,
He broke them, fearing punishment
He ran away from Earth—

1566①

努力攀抵那些昂贵的心
是他赋予它们价值,
他打碎了它们,害怕惩罚
便从地球逃离——

1567

The Heart has many Doors—
I can but knock—
For any sweet "Come in"
Impelled to hark—
Not saddened by repulse,
Repast to me
That somewhere, there exists,
Supremacy—

---

① 本诗是艾米莉·狄金森在侄子吉尔伯特1883年10月5日因伤寒症去世时写的,并把它寄给了嫂子苏珊(L870)。诗中的"He"应是指吉尔伯特。约5个月后的1884年春,艾米莉·狄金森又将本诗寄给文学导师希金森三岁的女儿玛格丽特,纪念玛格丽特的妹妹路易莎(Louisa W. Higginson, 1880—1880)一周年祭日。路易莎于1880年3月15日逝世。信的开头写道:"In memory of your Little Sister",随后是以散文体排列的本诗:"Who 'meddled' with the costly Hearts to which she gave the worth and broke them—fearing punishment, she ran away from Earth—"(L893)。

1567①

心有许多门扉——
我只能敲门轻轻——
任何一声甜美的"请进"
我都留神倾听——
被拒也不伤心,
我甘之如饴
假如某处,存在,
至高的威仪——

1568

To see her is a Picture—
To hear her is a Tune—
To know her an Intemperance
As innocent as June—
To know her not—Affliction—
To own her for a Friend
A warmth as near as if the Sun
Were shining in your Hand.

1568②

眼见她是一幅画——
耳听她是一支曲——
认识她难以自持
像六月一样无知——
不识她——苦恼不止——

---

① 这是艾米莉·狄金森在侄子吉尔伯特 1883 年 10 月 5 日因伤寒症去世后所写的诗,并把它寄给了嫂子苏珊。

② 霍兰夫人此前曾给艾米莉·狄金森寄来自己儿子和两位女婿的照片。本诗是艾米莉·狄金森 1883 年 3 月写给霍兰夫人一封回信的结尾部分。艾米莉·狄金森在信中谈了对照片的看法,随后是诗前引言:"May I present your Portrait to your Sons in Law?"(L802),紧接着是本诗。艾米莉·狄金森还在 1883 年 3 月把本诗寄给一位至今身份不明的朋友,诗前引言是:"I dream of your little Girl three successive Nights—I hope nothing affronts her—"(L809),信中写的另一首诗是第 1570 首。本诗也被寄赠给嫂子苏珊。

心怀她作为朋友
一股温暖近似太阳
正照耀在你手。

1569

The Clock strikes one that just struck two—
Some schism in the Sum—
A Vagabond from① Genesis
Has wrecked the Pendulum—

1569②

曾敲两次的钟只敲了一次——
数目有些不对——
是从创世纪来的一位浪子
弄坏了摆锤——

1570

Forever honored be the Tree
Whose Apple Winterworn
Enticed to Breakfast from the Sky
Two Gabriels Yestermorn.

---

① "from" 在 1960 年阅读版中为 "for"，应是印刷错误。
② 本诗是艾米莉·狄金森 1883 年 3 月 3 日写给霍兰夫人的一封信的部分内容。霍兰夫人的女儿凯特（Kate Holland）刚在 1882 年 9 月 27 日与布利克（Bleeker Van Wagenen）结婚，信中提到凯特此时应该知道什么是结婚的状态了，认为："Her question however is answered now—Please tell her from me—"（L805），紧接着是本诗。艾米莉·狄金森还在 1884 年 6 月初将本诗寄给朋友鲍尔斯的儿子鲍尔斯四世（Samuel Bowles Ⅳ，1851—1915），祝贺他于 1883 年 10 月与伊丽莎白（Elizabeth Hoar）订婚，但诗中的 "Vagabond" 改成了 "Sorcerer"（L902）。两人于 1884 年 6 月 12 日结婚。本诗还在 1883 年 5 月被寄给了朋友爱德华·塔克曼的夫人莎拉。《圣经·旧约·创世纪》第 2 章第 24 节记述："Therefore shall a man leave his father and his mother, and shall cleave unto his wife: and they shall be one flesh."［因此，人要离开父母与妻子连合，二人成为一体］（Genesis 2：24）。本诗即指涉此意。男女结婚后，由二合为一，以钟响比拟，也就由单身时的敲响两次变为婚后的敲响一次。诗中的 "Vagabond" 或指夏娃，"Sorcerer" 指上帝。

They registered in Nature's Book
As Robins—Sire and Son—
But Angels have that modest way
To screen them from Renown.

1570①
那棵树永为人称道
它的苹果在冬天残凋
从天上被诱来吃早餐
两位加百列天使②在昨日清早。

他们在大自然名册上登记
以知更鸟的身份——父与子——
但天使们自有谨慎的方式
避免他们为人所知。

1571
How slow the Wind—
how slow the sea—
how late their Feathers be!

---

① 艾米莉·狄金森1883年3月给一位身份不明的朋友寄了一封信,信中先写有第1568首诗,接着是本诗,本诗前写道:"Lest she miss her 'Squirrels,' I send her little Playmates I met in Yesterday's Storm—the lovely first that came—"(L809)。同样是1883年3月,艾米莉·狄金森也将本诗寄给霍兰夫人,作为一封信(L808)的结尾。本诗也被寄赠给嫂子苏珊。

② 加百列天使(Gabriel):大天使之一,是报喜天使。《圣经·新约·路加福音》第1章记述加百列奉神旨向童女玛丽亚预报耶稣将降生:"And in the sixth month the angel Gabriel was sent from God unto a city of Galilee, named Nazareth, To a virgin espoused to a man whose name was Joseph, of the house of David; and the virgin's name was Mary. And the angel came in unto her, and said, Hail, thou that art highly favoured, the Lord is with thee: blessed art thou among women…And the angel said unto her, Fear not, Mary: for thou hast found favour with God. And, behold, thou shalt conceive in thy womb, and bring forth a son, and shalt call his name JESUS."(Luke 1: 26-28, 30-31)。加百列也曾现身于但以理面前传话(Daniel 8: 16-26),参见第1483首诗注释。

1571①

风真慢——
海真慢——
它们的羽毛来得真晚!

1572

We wear our sober Dresses when we die,
But Summer, frilled as for a Holiday
Adjourns her sigh—

1572②

我们死时穿着素衣,
但夏日,装饰如庆假期
停止了她的叹息——

1573

To the bright east she flies,
Brothers of Paradise
Remit her home,
Without a change of wings,
Or Love's convenient things,
Enticed to come.

Fashioning what she is,
Fathoming what she was,

---

① 本诗是艾米莉·狄金森 1883 年夏天寄给朋友爱德华·塔克曼的夫人莎拉的一封短简的结尾,以散文形式写出,信全文如下:"Sweet foot—that comes when we call it! /I can go but a Step a Century, now—/How slow the Wind—how slow the Sea—how late their Feathers be!"(L832)。艾米莉·狄金森曾在 1883 年 6 月底写给朋友玛利亚(Maria Whitney of Northampton, 1830—1909)的一封信中提到她的脚扭伤未好:"With my foot in a sling from a vicious sprain, and reminded of you almost to tears by the week and its witness, I send this sombre word."(L830)。本诗最后一行可能是祈愿她脚伤好转的那天早点到来。关于玛利亚的身份,参见第 1493 首诗注释。

② 本诗 1883 年 8 月底被寄赠朋友爱德华·塔克曼的夫人莎拉。诗大意:我们死时都穿素衣,但夏日转入秋日,停止它最后的叹息之前,却被夏末之花装扮得如欢庆假期。

We deem we dream—
And that dissolves the days
Through which existence strays
Homeless at home.

1573①
她飞向明亮的东方,
兄弟们在天堂
接引她返回家园,
无须更换翅翼,
也无爱随身的东西,
不舍地跟在后面。

想象她现在的形象,
揣测她过去的模样,
我们恍若梦中——
就这样消融了日子
存在也因此迷失
在家中无所适从。

---

① 这是艾米莉·狄金森1883年春写给朋友玛利亚的一封信中的一首诗,为纪念1882年11月14日去世的母亲艾米莉·诺克罗斯(Emily Elizabeth Norcross, 1804—1882)而作,信中诗之前的引言是:"All is faint indeed without our vanished mother, who achieved in sweetness what she lost in strength, though grief of wonder at her fate made the winter short, and each night I reach finds my lungs more breathless, seeking what it means."(L815)。艾米莉·狄金森在1882年11月写给霍兰夫人的一封信中提到母亲去世的情况:"The dear Mother that could not walk, has flown. It never occurred to us that though she had not Limbs, she had Wings—and she soared from us unexpectedly as a summoned Bird—...After a restless Night, complaining of great weariness, she was lifted earlier than usual from her Bed to her Chair, when a few quick breaths and a 'Dont leave me, Vinnie' and her sweet being closed—"(L779)。两位女儿与久病的母亲的关系一向不亲密,但在母亲去世前的2年里,母女关系变得亲近了。艾米莉·狄金森的妹妹维尼在1882年12月中旬写给霍兰夫人的一封信中说:"Mother has now been gone five Weeks. We should have thought it a long Visit, were she coming back—...We were never intimate Mother and Children while she was our Mother—but Mines in the same Ground meet by tunneling and when she became our Child, the Affection came—"(L792)。

1574①

No ladder needs the bird but skies
To situate its wings,
Nor any leader's grim baton
Arraigns it as it sings.
The implements of bliss are few—
As Jesus says of *Him*,
"Come unto me" the moiety
That wafts the cherubim.

1574②

鸟儿需要天空而非梯子
以安置它的翅膀，
也没哪个指挥用冷酷的指挥棒
去审问它当它歌唱。
幸福的实现所需甚少——
正如耶稣谈及*他*时，
才半句"来我这里"
就令小天使③心往神驰。

1575

The Bat is dun, with wrinkled Wings—
Like fallow Article—

---

① 本诗最后 4 行与第 1586 首诗最后 4 行近似。
② 这是艾米莉·狄金森 1883 年 5 月写给朋友玛利亚的一封信中的结尾诗，玛利亚对儿童援助协会（Children's Aid Society）的事务特别热心，信中诗前的引言就与此有关："I can easily imagine your fondness for the little life so mysteriously committed to your care. The bird that asks our crumb has a plaintive distinction. I rejoice that it was possible for you to be with it, for I think the early spiritual influences about a child are more hallowing than we know. The angel begins in the morning in every human life. How small the furniture of bliss! How scant the heavenly fabric!"（L824）。
③ 小天使（Cherubim）：或称智天使，是基督教九等天使中的第二等级天使。九等天使从最高第一等至第九等分别为：Seraphim（炽天使），Cherubim（智天使），Thrones（Ophanim, 座天使），Dominations（Kyriotetes，主天使），Virtues（力天使），Powers（Exusiai，能天使），Principalities（权天使），Archangels（大天使），Angels（Holy Angels，圣天使）。

And not a song pervade his Lips—
Or none perceptible.

His small Umbrella quaintly halved
Describing in the Air
An Arc alike inscrutable
Elate Philosopher.

Deputed from what Firmament—
Of what Astute Abode—
Empowered with what Malignity
Auspiciously withheld—

To his adroit Creator
Ascribe no less the praise—
Beneficent, believe me,
His Eccentricities—

1575
蝙蝠暗褐，翅膀皱褶——
像淡棕色物件——
他双唇渗不出一首歌——
或没人能听见。

他的小伞奇特地分为两半
在空中绘出
一道难以捉摸的弧
令哲学家欢欣鼓舞。

受委派自怎样的天宇——
自怎样狡黠的居处——
被赋予怎样的恶意
又幸运地被撤除——

向他灵巧的创造者
依然献上赞誉——
都是善意,相信我,
他的所有怪癖——

1576①

The Spirit lasts—but in what mode—
Below, the Body speaks,
But as the Spirit furnishes—
Apart, it never talks—
The Music in the Violin
Does not emerge alone
But Arm in Arm with Touch, yet Touch
Alone—is not a Tune—
The Spirit lurks within the Flesh
Like Tides within the Sea
That make the Water live, estranged
What would the Either be?
Does that know—now—or does it cease—
That which to this is done,
Resuming at a mutual date
With every future one?
Instinct pursues the Adamant,
Exacting this Reply—
Adversity if it may be, or
Wild Prosperity,
The Rumor's Gate was shut so tight
Before my Mind was sown,
Not even a Prognostic's Push
Could make a Dent thereon—

---

① 本诗最后 4 行与第 1584 首第 5~8 行近似;最后 6 行与第 1588 首最后 6 行近似。

1576①

灵魂一直延续——但以什么方式——
在下界,肉体言说,
但由于是灵魂提供支持——
一旦分离,它就永远沉默——
小提琴的乐音
不会自己涌起
须与弹奏臂挽臂,而弹奏
单独——不成一支曲——
灵潜藏肉里
像潮寓居大海
使海水充满生息,一旦疏离
各自如何存在?
是否已明了——如今——或已不必——
即对此哪个已解决完毕,
可在某个共同日期
与每个未来的对方重新合一?
本能追求坚定,
苛求这个答复——
会是逆境,抑或
疯狂的坦途,
流言的大门如此紧闭
在我的思想播下之前,
即使一个预设的推力
也无法在上面造成凹陷——

1577

Morning is due to all—

---

① 这是艾米莉·狄金森1883年10月中旬寄给朋友詹姆斯·克拉克的弟弟查尔斯·克拉克的一首诗,诗之前写道:"These thoughts disquiet me, and the great friend is gone, who could solace them. Do they disturb you?"(L872)。艾米莉·狄金森的"尘世间最亲爱的朋友"(dearest earthly friend)、她心仪的牧师沃兹华斯于1882年4月1日逝世,而詹姆斯·克拉克是沃兹华斯的挚友。艾米莉·狄金森在沃兹华斯牧师去世后与詹姆斯·克拉克有书信往来,主题主要围绕沃兹华斯牧师。在詹姆斯·克拉克病重后,艾米莉·狄金森才开始写信给其弟弟查尔斯·克拉克。本诗应是为纪念沃兹华斯牧师而作。

To some—the Night—
To an imperial few—
The Auroral light.

1577①

清晨莅临所有人——
一些人——得到夜晚——
一小撮帝国成员——
得到曙光灿烂。

1578

Blossoms will run away,
Cakes reign but a Day,
But Memory like Melody
Is pink Eternally.

1578②

花儿终会凋残,
蛋糕只留驻一天,
但记忆像旋律
永远粉红如一。

1579

It would not know if it were spurned,
This gallant little flower—
How therefore safe to be a flower

---

① 这是艾米莉·狄金森1883年10月寄给朋友鲍尔斯的儿子鲍尔斯四世一封信（L864）中的一首诗，祝贺他于1883年10月与伊丽莎白订婚（另见第1569首诗注释）。
② 这是艾米莉·狄金森1883年夏天寄给朋友约翰·斯威策（John Howard Sweetser, 1835—1904）的妻子奈丽（Nellie, 即 Lucy Cornelia Peck, 1832—1907）的一封信里的一首诗，可能伴随一块蛋糕和一些花寄送。诗前写道："Blossoms, and Cakes, and Memory! 'Choose ye which ye will serve'! I serve the Memory."（L840），引言内的引文出自《圣经·旧约·约书亚记》第24章第15节："And if it seem evil unto you to serve the LORD, choose you this day whom ye will serve."（Joshua 24：15）。

If one would tamper there.

To enter, it would not aspire—
But may it not despair
That it is not a Cavalier,
To dare and perish there?

1579①
它不知道它会否被拒,
这朵小花真勇敢——
因此做一朵花儿多安全
如果有人在那里捣乱。

进入,它可没这心思——
但难道它不感到绝望
它不是骑士,
却要闯入并在那里灭亡?

1580
We shun it ere it comes,
Afraid of Joy,
Then sue it to delay
And lest it fly,
Beguile it more and more—
May not this be
Old Suitor Heaven,
Like our dismay at thee?

---

① 本诗写于1882年,是艾米莉·狄金森写赠哥哥奥斯汀和嫂子苏珊的某个孩子的诗,还随附了一枝花。诗歌大意:花儿替代自己去嫂子家,花儿更安全一点,万一有人在那里捣乱的话,总不会对花儿发难。花儿其实不想进入嫂子家,只是代人传意,因此,冒着死亡的风险勇闯险境,花儿难道不感到绝望吗?

1580①
它还没来我们就躲避，
对欢乐感到恐惧，
而后请求它推迟
又唯恐它飞远，
就一次次将它欺骗——
这难道不像
古老的求爱者上苍，
我们对你感到的惊惶？

1581
The farthest Thunder that I heard
Was nearer than the Sky
And rumbles still, though torrid Noons
Have lain their missiles by—
The Lightning that preceded it
Struck no one but myself—
But I would not exchange the Bolt
For all the rest of Life—
Indebtedness to Oxygen
The Happy may repay,
But not the obligation
To Electricity—

---

① 这是艾米莉·狄金森1883年初寄给约瑟夫·奇克林（Joseph Knowlton Chickering, 1846—1899）的一首诗，诗前写道："I had hoped to see you, but have no grace to talk, and my own Words so chill and burn me, that the temperature of other Minds is too new an Awe—"（L798）。约瑟夫·奇克林毕业于艾米莉·狄金森家乡阿默斯特镇的阿默斯特学院，1873—1885年在阿默斯特学院教授英国文学，1885年以副教授头衔去职。艾米莉·狄金森的母亲艾米莉·诺克罗斯1882年11月4日去世，其间，约瑟夫·奇克林多有协助，过后他提出想拜访艾米莉·狄金森，艾米莉·狄金森1882年底回复说等他外出旅行回来后再会面："Thank you for being willing to see me, but may I defer so rare a pleasure till you come again?"（L786），约瑟夫·奇克林外出返回后，艾米莉·狄金森乃陷入本诗所展现的惊惶心态之中。诗歌表达了艾米莉·狄金森想见人又怕见人的心态。自19世纪70年代起，艾米莉·狄金森怕见人的倾向日增，到此时，已至不再见人的地步（相同主题的诗参见写于1877年的1410首）。约瑟夫·奇克林几次尝试约访均未成功，两人一生从未见过面。

It founds the Homes and decks the Days
And every clamor bright
Is but the gleam concomitant
Of that waylaying Light—
The Thought is quiet as a Flake—
A Crash without a Sound,
How Life's reverberation
It's Explanation found—

1581①
我听到的最远的雷声
比天空还近前
隆隆声依旧,尽管酷热的正午
已放下它们的飞弹——
此前的闪电
只击中我自己——
但我不会用一道霹雳
换取我生命的剩余——
对氧气的亏欠
快乐者可以偿付,
但无法偿清
对电的义务——
它缔造了家园装扮了日子
每一次明亮的喧响
都是一次闪烁伴随
那道伏击的光芒——
思想如雪花般宁静——
一次无声的撞击,
生命的回音
如何找到它的释义——

---

① 艾米莉·狄金森1884年将本诗前4行寄给了嫂子苏珊,诗前的引言是:"Tell the Susan who never forgets to be subtle, every Spark is numbered—"(L814)在1884年9月写给朋友海伦的一封信里,艾米莉·狄金森提到自己的病情并说:"The Summer has been wide and deep, and a deeper Autumn is but the Gleam concomitant of that waylaying Light—"(L937)。

1582

Where Roses would not dare to go,
What Heart would risk the way—
And so I send my Crimson Scouts
To sound the Enemy—

1582

玫瑰不敢去的地方,
什么样的心会去冒险——
于是我派遣我深红的侦查员
去将敌人打探——

1583

Witchcraft was hung, in History,
But History and I
Find all the Witchcraft that we need
Around us, every Day—

1583

巫术已被绞死,在历史里,
但历史和我发现
我们所需的所有巫术
就在我们身边,每天——

1584①

Expanse cannot be lost—
Not Joy, but a Decree
Is Deity—
His Scene, Infinity—
Whose rumor's Gate was shut so tight
Before my Beam was sown,
Not even a Prognostic's push

---

① 本诗第 5~8 行与第 1576 首最后 4 行近似。

Could make a Dent thereon—

The World that thou hast opened
Shuts for thee,
But not alone,
We all have followed thee—
Escape more slowly
To thy Tracts of Sheen—
The Tent is listening,
But the Troops are gone!

1584①
浩瀚不可能失去——
不是欢乐，而是天命
具有神性——
无边无际，他的场景——
他流言的大门如此紧闭
在我的光束播下之前，
即使一个预设的推力
也无法在上面造成凹陷——

你打开的世界
为你关闭，
但并不孤单，
我们都已跟随你——
更缓慢地逃匿
到你光辉的领地——
营帐在倾听，
但军队已无影！

---

① 艾米莉·狄金森的侄子吉尔伯特 1883 年 10 月 5 日因伤寒症去世。艾米莉·狄金森 1883 年 10 月初给嫂子苏珊写了一封慰问信，本诗就是该信的结尾诗，诗前写道："Moving on in the Dark like Loaded Boats at Night, though there is no Course, there is Boundlessness—"（L871）。

1585

The Bird her punctual music brings
And lays it in it's place—
It's place is in the Human Heart
And in the Heavenly Grace—
What respite from her thrilling toil
Did Beauty ever take—
But Work might be electric Rest
To those that Magic make—

1585

鸟儿带来她准时的音乐
把它放在它的位置——
那个位置就在人类心上
以及上苍的恩典里——
从她令人激动的劳作里
美丽得到了怎样的喘息——
但工作或许是紧张的休息
对于那些人创造神奇——

1586①

To her derided Home
A Weed of Summer came—
She did not know her station low
Nor Ignominy's Name—
Bestowed a summer long
Upon a fameless flower—
Then swept as lightly from disdain
As Lady from her Bower—

Of Bliss the Codes are few—

---

① 本诗最后 4 行与第 1574 首诗最后 4 行近似。

As Jesus cites of Him—
"Come unto me" the moiety
That wafts the Seraphim—

1586
来到她受嘲笑的家
是一株夏天的杂草——
她不知她地位低下
也不了解她耻辱的名号——
给一朵默默无名的花
赐一个夏季漫长——
然后轻盈地从轻蔑中抽身
像女士离开她的闺房——

幸福的密码很少——
正如耶稣援引他的话时——
才半句"来我这里"
就令六翼天使①心往神驰——

1587
He ate and drank the precious Words—
His Spirit grew robust—
He knew no more that he was poor,
Nor that his frame was Dust—

He danced along the dingy Days
And this Bequest of Wings
Was but a Book—What Liberty
A loosened spirit brings—

---

① 六翼天使（Seraphim）：即炽天使。基督教九等天使中最高等级的天使。九等天使参见第1574首诗注释。

1587①

他饮食珍贵的文字——
他的灵魂变得强健——
他不再记得自己贫弱,
也不觉他躯体是尘烟——

他在暗淡岁月里起舞
而这羽翼的赠予
不过是一本书——多大的自由
一个无拘的灵魂孕育——

1588②

This Me—that walks and works—must die,
Some fair or stormy Day,
Adversity if it may be
Or wild prosperity
The Rumor's Gate was shut so tight
Before my mind was born
Not even a Prognostic's push
Can make a Dent thereon—

1588

这个我——行走和工作——必须死,
某个晴朗或暴雨的日子,
会是逆境的困苦
抑或疯狂的坦途
流言的大门如此紧闭
在我的思想诞生之前
即使一个预设的推力
也无法在上面造成凹陷——

---

① 其他有关书籍和阅读主题的诗歌参见第 371、第 604 和第 1263 首诗。
② 本诗最后 6 行与第 1576 首最后 6 行近似。

1589

Cosmopolites without a plea
Alight in every Land
The compliments of Paradise
From these① within my Hand

Their dappled Journey to themselves
A compensation fair
Knock and it shall be opened
Is their Theology

1589

世界公民没有请求
就降落各地
天堂的赞誉
来自这些在我手里

他们的斑驳之旅驶向自己
一次公平的补偿
叩门它就开启②
是他们的神学信仰

1590

Not at Home to Callers
Says the Naked Tree—
Bonnet due in April—
Wishing you Good Day—

---

① "these" 在 1960 年阅读版中为 "those"。
② 叩门它就会开启（Knock and it shall be opened）：参见《圣经·新约·马太福音》第 7 章第 7 节记述："Ask, and it shall be given you; seek, and ye shall find; knock, and it shall be opened unto you."（Matthew 7：7）。

1590①

对来访者无人在家
那秃树说话——
软帽会在四月出现——
恭祝你日安——

1591

The Bobolink is gone—　　the Rowdy of the Meadow—
And no one swaggers now but me—
The Presbyterian Birds can now resume the Meeting
He gaily **interrupted that overflowing Day**
　　boldly
When opening the Sabbath in their afflictive Way
He bowed to Heaven instead of Earth
　　　　to every Heaven above
　　　　to all the saints he knew
　　　　　every God he knew
And shouted let us pray—
and bubbled let us pray—

He recognized his maker—overturned the Decalogue—

He swung upon the Decalogue
And shouted Let us pray—

When supplicating mercy
In a portentous way—　　　　　portentous way

Gay from an unannointed Twig　　Sweet from a surreptitious Twig
He gurgled—　Let us pray—
bubbled

---

① 艾米莉·狄金森可能在 1883 年春将本诗寄赠当时 8 岁的侄子吉尔伯特。

1591①

食米鸟已离去——　　那草地的喧闹者——
如今除了我没人趾高气扬——
长老会的鸟儿们如今可以恢复集会
他曾愉快地打断那繁忙的日子
　　大胆地
当他们以痛苦的方式开启安息日
他躬身向天而非向地
　　　上界每一片天
　　　　他认识的所有圣徒
　　　　他认识的每位神灵
喊着让我们祈祷——
连续说让我们祈祷——

他认出他的造物主——推翻了十诫——

他猛烈抨击十诫
喊着让我们祈祷——

当恳求宽饶
以惊人的方式——　　　惊人的方式

欢乐来自一根未涂油的细枝　　甜蜜来自一根隐秘的细枝
他咯咯地说——　　让我们祈祷——
　　连续说

1592

The Lassitudes of Contemplation
Beget a force
They are the spirit's still vacation

---

① 这首写于1883年的诗稿未被艾米莉·狄金森再次整理。此处原文和译文中的黑体为译者所加，以示这是本诗在约翰逊1960年阅读版中的文本。

That him refresh—
The Dreams consolidate in action—
What mettle fair

1592
沉思的困倦
产生一种力
它们是精神的静谧休闲
使他心旷神怡——
梦想在行动中愈坚——
多迷人的勇气

1593
There came a Wind like a Bugle—
It quivered through the Grass
And a Green Chill upon the Heat
So ominous did pass
We barred the Windows and the Doors
As from an Emerald Ghost—
The Doom's electric Moccasin
That very instant passed—
On a strange Mob of panting Trees
And Fences fled away
And Rivers where the Houses ran
Those looked that lived—that Day—
The Bell within the steeple wild
The flying tidings told—
How much can come
And much can go,
And yet abide the World!

1593
一阵风吹来像号角——

瑟瑟穿过草地
炎热上方一股绿色寒气
打此经过不怀好意
我们闩上门窗
仿佛要将一个绿鬼阻挡——
厄运的闪电软鞋①
那一瞬间——
经过一丛喘息的怪林
篱笆已逃窜
河流中有房屋流淌
那些活着的在看——那天——
尖塔里的钟狂乱敲响
把翻飞的讯息传扬——
有多少来
又有多少往,
而世界依旧在!

1594

Immured in Heaven!
What a Cell!
Let every Bondage be,
Thou sweetest of the Universe,
Like that which ravished thee!

1594②

监禁在天堂!
那个牢房!
愿每个禁锢都是,

---

① 闪电软鞋（electric Moccasin）："electric Moccasin" 喻指雷闪电击（lightning strike）。"Moccasin" 原指软帮（拖）鞋，或指北美印第安人穿的鹿皮软鞋，还指一种生长在北美的大毒蛇。

② 这首写于1884年的诗可能在苏珊的儿子吉布于1883年10月5日因伤寒症去世后不久被艾米莉·狄金森寄赠给嫂子苏珊。

你宇宙中的最甜,
如从前那般令你沉迷!

1595

Declaiming Waters none may dread—
But Waters that are still
Are so for that most fatal cause
In Nature—they are full—

1595①

滔滔之水无人惧怕——
但平静之水
所以如此有其最致命的原因
在自然里——它们丰沛——

1596

Few, yet enough,
Enough is One—
To that ethereal throng
Have not each one of us the right
To stealthily belong?

1596②

少,也已足够,
足够就是一——
那空灵的集体

---

① 这是艾米莉·狄金森1884年寄赠嫂子苏珊的一首诗,诗前写道:"Wish I had something vital for Susan, but Susan feeds herself—Banquets have no Seed, or Beggars would sow them—"(L910)。本诗大意指苏珊对艾米莉·狄金森不言不语,令人害怕,这种安静对艾米莉·狄金森是致命的,因为正常而言,人不可能不言不语,正如自然中江河湖海的水,正常情况下是丰沛的。

② 这是艾米莉·狄金森1884年寄赠嫂子苏珊的一首诗。

难道我们每个人都没权利
暗地里属于?

1597

'Tis not the swaying frame we miss,
It is the steadfast Heart,
That had it beat a thousand years,
With Love alone had bent,
It's fervor the electric Oar,
That bore it through the Tomb,
Ourselves, denied the privilege,
Consolelessly presume—

1597①

我们怀念的不是摇晃的身影,
是那颗坚定的心,
假使它跳动了千年,
也只对爱动情,
它的激情是电浆,
载它穿越坟墓,
而我们,被剥夺了特权,
伤心徒然地揣度——

1598

Who is it seeks my Pillow Nights—
With plain inspecting face—
"Did you" or "Did you not," to ask—
'Tis "Conscience" —Childhood's Nurse—

---

① 本诗写于1884年,艾米莉·狄金森将它寄赠给嫂子苏珊,其主题应该与艾米莉·狄金森爱恋的洛德法官1884年3月13日逝世有关。

With Martial Hand she strokes the Hair
Upon my wincing Head—
"All" Rogues "shall have their part in" what—
The Phosphorus of God—

1598①

是谁找寻我安枕的夜晚——
以平常的审视的脸——
问,"你做了"或"你没做"——
是"良心"——孩提的保育员——

她用粗壮的手轻抚发丝
在我畏缩的额前——
"所有"恶棍"都有他们的份"在什么——
上帝的火焰——

1599

Though the great Waters sleep,
That they are still the Deep,
We cannot doubt—
No vacillating God
Ignited this Abode
To put it out—

---

① 这是艾米莉·狄金森写给嫂子苏珊的诗,写于1884年,表达了说话者良心的不安,可能是因为做了或没做过什么事,为此还提到了圣经里所说的坏人必要受火烧的情景。参见《圣经·新约·启示录》第21章第8节:"But the fearful, and unbelieving, and the abominable, and murderers, and whoremongers, and sorcerers, and idolaters, and all liars, shall have their part in the lake which burneth with fire and brimstone: which is the second death."(Revelation 21: 8)〔唯有胆怯的、不信的、可憎的、杀人的、淫乱的、行邪术的、拜偶像的,和一切说谎话的,他们的份就在烧着硫磺的火湖里。这是第二次的死。〕

1599①

尽管浩瀚之水已安睡，
它们依然深邃，
我们不会怀疑——
并没有哪个踌躇的天神
点燃这座寓所
又将它浇熄——

1600

Upon his Saddle sprung a Bird
And crossed a thousand Trees
Before a Fence without a Fare
His Fantasy did please
And then he lifted up his Throat
And squandered such a Note
A Universe that overheard
Is stricken by it yet—

---

① 本诗随附一封信，于 1885 年 2 月被寄赠一位波士顿律师——金博尔（Benjamin Kimball, 1850—?），他是艾米莉·狄金森爱恋的洛德法官的亲戚。洛德 1884 年 3 月 13 日去世前多年一直是艾米莉·狄金森家的好友。艾米莉·狄金森在 1884 年夏末写给嫂子苏珊的一封信里也抄录了本诗，成为信的一部分，诗前引言为："I can scarcely believe that the Wondrous Book is at last to be written, and it seems like a Memoir of the Sun, when the Noon is gone—You remember his swift way of wringing and flinging away a Theme, and others picking it up and gazing bewildered after him, and the prance that crossed his Eye at such times was unrepeatable—"（L908）。引言里提到的"him"指 1878 年 1 月 16 日去世的朋友鲍尔斯，提到的书指即将出版的鲍尔斯的回忆录。本诗还在 1884 年 11 月被抄录在寄给约瑟夫·斯威策（Joseph A. Sweetser）的妻子凯瑟琳（Catherine Dickinson, 1814—1895）的一封信里，信中诗前引言为："The beloved lilies have come, and my heart is so high it overflows, as this was mother's week, Easter in November. Father rose in June, and a little more than a year since, those fair words were fulfilled, 'and a little child shall lead them,' —but boundlessness forbids me."（L952）。凯瑟琳是艾米莉·狄金森的父亲爱德华的妹妹，她 1835 年嫁给约瑟夫·斯威策。艾米莉·狄金森在 1886 年春也给库伯（James Sullivan Cooper, 1802—1870）的夫人阿比盖尔（Mrs. James S. Cooper, 原名 Abigail Ingersoll "Abby" Girdler, 1817—1895）寄赠本诗，诗前引言为："It is too late to express my sorrow for my grieved friend? Though the first moment of loss is eternity, other eternities remain."（L1036）。

1600①

一只鸟跳上他马鞍
穿越千万棵树
在一道不收费的篱笆前
他的幻想得到了满足
他随即亮开嗓子
引吭高歌的那一曲
无意间听到的宇宙
也不禁为之着迷——

1601

Of God we ask one favor,
That we may be forgiven—
For what, he is presumed to know—
The Crime, from us, is hidden—
Immured the whole of Life
Within a magic Prison
We reprimand the Happiness
That too competes with Heaven.

---

① 本诗写于1884年末。艾米莉·狄金森的朋友海伦1884年6月28日在科罗拉多泉市（Colorado Springs, 属EI Paso County, Colorado）家中从楼梯跌下摔成臀部骨裂，艾米莉·狄金森1884年9月给海伦写了一封信，信中抄录了本诗的最后4行，诗前引言为："I hope you may be harmed no more—I shall watch your passage from Crutch to Cane with jealous affection. From there to your Wings is but a stride—as was said of the convalescing Bird."。诗之后，艾米莉·狄金森告诉海伦，自己的身体状况也不佳："I, too, took my summer in a Chair, though from 'Nervous prostration,' not fracture, but take my Nerve by the Bridle now, and am again abroad—Thank you for the wish—"（L937）。1884年8月艾米莉·狄金森已经在写给弗朗西斯·诺克罗斯和路易丝·诺克罗斯两位表妹的一封信里提到了自己在1884年6月14日周六中午烤蛋糕时的首次意外昏厥："Eight Saturday noons ago, I was making a loaf of cake with Maggie, when I saw a great darkness coming and knew no more until late at night. ...I had fainted and lain unconscious for the first time in my life. Then I grew very sick and gave the others much alarm, but am now staying. The doctor calls it 'revenge of the nerves'."（L907）。

1601[①]

我们求上帝一个恩惠,
让我们获得原谅——
为什么,想必他知道——
罪行,对我们,总是隐藏——
禁锢整个一生
在一个魔狱里
我们谴责那欢愉
它与天堂过分攀比。

1602

Pursuing you in your transitions,
In other Motes—
Of other Myths
Your requisition be.
The Prism never held the Hues,
It only heard them play—

1602[②]

在你过渡时期追寻你,
在别的尘埃里——
属于别的神话
就是你所需。
棱镜从未持有那些色彩,
只倾听它们嬉戏——

1603

The going from a world we know
To one a wonder still

---

① 这是艾米莉·狄金森 1885 年 3 月写给朋友海伦的一封信中的结尾诗,诗前引言为:"Knew I how to pray, to intercede for your Foot were intuitive—but I am but a Pagan."(L976)。

② 本诗和第 1600 首诗最后 4 行一样,同在 1884 年 9 月艾米莉·狄金森写给朋友海伦的一封信中,本诗是该信的结尾诗,诗前引言为:"The Summer has been wide and deep, and a deeper Autumn is but the Gleam concomitant of that waylaying Light—"(L937)。本诗中所指过渡时期或指海伦从受伤(海伦摔伤的情况参见 1600 首诗注释)恢复至痊愈的过渡期。

Is like the child's adversity
Whose vista is a hill,
Behind the hill is sorcery
And everything unknown,
But will the secret compensate
For climbing it alone?

1603①
从我们了解的世界
进入依然未知的彼岸
就像孩童遇到的困境
他的视野是一座山,
山后面是魔幻
一切都很陌生,
但这秘密会否补偿
独自攀登?

1604
We send the Wave to find the Wave—
An Errand so divine,
The Messenger enamored too,
Forgetting to return,
We make the wise distinction still,
Soever made in vain,

---

① 艾米莉·狄金森在1884年6月14日周六中午烤蛋糕时首次意外昏厥,8周后的1884年8月,她在写给弗朗西斯·诺克罗斯和路易丝·诺克罗斯两位表妹的一封信里提到此次事故(参见第1600首诗注释),还提到侄子吉尔伯特之死:"The little boy we laid away never fluctuates, and his dim society is companion still. But it is growing damp and I must go in. Memory's fog is rising."(L907),作为本诗引言。在1883年末写给霍兰夫人的一封信中,艾米莉·狄金森在谈起自己身体不适之后,描绘了自己想起吉尔伯特的情形:"The Physician says I have 'Nervous prostration.' Possibly I have—I do not know the Names of Sickness. The Crisis of the sorrow of so many years is all that tires me—Please, Sister, to wait—'Open the Door, open the Door, they are waiting for me,' was Gilbert's sweet command in delirium. Who are waiting for him, all we possess we would give to know—Anguish, at last opened it, and he ran to the little Grave at his Grandparents' feet—"(L873)。

The sagest time to dam the sea is when the sea is gone—

1604①

我们派波浪去找波浪——
这差事如此神圣,
竟然令信使迷上,
忘记了回程,
我们仍能明智区分,
怎么做都是白费,
筑坝拦海最佳时机是等大海消退——

1605

Each that we lose takes part of us;
A crescent still abides,
Which like the moon, some turbid night,
Is summoned by the tides.

1605②

每一次丧失都带走我们的一部分;
一弯弦月留守依然,
就像月亮,某个迷蒙的夜晚,
被潮汐召唤。

1606

Quite empty, quite at rest,

---

① 这是艾米莉·狄金森在1884年写赠弗朗西斯·诺克罗斯和路易丝·诺克罗斯两位表妹的一首诗,诗前引言是:"A Tone from the old Bells, perhaps might wake the Children—"(L934)

② 这是艾米莉·狄金森在1884年3月写赠弗朗西斯·诺克罗斯和路易丝·诺克罗斯两位表妹的一首诗,诗前引言是:"Thank you, dears, for the sympathy. I hardly dare to know that I have lost another friend, but anguish finds it out."(L891)。当年3月13日,艾米莉·狄金森的恋人洛德法官在萨勒姆(Salem)去世。在艾米莉·狄金森生命最后11年里,多位亲友相继离世,包括父亲(1874年6月16日)和母亲(1882年11月14日),侄子吉尔伯特(1883年10月5日),恋人洛德法官(1884年3月13日)和沃兹华斯牧师(1882年4月1日),朋友海伦(1885年8月12日)和鲍尔斯(1878年1月16日)。

The Robin locks her Nest, and tries her Wings.
She does not know a Route
But puts her Craft about
For *rumored* Springs—
She does not ask for Noon—
She does not ask for Boon,
Crumbless and homeless, of but one request—
The Birds she lost—

1606①

空荡荡，静悄悄，
知更鸟锁上巢门，拍翅试探。
它不认识线路
但使出浑身解数
飞向*传说中的*春天——
她不求午间——
她不求恩典，
无可充饥也无家可归，一心想要——
她失去的那些鸟——

1607

Within that little Hive
Such Hints of Honey lay
As made Reality a Dream
And Dreams, Reality—

---

① 这是艾米莉·狄金森在1884年3月写给霍兰夫人的一封信中的一首诗，信的开头就告诉对方，洛德法官去世了："When I tell my sweet Mrs Holland that I have lost another friend, she will not wonder I do not write, but that I raise my Heart to a dropping syllable—Dear Mr Lord has left us"，接着是安慰之语："Your last dear words seemed stronger, and smiling in the feeling that you were to be, this latest sorrow came—I hope your own are with you, and may not be taken—I hope there is no Dart advancing or in store—"（L890），然后紧接本诗。

1607①

在那小小蜂巢里
处处隐藏蜜的暗示
令现实变为梦想
梦想,成为现实——

1608

The ecstasy to guess
Were a receipted bliss
If grace could talk.

1608②

揣测的狂喜
不啻一种收讫的福气
假如天恩可以明言。

1609

Sunset that screens, reveals—
Enhancing what we see
By menaces of Amethyst
And Moats of Mystery.

1609③

遮蔽的落日,显露——

---

① 参见1606首诗注释。这是艾米莉·狄金森在1884年3月写给霍兰夫人的一封信（L890）中的结尾诗。信开头提到洛德法官之死,然后是1606首诗;信后半部艾米莉·狄金森提到妹妹维尼给自己和他人用药的事情,说药效良好,然后紧接本诗。此药里可能有本诗里所提到的蜂蜜。

② 本诗可能是艾米莉·狄金森于病中所作,她在1885年将本诗寄赠某位至今身份不明的人,诗之前附言:"Sweet friends. I send a message by a Mouth that cannot speak—"（L995）。

③ 这是寄赠艾米莉·狄金森的哥哥奥斯汀的情人托德夫人的一首小诗。写于1884年。托德夫人1879年与托德先生（David Peck Todd, 1855—1939）结婚,1881年随夫搬到阿默斯特,从而认识艾米莉·狄金森的哥哥奥斯汀,进而发展成情人关系。艾米莉·狄金森1886年去世后,是托德夫人和艾米莉·狄金森的朋友及文学导师希金森一起编辑出版了艾米莉·狄金森的第一和第二本诗选集（1890,1891）,随后托德夫人又独自编辑出版艾米莉·狄金森第一本书信选集（1894）和第三本诗选集（1896）。托德先生1875年毕业于阿默斯特学院,1881年起曾任阿默斯特学院天文台台长（Director of the Observatory）以及天文和航海学教授（professor of astronomy and navigation）。

使我们所见美不胜收
以紫晶的威逼
和神秘的壕沟。

1610

Morning that comes but once,
Considers coming twice—
Two Dawns upon a single Morn,
Make Life a sudden price.

1610①

只出现一次的清晨,
思忖着出现两次——
一个清晨两度黎明,
赋予生命意外的价值。

1611

Their dappled importunity
Disparage or dismiss—
The Obloquies of Etiquette
Are obsolete to Bliss—

1611②

对他们的胡搅蛮缠
要么轻视要么不理——
礼节的斥责
对幸福已过时——

1612

The Auctioneer of Parting

---

① 这是艾米莉·狄金森寄赠哥哥奥斯汀的情人托德夫人的一首小诗,写于1884年。
② 这是艾米莉·狄金森寄赠哥哥奥斯汀的情人托德夫人的一首小诗,写于1884年。本诗大意或是:对对方(托德夫人)的强索(诗歌),我(艾米莉·狄金森)要么轻视要么不理睬,不必进行礼节性的委婉斥责,因为这样并不能增加我的幸福快乐。

His "Going, going, gone"
Shouts even from the Crucifix,
And brings his Hammer down—
He only sells the Wilderness,
The prices of Despair
Range from a single human Heart
To Two—not any more—

1612①

别离的拍卖师
说"走,走,消失"
甚至在十字架上喊,
还落下锤子——
他只推销荒野,
绝望的价格
从一颗人类的心
到两颗——没有再多——

1613

Not Sickness stains the Brave,
Nor any Dart,
Nor Doubt of Scene to come,
But an adjourning Heart—

1613②

不是疾病玷污了勇士,
也不是任何箭镞,
也不是对未来情形的疑虑,
而是一颗心的踌躇——

---

① 这是艾米莉·狄金森寄赠哥哥奥斯汀的情人托德夫人的一首小诗,写于1884年。
② 这是艾米莉·狄金森1884年7月19日寄赠哥哥奥斯汀的情人托德夫人的一首小诗,诗前附言:"How martial the Apology of Nature! We die, said the Deathless of Thermopylae, in obedience to Law—"(L906)。关于"Thermopylae"(温泉关),参见第1554首诗注释。

1614
Parting with Thee reluctantly,
That we have never met,
A Heart sometimes a Foreigner,
Remembers it forgot—

1614①
与你别离依依,
因我们从未相遇,
心有时是异域人士,
才想起它已忘记——

1615
Oh what a Grace is this,
What Majesties of Peace,
That having breathed
The fine—ensuing Right
Without Diminuet Proceed!

1615②
啊这是何等的恩典,

---

① 1884 年秋天,托德夫人的父母埃本(Eben Jenks Loomis, 1828—1912)和玛丽(Mary Alden Wilder, 1831—1910)携女儿托德夫人到访阿默斯特。在他们离开之际,艾米莉·狄金森给托德夫人的父母写赠了本诗。诗后附言为:"In all the circumference of Expression, those guileless words of Adam and Eve never were surpassed, 'I was afraid and hid Myself.'"(L946)。附言中的引言出自《圣经·旧约·创世纪》第 3 章第 10 节中亚当对上帝的回话:"And he said, I heard thy voice in the garden, and I was afraid, because I was naked; and I hid myself."(Genesis 3: 10)。从诗内容看,艾米莉·狄金森似未与托德夫人的父母见面,因此心中更不舍别离。自己仿佛是异邦人,与周围环境甚为疏离,以至于别离之际,才想起自己忘记了一些事,比如曾邀请托德夫人的父母到访等。

② 这是艾米莉·狄金森 1884 年 11 月 19 日写给托德夫人的父母埃本和玛丽的一封信的结尾诗。诗前的信这样写道:"The atmospheric acquaintance so recently and delightfully made, is not, I trust, ephemeral, but absolute as Ether, as the delicate emblem just received tenderly implies. Thank you for the Beauty—Thank you too for Boundlessness—that rarely given, but choicest Gift. To 'know in whom' we 'have believed,' is Immortality."(L953)信中艾米莉·狄金森说他们之间的关系虽是"氛围中的相识"(atmospheric acquaintance)而非现实具体交流而成的相识,但并非短暂,而是绝对如苍天以太,这表明他们在现实中可能真的没见过面。艾米莉·狄金森还感谢对方送的漂亮礼物,感激对方的美意、宽广胸怀和对她的理解。本诗表达的或许就是对对方礼物的感激,虽然自己为对方所做的甚少。

这宁谧多么庄严,
闻吸
那美妙的——随之而至的特权
无须些许努力!

1616

Who abdicated Ambush
And went the way of Dusk,
And now against his subtle Name
There stands an Asterisk
As confident of him as we—
Impregnable we are—
The whole of Immortality
Secreted in a Star.

1616①

谁放弃了隐伏
出没在黄昏里,
如今在他敏感的名字旁边
打上了一个星形标记
如我们一般对他充满信心——
我们坚信不移——
永生的全部
隐匿于一颗星里。

1617

To try to speak, and miss the way
And ask it of the Tears,

---

① 参见第1525首,只有第1行和最后两行不同。艾米莉·狄金森1884年将本诗寄给了鲍尔斯四世,诗前写道:"A Tree your Father gave me, bore this priceless flower. Would you accept to because of him"(L935)。这封信是对鲍尔斯四世的父亲鲍尔斯的怀念,该信还随附了鲍尔斯以前从一棵树上摘下送给艾米莉·狄金森的一朵花。关于鲍尔斯一家父子孙三代的工作关系,参见第1453首诗注释。

Is Gratitude's sweet poverty,
The Tatters that he wears—

A better Coat if he possessed
Would help him to conceal,
Not subjugate, the Mutineer
Whose title is "the Soul."

1617①
想要开口，却不知所以
就向泪水问计，
这就是感激甜蜜的贫瘠，
他所披的破衣——

假如他有更好的外套
将有助于他藏好，
而非制伏，那叛逆者
"灵魂"是他的名号。

1618
There are two Mays
And then a Must
And after that a Shall.
How infinite the compromise
That indicates I will!

1618②
有两个可以
接着一个必须

---

① 这是艾米莉·狄金森1884年1月写赠爱德华·塔克曼的夫人莎拉的一首诗。
② 这是艾米莉·狄金森写赠迪克曼牧师的妻子伊丽莎白的一首诗。迪克曼牧师1883—1891年间任艾米莉·狄金森家乡阿默斯特镇第一公理会教堂（First Congregationalist Church）牧师。1886年艾米莉·狄金森去世时，迪克曼牧师与曾于1867—1877年间担任阿默斯特镇第一公理会教堂执行牧师（acting pastor）的詹金斯牧师共同主持了艾米莉·狄金森的葬礼。

随后是一个将欲。
这种折中多么宽泛
都意味着我愿意!

1619

Not knowing when the Dawn will come,
I open every Door,
Or has it Feathers, like a Bird,
Or Billows, like a Shore—

1619①

不知黎明何时来到,
我打开每扇门窗,
它是否像鸟,有羽毛,
或像海岸,带来巨浪——

1620

Circumference thou Bride of Awe
Possessing thou shalt be
Possessed by every hallowed Knight
That dares to covet thee

1620②

寰宇你这敬畏的新娘

---

① 本诗写于1884年。艾米莉·狄金森在1886年春写给文学导师希金森的一封信(L1042)中告诉对方关于朋友海伦于1885年8月12日去世的消息,表达了震惊和悲痛,描述了她与海伦的最后一次会面,接着就抄录本诗在信中,不过首行的"the Dawn"改成了"Herself",第三行的"it"改成了"she"。

② 这是艾米莉·狄金森1884年3月专门为雕塑家朋友丹尼尔·弗伦奇(Daniel Chester French, 1850—1931)写的诗,并于1884年4月寄给了对方,以祝贺他的雕塑作品约翰·哈佛(John Harvard)雕像在剑桥大学的大学学堂前揭幕。她在诗前附言:"We learn with delight of the recent acquisition to your fame, and hasten to congratulate you on an honor so reverently won. Success is dust, but an aim forever touched with dew. God keep you fundamental!",随后就是本诗,但标点有所不同:"Circumference, thou bride/Of awe,—possessing, thou/Shalt be possessed by/Every hallowed knight/That dares to covet thee."(L898)。丹尼尔·弗伦奇的父亲亨利·弗伦奇(Henry Flagg French, 1813—1885)曾担任位于艾米莉·狄金森家乡阿默斯特创办于1863年的马萨诸塞州农业学院(Massachusetts Agricultural College)首任校长,弗伦奇一家居住在阿默斯特的几年里,丹尼尔·弗伦奇认识了艾米莉·狄金森。

你占有也终究
被每一位胆敢觊觎你的
神圣骑士占有

1621

A Flower will not trouble her, it has so small a Foot,
And yet if you compare the Lasts,
Hers is the smallest Boot—

1621①

一朵花不会将她打扰，它的脚这么小巧，
但假如你拿鞋楦来比较，
她的靴子最小——

1622

A Sloop of Amber slips away
Upon an Ether Sea,
And wrecks in Peace a Purple Tar,
The Son of Ecstasy—

1622②

一艘琥珀单桅船悄悄驶离
在苍天的海域，
平静中撞亡了一名紫色水手，
这狂喜的后裔——

1623

A World made penniless by that departure
Of minor fabrics begs

---

① 本诗应该是随一朵作为礼物的花送人的。
② 本诗写于1884年，是准备送给爱德华·塔克曼教授（Professor Edward Tuckermam, 1817—1886）的，但最后并未寄出，诗前的附言是："Please accept a Sunset."。塔克曼是阿默斯特学院的植物学教授，自1858年起在该学院任教，直至逝世。

But sustenance is of the spirit
The Gods but Dregs

1623①
因那次别离而一文不名的世界
乞求次等的东西
但滋养来自精神
诸神都是渣滓

1624
Apparently with no surprise
To any happy Flower
The Frost beheads it at it's play—
In accidental power—
The blonde Assassin passes on—
The Sun proceeds unmoved
To measure off another Day
For an Approving God.

1624
显然不感到惊讶
对于任何快乐之花
寒霜在它嬉戏时斩首了它——
受意外之力激发——
那金发刺客扬长而去——
太阳漠然地继续
去丈量出另一天
为一个赞许的上帝。

---

① 本诗原稿与第 1599 首诗同在一页稿纸上。第 1599 首诗是纪念 1884 年 3 月 13 日去世的洛德法官的，它于 1885 年 2 月 20 日被寄给了洛德法官在波士顿的亲戚金博尔律师（见第 1599 首诗题注）。因此本诗应写于 1885 年 2 月，貌似原来准备用来替代第 1599 首寄出，但最终没被寄出。因此本诗主题极可能与洛德法官的逝世有关，大意是指洛德去世后，作者受到了巨大打击，不可能要求他回返，只能求次等的东西来支撑自己，即亟须获得精神上的安慰，而宗教并未起到安慰作用。

1625

Back from the cordial Grave I drag thee
He shall not take thy Hand
Nor put his spacious arm around thee
That none can understand

1625

从亲切的坟墓里我拽回你
他不会拉你的手
也不会用他宽阔的臂膀搂着你
这一点没人能参透

1626

No Life can pompless pass away—
The lowliest career
To the same Pageant wends its way
As that exalted here—

How cordial is the mystery!
The hospitable Pall
A "this way" beckons spaciously—
A Miracle for all!

1626①

没有生命可以平淡无奇地逝去——
最卑微的一生
也会参加同样的盛会
像这位在此被高捧——

这神秘多热情！
那殷勤的柩衣

---

① 本诗写于 1884 年，似乎是作者目睹某一次葬礼时有感而写。

大方地招呼"这边请"——
这是所有人的奇迹!

1627

The pedigree of Honey
Does not concern the Bee,
Nor lineage of Ecstasy
Delay the Butterfly
On spangle journeys to the peak
Of some perceiveless thing—
The right of way to Tripoli
A more essential thing.

(Version I)

The Pedigree of Honey
Does not concern the Bee—
A Clover, any time, to him,
Is Aristocracy—

(Version II)

1627①

蜜的谱系
蜜蜂并不在意,
狂喜的家世
也不能让蝴蝶延迟
闪光之旅
往某个无法察知物之顶——
去的黎波里的正道
是更重要的事情。

(版本1)

蜜的谱系

---

① 蜜蜂和蝴蝶并不在意花的出身与地位,对它们而言,如何能抵达花朵("去的黎波里的正道"),停在花之巅,是更重要的事情。花朵(红花草)任何时候在它们看来都是高贵的。

蜜蜂并不在意——
红花草,任何时候,对于他,
都有贵族气——

(版本 2)

1628

A Drunkard cannot meet a Cork
Without a Revery—
And so encountering a Fly
This January Day
Jamaicas of Remembrance stir
That send me reeling in—
The moderate drinker of Delight
Does not deserve the spring—
Of juleps, part are the Jug
And more are in the joy—
Your connoisseur in Liquours
Consults the Bumble Bee—

1628

醉汉不可能见到瓶塞
而不遐想连翩——
见到一只苍蝇也如此
这个一月天
记忆中的牙买加涌起
使我头晕目眩——
快乐的温和饮者
不配有春天——
冰镇薄荷酒,部分在酒罐
更多在欢乐中——
你这美酒鉴赏家
咨询大黄蜂——

1629

Arrows enamored of his Heart—

Forgot to rankle there
And Venoms he mistook for Balms
disdained to rankle there—

1629
箭簇迷恋他的心——
忘记在那里发作
他误以为香膏的毒液
不屑在那里发作——

1630
As from the earth the light Balloon
Asks nothing but release—
Ascension that for which it was,
It's soaring Residence.
The spirit looks upon the Dust
That fastened it so long
With indignation,
As a Bird
Defrauded of it's song.

1630
就像轻气球从地面
只求释放别无他索——
它存在本就为上升,
到它高耸的住所。
灵魂眼望尘土
把它拴了这么久
无比愤怒,
像一只鸟
被骗取了歌声。

1631
Oh Future! thou secreted peace

Or subterranean woe—
Is there no wandering route of grace
That leads away from thee—
No circuit sage of all the course
Descried by cunning Men
To balk thee of thy sacred Prey—
Advancing to thy Den—

1631
啊未来！你隐匿的宁静
或地下的悲哀——
难道没有蜿蜒的恩典路径
能从你身边引开——
难道全程没有明智的环道
被狡猾的人类看到
以阻止你得到你神圣的猎物——
走向你的窝巢——

1632
So give me back to Death—
The Death I never feared
Except that it deprived of thee—
And now, by Life deprived,
In my own Grave I breathe
And estimate it's size—
It's size is all that Hell can guess—
And all that Heaven was—

1632
那么请把我交还给死亡——
死亡我从不恐惧
除了它曾夺去你——
如今，被生活夺去，
我就在我墓里呼吸

并对它的大小做评估——
它的大小就是地狱能猜出的一切——
和天堂曾经的全部——

1633

Still own thee—still thou art
What surgeons call alive—
Though slipping—slipping I perceive
To thy reportless Grave—

Which question shall I clutch—
What answer wrest from thee
Before thou dost exude away
In the recallless sea?

1633

依然拥有你——你依然活着
一如外科医生所宣布——
尽管滑向——我觉察到滑向
你那无人提及的坟墓——

我该揪住哪个问题——
从你那里逼出什么答案
在你完全逸入
杳无回音的大海之前?

1634

Talk not to me of Summer Trees
The foliage of the mind
A Tabernacle is for Birds
Of no corporeal kind
And winds do go that way at noon
To their Ethereal Homes
Whose Bugles call the least of us
To undepicted Realms

1634
别跟我谈夏天的树木
心灵的枝叶
是一顶帐幕
给无肉躯的鸟儿停歇
午间风正是朝那边去
到它们太虚的宅邸
它们的号角极少召唤我们
去未描绘的疆域

1635
The Jay his Castanet has struck
Put on your muff for Winter
The Tippet that ignores his voice
Is impudent to nature

Of Swarthy Days he is the close
His Lotus is a chestnut
The Cricket drops a sable line
No more from yours at present

1635①
松鸦已敲起他的响板
请戴上你的袖套过冬
不理他声音的披肩
是对自然的不恭

他是昏暗日子的结束
他的莲花是一颗板栗
蟋蟀抛下一根黑线
当下再无你的声息

---

① 本诗描绘深秋转入初冬的景象：松鸦发出声音，宣告昏暗的日子结束，进入了冬天，需要披戴上暖手的护手筒和披肩。松鸦的食物是板栗，蟋蟀抛下一根黑线（一行黑色歌谣），逃匿而去，再无声息。

1636

The Sun in reigning to the West
Makes not as much of sound
As Cart of man in road below
Adroitly turning round
That Whiffletree of Amethyst

1636

驶向西方的太阳
它发出的声喧比不上
下界人驾的马车在路面
灵巧地旋转
那紫晶的车前横杆

1637

Is it too late to touch you, Dear?
We this moment knew—
Love Marine and Love terrene—
Love celestial too—

1637①

是不是太迟赶不上你了,亲爱的?
我们对此刻早有所知——
爱海洋及爱大地——
也爱天宇——

1638

Go thy great way!

---

① 本诗写于1885年,1885年3月2日被寄赠克洛韦尔教授(Edward Payson Crowell, 1830—1911)的夫人玛丽(Mary Hardy Warner, 1830—1903),就在他们一家出游欧洲的前夕。玛丽是艾米莉·狄金森儿时的友伴,玛丽的父亲华纳(Aaron Warner, 1794—1876)1844—1853年间在阿默斯特学院任教,是修辞、演讲和英国文学教授。玛丽于1861年嫁给克洛韦尔,1864—1908年他在阿默斯特学院任教,是拉丁文教授。

The Stars thou meetst
Are even as Thyself—
For what are Stars but Asterisks
To point a human Life?

1638①

走你的大道!
你所遇见的星辰
甚至就如你自己——
何谓星辰除了作为星号
将一个人生标记?

1639②

A Letter is a joy of Earth—
It is denied the Gods—

1639

信是人间一种欢愉——
它不对众神供给——

1640

Take all away from me, but leave me Ecstasy,

---

① 本诗写于1885年2月。大意指人死后升天,成为星星,每一颗星星代表一段曾经的人生。艾米莉·狄金森在1885年2月写给洛德法官在波士顿的亲戚金博尔律师的一封信中抄录了本诗,作为对1884年3月13日去世的洛德法官的纪念,信的开头写道:"To take the hand of my friend's friend, even apparitionally, is a hallowed pleasure. I think you told me you were his kinsman. I was only his friend—and cannot yet believe that",本诗前的引言写道:"On my way to my sleep, last night, I paused at the Portrait—Had I not loved it, I had feared it, the Face had such ascension—"(L967)。同样在1885年初,艾米莉·狄金森还把本诗寄给了库伯的夫人阿比盖尔,诗前引言写道:"Nothing inclusive of a human Heart could be 'trivial.' That appalling Boon makes all things paltry but itself—To thank you would profane you—There are moments when Gratitude is a desecration—"(L970)。另参见第1525和第1616首诗,其中也提到"asterisk"(星号;星形标记)。

② 这是艾米莉·狄金森在1885年1月2日写给哥哥奥斯汀的情人托德夫人的父母埃本和玛丽的一封信的结尾诗,该信对对方送来的圣诞贺卡表示感谢,信中的诗前引言写道:"And what *is* Ecstasy but Affection and what is Affection but the Germ of the little Note?"(L960)。

And I am richer then than all my Fellow Men—
Ill it becometh me to dwell so wealthily
When at my very Door are those possessing more,
In abject poverty—

1640①
把我的一切带走,但给我留下狂喜,
我就比我所有同胞都富有——
这并不合适我活得如此富裕
当我门口那些比我拥有更多的人,
陷入可怜的贫瘠——

1641
Betrothed to Righteousness might be
An Ecstasy discreet
But Nature relishes the Pinks
Which she was taught to eat—

1641②
许配于正义或许
是一种谨慎的狂喜
但大自然欢享石竹
她已被教怎么吃——

---

① 与第1639首诗一样,本诗是艾米莉·狄金森在1885年1月2日写给托德夫人的父母埃本和玛丽的一封信中抄录的一首诗。诗前引言写道:"I thought as I saw the exultant Face and the uplifted Letter"(L960)。此外,艾米莉·狄金森也在1885年将本诗寄给朋友鲍尔斯的儿子小鲍尔斯,诗前的留言写道:"Had I not known I was not asleep, I should have feared I dreamed, so blissful was their beauty, but Day and they demurred."(L1014)。本诗还在1885年3月被抄录在艾米莉·狄金森写给朋友海伦的一封信中,信中诗前的引言写道:"To reproach my own Foot in behalf of your's, is involuntary, and finding myself, no solace in 'whom he loveth he chasteneth' your Valor astounds me—It was only a small Wasp, said the French Physician, repairing the sting, but the strength to perish is sometimes withheld—though who but you could tell a Foot."(L976)。
② 本诗1885年被寄给了某位身份不明的人(L993)。

1642

"Red Sea," indeed! Talk not to me
Of purple Pharaoh—
I have a Navy in the West
Would pierce his Columns thro'—
Guileless, yet of such Glory fine
That all along the Line
Is it, or is it not, Marine—
Is it, or not, divine—
The Eye inquires with a sigh
That Earth sh'd be so big—
What Exultation in the Woe—
What Wine in the fatigue!

1642①

"红海,"确实! 别跟我讲
那紫袍的法老——
我有一支海军在西方
将穿破他的风浪——
无需伪装,就已威风八面
一路辉煌向前
它是,或它不是,海洋——
它是,或不是,神圣的地方——
眼睛叹声问起
竟有如此大的地球——
悲苦中多少欢愉——
疲惫中多少美酒!

1643

Extol thee—could I—   Then I will

---

① 前两行提到的红海和法老,可参见《圣经·旧约·出埃及记》第14章记述摩西带领以色列人逃离埃及,抵红海边时,蒙上帝护佑,海水往两边分开,以色列人得以从红海底穿行而过,随后跟来的法老的追兵则被海水淹没(Exodus 14)。

By saying nothing new—
But just the anti① fair—averring—fairest—**truest truth**
that thou art heavenly②
   tritest—brightest truth—
    Sweetest
   that tritest eulogy
   that thou are heavenly
Perceiving thee is evidence
That we are of the sky
Partaking thee a guar t y③ guaranty
of immortality

1643④
赞美你——如果可以—— 我会努力
说不出什么新意——
只有反公平的——宣称——最公平——最真的真理
说你来自天堂
  最陈腐的——最明亮的真理——
   最美妙
  那最陈腐的悼词
  说你来自天堂
感知你就证明
我们属于天上
分给你一份保证
关于永生

1644
Some one prepared this mighty show

---

① 本词在原稿中被划掉。
② 在 1960 年阅读版全集中 heavenly 后有句号。
③ 这是一首未完稿的诗，原稿如此。
④ 这是一首未完成的诗稿，原文和译文的黑体为译者所加，用以标示本诗在约翰逊 1960 年阅读版中的文本。1960 年阅读版中，本诗分为两节，前后两节各 4 行。

      To which without a Ticket go
      The nations and the Days—
      Displayed before the simplest Door
          Pass slow before the humblest Door
      That all may them—it—examine
                      and more
            witness it and more①
      The—of summer Days—
          pomp of summer Days②
      The Ethiopian Days

1644③
有人准备了这场盛大表演
没有门票就去看
那些国家和时光——
就在那最简朴的门前展现
    缓慢经过那最卑微的门前
让所有人可以他们——对它——检验
               以及更多
    将它以及更多饱览
那——夏季时光——
    夏季时光的盛况
那埃塞俄比亚的时光

1645

The Ditch is dear to the Drunken man
For is it not his Bed—

---

① 在约翰逊1960年阅读版中，本行末有逗号。
② 在约翰逊1960年阅读版中，本行末有句号。
③ 这是一首未完成的诗稿，原文和译文的黑体为译者所加，用以标示本诗在约翰逊1960年阅读版中的文本。1960年阅读版中，本诗分为两节，前后两节各3行。本诗描述夏季这段时光的盛况，各个国家和时光没有门票都去观看，该盛况也面对所有人开放，让所有人饱览这一切，还感受到更多。

His Advocate—his Edifice—①
How safe his fallen Head
In her disheveled Sanctity—
Above him is the sky—
Oblivion bending over him
And Honor leagues away②

1645
水沟是醉汉的挚爱
因为它不就是他的床——
他的拥护者——他的大宅——
他倒下的头必安然无恙
在她蓬乱的圣洁中——
他上面是苍天——
遗忘俯身向他
而荣耀在数里③之远

1646
Why should we hurry—why indeed④
When every way we fly
We are molested equally
By immortality⑤
no⑥ respite from the inference
That this which is begun⑦
Though where it's⑧ labors lie
A bland uncertainty
Besets the sight

---

① 在约翰逊1960年阅读版中，本行末为问号。
②⑤ 在约翰逊1960年阅读版中，本行末有句号。
③ 里（league）：实为里格，长度单位，1里格约为3英里或4.8千米。
④ 在约翰逊1960年阅读版中，本行末有问号。
⑥ "no"在约翰逊1960年阅读版全集中是"No"。
⑦ 在约翰逊1960年阅读版全集中，本行末有逗号。
⑧ "it's"在1960年阅读版中为"its"。

This mighty night①

1646
我们为何匆忙——为何这样
当我们逃往任何方向
我们受的骚扰都同等
被永生
根据推理不会停歇
已开始的这一切
尽管它劳碌在何处
一种漠然的变数
包围了眼前的一切
这盛大的暗夜

1647
Of Glory not a Beam is left
But her Eternal House—
The Asterisk is for the Dead,
The Living, for the Stars—

1647②
一束荣光也没留下
除了她永恒的门庭——
星号代表死者,
生者,代表星星——

1648
The immortality she gave

---

① 在1960年阅读版中,本行末有短横杠符号。
② 本诗和第1648首诗都是艾米莉·狄金森1886年4月末写给文学导师希金森的一封信(L1043)内抄录的诗,两首诗都与1885年8月12日逝世的朋友海伦有关。这封信的写作时间距艾米莉·狄金森5月1日病逝仅有2周多。此前不久的1886年春她写给希金森的一封回信中已说自己重病在身:"I have been very ill, Dear friend, since November, bereft of Book and Thought, by the Doctor's reproof, but begin to roam in my Room now—"(L1042)。

We borrowed at her Grave—
For just one Plaudit famishing,
The Might of Human love—

1648①

她永生的献出
我们借自她的坟墓——
就为一次饥肠辘辘的赞扬,
那人类爱的力量——

1649

A Cap of Lead across the sky
Was tight and surly drawn
We could not find the mighty Face
The Figure was withdrawn—

A Chill came up as from a shaft
Our noon became a well
A Thunder storm combines the charms
Of Winter and of Hell②

1649③

一顶铅帽跨过苍天
被画得又暗又紧
我们找不到那威武的脸
那轮廓已归隐——

---

① 本诗和第1647首诗都是艾米莉·狄金森1886年4月末写给文学导师希金森的一封信 (L1043) 内抄录的诗,都是为纪念1885年8月12日逝世的朋友海伦而作。本诗大意是海伦所展示给我们的人类爱的力量,自她逝世后我们就没再感受到了,因此我们自她的坟墓借来永生的她,就为了献上我们的喝彩,赞扬她那人类爱的力量。我们已经受此饥荒很久了。
② 在1960年阅读版中,本行末有句号。
③ 第1649~1709首诗均为苏珊的誊抄版,原稿已遗失。

一股寒气似从竖井里升起
我们的正午与一口井无异
一场雷雨兼容两种魅力
冬季和地狱

1650

A lane of Yellow led the eye
Unto a Purple Wood
Whose soft inhabitants to be
Surpasses solitude
If Bird the silence contradict
Or flower presume to show
In that low summer of the West
Impossible to know—

1650

一条黄色小径把目光带进
一片紫色树林深处
那里柔软的居民
即将超越孤独
是鸟儿打破沉寂
或花儿打算显耀
在那西边低迷的夏季
无法知道——

1651

A Word made Flesh is seldom
And tremblingly partook
Nor then perhaps reported
But have I not mistook
Each one of us has tasted
With ecstasies of stealth
The very food debated
To our specific strength—

A Word that breathes distinctly
Has not the power to die
Cohesive as the Spirit
It may expire if He—
"Made Flesh and dwelt among us①
Could condescension be
Like this consent of Language
This loved Philology

1651②
有血有肉的字很少
吃起来不禁哆嗦
恐怕也没人报告
但假如我没弄错
我们每人都曾尝试
怀着暗地的迷狂
这种争议的美食
对我们特定的力量——

一个生机盎然的字
无力去死
它像灵一样密实

---

① "Made Flesh and dwelt among us：诗原稿中双引号不全，本句源自《圣经·新约·约翰福音》第1章第14节："And the Word was made flesh, and dwelt among us, (and we beheld his glory, the glory as of the only begotten of the Father,) full of grace and truth."（John 1：14）[道成了肉身，住在我们中间，充充满满地有恩典，有真理。我们也见过他的荣光，正是父独生子的荣光。]

② 题解：有血有肉的生动的字我们都喜欢，也有过写出这样的文字的经验，这样的文字生机盎然、活力四射不会死，像灵一样虽然飘逸但密实具体可感，它的所谓断气其实只是像耶稣一样由圣灵化"成了肉身住在我们中间"，相当于有些屈尊、委屈了，就像语言屈尊同意由枯燥的符号变为有血肉、有活力的文字一样，这确实是令人爱慕的语言学。关于文字的活力问题，艾米莉·狄金森曾在1862年4月15日写给文学导师希金森的一封信中问对方是否觉得她的诗是"活的""有呼吸的"："Are you too deeply occupied to say if my Verse is alive? … The Mind is so near itself—it cannot see, distinctly—and I have none to ask—Should you think it breathed—and had you the leisure to tell me, I should feel quick gratitude—"（L260）。

它可能会断气假如他——
"成了肉身住在我们中间
确实委屈了些
就像这语言的应许
这令人爱慕的语言学

1652

Advance is Life's condition
The Grave but a Relay
Supposed to be a terminus
That makes it hated so—

The Tunnel is not lighted
Existence with a wall
Is better we consider
Than not exist at all—

1652

前进是生命的前提
坟墓不过一次接力
假定它是终点
就使它令人讨厌——

隧道漆黑无光
存在有一堵墙
我们想
也好过空空荡荡——

1653

As we pass Houses musing slow
If they be occupied
So minds pass minds
If they be occupied

1653

正如我们经过一座座房慢慢思量
是否它们已被占据
同样思想也经过思想
是否它们已被占据

1654

Beauty crowds me till I die
Beauty mercy have on me
But if I expire today
Let it be in sight of thee—

1654①

美拥挤我直至我死去
美请对我爱怜
但假如今天我断气
让它发生在你眼前——

1655

Conferring with myself
My stranger disappeared
Though first upon a berry fat
Miraculously fared
How paltry looked my cares
My practise how absurd
Superfluous my whole career
Beside this travelling Bird

1655

我正与自己商议

---

① 艾米莉·狄金森对美的看法,也见于她的书信中,如"In a World too full of Beauty for Peace, I have met nothing more beautiful."(L759),以及"How vast is the chastisement of Beauty, given us by our Maker!"(L965)。

我的陌生客就消失
尽管是首次用饱满的浆果
奇迹般地喂食
我的忧虑多么不足取
我的做法多么悖理
我的一生何等多余
与这只旅行的鸟儿相比

1656
Down Time's quaint stream
Without an oar
We are enforced to sail
Our Port a secret
Our Perchance a Gale
What Skipper would
Incur the Risk
What Buccaneer would ride
Without a surety from the Wind
Or schedule of the Tide—

1656
驶入时光奇异的河流
没有船桨
我们被迫起航
我们的码头是个秘密
我们或许遇上风浪
什么样的船长
会招致风险
什么样的海盗会袭扰
没有风的担保
或海潮的时间表——

1657
Eden is that old-fashioned House

We dwell in every day
Without suspecting our abode
Until we drive away①

How fair on looking back② the Day
We sauntered from the Door③
Unconscious our returning④
But discover it no more⑤

1657
伊甸园是那所老式房屋
我们每日其中安居
从不怀疑我们的住处
直至我们驱车离去

回首那天多美
我们信步迈出门外
不知不觉我们返回
但发现它已不再

1658
Endanger it, and the Demand
Of tickets for a sigh
Amazes the Humility
Of Credibility—

Recover it to Nature
And that dejected Fleet
Find Consternation's Carnival

---

① ⑤ 在1960年阅读版中，本行末有句号。
② 在1960年阅读版中，本词后有逗号。
③ 在1960年阅读版中，本行末有短横杠符号。
④ 在1960年阅读版中，本行末有逗号。

Divested of it's Meat①

1658
危害它，然后索要
叹息的票
令信誉的卑膝
惊异——

恢复它到自然
那队沮丧的舰艘
发现惊愕的欢宴
缺了它的肉

1659②
Fame is a fickle food
Upon a shifting plate
Whose table once a
Guest but not
The second time is set③
Whose crumbs the crows inspect
And with ironic caw
Flap past it to the
Farmer's Corn④
Men eat of it and die⑤

1659⑥
声名是无常的食物
在变换的盘子里

---

① ③ ⑤ 在1960年阅读版中，本行末有句号。
② 在1960年阅读版，中本诗分2节，各5行。
④ 在1960年阅读版中，本行末有短横杠符号。
⑥ 艾米莉·狄金森论及 fame（声名/名声）的诗有多首，包括第 228、713、866、1232、1475、1531、1659、1763 首。

它的餐桌一次
一位宾客但不会
摆放第二次
乌鸦检视它的残屑
发出冷嘲的聒噪
振翅从旁取道
飞向农夫的谷粒
人吃了它就死去

1660
Glory is that bright tragic thing
That for an instant
Means Dominion①
Warms some poor name
That never felt the Sun②
Gently replacing
In oblivion—

1660
荣耀是那光鲜可悲的东西
在某一瞬间
意味着统治权
温暖某个可怜的名字
它从未感受过阳光
又轻轻放回
进入遗忘——

1661
Guest am I to have
Light my northern room
Why to cordiality so averse to come

---

① 在1960年阅读版中,本行末有短横杠符号。
② 在1960年阅读版中,本行末有逗号。

Other friends adjourn
Other bonds decay
Why avoid so narrowly
My fidelity—

1661
我愿有客人
照亮我北边的房间
为何如此反感邂逅热忱
别的朋友推延
别的纽带不济
为何擦肩回避
我的忠贞不渝——

1662
He went by sleep that drowsy route
To the surmising Inn—
At day break to begin his race
Or ever to remain—

1662
他趁安眠沿那条困倦之道
到臆想中的客栈——
拂晓时开始他的赛跑
或永远流连——

1663
His mind of man, a secret makes
I meet him with a start
He carries a circumference
In which I have no part①

---

① 在 1960 年阅读版中，本行末有短横杠符号。

Or even if I deem I do
He otherwise may know
Impregnable to inquest
However neighborly—

1663
他的人类思想，由一个秘密造就
我见他时就惊惧
他携着一个宇宙
其中并无我参与

或即便我认为我有
他知道不是事实
经得起任何讯问
即使是邻里关系——

1664
I did not reach Thee
But my feet slip nearer every day
Three Rivers and a Hill to cross
One Desert and a Sea
I shall not count the journey one
When I am telling thee①

Two deserts② but the Year is cold
So that will help the sand
One desert crossed—
The second one
Will feel as cool as land
Sahara is too little price

---

① 在1960年阅读版中，本行末有句号。
② 在1960年阅读版中，本词后有逗号。

To pay for thy Right hand①

The Sea comes last—Step merry② feet③
So short we have to go④
To play together we are prone⑤
But we must labor now⑥
The last shall be the lightest load
That we have had to draw⑦

The Sun goes crooked—
That is Night
Before he makes the bend⑧
We must have passed the Middle Sea⑨
Almost we wish the End
Were further off⑩
Too great it seems
So near the Whole to stand⑪

We step like Plush⑫
We stand like snow⑬
The waters murmur new⑭
Three rivers and the Hill are passed⑮
Two deserts and the sea!
Now Death usurps my Premium
And gets the look at Thee—⑯

1664
我尚未抵达你

---

① ⑦ ⑧ ⑪ ⑭　在1960年阅读版中，本行末有句号。
②　在1960年阅读版中，本词后有逗号。
③ ⑤ ⑥ ⑫ ⑬　在1960年阅读版中，本行末有逗号。
④ ⑨ ⑩ ⑮　在1960年阅读版中，本行末有短横杠符号。
⑯　在1960年阅读版中，本行末是句号。

但我双足每天都滑近一些
有三条河和一座山要穿越
还有一片沙漠和一片海域
我不会把这旅程算作一个
当我把这些告诉你

两片沙漠但岁月寒冷
这样对沙子有好处
穿过了一片沙漠——
那第二片
会感觉凉爽如平陆
撒哈拉的价值不足以
作为对你右手的偿付

最后是那片海域——迈出轻快脚步
时间紧促必须出发
我们还想一起玩耍
但现在就得启程
最后的任务一定最轻
我们必须圆满完成

太阳绕弯——
那是夜晚
在它转弯前
我们一定越过了中部海域
我们几乎盼望终点
可以更远——
看起来多威武
能紧紧站在全体旁边

我们步履如鸿毛
我们站立似雪飘
海水呢喃着新奇。
穿越了三条河和一座山

两片沙漠和一片海域!
可如今死神抢去我的奖赏
得到了看你的权利——

1665

I know of people in the Grave
Who would be very glad
To know the news I know tonight
If they the chance had had①
'Tis this expands the least event
And swells the scantest deed②
My right to walk upon the Earth
If they this moment had③

1665

我认识墓中的人们
他们定会高兴非凡
听到我今夜知道的消息
假如他们有这个机缘
它能扩大最小的事件
使最细微的行为凸显
假如他们此刻拥有
我行走地面的特权

1666

I see thee clearer for the Grave
That took thy face between
No Mirror could illumine thee
Like that impassive stone—

I know thee better for the Act

---

① ③ 在1960年阅读版中,本行末有句号。
② 在1960年阅读版中,本行末有短横杠符号。

That made thee first unknown
The stature of the empty nest
Attests the Bird that's gone①

1666
我看你更清楚因那坟墓
把你的脸夹在中间
没有镜子如此映照你
如那漠然的墓碑——

我了解你更深因那行为
使你起初不为人知
空巢的地位
证明鸟儿已消失

1667
I watcher her face to see which way
She took the awful news②
Whether she died before she heard
Or in protracted bruise
Remained a few slow years with us③
Each heavier than the last④
A further afternoon to fail⑤
As Flower at fall of Frost—⑥

1667
我盯着她的脸想看从哪个渠道
她得到这可怕的消息
她在听说前死去
或忍着疼痛延续

---

①⑥ 在1960年阅读版中，本行末有句号。
②③④ 在1960年阅读版中，本行末有短横杠符号。
⑤ 在1960年阅读版中，本行末有逗号。

和我们再捱几年
一年比一年痛切
再过了一个下午终于凋谢
像花儿在霜降时节——

1668

If I could tell how glad I was
I should not be so glad—
But when I cannot make the Force①
Nor mould it into Word②
I know it is a sign
That new Dilemna be
From mathematics further off
Than for Eternity③

1668

如果我能说出我有多高兴
我就不会这么高兴——
但当我既无能造就那种力量
也无法形诸文字
我知道这表示
新的窘境真正
距离数学之远
超过距离永恒

1669

In snow thou comest④
Thou shalt go with the resuming ground⑤
The sweet derision of the crow⑥
And Glee's advancing sound⑦

---

① ② ⑤ ⑥　在1960年阅读版中，本行末有逗号。
③ ⑦　在1960年阅读版中，本行末有句号。
④　在1960年阅读版中，本行末有短横杠符号。

In fear thou comest①
Thou shalt go at such a gait of joy
That men② anew embark to live
Upon the depth of thee③—

1669④
你在风雪中来到
你将离去伴着复苏的大地
乌鸦甜美的嘲笑
还有欢乐前进的声息

你在恐惧中来到
你将离去以这般欢快的步幅
以致人们开启新生活
在你的深处——

1670
In Winter in my Room
I came upon a Worm⑤
Pink, lank and warm⑥
But as he was a worm
And worms presume
Not quite with him at home⑦
Secured him by a string
To something neighboring
And went along.

A Trifle afterward
A thing occurred

---

① ⑤ ⑥ ⑦ 在1960年阅读版中，本行末有短横杠符号。
② "men"在1960年阅读版中为"man"。
③ 在1960年阅读版中，本行末是句号。
④ 本诗有可能描写的是3月。

I'd not believe it if I heard
But state with creeping blood①
A snake with mottles rare
Surveyed my chamber floor
In feature as the worm before
But ringed with power②
The very string with which
I tied him—too
When he was mean and new
That string was there—

I shrank— "How fair you are"!
Propitiation's claw—
"Afraid he hissed
Of me"?③
"No cordiality" —
He fathomed me—
Then to a Rhythm *Slim*
Secreted in his Form
As Patterns swim
Projected him.

That time I flew
Both eyes his way
Lest he pursue
Nor ever ceased to run
Till in a distant Town
Towns on from mine
I set me down
This was a dream—④

---

①② 在1960年阅读版中，本行末有短横杠符号。
③ "'Afraid he hissed/Of me'?" 在1960年阅读版中为 "'Afraid,' he hissed/ 'Of me'?"。
④ 在1960年阅读版中，本行末是句号。

1670
在冬季我的房间里
我与一条蠕虫相遇
粉红细长且有暖意
但因他只是蠕虫而已
蠕虫们就猜
跟他不太合拍
我用一根绳把他系于
近旁的某个东西
然后照常做事。

转眼一件小事情
一样东西出现
耳闻我不会相信
但见胆战心惊间
一条蛇长着罕见的花斑
审视我房间的地板
似之前蠕虫的模样
但充满力量
我用来绑他的
那根绳——也如一
即便他一副难看的新长相
但绳子仍在那里——

我畏缩——"你真美丽"!
抚慰的爪——
"怕他对我
发嘶嘶"?
"没有诚意"——
他看穿我底细——
然后一阵节奏悉悉
隐入他的外形里
像一个图案游弋
凸现他自己。

我立时奔逃
两眼仍盯着他的方向
唯恐他追到
绝不停止狂奔
直到一个遥远城镇
距我的有数城之远
我才稍作停顿
这是一场梦魇——

1671

Judgment is justest
When the Judged①
His action laid away②
Divested is of every Disk
But his sincerity③

Honor is then the safest hue
In a posthumous Sun④
Not any color will endure
That scrutiny can burn—⑤

1671

审判最显正义
当被审判者
他的行为被搁置
剥掉每一副面具
只剩他的诚意

在死后的太阳里
荣誉是最保险的色调

---

① ② 在1960年阅读版中，本行末有逗号。
③ 在1960年阅读版中，本行末有句号。
④ 在1960年阅读版中，本行末有短横杠符号。
⑤ 在1960年阅读版中，本行末是句号。

不是任何颜色都经得起
细察的焚烧——

1672

Lightly stepped a yellow star
To it's lofty place①
Loosed the Moon her silver hat
From her lustral Face②
All of Evening softly lit
As an Astral Hall③
Father I observed to Heaven④
You are punctual—⑤

1672

一颗黄色的星轻轻迈步
朝向它高贵的位置
月亮自她皎洁的脸庞
解开她银白的帽子
整个夜晚被柔光照亮
仿佛一个星界的厅堂
我对着天空说父啊
你真守时不爽——

1673

Nature can do no more
She has fulfilled her Dyes
Whatever Flower fail to come
Of other Summer days
Her crescent reimburse
If other Summers be

---

① ② ③ 在1960年阅读版中,本行末有短横杠符号。
④ "Father I observed to Heaven"在1960年阅读版中为"Father, I observed to Heaven,"。
⑤ 在1960年阅读版中,本行末是句号。

Nature's imposing negative
Nulls opportunity—

1673
大自然不能再做什么
她已完成她的粉妆
不论什么花不能到场
在其他夏日里
她的新月会补偿
如果有其他夏季
大自然否定的威力
将机会消去——

1674
Not any sunny tone
From any fervent zone
Find entrance there①
Better a grave of Balm
Toward human nature's home②
And Robins near③
Than a stupendous Tomb
Proclaiming to the Gloom
How dead we are—

1674
没有任何阳光的乐曲
来自任何炽热的地域
在那里找到通道
宁愿一个慰藉的坟茔
通向人性的门庭
以及附近的知更鸟

①②③ 在1960年阅读版中，本行末有短横杠符号。

也胜过一座宏伟的坟墓
向幽暗去宣布
我们死得多糟——

1675

Of this is Day composed
A morning and a noon
A Revelry unspeakable
And then a gay unknown
Whose Pomps allure and spurn
And dower and deprive
And penury for Glory
Remedilessly leave①

1675

一天是这样构成
早晨和午间
一场难言的欢宴
随后是未知的欣喜
它的壮丽既引诱又唾弃
既赋予又夺取
贫困向着荣耀
无可救药地奔去

1676

Of Yellow was the outer Sky
In Yellower Yellow hewn
Till Saffron in Vermilion slid
Whose seam could not be shewn—②

---

① 在1960年阅读版中,本行末有句号。
② 在1960年阅读版中,本行末是句号。

1676

那黄色的是外太空
黄色把自己刷得更浓
直至橘黄滑进朱红
显不出一丝隙缝——

1677

On my volcano grows the Grass
A meditative spot—
An acre for a Bird to choose
Would be the General thought—

How red the Fire rocks below①
How insecure the sod
Did I disclose
Would populate with awe my solitude②

1677

我的火山上长着青草
一个引人遐思的地方——
一个供鸟儿选择的角落
普遍会这么想——

地下火山岩多通红夺目
草皮随时可能移位
假如我这样指出
我的孤独会平添敬畏

1678

Peril as a Possession
'Tis Good to hear

---

① 在1960年阅读版中，本行末有短横杠符号。
② 在1960年阅读版中，本行末有句号。

Danger disintegrates Satiety
There's Basis there—
Begets an awe
That searches Human Nature's creases
As clean as Fire①

1678
危险已是个人财物
很高兴听到这消息
危险可瓦解饱足
这有充分理据——
它会引起畏惧
去搜寻人性的缺陷
像火一样洁净

1679
Rather arid delight
If Contentment accrue
Make an abstemious Ecstasy
Not so good as joy—

But Rapture's Expense
Must not be incurred
With a tomorrow knocking
And the Rent unpaid—

1679
相当乏味的欢愉
如果满意累积
形成拘束的狂喜
未到快乐的层级——

---

① 在1960年阅读版中，本行末有句号。

但沉醉的费用
一定不能招致
明天有人敲门
房租未付讫——

1680
Sometimes with the Heart
Seldom with the Soul
Scarcer once with the Might
Few—love at all①

1680
有时用心
很少用灵魂
更罕见曾经用力
几乎没人——爱过

1681
Speech is one symptom of Affection
And Silence one—
The perfectest communication
Is heard of none②

Exists and it's indorsement
Is had within—
Behold said the Apostle③
Yet had not seen!

1681
言语是爱的一种表示

---

① 在 1960 年阅读版中，本行末有句号。
② 在 1960 年阅读版中，本行末有短横杠符号。
③ "Behold said the Apostle" 在 1960 年阅读版中为 "Behold, said the Apostle,"。

沉默也是其一——
最完美的交际
听不到一点声息

存在及其理据
是在里面——
使徒说请看仔细
却从没看见！①

1682

Summer begins to have the look
Peruser of enchanting Book
Reluctantly but sure perceives
A gain upon the backward leaves②

Autumn begins to be inferred
By millinery of the cloud
Or deeper color in the shawl
That wraps the everlasting hill③

The eye begins it's avarice
A meditation chastens speech
Some Dyer of a distant tree
Resumes his gaudy industry④

Conclusion is the course of All
At *most* to be perennial

---

① 最后两行参见《圣经·新约·彼得前书》第1章第8节里使徒彼得所言之众人看不见耶稣，但众人恒爱耶稣："Whom having not seen, ye love; in whom, though now ye see him not, yet believing, ye rejoice with joy unspeakable and full of glory."（1 Peter 1: 8）。
② 在约翰逊1960年阅读版中，本行末有短横杠符号。
③④ 在约翰逊1960年阅读版中，本行末有句号。

And then elude stability
Recalls to immortality—①

1682

夏季开始有一种神色
像位读者研读魅力之作
不情愿但确能察觉
向后叶子上的收获

秋季开始受推测
被一顶女帽在云中
或披巾上更深的颜色
包裹亘古的山峰

眼睛开启它的贪婪
一种沉思遏制了言谈
一棵远树的某位染色工
重操他花哨的劳动

终结是一切的航向
至多经历多年
随后便逃避稳定
回到永生之境——

1683

That she forgot me was the least
I felt it second pain
That I was worthy to forget
Was most I thought upon②

Faithful was all that I could boast
But Constancy became

---

① 在约翰逊1960年阅读版中，本行末是句号。
② 在1960年阅读版中，本行末有句号。

To her, by her innominate①
A something like a shame②

1683
她把我忘记最不值一提
我感到第二重难过
是我竟值得忘记
这令我思索最多

我唯一能吹嘘的是忠诚
但坚定不移
对于她，依她的无名
是一件类似耻辱的东西

1684
The Blunder is in estimate③
Eternity is there
We say as of a Station④
Meanwhile he is so near
He joins me in my Ramble⑤
Divides abode with me⑥
No Friend have I that so persists
As this Eternity⑦

1684
错误是在估计方面
永恒就在那里
我们说就像个车站
同时他近在咫尺

---

① 在1960年阅读版中，本行末有逗号。
②③⑦ 在1960年阅读版中，本行末有句号。
④ "We say as of a Station" 在1960年阅读版中为 "We say, as of a Station—"。
⑤⑥ 在1960年阅读版中，本行末有短横杠符号。

他和我一起漫步
与我分享住所
我没哪位朋友
像这永恒那么执着

1685
The butterfly obtains
But little sympathy
Though favorably mentioned
In Entomology—

Because he travels freely
And wea[r]s① a proper coat
The circumspect are certain
That he is dissolute②

Had he the homely scutcheon
Of modest Industry
T'were③ fitter certifying
For Immortality—

1685
蝴蝶所获取
几乎没有同情
虽然在昆虫学里
他受到好评——

因为他四处旅行
穿着体面的外衣
谨慎的人都确定
他是浪荡子无疑

---

① "wea[r]s"在1960年阅读版全集中为"wears"。
② 在1960年阅读版中，本行末有短横杠符号。
③ "T'were"在1960年阅读版全集中为"Twere"。

假如他穿大众的品牌
出产的企业普通
这才可证明
更适合永生——

1686

The event was directly behind Him
Yet He did not guess
Fitted itself to Himself like a Robe
Relished His ignorance①
Motioned itself to drill
Loaded and Levelled
And let His Flesh
Centuries from His soul②

1686③

事件就在他身后
但他并未猜到
它适合他就像一件长袍
享受他的无知
示意它去钻
装载又抚平痕迹
让他的肉体
离他的灵魂几世纪

1687

The gleam of an heroic Act
Such strange illumination
The Possible's slow fuse is lit
By the Imagination④

---

①②④ 在1960年阅读版中,本行末有句号。
③ 本诗可能描绘葬礼。

1687
英雄行为的光芒
如此奇异地照亮
可能的迟钝引信被点燃
通过想象

1688
The Hills erect their Purple Heads
The Rivers lean to see
Yet Man has not of all the Throng
A Curiosity①

1688
群山昂起紫色的头
百川倾身探视
但人对所有这一切
没一点好奇

1689
The look of thee, what is it like
Hast thou a hand or Foot
Or Mansion of Identity
And what is thy Pursuit②

Thy fellows are they realms or Themes
Hast thou Delight or Fear
Or Longing—and is that for us
Or values more severe—③

Let change transfuse all other Traits
Enact all other Blame

---

① 在1960年阅读版中,本行末有句号。
② 在1960年阅读版中,本行末有问号。
③ 在1960年阅读版中,本行末是问号。

But deign this least certificate①
That thou shalt be the same—②

1689
你的样子，像什么
你有无脚或手
或身份的大屋
你有什么追求

你的友伴他们是领域或主题
你有无快乐或恐惧
或渴望——是否是对我们
或有更重大的意义——

让改变注入所有其他特质
颁布所有其他惩诉
但请赐予这最轻微的证书
即你将不变如初——

1690
The ones that disappeared are back
The Phebe and the Crow
Precisely as in March is heard
The curtness of the Jay—
Be this an Autumn or a Spring
My wisdom loses way
One side of me the nuts are ripe
The other side is May.

1690
那消失的回来了

---

① 在1960年阅读版中，本行末有短横杠符号。
② 在1960年阅读版中，本行末是句号。

乌鸦和京燕
正如三月里听到
松鸦仓促的叫唤——
这是秋季还是春天
我的智慧难以分辨
我的一边坚果熟透
另一边是五月天。

1691

The overtakelessness of those
Who have accomplished Death
Majestic is to me beyond
The majesties of Earth①

The soul her "Not at Home"
Inscribes upon the flesh—
And takes her fair aerial gait
Beyond the hope of touch②

1691

那些人的无法超越
在完成死亡之后
其宏伟在我看来
胜过地球

灵魂把她的"不在家"
刻在肉身上——
迈出曼妙的凌虚微步
超越了接触的希望

1692

The right to perish might be tho't③

---

①② 在1960年阅读版中，本行末有句号。
③ "tho't"在1960年阅读版中为"thought"。

An undisputed right①
Attempt it, and the Universe
Upon the opposite
Will concentrate it's officers—
You cannot even die
But nature and mankind must pause
To pay you scrutiny—②

1692
死的权利或许被认为是
无可争议的权利
如若尝试,对面的
宇宙全体
会令其官员们全神注意——
你甚至无法死去
但自然和人类都得停下
将你看仔细——

1693
The Sun retired to a cloud
A Woman's shawl as big③
And then he sulked in mercury
Upon a scarlet log—
The drops on Nature's forehead stood
Home flew the loaded bees④
The South unrolled a purple fan
And handed to the trees⑤

1693
太阳退入一片云

---

①③④ 在1960年阅读版中,本行末有短横杠符号。
② 在1960年阅读版中,本行末是句号。
⑤ 在1960年阅读版中,本行末有句号。

大小如女士的披巾
随后他在水银中愠怒
在一根绯红的圆木——
露珠立在大自然额前
匆匆归巢是满载的蜜蜂
南面展开一把紫扇
递到丛林中

1694

The wind drew off
Like hungry dogs
Defeated of a bone①
Through fissures in
Volcanic cloud
The yellow lightning shone—
The trees held up
Their mangled limbs
Like animals in pain②
When Nature falls upon herself
Beware an Austrian③

1694

风撤离
像一群饿狗
被夺走一根骨头
穿过缝隙
在火山云里
那黄色的闪电熠熠——
树林挺起
凌乱的枝丫
像动物难忍疼痛

---

①② 在1960年阅读版中，本行末有短横杠符号。
③ 在1960年阅读版中，本行末有句号。

当大自然降临
小心一股南风

1695

There is a solitude of space
A solitude of sea
A solitude of death, but these
Society shall be
Compared with that profounder site
That polar privacy
A soul admitted to itself—
Finite infinity.

1695

有一种空间的孤寂
大海的孤寂
死亡的孤寂,但这些
都算是群体
比起那更深的地域
那极地的隐秘
一个灵魂承认自己——
有限的无边无际。

1696

These are the days that Reindeer love
And pranks the Northern star[①]
This is the Sun's objective[②]
And Finland of the Year[③]

---

① 在1960年阅读版中,本行末有短横杠符号。
② 在1960年阅读版中,本行末有逗号。
③ 在1960年阅读版中,本行末有句号。

1696

这是驯鹿喜爱的时光
北极星闪亮
这是太阳的目标
一年中的芬兰①

1697

They talk as slow as Legends grow
No mushroom is their mind
But foliage of sterility
Too stolid for the wind—

They laugh as wise as Plots of Wit
Predestined to unfold
The point with bland prevision
Portentously untold②

1697

他们交谈缓慢如传奇的生长
他们的思想不是蘑菇
而是不会结果的枝叶
对风太过麻木——

他们的笑聪明如机智的计谋
注定会展现那要义
其中平淡无奇的预知
自负地从未告示

---

① 艾米莉·狄金森曾在 1865 年 11 月初写给霍兰夫人的一封信中有这样的表述："November always seemed to be the Norway of the year."（L311）。
② 在 1960 年阅读版中，本行末有句号。

1698

T'is① easier to pity those when dead
That which pity previous
Would have saved②
A Tragedy enacted
Secures Applause
That Tragedy enacting
Too seldom does③

1698

对死者惋惜很容易
如果惋惜早一点
本可以挽救生命
一个悲剧演完
总能获得褒扬
正在上演的悲剧
极少有人夸奖

1699

To do a magnanimous thing
And take oneself by surprise
If oneself is not in the habit of him
Is precisely the finest of Joys—

Not to do a magnanimous thing
Notwithstanding it never be known
Notwithstanding it cost us existence once
Is Rapture herself spurn—

1699

做高尚的事情

---

① "T'is" 在1960年阅读版中为 "Tis"。
② 在1960年阅读版中, 本行末有短横杠符号。
③ 在1960年阅读版中, 本行末有句号。

让自己感到惊异
如果自己尚未养成这习性
正是快乐的极致——

不做崇高的事情
尽管它永不为人知
尽管它让我们付出一次生命
正是狂喜自己所唾弃——

1700

To tell the Beauty would decrease
To state the Spell demean①
There is a syllable-less Sea
Of which it is the sign②
My will endeavors for it's word
And fails, but entertains
A Rapture as of Legacies—
Of introspective Mines—

1700

说出美会减低
泄露魔咒会贬抑
有一片无声的海洋
这就是它的标志
我努力找描述它的言词
失败了,却乐享
沉醉好似一种遗赠——
一种内省的宝矿——

1701

To their apartment deep

---

①② 在1960年阅读版中,本行末有短横杠符号。

No ribaldry may creep
Untumbled this abode
By any man but God—

1701
他们深处的公寓
没有粗言会爬去
没人打搅这宅第
除了上帝——

1702
To-day① or this noon
She dwelt so close
I almost touched her②
Tonight she lies
Past neighborhood
And bough and steeple③
Now past surmise④

1702
今日或今日下午
她住得如此近
我几乎触到她
今夜她躺下
超过了四邻
粗枝和尖塔
如今超出了揣度

1703
T'was comfort in her Dying Room

---

① "To-day" 在 1960 年阅读版中为 "Today"。
② 在 1960 年阅读版中，本行末有短横杠符号。
③ 在 1960 年阅读版中，本行末有逗号。
④ 在 1960 年阅读版中，本行末有句号。

To hear the living Clock①
A short relief to have the wind
Walk boldly up and knock②
Diversion from the Dying Theme
To hear the children play③
But wrong the more
That these could live
And this of ours must *die*

1703

这是一种慰藉在她临终的房间
听到活生生的钟声
一阵短暂的解脱当有风
大胆走上去敲门
从死亡的主题转移
去听孩子们嬉戏
但错位更加剧
这些能存活于世
而我们这位必须*死*

1704

Unto a broken heart
No other one may go
Without the high prerogative
Itself hath suffered too④

1704

走进一颗破碎的心
没有别的心愿意
若无很高的特权
它自己也痛苦不已

---

①②③ 在1960年阅读版中,本行末有短横杠符号。
④ 在1960年阅读版中,本行末有句号。

1705

Volcanoes be in Sicily
And South America
I judge from my Geography①
Volcanos nearer here
A Lava step at any time
Am I inclined to climb②
A Crater I may contemplate
Vesuvius at Home③

1705④

火山在西西里
和南美洲
我据自己的地理位置
火山离此地更近
熔岩随时涌起
我若愿意爬上去
在火山口我就可畅想
维苏威在家里

1706

When we have ceased to care
The Gift is given
For which we gave the Earth
And mortgaged Heaven
But so declined in worth
'Tis ignominy now
To look upon—

---

① ② 在1960年阅读版中，本行末有短横杠符号。
③ 在1960年阅读版中，本行末有句号。
④ 题解：艾米莉·狄金森有可能是在家里对着地图上的维苏威火山作此遐想。

1706
我们已不在乎时
礼物送达
为了它我们曾献出地球
还以天堂作抵押
但其价值已大打折扣
如今感到丢脸
看上一眼——

1707
Winter under cultivation
Is as arable as Spring①

1707
培育中的冬天
如春天般适宜耕种

1708
Witchcraft has not a Pedigree
T'is② early as our Breath
And mourners meet it going out
The moment of our death—

1708③
巫术并无家谱
它早如我们的呼吸
哀悼者遇见它外出
在我们死亡之时——

---

① 在1960年阅读版中,本行末有句号。
② "T'is"在1960年阅读版中为"'Tis"。
③ 题解:巫术的源头无可考,我们出生时它已存在,我们死时它仍然存在。

1709①

With sweetness unabated
Informed the hour had come
With no remiss of triumph
The autumn started home—②
Her home to be with Nature
As competition done
By influential kinsmen
Invited to return③
In supplements of Purple
An adequate repast
In heavenly reviewing
Her residue be past—

1709④

怀着未减的甜蜜
被告知时辰已至
带着不懈的得意
秋天开启回家之旅——
她的家将与自然在一起
因为争夺已不再
德高望重的亲戚
盛邀他归来
除了紫色的云彩
还有丰盛的大餐
从天空的角度评判
她的残迹已消散——

---

① 本诗在1960年阅读版中分为3节，每节4行。
② 在1960年阅读版中，本行末没有短横杠符号。
③ 在1960年阅读版中，本行末有短横杠符号。
④ 题解：以秋天落日的景象表明秋天将带着辉煌离去，让位给冬天。当争夺之战已尘埃落定，是秋天该回归大自然之家的时候了，且它是被邀请回去的。最后，落日景象消弭，秋天也全无痕迹了。

1710

A curious Cloud surprised the Sky,
'Twas like a sheet with Horns;
The sheet was Blue—
The Antlers Gray—
It almost touched the lawns.

So low it leaned—then statelier drew—
And trailed like robes away;①
A Queen adown a satin aisle,②
Had not the majesty.

1710

一片奇特的云让天空惊叹,
它像一张带角的被单;
被单蓝——
鹿角灰——
它几乎触到芳草甸。

它俯下如此低——又更庄重地撤离——
像长袍拖曳而去;
女王走过铺着锦缎的通道,
也没这般威仪。

1711

A face devoid of love or grace,
A hateful, hard, successful face,
A face with which a stone
Would feel as thoroughly at ease
As were they old acquaintances—
First time together thrown.

---

① 在1960年阅读版中,本行末是逗号。
② 在1960年阅读版中,本行末没有逗号。

1711
一张缺乏爱或优雅的脸,
一张可恨,冷酷,成功的脸,
一张脸令一块石子
感到舒畅自由
仿佛他们相识已久——
首次被一同抛弃。

1712①
A Pit—but Heaven over it—
And Heaven beside, and Heaven abroad;②
And yet a Pit—
With Heaven over it.

To stir would be to slip—
To look would be to drop—
To dream—to sap the Prop
That holds my chances up.
Ah! Pit! With Heaven over it!

The depth is all my thought—
I dare not ask my feet—
'Twould start us where we sit
So straight you'd scarce suspect
It was a Pit—with fathoms under it③
Its Circuit just the same④
Seed—summer—tomb—⑤
Whose Doom to whom⑥

---

① 富兰克林版在本诗尾还多出5行,该5行在约翰逊版中则是第443首诗的第25~29行。
② 在1960年阅读版中,本行末是逗号。
③ 在1960年阅读版中,本行末有短横杠符号。
④ 在1960年阅读版中,本行末有句号。
⑤ 富兰克林版全集里没有这一行。
⑥ 在1960年阅读版中,本行末有问号。

1712
一个深渊——但苍天在上——
苍天在旁,苍天在外;
但还是一个深渊——
有苍天在其上。

动一动会滑下去——
看一眼会掉下去——
梦见——会削弱支撑力
我就靠它撑起我的希冀。
啊!深渊!苍天在其上!

其深度是我思想的全部——
我不敢要求我的双足——
那会惊吓我们在我们所坐之处
如此笔直你几乎不会怀疑
它一直是个深渊——其下深度
与它的周长无异
种子——夏季——和坟墓——
谁是谁的末日

1713
As subtle as tomorrow
That never came,
A warrant, a conviction,
Yet but a name.

1713
像明天一样缥缈
永远不会来到,
一个保证,一种信念,
但仅是一个名号。

1714

By a departing light
We see acuter, quite,
Than by a wick that stays.
There's something in the flight
That clarifies the sight
And decks the rays

1714

借助一束离去的光线
我们看得,更了然,
胜过借助留驻的烛焰。
飞行有一种特点
能使事物凸现
也将光线装扮

1715

Consulting summer's clock,
But half the hours remain.
I ascertain it with a shock—
I shall not look again.
The second half of joy
Is shorter than the first.
The truth I do not dare to know
I muffle with a jest.

1715

查验了夏日时钟,
只剩一半的时间。
我确认时感到震动——
我不会再去查看。
欢乐的后半段

比前半段短暂。
真相我不敢知道
我用一个玩笑遮掩。

1716
Death is like the insect
Menacing the tree,
Competent to kill it,
But decoyed may be.

Bait it with the balsam,
Seek it with the saw,
Baffle, if it cost you
Everything you are.

Then, if it have burrowed
Out of reach of skill—
Wring the tree and leave it,
'Tis the vermin's will.

1716
死亡就像昆虫
危及树木安全,
它有能力杀死它,
但可被诱骗。

诱它以香脂,
找它用铁锯,
刁难它,如果它令你
一切都失去。

最后，如果它已挖洞
技艺无能为力——
就拧断树木并离弃，
这正是害虫的心意。

1717

Did life's penurious length
Italicize its sweetness,
The men that daily live
Would stand so deep in joy
That it would clog the cogs
Of that revolving reason
Whose esoteric belt
Protects our sanity.

1717

是否生命贫瘠的长度
凸显了它的甜蜜，
活在当下的人们
如此沉溺于欢愉
以致卡住了
理智旋转的齿轮
是它隐秘的履带
将我们的清醒保护。

1718

Drowning is not so pitiful
As the attempt to rise.
Three times, 'tis said, a sinking man
Comes up to face the skies,
And then declines forever
To that abhorred abode,
Where hope and he part company—
For he is grasped of God.

The Maker's cordial visage,
However good to see,
Is shunned, we must admit it,
Like an adversity.

1718
溺亡并没那么可怜
比起浮起的尝试。
据说，一个正下沉的男人，有三次
浮上来脸对天宇，
随后永远沉入
那令人憎恶的住地，
在那里希望与他不再相依——
因他是被上帝抓去。
造物主亲切的面孔，
无论多宜人，
总被躲避，我们必须承认，
像躲避厄运。

1719
God is indeed a jealous God—
He cannot bear to see
That we had rather not with Him
But with each other play.

1719
上帝的确是个爱嫉妒的上帝——
他不忍心看见
我们不愿与他一起
而是我们彼此嬉戏。

1720
Had I known that the first was the last
I should have kept it longer.

Had I known that the last was the first
I should have drunk it stronger. ①
Cup, it was your fault,
Lip was not the liar. ②
No, lip it was yours,
Bliss was most to blame.

1720
假如我知道第一杯是最后一杯
我会留着它久一些。
假如我知道最后一杯是第一杯
我会喝得更猛烈。
酒杯,是你的错,
嘴唇并非撒谎者。
不,嘴唇,是你不对,
欢乐最该斥责。

1721
He was my host—he was my guest,
I never to this day
If I invited him could tell,
Or he invited me.

So infinite our intercourse
So intimate, indeed,
Analysis as capsule seemed
To keeper of the seed.

1721
他是我的主人——他是我的客人,
我直至今天都没能

---

① 在富兰克林全集版中,本行为"I should have mixed it stronger."。
② 在1960年阅读版中,本行末没有句号。

说清是我邀请了他,
还是他邀请了我。

我们的交流无边无际
确实,亲密无比,
分析看起来就如对种子囊一样
在保管种子的人眼里。

1722

Her face was in a bed of hair,
Like flowers in a plot—
Her hand was whiter than the sperm
That feeds the sacred light.
Her tongue more tender than the tune
That totters in the leaves—
Who hears may be incredulous,
Who witnesses, believes.

1722

她的脸在一丛毛发间,
像鲜花在一块地上——
她的手洁白胜过那元液
供养着圣光。
她的舌温柔胜过那乐曲
萦绕于叶荫——
听到的可能怀疑,
看见的,会相信。

1723

High from the earth I heard a bird;
He trod upon the trees
As he esteemed them trifles,
And then he spied a breeze,
And situated softly

Upon a pile of wind
Which in a perturbation
Nature had left behind.
A joyous going fellow
I gathered from his talk
Which both of benediction
And badinage partook.
Without apparent burden
I subsequently learned
He was the faithful father
Of a dependent brood.
And this untoward transport
His remedy for care, —
A contrast to our respites.
How different we are!

1723

在离地的高处我听到一只鸟叫；
他脚踩树梢
仿佛认为它们微不足道，
随后他察觉微风轻扫，
便悠然安置到
一阵风上边
在一阵烦乱中
被自然抛在后面。
他是一位快乐青年
我了解自他的话语
既有真诚的祝福
也有轻松的打趣。
不费多少力气
我随后便知道
他是位尽职的父亲
养育一窝待哺的鸟。
而这标新立异的沉迷

是他治愈忧虑的良方,——
与我们的喘息形成对比。
我们多么不一样!

1724

How dare the robins sing,
When men and women hear
Who since they went to their account
Have settled with the year! —
Paid all that life had earned
In one consummate bill,
And now, what life or death can do
Is immaterial.
Insulting is the sun
To him whose mortal light
Beguiled of immortality
Bequeaths him to the night.
Extinct be every hum
In deference to him
Whose garden wrestles with the dew,
At daybreak overcome!

1724

知更鸟竟敢歌唱,
当男男女女在倾听
自从他们去结账
已与岁月结清!——
为一生所得付了费
用一张完满的付款单,
如今,生或死之所为
均与物质无关。
无礼的是太阳
对他而言它的凡光
对永生迷恋

将他遗给了夜晚。
愿每一声嗡鸣都绝迹
为保障他安息
他的花园一直与露水搏击,
拂晓时取得胜利!

1725

I took one Draught of Life—
I'll tell you what I paid—
Precisely an existence—
The market price, they said.

They weighed me, Dust by Dust—
They balanced Film with Film,
Then handed me my Being's worth—
A single Dram of Heaven!

1725

我啜饮一口生命的玉液——
我告诉你我付出了什么——
刚好是我的存在——
市场价,他们说。

他们称量我,纤尘接纤尘——
他们衡量我皮囊对皮囊,
然后递给我生命的所值——
仅是一小杯天堂的琼浆!

1726

If all the griefs I am to have
Would only come today,
I am so happy I believe
They'd laugh and run away.

If all the joys I am to have
Would only come today,
They could not be so big as this
That happens to me now.

1726
如果我应有的全部悲伤
今天才会来,
我很高兴我相信
他们会大笑着跑开。

如果我应有的全部欢乐
今天才会来,
也不如我的这个重大
它发生在现在。

1727
If ever the lid gets off my head
And lets the brain away
The fellow will go where he belonged—
Without a hint from me,

And the world—if the world be looking on—
Will see how far from home
It is possible for sense to live
The soul there—all the time.

1727
假如盖子从我头上掉下
让大脑流失
这家伙会去往他所属的地方——
无须我暗示,

而世界——假如世界在看——

会看见离家有多远
理智可能存活
灵魂在那里————一直未变。

1728
Is Immortality a bane
That men are so oppressed?

1728①
难道永生是个灾祸
让人类备受压迫?

1729
I've got an arrow here.
Loving the hand that sent it
I the dart revere.

Fell, they will say, in "skirmish"!
Vanquished, my soul will know
By but a simple arrow
Sped by an archer's bow.

1729②
我有一支箭在这里。
因爱恋射出它的手
我对这飞矢有敬意。

倒下,他们会说,于"小冲突"!
被征服,我的灵魂会清楚

---

① 参见第1646首诗,也提到了永生的威力。
② 题解:别人以为我是在小冲突中倒下的,但我的灵魂清楚,我是被爱情之箭射中,被征服。由于我爱射箭的人,因而对身中的箭也就怀有崇敬之情。

是被一支简单的箭镞
由射手的弓射出。

1730
"Lethe" in my flower,
Of which they who drink
In the fadeless orchards
Hear the bobolink!

Merely flake or petal
As the Eye beholds
Jupiter! my father!
I perceive the rose!

1730
"忘川水"在我花里,
那些喝下的人
在永不凋谢的果园中
听到食米鸟的歌声!

眼睛所见
仅有花片或花瓣
朱庇特!我的父!
我能将玫瑰发现!

1731
Love can do all but raise the Dead
I doubt if even that
From such a giant were withheld
Were flesh equivalent

But love is tired and must sleep,
And hungry and must graze
And so abets the shining Fleet
Till it is out of gaze.

1731①

爱无所不能除了不能复活死人
我怀疑是否即使
未有如此一个巨人之身
也同样是肉躯

但爱累了必须安睡，
饿了必须进食
所以唆使那闪亮的舰队
直至它离开我们的凝视。

1732

My life closed twice before its close;②
It yet remains to see
If Immortality unveil
A third event to me,③

So huge, so hopeless to conceive
As these that twice befel④.
Parting is all we know of heaven,
And all we need of hell.

1732

我的生命结束前已结束过两次；
但它依然等着看
是否永生向我揭示
第三次事件，

---

① 题解：爱并非万能，不能令死者站起身复活，没有巨人之身，也是肉躯，也会累会饿，所以，要唆使那死亡的闪光舰队远离我们的视线，不要让它靠近，因为一旦有人死去，爱无法拯救死者。另参见第749首诗。
② 在1960年阅读版中，本行末是短横杠符号。
③ 在1960年阅读版中，本行末没有逗号。
④ "befel"在1960年阅读版中为"befell"。

像那两次降临时的这些
想来如此重大，如此无助。
分离是我们对天堂所知的一切，
也是我们对地狱所需的全部。

1733

No man saw awe, nor to his house
Admitted he a man
Though by his awful residence
Has human nature been.

Not deeming of his dread abode
Till laboring to flee
A grasp on comprehension laid
Detained vitality.

Returning is a different route
The Spirit could not show
For breathing is the only work
To be enacted now.

"Am not consumed," old Moses wrote,
"Yet saw him face to face" —
That very physiognomy
I am convinced was this①

1733

没人见过敬畏，他也不许任何人
进他房里面
虽然在他可怕的住处旁边
一直都有人烟。

---

① 在约翰逊1960年阅读版中，本行末有句号。

不相信他恐怖的住所
直至奋力逃匿
一种对理解的掌握
留滞了活力。

返回是不同的路
圣灵也无法指示
因为呼吸是唯一的事务
目前需要实施。

"我未消亡,"① 老摩西曾写道,
"却与他迎面相见"② ——
那个面相
我确信就是这样

1734

Oh, honey of an hour,

I never knew thy power,

Prohibit me

Till my minutest dower,

---

① 典故出自《圣经·旧约·出埃及记》第3章第2节:"And the angel of the LORD appeared unto him in a flame of fire out of the midst of a bush: and he looked, and, behold, the bush burned with fire, and the bush was not consumed."(Exodus 3:2)[耶和华的使者从荆棘里火焰中向摩西显现。摩西观看,不料,荆棘被火烧着,却没有烧毁。]原文指荆棘未被烧毁,而非指摩西未消亡,艾米莉·狄金森记忆有误。

② 典故出自《圣经·旧约·出埃及记》第33章第20～23节:"And he said, Thou canst not see my face: for there shall no man see me, and live. And the LORD said, Behold, there is a place by me, and thou shalt stand upon a rock. And it shall come to pass, while my glory passeth by, that I will put thee in a clift of the rock, and will cover thee with my hand while I pass by. And I will take away mine hand, and thou shalt see my back parts: but my face shall not be seen."(Exodus 33:20-23)[又说,你不能看见我的面,因为人见我的面不能存活。耶和华说,看哪,在我这里有地方,你要站在磐石上。我的荣耀经过的时候,我必将你放在磐石穴中,用我的手遮掩你,等我过去,然后我要将我的手收回,你就得见我的背,却不得见我的面。]原文记载摩西并未得见耶和华的脸,艾米莉·狄金森记忆有误。

My unfrequented flower①

Deserving be.

1734②

啊,一小时的甜言蜜语,
我从不知你的威力,
请禁我领受
直至我最微小的天赐,
我那备受冷落的花枝
值得拥有。

1735

One crown that no one seeks
And yet the highest head
Its isolation coveted
Its stigma deified

While Pontius Pilate lives
In whatsoever hell
That coronation pierces him
He recollects it well.

1735

一顶王冠没人求取
但那至高的头颅
垂涎它的孤离
神化它的耻辱

---

① 在1960年阅读版中,本行末有逗号。
② 题解:一朵花让蜜蜂等一等,等到她值得享有蜜蜂一小时的甜言蜜语之时。这里"honey"是双关语。

只要本丢·彼拉多①还活着
不论在地狱某处
那加冕礼②会刺痛他
他还记得一清二楚。

1736

Proud of my broken heart, since thou didst break it,
Proud of the pain I did not feel till thee,

Proud of my night, since thou with moons dost slake it,
Not to partake thy passion, *my* humility.

Thou can'st not boast, like Jesus, drunken without companion
Was the strong cup of anguish brewed for the Nazarene

Thou can'st not pierce tradition with the peerless puncture,
See! I usurped *thy* crucifix to honor mine!

---

① 本丢·彼拉多（Pontius Pilate）：《圣经·新约·路加福音》第3章第1节记述本丢·彼拉多曾任古代罗马犹太行省朱迪亚（Judea）的总督："Now in the fifteenth year of the reign of Tiberius Caesar, Pontius Pilate being governor of Judaea."（Luke 3：1）。朱迪亚是古巴勒斯坦的南部地区，是犹太人故土，包括今巴勒斯坦的南部地区和约旦的西南部地区，是耶稣生活、传教、受难、复活之地（参见《圣经·新约·路加福音》第1～24章记载）。《圣经·新约·马太福音》第2章第1节记载耶稣出生地："Now when Jesus was born in Bethlehem of Judaea in the days of Herod the king, behold, there came wise men from the east to Jerusalem."（Matthew 2：1）彼时，彼拉多迫于当地犹太人的压力，下令将耶稣钉死在十字架上（见《圣经·新约·马太福音》第27章）。本丢·彼拉多死于公元36年。

② 加冕礼（coronation）：《圣经·新约·马太福音》第27章第27～31节记载了总督彼拉多被判处耶稣钉十字架后，卫兵们戏弄性地对耶稣施行加冕礼的情形："Then the soldiers of the governor took Jesus into the common hall, and gathered unto him the whole band of soldiers. And they stripped him, and put on him a scarlet robe. And when they had platted a crown of thorns, they put it upon his head, and a reed in his right hand: and they bowed the knee before him, and mocked him, saying, Hail, King of the Jews! And they spit upon him, and took the reed, and smote him on the head. And after that they had mocked him, they took the robe off from him, and put his own raiment on him, and led him away to crucify him."（Matthew 27：27 - 31）[巡抚的兵就把耶稣带进衙门，叫全营的兵都聚集在他那里。他们给他脱了衣服，穿上一件朱红色袍子。用荆棘编作冠冕，戴在他头上，拿一根苇子放在他右手里。跪在他面前戏弄他说，恭喜犹太人的王啊。又吐唾沫在他脸上，拿苇子打他的头。戏弄完了，就给他脱了袍子，仍穿上他自己的衣服，带他出去，要钉十字架。]

1736
为我破碎的心自豪,既然你将它打碎,
为直至你来我才感受到的痛苦自豪,

为我的夜晚自豪,既然你用月光使它衰颓,
*无须*分享你的激情,*我的*谦卑。

你可以自吹,像耶稣一样,沉醉无人陪
难道那杯痛苦的烈酒专为那位拿撒勒人酿造

你可用无与伦比的穿孔刺破传统,
看!我篡夺了*你的*十字架以令我荣耀!

1737
Rearrange a "Wife's" affection!
When they dislocate my Brain!
Amputate my freckled Bosom!
Make me bearded like a man!

Blush, my spirit, in thy Fastness—
Blush, my unacknowledged clay—
Seven years of troth have taught thee
More than Wifehood every may!

Love that never leaped its socket—
Trust entrenched in narrow pain—
Constancy thro' fire—awarded—
Anguish—bare of anodyne!

Burden—borne so far triumphant—
None suspect me of the crown,
For I wear the "Thorns" till *Sunset*—
Then—my Diadem put on.

Big my Secret but it's *bandaged*—
It will never get away
Till the Day its Weary Keeper
Leads it through the Grave to thee.

1737
重新调整一位"妻子"的爱!
当他们移走我的脑子!
截除我斑驳的胸脯!
让我长胡子像一位男士!

羞愧,我的灵,于你的坚定——
羞愧,我未被赏识的身躯——
七年婚约所教与你
多于妇道所给予!

爱从未移位——
信任扎根在彻痛里——
换来——浴火后的始终如一——
痛楚——没有止痛剂!

重负——至今胜利承受——
没人怀疑我会加冕,
因我头戴"荆棘"① 直至*日落*——
而后——戴上我的冠冕。

我的秘密重大但已*被包扎* ——
它绝不会露底
直到那一天它疲惫的看守者
引领它穿越坟墓抵达你。

---

① 这里应指耶稣被钉十字架前头上被戴上的用荆棘做的王冠(crown of thorns),参见第 1735 首诗注释。

1738

Softened by Time's consummate plush,
How sleek the woe appears
That threatened childhood's citadel
And undermined the years.

Bisected now, by bleaker griefs,
We envy the despair
That devastated childhood's realm,
So easy to repair.

1738

被时间完美的毛绒软化,
悲伤显得多么柔滑
它曾威胁孩提时的城堡
让那段岁月几乎崩塌。

如今被更凄惨的悲伤,一分为二,
我们对绝望感到嫉妒
它摧毁了孩提时的王国,
轻易又可修复。

1739

Some say goodnight—at night—
I say goodnight by day—
Good-bye—the Going utter me—
Goodnight, I still reply—

For parting, that is night,
And presence, simply dawn—
Itself, the purple on the height
Denominated morn.

1739

有人道晚安——在夜晚——
我道晚安在白天——
再见——离去的人对我说——
我仍旧回答,晚安——

因为分别时,是夜晚,
而现身,就在黎明时分——
它,那高处的紫彩
表明是清晨。

1740

Sweet is the swamp with its secrets,
Until we meet a snake;
'Tis then we sigh for houses,
And our departure take
At that enthralling gallop
That only childhood knows.
A snake is summer's treason,[①]
And guile is where it goes.

1740

充满秘密的湿地很美丽,
直至我们与一条蛇相遇;
此时我们才渴望房子,
才抽身离去
那迷人的飞奔
只有童年知悉。
蛇是夏季的叛逆,
到哪儿都耍诡计。

---

① 在富兰克林版全集中,本诗最后两行为:"A snake is nature's treason/And awe is where it goes."。

1741

That it will never come again
Is what makes life so sweet.
Believing what we don't believe
Does not exhilarate.

That if it be, it be at best
An ablative estate—
This instigates an appetite
Precisely opposite.

1741

正是它一去不返
才让它如此美丽。
信我们所不信
并不能令人欣喜。

假如它在，至多只是
一个短暂的庄园——
这会激起一种欲望
与它正好相反。

1742

The distance that the dead have gone
Does not at first appear;①
Their coming back seems possible
For many an ardent year.

And then, that we have followed them,
We more than half suspect,
So intimate have we become

---

① 在1960年阅读版中，本行末是短横杠符号。

With their dear retrospect.

1742
死者已走的距离
起初并未显现；
似乎他们还会回来
这样渴望了多年。

随后，直至我们尾随而去，
我们才大感怀疑，
我们如此熟悉
对他们的珍贵回忆。

1743
The grave my little cottage is,
Where "Keeping house" for thee
I make my parlor orderly
And lay the marble tea.

For two divided, briefly,
A cycle, it may be,
Till everlasting life unite
In strong society.

1743
坟墓是我的小屋，
在那里为你"管家"
我把我客厅收拾干净
摆上大理石茶。

短暂的，两人分离，
或许只是，一个轮回，
直至永恒的生命统一
在牢固的社会。

1744

The joy that has no stem no core,
Nor seed that we can sow,
Is edible to longing,
But ablative to show.

By fundamental palates
Those products are preferred
Impregnable to transit
And patented by pod.

1744

无茎无核的欢乐,
也无种子供我们种植,
渴望可以享用,
但只短暂的显示。

原生的嘴①
偏爱那些产品
无法运走
只能由荚专有。

1745

The mob within the heart
Police cannot suppress
The riot given at the first
Is authorized as peace

Uncertified of scene
Or signified of sound
But growing like a hurricane
In a congenial ground.

---

① 嘴(palate): "palate" 本指上颚, 此处喻指嘴, 或味觉, 或渴望。

1745
内心深处的暴徒
警察无法平定
暴动在最初
被认可为和平

没有确定的场景
或预示的声息
而是像飓风一样发展
在宜人之地。

1746
The most important population
Unnoticed dwell,
They have a heaven each instant
Not any hell.

Their names, unless you know them,
'Twere useless tell.
Of bumble-bees and other nations
The grass is full.

1746
最重要的居民
居处不为人注意,
他们时时享有天堂
没有地狱。

他们的名字,除非你认识他们,
无须一一说出。
大黄蜂和其他群类
在草地上遍布。

1747

The parasol is the umbrella's daughter,
And associates with a fan
While her father abuts the tempest
And abridges the rain.

The former assists a siren
In her serene display;
But her father is borne and honored,
And borrowed to this day.

1747

阳伞是伞的女儿,
与扇子有关联
而她父亲紧靠暴风雨
把雨量缩减。

前者协助塞壬①
使她展示宁静;
但她父亲生来便受尊敬,
并被借用至今。

1748

The reticent volcano keeps
His never slumbering plan;②
Confided are his projects pink
To no precarious man.

If nature will not tell the tale
Jehovah told to her

---

① 塞壬(siren):塞壬是古希腊神话中半人半鸟或半人半鱼的女海妖,以美妙歌声诱使航海者驶向礁石或进入危险水域。
② 在1960年阅读版中,本行末是短横杠符号。

Can human nature not survive
Without a listener?

Admonished by her buckled lips
Let every babbler① be
The only secret people② keep
Is Immortality.

1748
沉默寡言的火山坚持
他永不休眠的宏图；
他激进的方案
决不向靠不住的人透露。

假如大自然不肯讲述
耶和华讲给她的内容
是否人性无法存活
如果没有听众？

让她紧闭的双唇告诫
给每位饶舌者听
人们保守的唯一秘密
是永生。

1749
The waters chased him as he fled,
Not daring look behind;③
A billow whispered in his Ear,
"Come home with me, my friend;④
My parlor is of shriven glass,

---

① "babbler" 在富兰克林全集版中为 "prater"。
② "people" 在富兰克林全集版中为 "neighbors"。
③④ 在1960年阅读版中，本行末是短横杠符号。

My pantry has a fish
For every palate in the Year," —
To this revolting bliss
The object floating at his side
Made no distinct reply.

1749
他逃跑时大水紧追不舍,
他不敢看身后;
一个巨浪对他耳语,
"跟我回家吧,我的朋友;
我客厅有赦免过的酒杯,
我储存室有一条鱼
为一年中每一次口味而备," ——
对这令人厌恶的福气
漂浮在他身边之物
未作明确答复。

1750
The words the happy say
Are paltry melody
But those the silent feel
Are beautiful—

1750①
愉快说出的话语
是无足轻重的旋律
但默默感受到的那些
美妙无比——

---

① 类似主题的诗可参见第 1668 和 1700 首诗。

1751

There comes an hour when begging stops,
When the long interceding lips
Perceive their prayer is vain.
"Thou shalt not" is a kinder sword
Than from a disappointing God
"Disciple, call again."

1751①

有一个时辰恳求止声,
当长时哀告的双唇
发现他们的祈祷是徒劳。
"你不该"是一把更仁慈的剑
比起来自令人失望的上帝那边
"信徒,再叫。"

1752

This docile one inter
While we who dare to live
Arraign the sunny brevity
That sparkled to the Grave

On her departing span
No wilderness remain
As dauntless in the House of Death
As if it were her own—

1752

请将这温良的一位埋葬
当敢于活着的我们
指责阳光的短暂

---

① 题解:信徒长期祷告而无效,不如说不该再叫唤上帝了,这比要求信徒再叫要仁慈得多。

向着坟墓闪光

她离去的这段时间
没有荒原能保持
凛然无畏在死亡之屋
如在她自己家里——

1753

Through those old Grounds of memory,
The sauntering alone
Is a divine intemperance
A prudent man would shun.
Of liquors that are vended
'Tis easy to beware
But statutes do not meddle
With the internal bar.
Pernicious as the sunset
Permitting to pursue
But impotent to gather,
The tranquil perfidy
Alloys our firmer moments
With that severest gold
Convenient to the longing
But otherwise withheld.

1753

沿那些记忆的故地,
独自浪迹
是一种神圣的放纵
谨慎的人会回避。
公开贩卖的酒
很容易被注意
但内心的酒吧
法律不会干预。

一如落日之害
在于可以追击
却无法获取,
这宁静的叛逆
把我们更坚定的时刻
混与那最严苛的金子
仅渴望很容易
但实际却被拒。

1754

To lose thee—sweeter than to gain
All other hearts I knew.
'Tis true the drought is destitute,
But then, I had the dew!

The Caspian has its realms of sand,
Its other realm of sea.
Without the sterile perquisite,
No Caspian could be.

1754

失去你——其甜蜜胜过获取
我认识的其他所有人的心。
确实已干旱得一贫如洗,
但至少,我曾有露滴!

里海有自己的沙地,
其余部分是海域。
没有这不毛的特权,
里海成不了自己。

1755

To make a prairie it takes a clover and one bee,
One clover, and a bee,

And revery.
The revery alone will do,
If bees are few.

1755

造一片草原需一棵红花草和一只蜜蜂,
一棵红花草,一只蜜蜂,
还有幻梦。
光有幻梦也能办到,
如果蜜蜂寥寥。

1756

'Twas here my summer paused
What ripeness after then
To other scene or other soul
My sentence had begun.

To winter to remove
With winter to abide
Go manacle your icicle
Against your Tropic Bride①

1756

我的夏季就在此暂停
往后的成熟是什么样子
对于其他场景和魂灵
我的刑期已开始。

迁移到冬季
与冬季同驻

---

① 在1960年阅读版中,本行末有句号。

去铐住你的冰凌
给你热带新娘以保护

1757

Upon the gallows hung a wretch,
Too sullied for the hell
To which the law entitled him.
As nature's curtain fell
The one who bore him tottered in, —
For this was woman's son.
"'Twas all I had," she stricken gasped—
Oh, what a livid boon!

1757

绞刑架上吊着一个卑鄙的人,
连地狱都嫌他肮脏
虽然按理他该被罚下去。
当大自然的帐幕下降
生育他的人踉跄到场,——
因为他是这妇人的儿子。
"这就是我得到的" 她气喘吁吁地讲——
啊,多悲惨的恩赐!

1758

Where every bird is bold to go
And bees abashless play,
The foreigner before he knocks
Must thrust the tears away.

1758

那里每只鸟儿都敢去
蜂儿无拘无束逍遥,
外来者在敲门之前
一定要把眼泪擦掉。

1759

Which misses most,
The hand that tends,
Or heart so gently borne,
'Tis twice as heavy as it was
Because the hand is gone?

Which blesses most,
The lip that can,
Or that that went to sleep
With "if I could" endeavoring
Without the strength to shape?

1759①

哪一个思念最深,
是看护的手,
还是天生温柔的心,
比从前倍加沉重
因那只手已无踪影?

哪一个祝福最多,
是畅所欲言的唇,
还是那已然入睡
想说"假如我能"
却无力说出的嘴?

1760

Elysium is as far as to
The very nearest Room
If in that Room a Friend await
Felicity or Doom—

---

① 题解：是实际看护你的手，还是天生温柔的心对你的思念最深？如果那只手不见了，是否会倍感沉重？是想说就说，还是想说却没有说的嘴，对你的祝福最多？

What fortitude the Soul contains,
That it can so endure
The accent of a coming Foot—
The opening of a Door—

1760
极乐世界之远
如至那最近房间
假如房内有位朋友等待
幸福或祸患——

灵魂有多坚强,
它能如此忍耐
一阵逼近的足音——
一扇门的打开——

1761
A train went through a burial gate,
A bird broke forth and sang,
And trilled, and quivered, and shook his throat
Till all the churchyard rang;

And then adjusted his little notes,
And bowed and sang again.
Doubtless, he thought it meet of him
To say good-by to men.

1761[①]
一行人穿过墓地大门口,

---

① 本诗描写送葬队伍进入墓园的场景。艾米莉·狄金森曾在1846年3月28日写给自己的童年女伴阿比亚·鲁特(Abiah Palmer Root, 1830—?)的一封信里写道:"Yesterday as I sat by the north window the funeral train entered the open gate of the church yard, following the remains of Judge Dickinson's wife to her long home."(L11)。狄金森一家1840—1850年间住在阿默斯特镇快乐北街(North Pleasant Street)上的一栋木头房子里,可以俯瞰附近的墓园。1855年11月,全家搬回到主街上的"家宅"(The Homestead on main street)居住。

一只鸟打破沉默引吭歌唱，
嗓音微颤，战栗，继而发抖
直至教堂墓园四处回响；

他这才调整细小的歌喉，
鞠躬致意重唱一遍。
无疑，他以为该是他
向人们说再见。

1762

Were nature mortal lady
Who had so little time
To pack her trunk and order
The great exchange of clime—

How rapid, how momentous—
What exigencies were—
But nature will be ready
And have an hour to spare.

To make some trifle fairer
That was too fair before—
Enchanting by remaining,
And by departure more.

1762
假如自然是个凡间女子
只有一点点时间
收拾她的行李箱和安排
季节的重大变换——

多么仓促，多么重要——
又多么紧急——
但自然会妥善应对

会拿出一个小时。

让一些细碎事物更美
虽然它们本已美丽无比——
通过长驻保持魅力,
更通过别离。

1763
Fame is a bee.
It has a song—
It has a sting—
Ah, too, it has a wing.

1763
名声是一只蜂。
它有自己的歌声——
它有一根刺——
啊,它还有,翅膀一只。

1764
The saddest noise, the sweetest noise,
The maddest noise that grows, —
The birds, they make it in the spring,
At night's delicious close.

Between the March and April line—
That magical frontier
Beyond which summer hesitates,
Almost too heavenly near.

It makes us think of all the dead
That sauntered with us here,
By separation's sorcery
Made cruelly more dear.

It makes us think of what we had,
And what we now deplore.
We almost wish those siren throats
Would go and sing no more.

An ear can break a human heart
As quickly as a spear,
We wish the ear had not a heart
So dangerously near.

1764
最悲伤的聒噪,最甜美的聒噪,
最狂乱的聒噪响起,——
由众鸟,在春天制造,
在黑夜欣然闭幕时。

在三月和四月边线之间——
那条魔幻的界线
远处夏天踟蹰,
几乎就在天堂旁边。

我们不禁想起所有死者
曾经在这里和我们漫步,
因为分离的巫术
显得愈加美丽而残酷。

我们不禁想起我们曾经的拥有,
以及我们如今所哀伤。
我们简直希望那些妖惑的歌喉
离去不再歌唱。

一只耳朵能伤人心
迅疾如标枪,

我们希望耳朵没有心
如此危险地近旁。

1765
That Love is all there is,
Is all we know of Love;
It is enough, the freight should be
Proportioned to the groove. ①

1765②
爱就是现有的一切,
是我们对爱的全部认识;
这已足够,这货物应该与
心态③成正比。

1766
Those final Creatures, —who they are—
That, faithful to the close,
Administer her ecstasy,
But just the Summer knows.

1766④
那些最后的生灵,——他们是谁——
他们,坚持到结束,

---

① 在1960年阅读版中,本行末没有句号。
② 艾米莉·狄金森曾在1862年初写给朋友鲍尔斯的一封信里抄录了这几句诗在信末,作为信的结尾:"'Speech'—is a prank of Parliament—/'Tears'—a trick of the nerve—/But the Heart with the heaviest freight on—/Does'nt—always—move—"(L252),信中的这几行诗被约翰逊编入狄金森诗歌全集,序号为第688首。艾米莉·狄金森也曾将信中这几行诗寄给弗朗西斯·诺克罗斯和路易丝·诺克罗斯两位表妹。这几行诗和本诗都提到"freight",可参照理解。
③ 心态:原文"groove"可指 channel(渠道),carved slot(刻槽),[fig.] typical state of mind(典型心态),usual train of thought(惯常思路),normal track of cognition(正常认知轨迹)。
④ 题解:可能指蟋蟀。

管理她的狂喜,
但只有夏季清楚。

1767

Sweet hours have perished here;
This is a mighty① room;
Within its precincts hopes have played, —
Now shadows② in the tomb.

1767

甜美的时光在此消逝;
这是一个巨大的房间;
多少希望曾在其中嬉戏,——
如今变成墓中的昏暗。

1768

Lad of Athens, faithful be
To Thyself,
And Mystery—
All the rest is Perjury—

1768③

雅典的小伙,要忠实
对你自己,
和神秘——
其余都是虚情假意——

1769

The longest day that God appoints

---

① "mighty"在富兰克林版全集中为"timid"。
② "shadows"在富兰克林版全集中为"fallow"。
③ 本诗约写于1883年,随附于一封写给身份不明的人的信中。据猜测可能是艾米莉·狄金森寄给朋友鲍尔斯的儿子鲍尔斯四世,给他忠告。他于1883年10月与伊丽莎白订婚(参见寄给鲍尔斯四世祝贺其订婚的第1577首诗)。

Will finish with the sun.
Anguish can travel to its stake,
And then it must return.

1769①

上帝指定的最长的一天
会随太阳一同结束。
痛苦巡游到它的火刑柱,
随后必定返回原处。

1770

Experiment escorts us last—
His pungent company
Will not allow an Axiom
An Opportunity

1770②

实验护送我们到最后——
有他殷切的陪侍
不会给公理
可乘之机

1771

How fleet—how indiscreet an one—
How always wrong is Love—

---

① 本诗包含在 1868 年末艾米莉·狄金森写给弗朗西斯·诺克罗斯和路易丝·诺克罗斯两位表妹的一封信（L329）中，该信表达了对对方的安慰之情，貌似对方陷入了某种困境。约 20 年后当托德夫人编辑出版艾米莉·狄金森的书信集时，她写信向两位表妹询问本诗的缘起，弗朗西斯·诺克罗斯回信说早已忘记具体缘起了："All this trouble has become only a myth now; it must have been some illness, or other forgotten calamity."（参见 Dickinson, Emily. *Letters of Emily Dickinson*. Ed. Mabel Loomis Todd. Boston: Roberts Brothers, 1894: 257.）诗中提及的"stake"可指火刑柱（即落日）或界桩。

② 本诗包含在 1870 年 10 月艾米莉·狄金森写给文学导师希金森的一封信（L353）中。

The joyful little Deity
We are not scourged to serve—

1771①
多迅疾——多轻率的一次——
爱怎么总是错误百出——
快乐的小神
我们并非被鞭笞去服务——

1772
Let me not thirst with this Hock at my Lip,
Nor beg, with Domains in my Pocket—

1772②
别让我口含霍克酒依然干渴,
也别让我袋中有地产依然乞讨——

1773
The Summer that we did not prize,
Her treasures were so easy
Instructs us by departing now
And recognition lazy—

Bestirs itself—puts on it's Coat,
And scans with fatal promptness
For Trains that moment out of sight,
Unconscious of his smartness.

---

① 本诗是艾米莉·狄金森约 1881 年写给她爱恋的洛德法官的一封信的草稿的结尾诗，信并未寄出。诗前的信写道："My little devices to live till Monday would woo（win）your sad attention—（fill your eyes with Dew）—Full of work and plots and little happinesses the Thought of you protracts（derides）them all and makes them sham and cold—"（L695）。由此推测，洛德法官的来信一般在周一抵达，而在其他时间里艾米莉·狄金森在忙乱地做其他事情，渴待周一的到来。她的爱是自愿的，不是被胁迫的。

② 这是艾米莉·狄金森约 1881 年写给她爱恋的洛德法官的诗。

1773①
我们不曾珍视的夏季，
她的财宝唾手可取
如今将离去才给我们指示
确实太懒得在意——

赶紧行动——穿上外套，
以致命的快速扫视
那一刻已在视线外的火车，
意识不到他的机智。

1774
Too happy Time dissolves itself
And leaves no remnant by—
'Tis Anguish not a Feather hath
Or too much weight to fly—

1774②
过于欢乐的时光自行消散
不剩一丝残迹——
痛苦要么没一根羽毛
要么太重无法飞起——

1775
The earth has many keys.
Where melody is not
Is the unknown peninsula.

---

① 这是艾米莉·狄金森约1883年写给她爱恋的洛德法官的诗，本诗可能指洛德法官夏天到访，艾米莉·狄金森快乐无比，直至对方将要离去这个事实来临，才教会她认识到过去确实太懒惰，没去注意到和对方在一起的不易，未曾珍惜。如今赶紧穿衣往火车站赶，急急查看那一刻已在视线以外的火车，没有意识到火车也很机智地躲开了她，已经开走，不让她看到。

② 本诗包含在艾米莉·狄金森1870年10月写给文学导师希金森的一封信（L353）中。信内共抄录了4首诗，除了本诗，还有第1222、第1770首，以及第1039首诗的最后一节。

Beauty is nature's fact.

But witness for her land,
And witness for her sea,
The cricket is her utmost
Of elegy to me.

1775①
地球有许多曲调。
那没有旋律之地
都是未知的半岛。
美丽是大自然的事实。

但见证了她的大地,
见证了她的海洋,
蟋蟀是她最后
送给我的绝唱。

---

① 参见第1068首诗描绘蟋蟀唱晚的情形。

附录 1955年集注版与1960年阅读版词汇和标点差异一览表

序号	1955年集注版	1960年阅读版	诗序号
1	it's	its	1501、1508、1527、1537、1558、1581、1585、1597、1624、1630、1632、1646、1658、1672、1681、1682、1692、1700、1773
2	stepping	standing	1507
3	burden	mountain	1507
4	does'nt	doesn't	1510、1521
5	has'nt	hasn't	1521
6	our's	ours	1544
7	from	for	1569
8	these	those	1589
9	heavenly	heavenly.	1643
10	witness it and more	witness it and more,	1644
11	summer Days	summer Days.	1644
12	Edifice—	Edifice?	1645
13	away	away.	1645
14	indeed	indeed?	1646
15	immortality	immortality.	1646
16	no	No	1646
17	begun	begun,	1646
18	mighty night	mighty night—	1646
19	Hell	Hell.	1649
20	away	away.	1657
21	back the Day	back, the Day	1657

续表

序号	1955年集注版	1960年阅读版	诗序号
22	from the Door	from the Door—	1657
23	our returning	our returning,	1657
24	it no more	it no more.	1657
25	it's Meat	its Meat.	1658
26	is set	is set.	1659
27	Corn	Corn—	1659
28	die	die.	1659
29	Dominion	Dominion—	1660
30	the Sun	the Sun,	1660
31	no part	no part—	1663
32	telling thee	telling thee.	1664
33	Two deserts but	Two deserts, but	1664
34	Right hand	Right hand.	1664
35	Step merry feet	Step merry, feet,	1664
36	to go	to go—	1664
37	we are prone	we are prone,	1664
38	labor now	labor now,	1664
39	had to draw	had to draw.	1664
40	the bend	the bend.	1664
41	Middle Sea	Middle Sea—	1664
42	further off	further off—	1664
43	to stand	to stand.	1664
44	like Plush	like Plush,	1664
45	like snow	like snow,	1664
46	murmur new	murmur new.	1664
47	are passed	are passed—	1664
48	at Thee—	at Thee.	1664

续表

序号	1955 年集注版	1960 年阅读版	诗序号
49	had had	had had.	1665
50	deed	deed—	1665
51	moment had	moment had.	1665
52	gone	gone.	1666
53	news	news—	1667
54	with us	with us—	1667
55	last	last—	1667
56	fail	fail,	1667
57	Frost—	Frost.	1667
58	Force	Force,	1668
59	Word	Word,	1668
60	Eternity	Eternity.	1668
61	comest	comest—	1669
62	ground	ground,	1669
63	crow	crow,	1669
64	sound	sound.	1669
65	comest	comest—	1669
66	men	man	1669
67	thee—	thee.	1669
68	Worm	Worm—	1670
69	warm	warm—	1670
70	home	home—	1670
71	blood	blood—	1670
72	power	power—	1670
73	"Afraid he hissed/Of me"?	"Afraid," he hissed/"Of me"?	1670
74	dream—	dream.	1670
75	Judged	Judged,	1671

续表

序号	1955 年集注版	1960 年阅读版	诗序号
76	away	away,	1671
77	sincerity	sincerity.	1671
78	Sun	Sun—	1671
79	burn—	burn.	1671
80	place	place—	1672
81	Face	Face—	1672
82	Hall	Hall—	1672
83	Father I observed to Heaven	Father, I observed to Heaven,	1672
84	punctual—	punctual.	1672
85	there	there—	1674
86	home	home—	1674
87	near	near—	1674
88	leave	leave.	1675
89	shewn—	shewn.	1676
90	below	below—	1677
91	solitude	solitude.	1677
92	Fire	Fire.	1678
93	all	all.	1680
94	none	none—	1681
95	Behold said the Apostle	Behold, said the Apostle,	1681
96	leaves	leaves—	1682
97	hill	hill.	1682
98	industry	industry.	1682
99	immortality—	immortality.	1682
100	upon	upon.	1683
101	innominate	innominate,	1683
102	a shame	a shame.	1683

续表

序号	1955 年集注版	1960 年阅读版	诗序号
103	estimate	estimate.	1684
104	We say as of a Station	We say, as of a Station—	1684
105	Ramble	Ramble—	1684
106	me	me—	1684
107	Eternity	Eternity.	1684
108	wea[r]s	wears	1685
109	dissolute	dissolute—	1685
110	T'were	'Twere	1685
111	ignorance	ignorance.	1686
112	soul	soul.	1686
113	Imagination	Imagination.	1687
114	Curiosity	Curiosity.	1688
115	Pursuit	Pursuit?	1689
116	severe—	severe?	1689
117	certificate	certificate—	1689
118	same—	same.	1689
119	Earth	Earth.	1691
120	touch	touch.	1691
121	Tho't	thought	1692
122	right	right—	1692
123	Scrutiny—	scrutiny.	1692
124	big	big—	1693
125	bees	bees—	1693
126	trees	trees.	1693
127	bone	bone—	1694
128	pain	pain—	1694
129	Austrian	Austrian.	1694

续表

序号	1955 年集注版	1960 年阅读版	诗序号
130	star	star—	1696
131	objective	objective,	1696
132	Year	Year.	1696
133	untold	untold.	1697
134	T'is	'Tis	1698
135	saved	saved—	1698
136	does	does.	1698
137	demean	demean—	1700
138	sign	sign—	1700
139	To-day	Today	1702
140	her	her—	1702
141	steeple	steeple,	1702
142	surmise	surmise.	1702
143	Clock	Clock—	1703
144	knock	knock—	1703
145	play	play—	1703
146	too	too.	1704
147	Geography	Geography—	1705
148	climb	climb—	1705
149	Home	Home.	1705
150	Spring	Spring.	1707
151	T'is	'Tis	1708
152	home—	home	1709
153	return	return—	1709
154	away;	away,	1710
155	aisle,	aisle	1710
156	abroad;	abroad,	1712

续表

序号	1955年集注版	1960年阅读版	诗序号
157	it	it—	1712
158	same	same.	1712
159	whom	whom?	1712
160	liar.	liar	1720
161	close;	close—	1732
162	me,	me	1732
163	befel	befell	1732
164	this	this.	1733
165	flower	flower,	1734
166	appear;	appear—	1742
167	plan;	plan—	1748
168	behind;	behind—	1749
169	friend;	friend—	1749
170	Bride	Bride.	1756
171	groove.	groove	1765

后　记

　　自 1991 年专注于研究艾米莉·狄金森，1994 年发表首篇艾米莉·狄金森研究论文，迄今逾 30 载。忆青葱岁月，尚诗歌青年，神采飞扬，如彼时诸多文艺青年一般，如饥似渴，遍阅诗歌杂志、报纸、民间诗刊，参与各种诗歌文学聚会，读诗写诗，不舍昼夜，乐在其中。初时读到艾米莉·狄金森，泪如雨下，自此不懈不弃，至今。

　　艾米莉·狄金森乃是一位正常写诗的普通女子，其人其诗所有特点，均可在此认识框架下加以理解与把握。总体而言，她非思想家、哲学家、智者、道姑、浪漫主义者等，虽然多少有诸如此类之特点。她如一般诗人正常地写诗，其诗歌特点及由诗歌影响或选择的人生，其内在逻辑，与其他写诗者一样正常，虽有其个性，正如每位写诗者都有个性一样，但并无异样；她也如一位普通女子，她的生活、思想、情感，其内在逻辑，一如我们普通人、普通女子的人生逻辑，不值特别惊奇。本译文中的艾米莉·狄金森，正是如此一位正常写诗的普通女子。同为写诗者的译者，对其人其诗体现的思想与心路历程曲折，似曾相似，并无陌生。

　　对艾米莉·狄金森诗歌的评论众多，其中美国评论家布鲁姆（Harold Bloom）在《西方正典》（*The Western Canon: The Books and School of the Ages*）一书中所言甚为精当，他也指出了过往评论家们所不够重视者："What her critics almost always underestimate is her startling intellectual complexity."[①] 艾米莉·狄金森诗歌往往逃脱肉眼所见，甚至逃避理性抓取，其真正个性的精髓无法解读，只能共鸣，对读者的诗性有很高要求，故其难懂。艾米莉·狄金森的诗歌像一张满是皱褶的布，其真正的特性在纵横四处的皱痕深处，精而细。

　　晚近二十余年来，译者的行为日益自由，有以自我为中心，视原作为媒介，依靠灵感抒发了自己；有以读者为中心，理顺文字，美化语

[①] Bloom, Harold. *The Western Canon: The Books and School of the Ages*. New York: Harcourt Brace & Company, 1994: 291.

言，令读者满意；而本译者更乐于关注原作，甚至拘泥于原作的形式、内容及风格，因为，这是译诗，尤其是狄金森的诗。企望本译文尽量忠实，在语言形式和语言内容，也在语气、语调、节奏、氛围等风格，更在精而细处。原文凝练，译文不宜松散；原文断裂跳跃，译文不宜顺畅流利，反之依然；总尽力亦步亦趋，望得形似而后神似，虽亦时时力有不逮。

艾米莉·狄金森诗歌之晦涩，除表现形式或微妙内涵，亦时常与当时外部语境及诗人内部心境相关，今日读者捧读，未知诗歌源出之语境，自是难懂。然诗者，其是也，它自在，自足，自言，何需强解？然译者而后意识到，译者终需对读者负责，对读者而言，无从解读的天书，毫无意义。故译本的后几个选本，适当提供注释或解读指引，对读者有益，对诗歌无礼，是为无奈。

2003 年，前辈诗歌翻译家嘱译者翻译艾米莉·狄金森诗歌，不从，因翻译难免肢解，诗人译者亦常感如自戕，故而不忍。随后几年，不论见面还是在电话里，前辈总不忘敦促译者翻译艾米莉·狄金森诗歌，最终，其"责任"之说将译者说服。于是，2010 年译者译完约翰逊版 1775 首艾米莉·狄金森诗歌，随后听从另一位前辈学者建议，分辑出版。随后便是分辑出版，至最后一个选辑出版的今天，时光已逝去 14 年有余。

最后一辑出版，诗人译诗之解剖及自我解剖暂告结束，然免于研究诗歌之幸似未可期。从初时的黑发至如今的白头，人生流逝，多与艾米莉·狄金森有关，凝望镜中的自己，唯有一声叹息……

译者
2024 年 10 月 10 日